The Emergent
in Curriculum

The Emergent in Curriculum

GAIL M. INLOW
Professor of Education
Northwestern University

John Wiley & Sons, Inc.   *New York*   *London*   *Sydney*

DEDICATED TO

The mental-health movement throughout the world. Through its efforts, may
the true increasingly supplant the false.

Preface

This book is a blend of the old and the new in curriculum theory and practice. While respecting the time-tested as an indispensable criterion of educational quality, I look to the innovational for possible significant improvement.

My purpose from the start was not to bring into being just another conventional book on curriculum. An oversupply of these may already exist. Neither was it to bring into being yet another of the many anthologies on the curriculum innovational. Although currently the fad, these often offend by their lack of unity while alluring by their immediacy.

My purpose rather was to reveal the new while at the same time appraising its educational significance. The criterion of significance applied throughout was the size of the contribution that curriculum in any of its forms makes to the cause of individual fulfillment. A culture necessarily transmits, and man necessarily adapts, but both processes remain pedestrian unless they contribute substantially to the ultimate of total personality development.

The first three chapters set the stage for the remainder of the book. The final thirteen chapters carry the weight of the book's curriculum substance.

I profess in no way to have covered all, or even nearly all, of the current innovational in curriculum. The field is too vast and the book is too selective to warrant any such grandiose claim. When in doubt about what content to select, I employed the criteria of timeliness and significance. Both sanctioned coverage of mental health, creativity, problem solving, current large-scale subject-matter experimentation, emergent social issues, the status of electronics in education, and the innovational in organizational practices.

The book is aimed at three audiences or audience sources: colleges and universities, elementary and secondary schools, and the general public. For colleges and universities, *The Emergent In Curriculum* has significance for courses bearing such labels or partial labels as curriculum, school administration, educational issues, and the school in modern society. For public and private schools, it brings a practical orientation to the on-going curriculum concerns of teachers and school administrators. For the lay public, it communicates a timely and lucid message to citizens who are interested in keeping abreast of educational affairs.

Several individuals were extremely helpful while the manuscript was taking shape. The most noteworthy of these was my colleague, Mrs. Joan Smutny. Her friendship and encouragement were matched only by her insightful criticism. Four other colleagues—George Beauchamp, George Giles, Claude Mathis, and Edward Victor—were generous with their time, suggestions, and private libraries.

I also wish to recognize two Deans, B. J. Chandler and E. T. McSwain, who have consistently demonstrated their faith in a moderate teaching load as motivational to professional writing and research.

To my immediate family: Joanne, Rick, Ron, and Bev; and to my sister and brother-in-law, Muriel and Ray Olson, respectively, I extend thanks for their interest and encouragement.

Finally, I offer a special thanks to my co-worker Mrs. Helen Meyer, whose assistance, in many ways, proved invaluable.

G. M. I.

Contents

the unknown 74. Creativity and the posture of agnosticism 75. From divergence to convergence 75. From convergence to closure 76. The distorted genius issue 76. Education's role in creativity 77. A classroom synthesis 82. Intelligence testing and creativity 83. A final word 87. Suggested readings 87. For further thought 88. References 89.

The thinking dimension 91. The action dimension 95. Steps in problem solving 96. Can problem solving be taught? 99 Does problem solving as a learning process transfer? 100 Problem solving and the school 102. Recommended readings 107. For further thought 108. References 107.

PART III.   *Current Experimentation in Content and Method*

The scope of experimentation is broadening 113. Selected curriculum experimentation 121. A final statement 136. For further thought 137. References 137.

Claims regarding television as an educational medium 139. Issues inherent in instructional television 140. Principles underlying the employment of instructional television 143. Advantages of television instruction 144. Disadvantages of television instruction 144. CTV as an instructional medium 145. Selected readings on CTV 150. ETV as an instructional medium 150. Selected readings on ETV 155. CCTV as an instructional medium 155. Selected readings on CCTV 158. Administrative responsibilities in television instruction 158. An evaluation of television instruction 160. For further thought 161. References 162.

The program 165. The machine 172. "Pros" of programmed learning 173. "Cons" of programmed learning 175. An overall evaluation 176. Final conclusions 179. A final word 180. Recommended readings 181. For further thought 182. References 182.

evaluation of nongrading 315.   A point of view 319.   For further thought 320.   References 320.

16. *The Advanced Placement Program* 322

part *I*

A Curriculum Position

chapter 1

A Curriculum Position
on Goals

At the start of this venture in curriculum, we take the reader briefly
into the world of make-believe by asking him to relate to the following
situation. In some mysterious but unexplained manner, a complete
society awakens one morning without its structure of formal education.
The people remember nothing about the previously existent educational
curriculum, about school buildings, about textbooks, about reference materials, or about school organization. Other components of the culture:
family groups, business and industry, religion, government, social mores,
and all previously existing knowledge (except that pertaining to formal
education) remain unchanged. This fancifully conceived society might
even be a replica of America today without its educational system.

On that first morning after the metamorphosis, the people arise to meet
the demands of the new day. Businessmen go to their offices as usual.
Professional men assume their customary obligations. Housewives
pursue their daily routines, but with one significant difference: mothers
do not send their children to school, because there is no school. And
the ranks of the unemployed are at least temporarily reinforced by the
addition of one entire category of adults: the people who had been employed in the enterprise of education.

As previously indicated, the holocaust, even though obliterating all
traces of formal education, left knowledge itself intact. Thus the society,
dispossessed of its previously existing educational system, has the necessary ingredients to build another. Before long, the former teacher-schol-
ars and researchers, with time on their hands, begin to probe informally

3

and formally into such questions as these: How can individuals and the society survive unless the society conceives some organized means of channeling a flow of knowledgeable personnel into its social institutions? How can individualism reach fulfillment, and thereby help society to reach its own fulfillment, short of an enlightened collective effort? And finally, what organizational arrangement will serve the society best as it pursues its educational purposes?

As the educators of our mythical society address themselves to these questions and attempt to implement their answers, in effect they would be replicating both the historical and the current efforts of almost every society of the Western World. The only basic difference would be the factor of time. Whereas the hypothetical society, in order to survive, would have had to forge immediate answers, actual cultures have been able, fortunately, to employ more gradual processes.

Whatever the pace of its development, education in every culture, consciously or unconsciously, pursues the dual objectives of perpetuation and change. In an exact semantic sense, these outcomes are contradictory and therefore irreconcilable. In an operational frame, however, they are congenial in that only in a milieu of structural stability, can orderly and sustained change take place. The constructive compromise thus is for education to accord the time-tested values a privileged status while holding them up for continuous examination and re-examination.

Time-tested Cultural Values

The most vital aspect of the structural stability of any society is the values by which it lives. These values evolve slowly, change slowly, and constitute, at any given time, a bedrock foundation for an educational program. Thus, early in this chapter we identify the fundamental values that characterize life in the United States and in most of the Western World as well. A list of such values follows:

1. The individual is at the center of all other values. In the United States, no less than the Constitution of the land attests to this tenet. In a religious-ethical frame of reference, the Judeo-Christain ethic is no less emphatic. And in a mental-health frame of reference, individualism lies at the heart.

2. The quality of man's humanness obligates him to achieve optimum personality development. The range of expected development extends along the several dimensions of the mental, the social, the emotional, the ethical, the esthetic, and the physical. The idealistic expectation is that each indivdual will achieve adequacy in all of these categories as a satisfactory base for extended vertical growth in any single

category. The goal is not to limit specialized excellence but to give it authenticity by casting it in a universal perspective.

3. At a functional level, man most nearly attains this projected optimum of personality development in an ever expanding world of people to whom he relates and who, in turn, relate to him. Religion, most mental-health orientations, and pragmatism particularly attest to the validity of this concept. In all three, man achieves his ultimate only in an expanding social milieu. This value tenet increases daily in significance across the world scene as frontiers recede, as mobility increases, as communications media expand, as new nations form, and as all social groups progress toward the ideal of an open encounter with other groups.

4. Also at a functional level, man most nearly attains this optimum of personality development when, through the rational and affective processes, he extends his horizons of knowledge, understanding, assessment, and application into an ever expanding universe.

5. At a political level, man most nearly attains this optimum of personality development under a governmental arrangement whose traditions derive from individualism. Within such an arrangement, the ruling body represents the collective will of the electorate. Furthermore, the ruling body acts to delimit the personality rights of any single person only when such curtailment is necessary, (a) to protect the personality rights of others, and (b) to protect the personality rights of an individual or the group during periods of emergency.

6. The index of growth attained at any time by the society is the growth evidenced at any time by its indvidual members. In and of itself, the state or the ruling power has no inherent significance. Its role exclusively and indisputably is service.

7. Within this humanistic-cosmic-political framework, the status quo is no more or no less than a point of departure for change. The *what is* continuously concedes to the *what should be*. All life is dynamic and evolving.

How the Time-tested Values Developed

These fundamental values collectively constitute the nerve center of our national way of life. At the governing controls of the nerve center are these convictions: that individualism is of supreme essence; that its total development constitutes a moral mandate; that individualism flowers in a mature social order; that development must take place along lines of the affective as well as the rational; that government exists to serve individualism; and that life is an evolutionary process of dynamic change.

How did these and related values evolve? Succinctly put, they have their origins in three sources: (1) in the conditions of practical living throughout the ages, (2) in man's progressive and cumulative assessment of these conditions, and (3) in a progressively growing body of theoretical dogma which, at one and the same time, reflects the existent while pointing toward the possible. Each successive generation receives from each preceding one a cumulative inheritance of practice and theory. Both of the latter undergo change in any kind of culture by the subjective nature of the transmission process itself. But in an Anglo-Saxon culture, they undergo significant change because change itself is an indelibly imprinted cultural value. Each generation thus receives, distills, evaluates, transmits, and changes.

An illustration is in order here. The generation of the forties, for instance, inherited from antecedent generations a controversial body of practices and theory pertaining to the issue of race relations. At the level of practice, segregation was the more-or-less accepted social order of the day. At the level of theory, segregation was only debatably acceptable, if acceptable at all. Once again at the practical level, such motivators as the nation's need to emerge victorious in World War II, its need to project an authentic democratic image before the world, and its need to make the best economic use of its human resources—all these led to a transformed posture toward racial equality. Once again at the level of theory, the rational and affective processes of the society bestirred themselves. The combined result was a racial inheritance distilled to fit a new set of circumstances. Selected tangible sequels were the case of *Brown v. Board of Education* in 1954, the Civil Rights Law of 1964, and a nation struggling on many fronts to wrest peace from potential anarchy. Each of these events reflects a generation which inherited a body of practice and theory, a generation which agonizingly assessed its inheritance, and, as a consequence, a generation which transmitted a new value emphasis to the next generation.

Interestingly but not surprisingly, the nation's current assessment of racial attitudes and practices is taking place within the framework of the fundamental values introduced earlier in the chapter. Emerging with increased stature are individualism, which now has a broader base; government, which is acting more vigorously to put into practice the theory on which it rests; and the phenomenon of change, which is undergoing renewed validation as an inherent cultural value. At stake, in a very realistic way, is the fundamental way of life of the entire nation.

Education Translates Cultural Values

Cultural values exist in all societies. And in a democratic society, they exist as the cumulative fruits of the rational-affective processes. This has been the thesis developed to date. We now proceed to describe and to analyze education's posture before these values.

A starting truism is that the values of any culture automatically frame the values of the educational system that exists to serve the culture. Thus a communist society creates and maintains an educational system that mirrors the ideals of totalitarianism. A closed system of education results. By the same logic, a democratic society creates and maintains an educational system that mirrors the ideals of individualism, total personality growth, and social change. An open system results wherein education, by the very nature of the dynamic and surcharged values that frame it, becomes an important instrument of change as well as of adaptation and transmission.

However, any educational enterprise endowed with inherent power achieves the full realization of that power only to the extent that it translates cultural values into a meaningful educational totality of many parts, and into a meaningful curriculum as the most important part. Throughout the book, curriculum will carry the connotation of *the planned composite effort of any school to guide pupil learning toward predetermined learning outcomes.* This definition is similar to ones espoused, among others, by Doll,[1] Ragan,[2] and Saylor and Alexander.[3]

Along the *process dimension,* we conceive curriculum as including such efforts of educational personnel as the following: (1) determining educational goals; (2) translating the goals into the substance of learning; (3) selecting and employing instructional methods designed to make learning effective and economical; and (4) evaluating how well any educational echelon has achieved its predetermined goals. Along the *product dimension,* we conceive curriculum as including the tangible manifestations of educational planning and implementation. Illustrative are statements of goals; lesson plans, unit plans, and complete course guides; the tangible results of instruction such as homework and class projects; and instruments and profiles of evaluation.

Education Determines Its Goals

Ever desirous of constructing curriculum along defensible lines, education has developed over the years a curriculum-building sequence that consistently starts with goal determination and progresses toward goal implementation. Thus this century has seen formulation after formulation of educational objectives. One of the earliest and most influential—in the sense that it moved education off the strictly intellectual center—was that of 1918 which promulgated the so-called seven cardinal principles. Actually more categories than goals, these appeared as the following

[1] Donald C. Doll, *Curriculum Improvement: Decision Making and Process* (Boston: Allyn and Bacon, 1964), p. 15.
[2] William B. Ragan, *Modern Elementary Curriculum* (New York: The Dryden Press, Inc., 1953), p. 3.
[3] J. Galen Saylor and William M. Alexander, *Curriculum Planning for Better Teaching and Learning* (New York: Holt, Rinehart, and Winston, 1954), p. 5.

captions: health, command of fundamental processes, worthy home membership, worthy use of leisure, vocation, citizenship, and ethical character.[4] Drawing heavily on Herbert Spencer, these principles highlighted education's growing interest in a program, conceived broadly, that would be appropriate for the masses as well as for the intellectual elite.

In 1938, the Educational Policies Commission elaborated what was probably the second most influential statement of goals. This formulation included a lengthy set of objectives grouped under the four categories of: Self Realization, Human Relationship, Economic Efficiency, and Civic Responsibility.[5] In this promulgation, the mental-health objective of self realization received, for the first time, signal attention.

Then in 1945, the so-called Harvard Committee adopted and announced a composite objective that committed education "to prepare an individual to become an expert both in some particular vocation or art and in the general art of the free man and the citizen."[6] Despite the inclusion of specialism, the Committee was vague about how to implement it.

Ten years later, the White House Conference on Education came close to replicating the goals included in most previous pronouncements. However, it also high-lighted an emergent one in deference to education's growing espousal of reflective thinking and creativity. The Conference stated this goal as the "Ability to think and evaluate constructively and creatively."[7]

More recently, in 1961, the Educational Policies Commission in collaboration with the American Association of School Administrators, while coming out in support of a more virile curriculum that would place proper stress on abstract thinking, made this provocative interpretation of its stand. "These Abilities [to analyze, to deduce, to infer] may be developed in the course of mathematical study, but they may be developed as well through experiences in aesthetic, humanistic, and practical fields, which also involve perception of form and design. Music, for example, challenges the listener to perceive elements of form within the abstract."[8]

[4] Commission on Reorganization of Secondary Education, *Cardinal Principles of Secondary Education* (Washington, D.C.: Government Printing Office, 1918).
[5] Educational Policies Commission, *The Purposes of Education in American Democracy* (Washington, D.C.: National Education Association, 1938).
[6] The committee on the Objectives of a General Education in a Free Society, *General Education in a Free Society* (Cambridge, Mass.: Harvard University Press), 1945, p. 54.
[7] The Committee for the White House Conference on Education, *A Report to the President* (Washington, D.C.: U.S. Government Printing Office, 1956), p. 90.
[8] Educational Policies Commission and American Association of School Administrators, *The Central Purpose of American Education* (Washington, D.C.: National Education Association, 1961), pp. 17–18.

Professor Downey, in 1960, put together what is probably the best synthesis of educational goals prepared to that time. Analyzing pronouncements from Horace Mann to 1960, he ended up with the following composite.

A. *Intellectual Dimensions*

1. Possession of Knowledge: . . .
2. Communication of Knowledge: . . .
3. Creation of Knowledge: . . .
4. Desire For Knowledge: . . .

B. *Social Dimensions*

5. Man to Man: . . .
6. Man to State: . . .
7. Man to Country: . . .
8. Man to World: . . .

C. *Personal Dimensions*

9. Physical: . . .
10. Emotional: . . .
11. Ethical: . . .
12. Aesthetic: . . .

D. *Productive Dimensions*

13. Vocation—Selective: . . .
14. Vocation—Preparative: . . .
15. Home and Family: . . .
16. Consumer: . . .[9]

Because conditions at the national and world levels differ from time to time, and because conditions at local levels differ from place to place as well as from time to time, we agree with the Harvard Report that any single goal composite "can claim neither completeness nor originality. The size of the subject precludes the former, and its character at once ageless and contemporary, the latter."[10]

Nevertheless, without any pretense either of completeness or originality, we operate from a point of view that goes something like this. Basically, education has three major purposes: the *Transmissive*, the *Adap-*

---

[9] Lawrence W. Downey, *The Task of Public Education* (Chicago: Midwest Administration Center, 1960), p. 24.
[10] Report of the Harvard Committee, *General Education In A Free Society* (Cambridge, Mass.: Harvard University Press, 1955), pp. 5–6.

tive, and the *Developmental.* To fulfill its transmissive purpose, education gives continuing stability to life by passing on to each new generation the tried, if not necessarily the true. With the tried becoming ever more voluminous, however, increasingly wise educational selection of what the curriculum should transmit becomes more and more essential.

To fulfill its adaptive purpose, education helps the individual to acquire the skills, the knowledge, and the emotional adjustment needed by him to relate successfully to himself and to his world. Education, in this regard, helps him to relate along the several dimensions of the cognitive, the emotional, the social, the ethical, the esthetic, and the motor.

To fulfill its developmental purpose, education guides the individual toward his optimum of growth, along these same dimensions, at each maturational level.

The transmissive, the adaptive, and the developmental are not serially related, rather mutually interacting and reinforcing. All three relate to man as a holistic organism made up of many parts and to a social order which is, and has ever been, multifaceted and complex. Within the framework of the three, education in the United States operates out of the values that the nation lives by at any given time. These values education progressively passes down to each succeeding generation so that the new can always start from the old. But because the goal of change is a value with universal status in the culture, the ultimate goal of education in the nation is the emerging man—and, as a sequel, the emerging society.

For Further Thought

1. React to the seven so-called time-tested values listed early in the chapter. Are they valid? Should any be added?

2. If one major goal of education is change, how can this goal be realized when the values of a local community are out of step with the times?

3. Change involves an attitude of questioning, open-mindedness, and even, at times, skepticism. Are these values to be encouraged in pupils? Discuss this issue from the point of view of age and maturation.

References

Commission on Reorganization of Secondary Education, *Cardinal Principles of Education.* Washington, D.C.: U.S. Government Printing Office, 1918.

Downey, Lawrence W., *The Task of Public Education.* Chicago: Midwest Administration Center, 1960.

Educational Policies Commission, *The Purposes of Education in American Democracy.* Washington, D.C.: National Education Association, 1938.

Educational Policies Commission and American Association of School Administrators. *The Central Purpose of American Education.* Washington, D.C.: National Education Association, 1961.

The Committee for the White House Conference on Education, *A Report to the President.* Washington, D.C.: U.S. Government Printing Office, 1956.

The Committee on the Objectives of a General Education in a Free Society, *General Education in a Free Society.* Cambridge, Mass.: Harvard University Press, 1945.

The President's Commission on National Goals, *Goals for Americans.* New York: The American Assembly, Columbia University, 1960.

chapter 2

A Curriculum Position on Content: Sources and Selection Criteria

In Chapter 1 it was contended that education transmits the past to provide individuals a locus in the present, so that they and their respective societies can progress satisfactorily toward developmental maturity in the future. It was emphasized, and will continue to be emphasized, that education's goal is primarily individual development, and only secondarily societal development. I do not mean to downgrade the importance of any group or to deny that individual welfare must occasionally, or even often, defer to group welfare, but rather to reaffirm the democratic conviction that groups, including the state, exist to fulfill individuals, not vice versa.

This concept grows in importance by the day as bigness looms increasingly as a cosmic characteristic. What is one man in a world of three billion? What influence can one individual have on civic and political causes which, by their very size, seem impervious to change? How can the worker find job fulfillment when circumstances alienate him from those who hold his destiny?[1] Although without ready answers to these and related instances of man's loss of individualism, education must continue fearlessly as the champion of individualism. This has been education's role in the past and must continue to be its role in the future.

[1] Erich Fromm develops this concept of alienation particularly well in *Sane Society* (New York: Rinehart and Winston, Inc., 1955), pp. 124–125.

Three Primary Curriculum Sources

Confronted with the three objectives of transmission, adaption, and development, education draws on three sources for curriculum substance. These are: (1) the age-old disciplines, (2) the emerging disciplines, and (3) the contemporary world. We do not include the child himself as a source of content, for, in our opinion, he does not produce content in the same sense as the others do. Rather, by his focal position he determines the nature and the directions of the content that education draws from the three primary sources.

The Traditional Disciplines. The most unassailable of the three are the traditional disciplines, which, some for years, others for centuries, have been the foundation of formal education in every civilized land.

First, however, the logical question: What is a discipline? As would be expected, the word has a variety of interpretations depending on the user. Phenix approaches the term etymologically, tracing it from the Latin noun *discipulus,* which, in turn, derives from the Latin verb, *discere* (to know). A discipline, then, says he, "may be construed as knowledge the special property of which is its appropriateness for teaching and its availability for learning. A discipline is knowledge organized for instruction."[2] Foshay defines it "as a way of making discoveries, or generalization, within a particular domain . . . a way of knowing." And he ascribes to it three elements: a domain, a set of rules, and a history.[3] Fraser defines it as "a body of knowledge organized around basic concepts. These basic concepts form the structure of a discipline . . . Each discipline has its particular approaches, tools, and methods for discovering and ordering information."[4] To me, a discipline possesses three characteristics: it consists of knowledge and concepts that emanate from and relate to a given life area; it consists of demonstrable and describable methods of discovering and validating knowledge and hypotheses within that life area; and it is ever evolving.

Because the totality of knowledge is too great at any time for man to fathom it as a single entity, he customarily divides it for purposes of analysis and interpretation. First, he classifies it into broad categories—for example: natural sciences (biological and physical), social sciences, and humanities; or investigative, decision making, and apprecia-

---

[2] Philip H. Phenix, "The Disciplines as Curriculum Content," in A. Harry Passow, *Curriculum Crossroads* (New York: Teachers College Press, Columbia University, 1962), pp. 57–58.
[3] Arthur W. Foshay, "Discipline-Centered Curriculum," in Passow, *Curriculum Crossroads*, p. 68.
[4] Dorothy M. Fraser, *Deciding What to Teach* (Washington, D.C.: Project on the Instructional Program of the Public Schools, N.E.A., 1963), pp. 21–22.

tive.[5] With these classifications still too encompassing to be manageable, he subdivides each. Thus the natural sciences emerge as astronomy, biology, chemistry, geology, mathematics, physical geography (perhaps), and physics; the social sciences, as athropology, economics, history, human geography, political science, psychology, and sociology; and the humanities as the kinetic arts, fine art, language, literature, music, and philosophy.

These subdivisions, with minor variation, constitute the disciplines. Some like astronomy, mathematics, and music were members of the original seven liberal arts. Others like anthropology, psychology, and sociology are relatively new. Combined, all serve the purpose of cultural transmission. They transmit the past in an organized way including: knowledge, attitudes, mores, institutions, appreciations, and methods of bringing knowledge into being. Without the disciplines, transmission would be at the mercy of word-of-mouth evidence, unassembled written communications, empirical inference, and superstitous conjecture.

The disciplines not only serve the purpose of cultural transmission but of individual development as well. As they transmit knowledge and methods of discovery, they provide man with the basic ingredients of developmental growth. Language, for instance, opens the door to knowledge, and knowledge liberates. The more extensive and mature the knowledge, the more authentic the encounter with life. The less extensive and mature the knowledge, the more distorted the encounter. And the devious companions of distortion are always cognitive falsity, social narrowness, and egocentricity.

For one to say, however, that the disciplines transmit the culture and nurture individual development is to beg the question of what disciplines are really essential to either function. The problem is one of selection. Education's historical response has been a program of general education drawn from the content areas of the language arts, mathematics, the natural sciences, the social sciences, and the fine and practical arts. The underlying thesis is that individuals can adequately adapt to their cultures and progress developmentally toward their potentials only if operating from a common base. General education constitutes just such a base—but only if the mosaic is properly woven.

Selection for this mosaic, chronically difficult, has become acutely difficult with the advent of the knowledge explosion. Whether knowledge has doubled in the past fifteen to twenty years, as many are postulating, is a debatable point. But as the storehouse of knowledge increases, priorities of importance must be established so that only the most justifiable gets into education's curriculum.

[5] Joseph J. Schwab, in an unpublished address reported in Fraser, *Deciding What to Teach*, p. 24.

Challenged by this growing problem of selection, education in the 1950's became more diligent in its search for defensible selective criteria. The search, although not consistently rewarding, uncovered a number of leads, one of which has become probably the most controversial curriculum issue of the day: the postulate about the learning value of structure in a discipline. The proposition is that the inherent structure of any discipline is the only proper source of learning content; that the learner who understands the structure of any discipline will be able to contend with any aspects of the discipline. This concept and the growing theory to support it, say many, provide education with the answer to the knowledge explosion. Nurtured, if not conceived, in the mind of Jean Piaget, the concept became full blown when elaborated by, among others, Jerome Bruner and Philip Phenix.

Basic to the entire issue, of course, is the meaning that the respective theorists ascribe to the word structure. In searching for an answer, I often felt that the theorists, like the fabled six blind men of Indostan, were reacting to different parts of the academic elephant. Yet from the welter, the following specifics seemed to emerge.

1. Each discipline has its own unique structure.

2. Structure within each discipline consists of the fundamentals (and/ or concepts, and/or powerful ideas) that are sequential and related.

3. Because mastery of copious detail is impossible and undesirable, details should be grouped into a structured pattern of concepts, formulas, and theory from which nonspecific as well as specific transfer may be made.

4. Each discipline has its own methods and tools of discovery—sometimes discrete, sometimes shared with other disciplines.

5. Teaching and learning should follow the methods that brought the discipline into being in the first place, and act, on a continuing basis, to refine its conceptualizations.

6. A discipline is never to be converted into a teaching arrangement; *it is* the teaching arrangement. It is to be learned as the scholars learned it and developed it.

7. A study of, and in, the disciplines should constitute educational effort from the earliest elementary grades until general education terminates. And study at all levels should be organized around the central themes of each discipline. Bruner, for instance, cites these two concepts as germane for the primary grades: that all things are connected and that all things serve a function.[6]

Current writings and practices pertaining to the academic disciplines and their structure lead to this inevitable conclusion: if in the past several

[6] Jerome S. Bruner, *The Process of Education* (Cambridge, Mass.: Harvard University Press, 1960), p. 33.

decades, education paid too much attention to the learner and to his environment, at present it is correcting the imbalance. Whether it is over-correcting, only future developments will reveal. At the turn of the century, education was in the hands of academic scholars who, while promulgating scholarship, undoubtedly paid too little attention to the learner and to the learning process. For a half century thereafter, education was in the hands of teachers, albeit usually scholarly teachers, who conceivably let their concerns for the learner, his environment, and teaching methods detract from learning content. With the pendulum again reversing itself, education must be ready to counter possible compensatory excesses.

It is true that the time-tested disciplines are conveyors of the past, and unquestionably the best organized and the most reliable of the many conveyors. It is equally true that they, of all the learning sources, come closest to providing universal models for study and emulation, thereby serving the cause of development. In fact, if by some disaster the disciplines were destroyed, they assuredly would have to rise again. Thus our curriculum position is far from antidiscipline.

But we are not yet ready to go the whole way with those who portray the disciplines as the one and only source of learning content. A case in point is Phenix who, although one of the more organized and articulate thinkers in this field of curriculum, goes so far as to declare that "if learning time is to be economized, *all* material should come from the disciplines, and *none* from other sources."[7] Bruner has comparable convictions. This point of view is a radical departure from professional theory developed and practiced during the past fifty years. Rallying around the point of view, in addition to the older perennialists, is a modern coterie of free-wheeling thinkers from the fields of philosophy, psychology, education, and the many content disciplines. These individuals, sharing education's own discontent with the status quo, call through the window of structure for the disciplines to lead education into the promised land. We question, at this point: (1) whether the disciplines are the only way, and (2) whether the theory of structure has been sufficiently developed to serve as the sole axis of the disciplines.

Regarding the disciplines as the "be all and end all" of curriculum, a fundamental question is this: Specifically what disciplines do the advocates of this concept have in mind? For instance, in the field of the social studies, should elementary and secondary education go down the path of each of the several disciplines of anthropology, economics, geography, history, political science, sociology, and social psychology? Obviously not! But if not, barring some pattern of fusion, what criteria

[7] Philip H. Phenix, *Realms of Meaning* (New York: McGraw Hill Book Company, 1964), p. 54.

will determine the selection of one or several of the disciplines and the rejection of the others? And if fusion becomes the solution, will structure be sacrificed by it?

A second equally fundamental question is whether the disciplines, as discrete entities, are as relevant to learning in the earlier as in the later school grades. When distilled through the structural approach, Bruner thinks that they are, but his justifications are Piaget's findings, his own logical conclusions, and the alleged lack of substantial evidence to refute his conclusions—scarcely the kind of solid support on which to base a sweeping theory.[8]

Selected other questions pertaining to the current dialog on the disciplines and their structures are these: Does not the single disciplinary approach segment? If it does, through what methods will education supply needed integration? Who is to build curriculum: teachers, scholars, or both? If the disciplines are to be taught in the sequential and logical manner in which they initially developed, can the current crop of teachers, who are not necessarily scholars in all the fields in which they teach, get the desired job done? If not, what are the alternatives? And how do the disciplines relate to such educational problems as these: a young lady, upset by her first menstrual period, who needs counseling, not organized theory; a seventy-five word per minute reader who cannot keep up in physics; a sadistic child who physically harms others; a fifth grader who lacks library skills; a withdrawn kindergartner; or an adolescent who is rejected by his peer group because he lives in the wrong neighborhood?

In specific reference to the structural postulate itself, what education needs now more than anything else is tangible evidence that the thesis of structure can leave the realm of theory and become translated effectively into practice. An experimental sequence such as the following we have in mind:

1. One discipline to be singled out for experimental purposes.

2. Selected teachers and scholars from that discipline to identify and to rank independently, each in his own way, the ideas and concepts that give the discipline meaning.

3. The same individuals to identify and describe, independently, the methods and tools of discovery that characterize the discipline.

4. Objective evaluators to assess the extent of agreement among the evaluators in No. 2 and No. 3 above.

5. Assuming agreement, materials for teaching purposes to be prepared for all learning levels, from kindergarten up.

6. Teachers to be trained in the use of the materials.

[8] Bruner, *The Process of Education,* p. 33.

7. The experiment to continue until the approach is proved valid or specious.

In one sense, many of the more recent experiments in the curriculum content fields have followed much of this procedure—Chem Bond and Chem Study, for one instance; and the yellow, green, and blue text books in biology, for another. However, none of these reaches from the early primary grades to high school. Furthermore, the fact that competent scholars in each of the two disciplines of chemistry and biology went in more than one experimental-conceptual path casts serious doubt on whether structure in a discipline is as discretely apparent as many would have us believe.

In summary, the traditional disciplines are the foundation of education—so much so that without them education would become very narrow. The disciplines transmit the past. They reveal the universal in knowledge and behavior. They train individuals to generalize when valid authority so authorizes and to resist generalization when such authority is lacking. Without them, mature development is impossible. Yet, the disciplines are not, never will be, and never can be the only source of curriculum content. To conclude otherwise is to ignore the existent and the emergent world of the society and the individual.

However, the issue should not be a forced choice between a curriculum based entirely on the disciplines and a curriculum that rests exclusively in problems of the present. Instead the traditional disciplines should be utilized in such a way that they accomplish their fundamental purpose. That purpose is to develop in individuals disciplined thinking and disciplined attitudes, with the outcome a disciplined way of life. The traditional disciplines are both ends and means. As the former, they liberate, they satisfy, and they fulfill. As the latter, they prepare individuals to deal more effectively with life's problems. But they are not the totality of learning.

The Developing Disciplines.   An inherent characteristic of the disciplines is their dynamic quality. The existent ones are aways sloughing off or revising the old while adding the new. And a few emerging ones are always competing for status. These newer disciplines will be discussed in this section.

At the beginning, we note again that some of the so-called traditional disciplines go back as far as antiquity, whereas others have evolved more or less recently. The original liberal arts, seven in number, consisted of grammar, logic, and rhetoric, as the trivium; and geometry, astronomy, arithmetic, and music, as the quadrivium. Of these seven, logic and rhetoric have more tenuous status today, as disciplines, than they had in earlier days. But addition more than subtraction has characterized development in the disciplines, as any analysis of the several categories of the natural sciences, the social sciences, and the humanities will testify.

One of education's major tasks, as previously indicated, is to keep abreast of new knowledge and of new knowledge areas, as a preliminary to determining what of the new, at any given time, should replace or be given the recognition accorded to the old. Change within an already existent discipline is always easier to effect than the addition of a new discipline; yet over the years, new ones from time to time have become incorporated into education. One receiving serious consideration today is the evolving discipline of mental hygiene. It already exists in various forms in every school. Biology touches on some of its content, the conventional high-school health course does also, and the elementary-school curriculum weaves a substantial part of it into many program facets. Mental hygiene also appears universally in the guidance program and in an occasional course in psychology at the high-school level. As yet, however, it does not have the respected status of an organized discipline.

We predict that it is just around the corner from full curriculum status. Our reasons are these: it is an inseparable part of the whole-man, total-personality concept of educational purpose; its content is gradually jelling into an organized system of conceptual knowledge; its methods are identifiable; and it meets a definite growth need. These are potent reasons why education should recognize mental hygiene as a separate and important field of study.

Selected other of the newer disciplines which throughout the country have indirect, rather than direct, status are anthropology, astronomy, economics, geology, psychology (if this can be separated from mental hygiene), and sociology. Two of these, astronomy and psychology, because of their mounting timeliness, may soon appear in secondary education as independent courses. They already have appeared in a few schools. Most of the newer and emergent disciplines, however, will continue to be absorbed, in one form or another, into those now in operation. This outcome is inevitable for two reasons. First, the disciplines in their totality are much too numerous for each to be accorded separate status. Second, because many of them share common concepts and methods of inquiry, they are not really distinctive to begin with.

Even certain of the discipline structuralists subscribe to this point of view, Phenix for one when he declares: "The discipline principle is not an argument, for example, for a departmentalized curriculum in the elementary school—or, for that matter, in the high school or college. It is possible to use knowledge from the disciplines in connection with studies that cut across several disciplines."[9]

[9] Phenix, *Realms of Meaning*, p. 319.

The On-Going World.   A third source from which education draws learning essence is the on-going world of practical affairs. From this world, education extracts substance for one of two purposes: to give theory clearer meaning, or to expedite the learner's adaption to his environment by directly acquainting him with it. The first unites the abstract with the concrete, or the pure with the applied; the second communicates to the learner the immediacy of the practical world—its resources, limitations, and demands. The fundamental issue, we are convinced, is not whether the practical should enter formal education, for it cannot remain outside; the issue rather is over amount and purpose.

In the area of general education—which consists of those curriculum experiences needed by all to adapt to life and to find meaning in it—the practical appears in many places. Kindergartners whom teachers guide through the school building, first-graders who bring objects from home for "show-and-tell" purposes, a fifth-grade class which visits a science museum, and ninth-graders who in a year-long course explore alternately the applied areas of woodwork, metal work, electricity, and ceramics—these are all examples of education's use of the on-going practical.

In this regard, I refer once more to those who would insist that general education should flow only from the disciplines; that the practical becomes admissible only as a derivative of the disciplines. In my considered opinion, general education is what it is, not as a result of its source, but because of its inherent nature and purpose. If, for instance, all males need a modicum of proficiency in the tools of carpentry, and the school is the best agency to effect this outcome, a program in woods thus becomes general education because it satisfies a developmental purpose. Comparably, such curriculum components as safety education, personal hygiene, physical education, and library orientation are general education because all individuals need adequacy in them. Their direct relationship or lack of direct relationship to a discipline is beside the point.

In the area of special, as distinct from general, education, the on-going world of practical affairs is posing some knotty problems for education to solve, most of which relate to secondary education's proper role in vocational education. The pivotal issue is this: With education committed to helping pupils adapt to the culture, what, exactly, should be its specific function in helping pupils adapt to the single vocational aspect of the culture? Traditionally, education has pursued one of these paths: (1) offered general academic education only and made vocational training a post-school project for business and industry; (2) offered general academic education for all, but provided, for some, technical training in selected vocational areas where the greatest number of placement opportunities existed; (3) offered mostly technical training in a vocational type school with general academic education more or less supplementary.

Limited in resources, formal education has to invest its efforts in curriculum areas deemed most important at any given time. One of the perennial problems of secondary education has been the establishing of priorities among general education, exploratory education, and vocational education. When it assigns highest priority to general education, as it customarily does, rare indeed is the protest, but when it expands its program of specialized vocational education, protest is almost automatic except in submiddle-class communities.

The manner in which secondary education should spread its efforts is determined by educational purposes, the breadth of the academic curriculum in any given school, and local community attitudes about what knowledge is of most worth.

In reference to the first, secondary education should assess how well a vocational curriculum serves the purposes of transmission, adaption, and developmental growth. Its relationship to cultural transmission is admittedly limited. Its relationship to cultural adaption has been the major justification for the existence of vocational education. Yet how many graduates of a vocational curriculum actually have become printers, woodworkers, metal workers, or electricians? A small percentage, probably, if the truth were known. How much transfer, then, takes place between a vocational program in a school and a later vocational outcome involving different experiences and skills? Unable to quantify or authenticate an answer, we conjecture that until a decade or so ago, a considerable amount of transfer took place. More recently, with the advent of the electronics age and the associated need of industry for countless skills not introduced or practiced in the woods, metals, or machine shop, I conjecture that the amount of transfer has shrunk significantly.[10] Next, what has been vocational education's contribution to the developmental purpose of education—specifically to such sophisticated outcomes as reflective thinking and creativity? The answer is probably "very little," but not because these outcomes are impossible of achievement in a vocational program; rather because most schools have not projected these outcomes as expected purposes and have not hired teachers qualified to achieve them.

This leads to the second consideration, namely, the educational value which the existent academic program holds for students who customarily enroll in an applied-arts program. A candid answer is that too often the cognitive complexity of the academic curriculum drives many students to a vocational curriculum. The choice, actually, should be between an academic curriculum broad and flexible enough to relate to all categories of students and a practical-arts curriculum equally broad and flexible.

[10] This topic receives excellent treatment in Harry S. Broudy, B. Othanel Smith, and Joe R. Burnett, *Democracy and Excellence in American Secondary Education*, (Chicago: Rand McNally and Company, 1964), pp. 13–17.

A vocational curriculum no longer can, if it ever could, justify its existence as an escape from an ill-advised academic curriculum.

Now for the final consideration, namely, the attitudes and expectancies of local communities for vocational programming in the schools. These affective factors, deeply rooted in traditional practices, constitute powerful curriculum determinants, and they change slowly. Yet despite their depth and tenacity, education must not forget that any school program that assures immediate employment is inevitably integrated with a labor market of the unskilled and semi-skilled; a market that is shrinking before the onslaught of electronics, and a market that is becoming more overcrowded by the day. Thus community pressures alone should not govern.

All things considered, our conclusion is that vocational education needs updating to keep pace with the times. The first requirement is for a heavier weighting of academic education, properly conceived and implemented. A recommended rule of thumb, in this regard, is that in grades nine through twelve, nonvocational education should consume a minimum of from two-thirds to three-fourths of any pupil's program. The result will be education in breadth, which, it is hypothesized, will enhance, not decrease, future job-placement possibilities.

I recommend the updating of the vocational part by the shift, whenever community facilities permit, of its operational base from the school itself to local business and industry. Under such an arrangement, the individual school would plan, develop, and administer the vocational program but would utilize the training opportunities already existing outside the school. In this way, education would relinquish none of its control but would gain facilities more elaborate and more in line with space-age specifications than the school could possibly provide. This plan obviously is not feasible for schools located off the beaten paths of business and industry. In such instances, the schools should determine through the medium of business and industrial analyses what the most marketable skills are at any given time and build, within the schools themselves, a modest vocational program around them.

In urban areas, the coordinated school-business-industry arrangement may provide an increasingly satisfactory answer to the drop-out problem. Not distinctly different from the many work-study cooperative programs that have operated in a number of schools for several decades or more, the newer approach expands the work base into more job possibilities and usually increases the length of time on the job itself. It is having a number of experimental runs throughout the country and is achieving, in most instances, at least nominal success.[11] It provides the two-fold benefits of additional academic education and practical work experience. When

[11] See U.S. Department of Health, Education, and Welfare, *The 1963 Dropout Campaign* (Washington, D.C.: U.S. Government Printing Office, 1964).

both are realistically conceived, they constitute a potent educational partnership.

Criteria of Content Selection

It has been established that education, within the framework of approved cultural values, first carves out its operational goals and then implements them by selecting content from the traditional disciplines, from the emerging disciplines, and from the on-going social order. The criteria governing this process of selection constitute the theme of the present section.

The Pivotal Criterion of Educational Goals. By the very nature of their centrality in the entire curriculum-making process, educational goals are the most fundamental of all criteria. They establish learning directions and emphases, they generate activity, and they reveal illogic as well as logic in curriculum builders, and inconsistency as well as consistency in programs. Specifically, when education at the operational level announces its three-way goals to be cultural transmission, adaption of the individual to the society, and total-personality development of the individual, it commits curriculum makers to select only that content (and teachers only those methods) that will foster these ends economically and efficiently.

The Criterion of Essentiality and Universality. A limitation of central goals and purposes, however, is that although they chart a procedural course broadly, they leave undone the many tasks of translation. And it is in this latter process that curriculum makers have to distinguish between the imperative and the undemanding, the more significant and the less significant. Generally speaking, societies and education always have had and still continue to have the following focal concerns. The first is basic survival; the second, survival attuned to social conformity; and the third, fulfillment.

Because instinct itself cries out for survival, this concern and the curriculum essentials which nourish it always have, and should have, universal support. Thus physical health, the skills of communication, the physical universe as it impinges on everyday living, and social realities consistently should have top priority in any curriculum.

The second concern, survival attuned to social conformity, becomes controversial as soon as it leaves the hard core of general education and steps over into the ornamental. Examples of this latter are knowledge for knowledge's sake, a classical language justified by its status in a social group, or learning of any kind for nonintrinsic reasons. The ornamental has a place in education but is always more defensible when elected by, not forced on, students. And a curriculum that too consistently revolves around the values, behavior patterns, and aspirations of a single social class—usually the middle class—easily appears merely ornamental to the nonmiddle-class members. The criterion of essentiality instructs education to accord a lesser status to the socially ornamental than to the essential and the universal.

The third concern, fulfillment—total personality development, that is—has too often conceded to the more pedestrian individual and social essentials. Important though these are, they are means to greater ends more than they are ends in themselves. And these greater ends are mentally healthy individuals, reflective thinkers in search of truth, and truly creative personalities. Thus curriculum selection that ignores these is selection that has not matured; it is selection that eschews the universals. The criterion of essentiality and universality instructs education to accord these developmental outcomes the highest possible status because they encompass the highest possible values.

The Criterion of the Nature of Man.   A third criterion, which although general in nature is most fundamental, is that which relates to the nature of man. Contemporary education consistently graduates young people who have rarely squared off before such vital questions as: What is man? Why does he act as he does? What controls does he have over what he does? Can he change for the better? These used to constitute important focal concerns of philosophy when it was a tenant in good standing in education. But today, with philosophy generally having gone the way of organized religion, most school curricula touch these ontological issues not at all, or so much by indirection that the issues get lost along the way.

Yet this is not an inevitable consequence. If philosophy no longer exists as a direct vehicle of curriculum implementation, other disciplines, wisely selected and integrated, can do the job collectively almost as well. Biology, for instance, sees man as an evolutionary animal; dynamic psychology sees him as psychic energy swayed by tensions within his environment; behavioral psychology sees him as a physiological-neurological organism; sociology sees him as a product of group patterns and vectors; political science sees him as a product of, and a contributor to, political power blocks; and anthropology views him comparatively across cultural lines.

Several conclusions are in order here. One is that the several disciplines project man and his behavior in varying ways. Somewhere, then, education must reconcile these differences, which usually are more nominal than real. The teacher who is specialized but also broad in scholarship can reveal man both through the single discipline and across disciplinary lines. When teachers lack this essential breadth, however, a molar approach outside the framework of the specialized disciplines needs to be taken. This proposal will be developed more fully in Chapter 3.

The Criterion of the Nature of the Universe.   A further determiner of curriculum selection relates to the physical universe. In effect, it commits the schools to immerse pupils in the important phenomena of the universe and to engender in pupils an optimum of understanding of these phenomena. It is the criterion that admitted the physical sciences in the first place and is demanding their updating to space-age specifications today. The demand for authenticity engenders a progression from memorized fact to meaning, from a priori absolutism to statistical probabilities, from physical separateness to physical relatedness, and from postulates that set man apart from his physical universe to others that bring him together with his physical universe.

The Criterion of Balance.   With education committed to achieve many outcomes along many growth dimensions, the need for balance in education's curriculum is becoming increasingly apparent and essential. We speak not of a balance that dilutes any of the significant but of one that protects *all* of the significant: a balance that resists the single-minded and protects against the one-sided and momentary. Each generation spawns critics who advocate the single-track approach to curriculum improvement. Their capsuled proposals, although usually shortsighted, entice by very reason of their simplicity. Their stock in trade is the easy remedy: "All we need to do is to raise standards, or be rigorous, or let children grow, or take care of the gifted, or abolish teacher certification, or increase budgets, or trim the frills, or just get back to the good old days. Of course, the single-trackers never agree on how the train should be routed, but each knows that his right-of-way is the main line."[12]

When one-sidedness threatens any school's curriculum, the criterion of balance becomes the antidote. In effect, the school announces that because the entire enterprise of education stands forthrightly behind a well-defined core of goals and values, all efforts to change them in any radical way will be resisted.

These goals and values commit education to maintain a balance among the following:

1. *The goals themselves.*   The transmissive, the adaptive, and the developmental all have fundamental importance and are interrelated. Thus each must have legitimate status; no one can be neglected.

2. *The several growth dimensions.*   The cognitive, the affective (emotional, social, esthetic and ethical), and the motor-physical all have fundamental importance and are interrelated. Thus each must have legitimate status; no one can be neglected.

[12] John H. Fischer, "Curriculum Crossroads?" in Passow, *Curriculum Crossroads,* p. 3.

3. *The values of the various political levels.*   National, state, and local values all impinge on any given curriculum. Thus they must be reasonably homogeneous; major differences must be reconciled. Humanism should be the arbitrator when attempts at reconciliation reach the point of conflict.

4. *The spread of the disciplines.*   The several areas of the learning disciplines—the humanities, the social sciences, and the physical sciences—should always be in reasonable curriculum balance, with none dominating.

5. *Learning methods.*   The various methods of learning—memory, discovery, and reflective thought—should always be in reasonable curriculum balance, with none dominating.

6. *The immediate and the ultimate.*   A well-designed curriculum should relate both to the present and to the future; it should reward students not only with immediate but with delayed benefits; it should reveal specific evidences of mastery while progressing down a path of long-term development.

The Criterion of Vertical Sequence and Pupil Readiness.   The criterion counterpart of balance across the many dimensions of a curriculum is vertical sequence within the framework of any single dimension. To insure pupil readiness, content must flow from the simple to the complex. To stimulate emotional maturity, content must flow from self- to other-relatedness. In accordance with good teaching method, content must flow from imitation to discovery and from discovery to reflective thought. For instance, when children in their early years first learn about immigration, they accept it matter-of-factly as just another phenomenon of social living. Then when they superficially think about it in a value frame of reference, they relate it egocentrically to their own interests and to those of their native country. But as they move toward greater maturity, they increasingly examine the practice in terms of ethical as well as utilitarian considerations, in terms of world as well as of national attitudes and consequences.

The so-called discipline structuralists envision vertical sequence as extending from a less sophisticated handling, in the earlier developmental years, of selected important concepts to a more sophisticated handling, in the later developmental years, of the same concepts—with, of course, subordinate ideas and concepts injected as developmentally appropriate. This approach allures by reason of its concern for the significant at all learning levels and by reason of its concern for qualitative growth in depth rather than for quantitative growth in breadth. The approach allures so much, in fact, that we await with interest its future translation into more extensive operational practice.

The Criterion of Agency Appropriateness.   Yet another criterion in the selection of curriculum content and practice is whether the school is the most appropriate agency to accomplish the intended curriculum purpose or purposes. One aspect of this criterion is curriculum appropriateness adjudged by the school's ability to do. For instance, if sex education were under consideration and the school was deemed the proper agency to assume responsibility for it, the question would still remain: Could the school perform the assignment with proficiency? In this connection, teacher qualifications and curriculum-organization issues would require assessment before a final answer could be forthcoming.

A second aspect of this criterion is agency appropriateness adjudged in the light of community attitudes. As will be discussed in the chapter dealing with delinquency, Passaic, New Jersey, for over twenty years, has seen fit to entrust to the local public school system the problem of juvenile delinquency, both prevention and correction. The plan is reported as working well in Passaic. It would work not at all well in a different municipality that withheld its support from a similarly conceived project.

Selected Additional Criteria.   Selected other criteria are included here in the form of questions. And, almost, without exception, any school engaged in curriculum development or analysis should respond to each with an affirmative answer. Is the curriculum in its totality extensive enough and flexible enough to relate to the uniqueness of each pupil? Does the curriculum, or curriculum component, have the sanction of such agencies of assessment as the state, the federal government, and professional groups? Does it have unity? Does it lend itself to systematized instruction? Does it lead to further learning? Are needed materials of instruction available in sufficient quantity? Are curriculum content and curriculum organization in harmony?

A Final Word

These and related criteria serve education's diagnostic purposes as the X-ray serves medicine. Individually and collectively, criteria permit professional curriculum personnel to penetrate into the vitals of curriculum substance and related practices to the end of detecting and setting apart the pathological from the healthy. Although no criterion constellation is infallible, any one that is reasonably thought out cannot help purifying, at least in part, the process of curriculum development or curriculum change. The schools that refuse to look at themselves in some approved systematized way invariably are schools that offer the same content year after year, believe in the same things year after year, and make the same mistakes year after year. Society's current mood may not be one to condone, for very long, such indifference and sloth.

For Further Thought

1. React in general to the theory of discipline structure, listing and defending the pros and cons.

2. Draw from any single discipline what you believe to be its fundamental concepts. Then rank-order them from the simple to the complex. In your opinion, are all teachable, in some meaningful form, to all children of school age?

3. For any single grade level, list the important elements (if any) of curriculum content that you think lie outside the direct framework of the disciplines.

4. Which of the newer disciplines, if any, do you think education in the future will incorporate as independent entities into the schools' curricula?

5. Identify any criteria of curriculum selection that you think have been omitted.

Selected Readings

Broudy, Harry S., B. Othanel Smith, and Joe R. Burnett, *Democracy and Excellence in American Secondary Education.* Chicago: Rand McNally and Company, 1964.

Bruner, Jerome S., *The Process of Education.* Cambridge, Mass.: The Harvard University Press, 1960.

Editors of Education U.S.A., *The Shape of Education for 1963–1964*—Wash. D.C.: National Education Association, 1964.

Elam, Stanley (ed.), *Education and the Structure of Knowledge.* Chicago: Rand McNally and Company, 1965.

Frazier, Alexander (ed.), *New Insights and the Curriculum: Yearbook, 1963.* Wash. D.C.: Association For Supervision and Curriculum Department, 1963.

Goodlad, John I., *Planning and Organizing for Teaching.* Wash. D.C.: National Education Association, 1963.

Huebner, Dwayne, (ed.), *A Reassessment Of The Curriculum.* New York: Bureau of Publications, Teachers College, Columbia University, 1964.

National Education Association, *Schools for the 60's.* Wash. D.C.: N.E.A. 1963.

National Education Association, *The Principals Look at the Schools.* Wash. D.C.: N.E.A., 1962.

National Education Association, *The Scholars Look at the Schools.* Wash. D.C.: N.E.A., 1962.

Passow, A. Harry (ed.), *Curriculum Crossroads.* New York: Bureau of Publications, Teachers College, Columbia University, 1962.

Phenix, Philip H., *Realms of Meaning.* New York: McGraw Hill Book Company, 1964.

Smith, B. Othanel and Robert H. Ennis, (eds.), *Language and Concepts in Education.* Chicago: Rand McNally and Company, 1961.

Taba, Hilda, *Curriculum Development, Theory and Practice.* New York: Harcourt Brace and World, Inc., 1962.

chapter 3

A Curriculum Position
On Implementation

The theme of the first two chapters was that education, within the governing frame of cultural values, develops a curriculum in a predictable and logical way. The first step consists of the determination of educational goals; and the second step consists of the development of standards to guide the process of content selection. The third step, which constitutes the theme of the present chapter, consists of creating a curriculum that conforms to the goals and that stays within the limits of the standards of selection.

Content Is First Broadly Classified

Curriculum makers, early in their operational efforts, usually classify content into broad subject categories. In so doing, they give perspective to the more detailed processes of curriculum development that follow. The progression invariably is from the theoretical-general to the operational-specific. The greater the psychological distance from the classroom, the broader the design tends to be; the closer to the classroom, the more specific the design has to be.

In this connection, innovation characterizes a few recent proposals for curriculum classification. Phenix, for instance, suggests that any curriculum should issue from six "fundamental patterns of meaning . . . designated respectively as symbolics, empirics, esthetics, synnoetics [personal knowing and insight], ethics, and synoptics [such subjects as philosophy or religion which interpret knowledge broadly]."[1] This proposal, as

[1] Philip H. Phenix, *Realms of Meaning* (New York: McGraw Hill Book Company, 1964), p. 6.

Phenix develops it, is undeniably controversial, but also commendatory because of its preoccupation with life's fundamental meanings rather than with its fragmented elements. Broudy, Smith, and Burnett, also eschewing the traditional, recommend an educational curriculum developed around the categories of symbolic studies, basic sciences, developmental studies, aesthetic studies, and molar problems.[2]

Reflecting along the same dimension, we propose a curriculum organized into the following six categories: (1) symbolics, (2) esthetics, (3) the natural sciences, (4) the behavior of social groups, (5) the behavior of the individual, and (6) a synthesis of knowledge and behavior. The first four are common to schools throughout the country, the fifth is moving uncertainly toward status, and the sixth is only knocking at education's door.

Because of my announced intent to present a curriculum position in breadth, I shall develop none of these in detail. This assignment I leave for other theoreticians and for operational practitioners. Furthermore, because the first four of the six categories deal with curriculum content and practice that have been commonplace in the nation's schools for years, I shall limit my brief evaluative comments here to categories (5) and (6).

In reference to category (5) pertaining to behavior of the individual, education, until recently, has entrusted this component to the broad province of the many academic disciplines. The underlying assumption has been that insight and self-acceptance will flow inexorably from a student's extensive exposure to the humanities, to the natural sciences, and to the social sciences. The same assumption, elaborated, is that pupils who travel vicariously to many places, who identify with people of diverse interests and experiences, who penetrate into many thought-provoking situations, and who relate to many phenomena of the universe will automatically become well adjusted, mature personalities. This is a long-range, indirect approach to personality development, and, without a doubt, it is one that has no substitute.

However, even though this indirect approach to adjustment cannot be replaced, it needs to be supplemented. The supplement appears in the evolving theory of the mental-health movement. This body of theory commits teachers and school administrators to address themselves directly, while the academic curriculum is addressing itself more indirectly, to such eminently desirable outcomes as self-understanding, self-acceptance, and altruism. The commitment is for pupil-centered teachers and specialized guidance personnel, through the avenues both of teaching and counseling, to relate at all grade levels to the psyches as well as to the mentalities of individual learners.

[2] Harry S. Broudy, B. Othanel Smith, and Joe R. Burnett, *Democracy and Excellence in American Education* (Chicago: Rand McNally and Company, 1964), p. 78.

Although the topic of mental health will receive more complete treatment in the next chapter, I wish to emphasize here that the educational path of the future needs to be the mental-health path. What, indeed, is more essential in life than self understanding, self acceptance, and empathy? Only those who remain moderately free of emotional distortion are able to view life authentically. It is these same individuals who are able to understand and relate to others because they first have understood and have related to themselves.

A possible future adjunct of mental health approached through the disciplines and through individual counseling might well be the same outcome attempted through the direct teaching of mental-health theory. This teaching conceivably would embrace the following: the technical vocabulary of the field; what mental health is; what it is not, including coverage of the pathological states; how mental health releases the creative powers; and ways of maintaining a healthy emotional life. In this regard, a study I made several years ago revealed analysts, psychiatrists, and clinical psychologists to be generally supportive of such a curriculum endeavor.[3] Regardless of the exact specifics of any future attempts, education needs to become actively engrossed in what is probably the world's greatest need: the mental health of all the people, especially people in leadership positions. It is for this reason that I propose addition of "the behavior of the individual" to curricula that are without it and its amplification in curricula that have already endowed it with status.

In reference to the sixth listed content category—a synthesis of knowledge and behavior—education characteristically fragments learning for operational purposes but often stops short of putting the pieces back together. This criticism holds less for elementary than secondary education. In the former, particularly where the self-contained classroom is the organizational pattern, competent teachers consistently interrelate the various parts of a curriculum. Whether the several subjects of the fine arts, arithmetic, the language arts, science, and social studies appear as separate entities or in some combined arrangement, they become holistic under the direction of a truly professional teacher. However, in the later elementary and throughout the secondary grades, where departmentalization is the organizational pattern, rare indeed is the teacher who relates the single subject to the totality of knowledge.

It is for this reason that a curriculum, particularly for the upper secondary-school grades, needs an arrangement wherein the many concepts and methods of the several disciplines converge on selected molar problems. Focal possibilities here are interdisciplinary topics such as bigotry, nationalism, delinquency, neuroticism, dominance, or political immoral-

[3] Gail M. Inlow, "Can the School Curriculum Make a Frontal Approach to Mental Health?" *The Journal of Educational Research*, **56** (April 1963), pp. 395–402.

ity. Possibilities at a more ambitious level are the nature of man or the nature of values. More important than the exact substance of any single topic would be its effectiveness in precipitating both analysis in breadth and depth, and evaluation in a field of many alternatives.

The issue of delinquency, for instance, impinges on biology, economics, philosophy, political science, psychology (or psychiatry), and sociology, not to mention religion. Thus any student or group in search of truth about delinquency would need to study it across the spectrum of many content areas, employing the methods of inquiry of the many disciplines. Only in this way could an authentic synthesis emerge. This kind of integrated curriculum experience, geared appropriately to readiness levels, should characterize learning at all developmental stages; and it becomes mandatory in the upper secondary-school grades. Under any circumstances, the primary requisite would be a teacher qualified to assume this demanding assignment. The primary opposition would come from the single-discipline specialists. The primary gain would be the reintegration of knowledge long fragmented.

Content Reflects the Moods of the Society and the Profession

As any curriculum expands developmentally from the broadly theoretical to the operational, it inevitably, at any given time, absorbs the temperament and convictions both of the society and of the profession. At the political-social level it incorporates national, state, and local expectancies; at the professional level it incorporates the expectancies of educational and quasi-educational groups and agencies.

The National Community. Nationally, influences on curriculum consist of both the intangibles of tradition and the tangibles of the moment. As discussed in Chapter 1, the intangibles have expression in the fundamental values that Western man lives by: his freedoms, his rights, his obligations. The national community, in effect, communicates to lower political echelons that educational endeavor in the latter must operate within the bounds of national unity and expectancy. When states and local communities fail this expectation, the federal power, although painfully slowly at times, acts to bring them back into line. Instances of this corrective process in operation are the case of *Brown versus Board of Education* 1954 pertaining to the educational rights of Negroes, and assorted recent legal decisions pertaining to religious practices in schools.

The national community injects into education the serious social concerns that it has at any given time. For example, the federal government, recently convinced of a social lag in the natural sciences and modern languages, produced, in 1958, an intended antidote in the form of the National Defense Education Act. This act, through its extensive appropriations, has played a telling role in curriculum change throughout the nation's schools. One result, a laudable one, has been the upgrading of these content areas. A second result, not at all laudable, has been at least a temporary downgrading of the humanities, the social sciences, and the applied arts. Regardless of immediate or long-term results, the 1958 act stamps the national community as an active participator in the educational process.

The State Community.   Whereas the national community operates in educational affairs without clear-cut definition, each of the fifty states operates with designated legal powers. The state is the legal unit of education by virtue of the Tenth Amendment, which reserves for the states all powers not specifically delegated to the federal government nor prohibited to the states. The extent to which the several states exercise their educational prerogatives varies widely. Each tends to prescribe minimum curriculum essentials for such content areas as English, United States History, government, and the learning skills. Generally speaking, some states prescribe more than others, but none has prescribed oppressively over any extended period. Yet, in specific instances, all states have acted and continue to act impulsively over selected volatile social issues, leading often to legislation on curriculum that is offensive to some local communities and their schools. A case in point, today, is the legal stand taken by a few states on teaching about communism in the schools—a stand which insists, among other things, that only the evils of communism are proper curriculum content. More generally, however, the pattern is for states to establish minimum essentials, to supervise broadly, and then to allow local autonomy to operate.

Professional, Quasi-professional, and Nonprofessional Influences. Curriculum influences that cut across political and geographical lines are those exerted by agencies and individuals within the profession itself and within quasi- or nonprofessional groups.

Selected agencies such as the National Education Association, the accrediting agencies, learned professional societies, and institutions of higher learning, all fall into the first category. Although not always in agreement, these agencies provide channels through which recognized scholars and practitioners transmit instructional practices and make known their points of view. Illustrative here, the National Education Association has described its recent Project On Instruction, as "one of several major efforts . . . in this century to upgrade the quality of American Education and to give it direction." And this is just one of many instances where the NEA through a seminar, through a publication, or through direct representation on a governmental or some other professional project has attempted to shape the course of education's curriculum. It should be noted here that the NEA operates through persuasion, for it lacks the power to command. The accrediting associations operate more sure-footedly in an administrative staff capacity, but they too "sell" ideas more often than they exercise their modest powers to coerce.

Learned professional societies and leading universities, like the first two professional groups already commented upon, similarly play a vital role in curriculum development. Particularly contributive are professional organizations which represent the various content areas or disciplines. These customarily assess selected curriculum content and teaching methods, distilling the approved from the doubtful or the unapproved. The curriculum influence, for example, of the National Council of Teachers of English, through conferences and its three periodicals, is inestimable. Comparably inestimable is the influence that leading universities such as Harvard and Stanford have had, and continue to have, on curriculum decision making. Significantly, "The Harvard Report," now a quarter-century old, is still reverberating in educational thinking and writing.

Quasi-professional organizations, in the process of curriculum development, supplement the efforts of their more strictly professional counterparts. Noteworthy in this category are the philanthropic foundations which, through monetary grants, large and small, often upset curriculum balance by supporting certain causes and withholding support from others. Fortunately, in this regard, certain of the foundations—the Carnegie and Sloan, for example—are currently reacting strongly against the government's overemphasis on the natural sciences by giving considerable countersupport to the social sciences and to the humanities. And other organizations which have educational interests but are not even quasi-educational—such as The American Legion, NAACP, and ADA—pressure, each in its own way, for curriculum change in the nation's schools.

Selected individuals, like agencies, likewise cast their lengthened shadows on curriculum. Messrs. Bruner and Conant are cases in point. Both, operating out of status positions in education, have employed oral and written media in an attempt to change the beliefs of teachers, school administrators, and professional educators about curriculum issues. That their contributions are controversial is beside the point. Still other individuals such as Rickover, Woodring, and Bestor have operated with the same purpose in mind but have remained more detached from curriculum practicalities.

The Local Community.   The organizational unit with the most commanding position in educational endeavor is the local community. This is the place where all other influences and pressures converge. This is the place where agencies and individuals exert the most direct influence on education. This is the place where human emotions work up to the highest pitch. This is the place where both success and failure stand out as dramatic realities. This is the place where children, not statistics, come to school, bringing with them their differences in abilities, in potentials, in interests, and in backgrounds. And at the point when these children arrive at a local school, a curriculum becomes a living, pulsating force not only in the lives of the children, but in the total life of the community. This is a truism for a large city like New York, for a medium-sized one like Cheyenne, or for a small town like Little-town, U.S.A.

Curriculum Is Detailed at the Building Level

Curriculum makers, sensitized to the values and aspirations, both lay and professional, of the national, state, and local communities, next move toward the task of delineating a curriculum. This assignment demands that they elucidate educational goals; select curriculum content; reflect broadly about teaching method (the specifics of method are the province of a teacher); and evaluate the curriculum both as it develops, and later, when it gets into operation.

Where Should Basic Loyalties Lie?   Early in this discussion, readers need to square off before one of the most basic of all questions in curriculum development and implementation: When differences among value sources exist, which should control and which should concede? Where, for instance, should loyalties lie when the national, local, and professional climates are out of joint? Van Til pinpoints the issue this way: "Suppose the people of community X want indoctrination of a set of not-to-be-examined but claimed-to-be-good answers on certain economic, social, religious, or political issues. Yet the educators in school leadership positions in community X believe that there can be no freedom without freedom of the mind and consequently support the method of intelligence . . . . What then is the modern democratic educator's highest loyalty?"[4] This obviously is a situation which resists ready cliché.

At the operational (and even legal) level, one-sided local values can operate coercively—sometimes for extended periods. Illustrative are school boards that censored social-studies books during the McCarthy era, and pressure groups in any era that oppose education's entertainment of the controversial. Local communities tend to get by even with the unreasonable when the state and national climates are divided, but these same communities become more accountable when the climates of higher political echelons are reasonably unified. A phenomenon that stirs the waters, in this regard, is that teachers tend more to conform to liberal viewpoints held nationally than to conservative viewpoints held locally.

There is no easy answer to the issue. However, in my opinion, teachers and school administrators have no choice but to remain loyal at all times

[4] William Van Til, "Editorial: Curriculum Improvement—Who Participates?" *Educational Leadership,* 11 (March 1954), p. 336.

to the basic values—the ones detailed in Chapter 1—that have shaped and that continue to shape the American way of life. While conceding that education basically is a local function, educators must have loyalties higher than those of any given locale at any given time. It is important for teachers and school administrators never to sell short the art of compromise, but it is even more important for them not to compromise the fundamental principles that they and the nation cherish. Fortunately, however, differences tend to remain tolerable when individuals respect one another. Thus resolutions of ideational differences often may lie as much in the intangibles of human relations as in the specifics of the differences themselves.

Who Are the Participants. Almost as controversial as the sources of primary and secondary loyalties in curriculum development is the question of exactly what categories of personnel should participate in the organizational process. Singly, there are three possibilities, and collectively several more. The single possibilities are: (1) public-school personnel—teachers and administrators; (2) learned scholars in the content fields, from universities or industry, or both; and (3) lay (noneducational) personnel from the local community.

Regarding the first category, few can argue logically against participation in curriculum development by those closest to the scene of learning. But many can debate the issue of *selected* of these individuals as participants versus *all* of them as participants. My stand on this matter is identical with Beauchamp's, namely: "that curriculum planning is part of the work of the teacher. It is believed that teachers have three basic functions. One is to participate in planning the curriculum that is to be their point of departure for teaching. The second is to teach. The third is to evaluate what was planned and taught and to interpret those results."[5]

However, the extent of curriculum involvement by any single teacher or administrator is always a function of the size of the school or school system and of other related circumstances of the moment. A rule of thumb is that the larger the planning group and the further away from the classroom that curriculum planning takes place, the greater the need for the representative process to operate. Conversely, the smaller the planning group and the closer to the classroom that curriculum planning takes place, the greater the necessity of total involvement. And I stress here that not only administrators, but also teachers, are responsible for curriculum planning. The underlying management thesis is that those engaged in the execution of an operation should have a hand in planning the operation.

[5] George A. Beauchamp, *The Curriculum of the Elementary School* (Boston: Allyn and Bacon, Inc., 1964), p. 269.

The exact role of learned scholars in curriculum development is also a controversial topic of the current educational debate. At one pole, the more absolute among the discipline-structuralists conceive the discipline itself to be the curriculum. Say they: "Turn over to teachers the substance and methods of the disciplines, and have them go down the same paths that the scholars originally trod." As indicated in Chapter 2, I believe this to be a too patent simplification. First, it conceives of the disciplines as the only avenues to learning. Second, it assumes that the paths taken by the scholars who developed the disciplines in the first place are necessarily the paths that all learners must follow. Third, it glosses over the differential nature of the learning process in respect to such factors as age, ability, and maturity. Fourth, it makes teaching a process of imitative and mechanical dimensions.

At the opposite pole, the more fearful or myopic in the ranks of public-school practitioners accord subject-matter scholars grudging status, if any status at all, in the process of curriculum planning and development. The reason is understandable: the scholars dominated public education until the turn of the century; then they turned their backs on it for a half century; and, as a result, they ultimately became suspect in the ranks of those who took up the neglected burden.

In the 1950's and '60's, however, the practitioner-scholars and the "pure" scholars once more joined hands. Brought together by the federal government and related agencies to update education, the two groups rediscovered each other. And each group found its counterpart to be very much complementary, very little antagonistic. This discovery, however, has remained primarily a phenomenon of the large-scale regional and national educational projects. It has yet to become an equally common phenomenon at the local-school level.

Yet at the latter level, professional school personnel have to take some kind of stand regarding what role, if any, subject-matter scholars are to play in curriculum making. Our position is forthrightly in favor of their playing an increasingly active advisory and participatory role as the curriculum progresses upward through the respective school grades. The contemporary knowledge explosion, in fact, may not tolerate, for long, any other position. But just as forthrightly, we see need for scholars to make serious preparation for this evolving role. The irreducible requirements are that they become acquainted with what children actually are like at various growth stages; that they test concepts and methods of inquiry, under experimental conditions at the various grade levels, before recommending them to schools; and that they have close psychological contact with any school group with which they identify. In essence, the practitioner-scholars and the pure scholars need to relate so closely that the wall of partition which for decades has divided university scholarship and public-school scholarship will ultimately disappear. At the moment, there are hopeful signs that the academic "Berlin Wall" is at least cracking. Conceivably, then, a true rapprochement is not far away.

Now we turn to the issue of lay participation in curriculum planning, which is volatile, to say the least. One popular position is that because the schools "belong" to the people, the latter allegedly have the right to make curriculum decisions ranging from top-policy matters to such operational decisions as whether set theory, phonics, or communism should be taught in the schools. This position entrusts decisions to individuals who ostensibly may be totally uninformed and even undesirous of becoming informed. It likewise casts the need for teacher scholarship into serious doubt. The opposite position is that education resides in the province only of professionals; thus lay opinion should have no more status in education than it should have, for example, in surgery. This analogy, however, ignores the fact that education is a direct public enterprise, whereas medicine, at least at present, is not comparably so. The oversimplified middle-of-the-road compromise taken by theory, for years now, has been that lay personnel should determine the ends of education, whereas professional personnel should determine the means. This also is a too pat generalization to be convincing.

The issue here, again, is one which defies easy solution but yet is one about which any writer on curriculum needs to project a point of view. The following series of statements, taken collectively, represents mine:

1. Education is a public enterprise and therefore must conform to the will of the people—but to the will of the nation as well as to that of a local group.

2. The will of a local group has its legal expression in a lay board of education. This body should establish broad curriculum limits but, barring emergencies, should delegate to the professional faculty all other curriculum rights of decision. In this connection, any given school board should confine its recommendations on curriculum to the dimensions of urgent local needs and demands. Thus a school board in a predominantly agricultural community might insist on a course being offered in the field of agriculture, but it would not, with the same conviction, insist on a course being offered in an academic field.

3. Any school faculty has a legal mandate from the state, and a professional mandate from the larger social order, to uphold the values that the American society lives by.

4. Within the framework of 2. and 3. above, a faculty engaged in the process of curriculum development or change should draw on the services of selected lay (nonschool-board) personnel, but should regard and treat them as advisory in nature. This is not to downgrade the impor-

tance of the lay personnel; it is rather to pay proper respect to the representative process and to the professionalism of the teaching faculty.

The Role of Leadership.   With participants in the process of curriculum-making as diverse as professional faculties, university representatives, and lay individuals, the quality of leadership is always a serious concern. And leadership quality needs to reside in a professional faculty because that is the primary source from which leadership must emanate. It generally has tangible expression in all-school, or all-school-system, committee as well as in an individual leader. The functions of leadership are these:

1. Motivating interest.
2. Encouraging participation.
3. Arbitrating differences.
4. Synthesizing points of view.
5. Identifying common goals and purposes.
6. Capitalizing on professional differences: encouraging a professional faculty to keep scholars within the framework of school realities; the scholars to extend the conceptual horizons of a professional faculty; and lay personnel to refine the contributions of both.
7. Converting subgroup separateness into total-group unity.
8. Effecting the translation of abstract considerations into concrete proposals, leading ultimately to a final operational plan.
9. Organizing and administering an in-service program to ready operational personnel for their intended roles and tasks.
10. Assuring that materials of instruction are prepared, available, and properly disseminated.

The specifications of leadership in curriculum making have altered of late as groups have become more diversified. Unchanged are the conventional attributes germane to leadership in any group situation. In ascendancy is the demand for scholarliness as a leadership attribute. The assumption, in this connection, is that scholarliness in a leader breeds and appeals to scholarliness in a group. And, if not carried to a pedantic extreme, the assumption rises above criticism.

Movement toward the Specifics.   Curriculum personnel readied with goals, content categories, and a leadership scheme eventually move increasingly toward the specific. The term "symbolics," for instance, although descriptively useful to professional individuals, would remain operationally sterile unless converted into curriculum specifics. Thus as any curriculum gets closer to the classroom, generalities are more and more translated into specifics, and the abstract into the concrete.

In the hands of curriculum workers, symbolics would undergo division into reading, speaking, listening, writing, and computing. And each of these, in turn, would undergo further division into smaller units. Reading is sensing, perceiving, thinking, evaluating, analyzing, feeling, imagining, experiencing, and making motor movements. Embracing all these, a well conceived curriculum would weave them into an operational plan—a plan that would give structure to the topic, and guidance to teachers.

For "behavior of the individual" to become operationally functional at the high school level, it also would have to undergo analysis, division, and development. Such questions as these would need answering and implementing: Should the content take the form of a course in psychology or become part of the more informal guidance program, or both? Should the content relate to self-understanding broadly conceived—including such personality facets as self-hate and sadism toward others—or relate only to more socially approved content? Should the content expose and face up to Oedipal conflicts or avoid these as too laden with danger to public relations? Should the coverage assume only didactic characteristics or therapeutic characteristics as well?

My point here is that a curriculum is more than philosophical, although it must rest on a base of philosophy. So grounded, it must eventually culminate in an operational plan that guarantees structure for teachers and pupils alike. The ideal is for structure to be substantial enough to guide but flexible enough to allow spontaneity and creativity. It is within this framework that theory properly translates into the practical.

Curriculum plans vary widely from school system to school system. Some are general guides only, identifying little more than broad areas of content coverage. Others elaborate the specifics of educational goals, subject-matter content, teaching methods, and evaluation. A curriculum plan "in general" is probably no curriculum at all, and a curriculum plan in minute detail tends to defeat its intended purpose by over-structuring. Somewhere in between is the well-conceived curriculum plan that guides skillfully without stifling.

At a school-system or building level, a curriculum performs best when it satisfies these specifications: (1) identifies the significant concepts, skills, and attitudes that professional personnel regard as desirable outcomes for students; (2) organizes subject matter by topic or units; and (3) suggests experiences in which students can or should engage. A teacher, then, elaborates each of these by (4) selecting teaching methods which offer the most promise in the accomplishment of learning and evaluative outcomes.

Beauchamp, in deference to the need for specificity in curriculum development, has woven the first three of the above into the following Instructional Guide.[6].

[6] George A. Beauchamp, *Instructional Guide Worksheets* (Wilmette, Illinois: The Kagg Press, 1964).

Instructional Guide

Subject or Unit_____ Grade_____

Subject Matter Breakdown in Topics or Units	Suggested Activities for Children to Perform	Expected Outcomes in Changed Pupil Behavior		
		Concepts, Facts, or Generalizations to Be Learned	Skill Performances to Be Developed	Developmental Values to Be Acquired

Organizational Issues

Throughout the entire process of curriculum construction, a school makes decisions on the organizational patterns that will best serve the curriculum's intended purposes. And in this connection, organization relates to the curriculum scheme itself, to the methods of grouping children for learning, and to the methods of employing teachers in the instructional process.

With respect to the curriculum, education traditionally has organized learning around: (1) the separate subjects such as reading, music or biology; (2) around broad fields, such as language arts or social studies; (3) around correlated content wherein two or more subject areas, such as English and social studies, merge into a unified category; and (4) around social functions that appear under such captions as conservation, consumption, or transportation. For years, the separate-subjects approach was the vogue. Then, in the 1930's, education at the elementary level moved strongly in the direction of fusion or correlation. Secondary education, a decade later, followed suit, although to a much lesser extent.

The structuralists to the contrary, it is our opinion that narrow compartmentalization will continue to fight a losing action against curriculum breadth. In support of this opinion, we cite the growing integration of such related areas or disciplines as chemistry and biology; anthropology, economics, geography, history, political science, and sociology; English and social studies in a core program; and language structure and written expression. Actually, education can have its cake and eat it too by approaching learning both through selected of the individual disciplines and through molar problems that cut through the content and methods of inquiry of the many disciplines. Education, like life itself, has a place for both diagnostic analysis and synthesis. For this reason, education should reject the simplicity of an either-or proposition, and elect, instead the best from both.

Such topics as school organizational schemes for the grouping of pupils and the utilization of teachers for instruction are left for others to develop in detail. However, each of the last three chapters treats an aspect of these broader fields of thought: team teaching, the nongraded classroom, and the Advanced Placement Program.

A Schematic Design

Reserved for this last section is a schematic presentation of curriculum development that condenses the content of these first three chapters. The presentation, although stopping short of building-level detail in curriculum development, is projected as a preliminary for such an effort. It is from this frame that we shall continue to analyze selected of the emergent in curriculum trends, content, and teaching method.

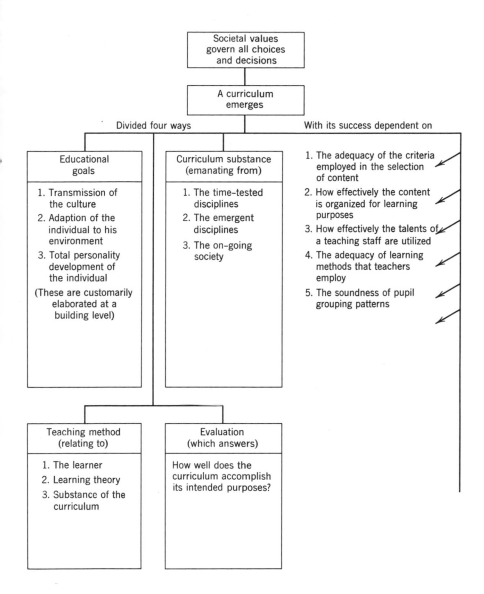

For Further Thought

1. React to the suggestion that "the behavior of the individual" and "a knowledge synthesis" should be a part of all curricula. Agree or disagree and state your reasons.

2. What qualifications would a teacher need in either area to be regarded as competent?

3. Do you know of a local community whose views are appreciably out of line with those of the national community? If you know of such a community, what problems is the rift making for the local school system?

4. Where would your basic loyalties lie in 3. above? why?

References

Alberty, Harold B. and Elsie J. Alberty, *Reorganizing The High-School Curriculum*. New York: The Macmillan Company, 1962.

Associction for Supervision and Curriculum Development, *New Insights and the Curriculum*. Washington, D.C.: A.S.C.D., 1963.

Association for Supervision and Curriculum Development, *Role of Supervisor and Curriculum Director in a Climate of Change*. Washington, D.C.: A.S.C.D., 1965.

Beauchamp, George A., *The Curriculum of the Elementary School*. Boston: Allyn and Bacon, Inc., 1964.

Doll, Ronald C., *Curriculum Improvement: Decision-making and Process*. Boston: Allyn and Bacon, Inc., 1964.

Douglass, Harl R. (ed.), *The High School Curriculum*. New York: The Ronald Press Company, 1964.

Huebner, Dwayne (ed.), *A Reassessment of the Curriculum*. Washington, D.C.: Teachers College Press, Columbia University, 1964.

Jameson, Marshall C. and Wm. V. Hicks, *Elementary School Curriculum: from Theory to Practice*. New York: American Book Company, 1960.

Krug, Edward A., *The Secondary School Curriculum*. New York: Harper and Brothers, 1960.

Oliver, Albert I., Curriculum Improvement: *A Guide to Problems, Principles, and Procedures*. New York: Dodd, Mead and Company, 1965.

Passow, A. Harry (ed.), *Curriculum Crossroads*. New York: Teachers College Press, Columbia University, 1962.

Shuster, Albert H. and Milton E. Ploghoft, *The Emerging Elementary Curriculum*. Columbus, Ohio: Charles E. Merrill Books, Inc., 1963.

Taba, Hilda, *Curriculum Development, Theory and Practice*. New York: Harcourt, Brace and World, Inc., 1962.

Wiles, Kimball, *The Changing Curriculum of the American High School*. Englewood Cliffs, N.J.: Prentice-Hall, Inc., 1963.

part **II**

Newer Curriculum Directions

chapter 4

Mental Health and Education

Committed to the purposes of cultural transmission, individual adaption, and total personality development, education needs a guiding frame within which to pursue them. Mental health provides just such a frame, operating as it does from these two fundamental principles: (1) that all human behavior stems from basic needs and drives, and (2) that the ultimate of growth is the total development of human personality.

Both mental health and education are grounded in the concept of individualism. Both conceive of contact with reality as essential to individual fulfillment. Both view well-being as a cherished end. Both seek the release of the positive psychic energy that resides in every one. And both strive along diversified dimensions to help every individual grow to his optimum. The case for mental health is this simple but also this fundamental: the emotionally healthy, not enervated by conflict and tension, are able to attack life's important tasks economically and efficiently. In contrast, the emotionally disturbed, enervated by the negative in life, have proportionately less reserve left for the positive. The communication to education here is obvious: a mentally healthy student body is a happy and a productive student body; a less healthy one is commensurately less happy and therefore less productive.

Before going any further, I pause to define three key terms. The first is *mental hygiene* which, simply stated, is the science of mental health. Its functions are prevention and cure of emotional illness. Its laboratory is human relationships. A second term, equally basic, is *mental*

47

health, which denotes a state of emotional equilibrium. The term characterizes those balanced, well-adjusted individuals who view themselves and life realistically; who, although critical of both, are also accepting of both. Mental health, like physical health, is a relative term existing always as more or less, never as all or none. A third basic term is *psychotherapy,* which is the process of psychological treatment.

Conceivably one of mental hygiene's most noteworthy contributions is that it transplants human behavior from the dead center of puritanical goodness and badness to the realm of the psychological. In this connection, orientations as divergent as psychoanalysis, neuropsychiatry, existential psychiatry, and clinical psychology share these common tenets. All concur to a degree that unconscious as well as conscious motivation constitutes the basis of decision making. All, despite differences of emphasis, concur that both genetic and environmental factors affect behavior. All likewise concur that, except for the acutely disturbed, every person needs to accept some or extensive responsibility for his own behavior. Thus, mental hygiene like religion is concerned with goodness and badness, but mental hygiene deals with them almost exclusively in a psychological frame of reference.

The respective mental-health orientations not only explain human behavior, but they make therapy available—at least to a selected extent—for those in need of it. In this regard, the past several generations are the first to have, at one and the same time, both a body of organized theory and a reasonably adequate system of therapy. The two in combination hold out modest hope to the world that man through improved insight will be able to relate more positively to his fellow man. And as mental health in individuals multiplies to a point of cumulative significance, the greater society will increasingly assume more pronounced characteristics of maturity.

Conversely, to the extent that individuals and the society accord the promising new theory only grudging support and succeed in circumventing the therapeutic methods, life will replicate its past mistakes. The neurotic will continue to succumb to his anxieties, and the psychotic to his fears. Traumatic as these outcomes inevitably will be for the disturbed themselves, they will not confine themselves to those individuals alone. Unfortunately, the anxieties and fears will splash over also on other members of primary reference groups including new offspring. Thus the sins of the fathers will continue to become the tainted inheritance of children of succeeding generations.

The emotionally disturbed person who feels inadequate and is menaced by this feeling tends to drain it off or to act it out in one of two ways. Either he withdraws into a protective shell, or he projects his negative emotions inappropriately and aggressively on others. Even so-called normal individuals follow one or both of these patterns on occasions, but the less normal pursue them more habitually.

The withdrawal syndrome can be observed to varying degrees in each of the following examples: the child who, having fought a losing battle with overpowering parents for personality status, retreats into introversion; the would-be little leaguer who, failing to make the team, escapes into autism; the stereotyped adult wall-flower who, apprehensive of close social involvement, remains always on the sidelines; or the agorophobic who, fearful of open spaces, stays in the unthreatening familiar. A surface reaction to these and comparable behavior manifestations may be that they are inoffensive and harmless. A penetrating analysis, however, predictably would reveal them as more harmful than they superficially appear. Actually, their more-or-less benign exteriors not infrequently serve as cover-ups for hostile affective content which, although bottled up temporarily, is capable of erupting at any time—and as often as not in the wrong place and at the wrong time. In any event, individuals who engage in such behavior shortchange themselves and society by falling short of their potentials.

Instances of the aggression syndrome are the bully who converts his inadequacy into belligerence; a counterpart of the child mentioned above who, instead of withdrawing from his overpowering parents, goes through life bristling both at them and at other authority figures; the unfulfilled person who, given power for the first time, abuses it; or the uninformed person who, plagued by a deflated ego, insists on being "the voice of authority." These individuals compensate for their inadequacies by attempting, consciously or unconsciously, to be what they are not. In the process, they remove themselves from reality and thus from the reach of logic and reason. The only avenue open to them is through their emotions.

At the group level, neurotic symptoms also abound, because the whole cannot divorce itself from its constituent parts. What, for instance, is imperialism but individual egocentricity compounded? At best, it reflects a thoughtless internalization of attitudes removed in time and place; at worst, it reveals a callous unconcern for the rights of others. Obviously neither is congenial in any sound value system. Also, what is die-hard nationalism but narcissism on a large scale? And what lies at the heart of most international misunderstandings but a provincial kind of self-righteousness which bars the door to tolerance and understanding? At a more mundane level, what is knee-bending to titles, social position, and foolish protocol but the acting out of juvenile emotions?

If we are correct in assuming that immaturity, often to the point of neuroticism, characterizes much individual and group behavior, education is remiss when it ignores the contagion. In view of the destructive potential of today's weapons of war, education may not much longer have a choice. The alternative even at this moment may well be either more altruism among the world's peoples or the end of an era.

Selected Statistics

Those who remain unconvinced by the cosmic justifications for mental health may be more impressed by these national statistics.

1. One person in 10, in the course of his lifetime, will be emotionally ill.[1]

2. One in every 20, in the course of his lifetime, will be a patient in a mental hospital.[2]

3. The population of disturbed children in school ranges from 4 per cent, as reported in certain studies, to as high as 12 per cent, as reported in others.[3]

4. The number of the emotionally ill in hospitals today is in excess of 750,000; these occupy 55 per cent of all hospital beds.[4]

5. The new-patient admission rate of the emotionally ill is 200,000 yearly.[5]

6. The ratio of first-admission psychotics is approximately 2 Negroes to 1 White. Admissions are also high among the Irish; lowest among Jews.[6]

7. Of medical discharges issued to defense personnel in World War II, 43 per cent were for psychiatric reasons.[7]

8. Approximately 4,000,000 persons in the country are alcoholics.[8]

9. Approximately 17,000 persons in the U.S. commit suicide yearly.[9]

10. In the nation's schools, three times as many boys as girls have serious mental-health problems.[10]

[1] William C. Menninger, *Psychiatry, Its Evolution and Present Status* (Ithaca: Cornell University Press, 1948), p. 98.
[2] Edward J. Shoben, "The Clinic And the Curriculum" in Dwayne Huebner (ed.), *A Reassessment of the Curriculum* (New York: Teachers College Press, Columbia University, 1964), pp. 55–56.
[3] W. D. Wall, *Education and Mental Health* (Paris: UNESCO, 1955), p. 240.
[4] August B. Hollingshead and Frederich C. Redlich, *Social Class and Mental Illness* (New York: John Wiley & Sons, 1958), Chapter 1.
[5] Harry S. Rivlin, "The Role of Mental Health in Education," *The Fifty-Fourth Year Book of the National Society for the Study of Education* (Chicago: University of Chicago Press, 1955), p. 12.
[6] Benjamin Malzberg, "Important Statistical Data About Mental Illness," *Handbook Of American Psychiatry* (ed. Silvano Ariete) (New York: Basic Books, Inc., 1959), pp. 171–172.
[7] Hollingshead and Redlich, Social Class and Mental Illness, Chapter 1.
[8] *Ibid.*
[9] *Ibid.*
[10] Carl Rogers, "Mental Health Findings in Three Elementary Schools," *Educational Research Bulletin* 21 (March 1942).

These data, indicative as they are of pathological conditions in the American society, should leave only the hardened unconcerned. In the first place, they weave a picture of human unhappiness and misery. In the second place, they reveal what undoubtedly is a lackadaisical approach by the society to illness prevention. In the third place, they reveal a society profligate of its most cherished possession, manpower. In this regard, whatever energy the emotionally ill expend in fruitless negative ways constitutes a serious and irrevocable loss of the positive in the total social order. For these and other reasons, America needs an all-out effort at the prevention of mental illness. And with ignorance no excuse, the society should settle for no less than such an effort.

Mental-Health Criteria

Against this introductory background, we now pose what is probably the most fundamental question of all. What are acceptable criteria for the assessment of mental health? A forthright answer is that no one knows for an absolute certainty. But neither does scholarship know for a certainty what constitutes intelligence or personality; yet, despite such admitted vagueness, activity in these areas does not stand still. Our constructive escape from the dilemma is into a listing of descriptive statements that leading mental-health theorists and practitioners would agree characterize the well-adjusted individual.[11]

These writers would concur that such an individual:

1. is independent; relies on others but not until he has first utilized his own resources.

2. lives by the reality principle; faces problems head on rather than circumventing or postponing attempts at solution.

3. stands behind his actions.

4. accepts himself including those limitations which he is unable to overcome.

5. yet is ever emergent in those areas where growth and change are possible, moving toward the goal of optimum development.

6. is flexible; is not easily upset by changes in living routines.

7. is uncompartmentalized, applying values in a consistent way in all of life's areas.

[11] The following we recommend as particularly germane to the criterion issue. Marie Jahoda, *Current Concepts of Positive Mental Health: A Report to Staff Director, Jack R. Ewalt* (New York: Basic Books, Inc., 1959), p. [xi]; Gail M. Inlow, *Maturity in High School Teaching* (Englewood Cliffs, N.J.: Prentice-Hall, Inc.; 1963), Ch. 1; Lawrence S. Kubie, *Neurotic Distortion of the Creative Process* (Lawrence: University of Kansas Press, 1958), p. 20; Abraham H. Maslow, *Motivation and Personality* (New York: Harper and Row, 1954), Ch. 12; and Ruth Strang, "Many Sided Aspects of Mental Health," *Fifty Fourth Yearbook*, National Society for the Study of Education (Chicago: University of Chicago Press, 1955); p. 36.

8. relates effectively to others.

9. keeps basic needs satisfied, as best he can, so as to increase his effectiveness in solving life's problems.

10. remains free of debilitating guilt.

11. works in the present but makes reasonable plans for the future.

12. has a high tolerance for frustration.

The above qualities admittedly characterize only a mythical entity who relies on others not until he has utilized his own resources, but yet who is fulfilled through others; who, without apology, accepts his current endowments, including the negative ones, but who works toward optimum growth; who speaks and acts and stands behind his words and actions; who accommodates well to reality, even unpleasant reality, when he is unable to change it for the better; who is flexible; whose life pattern is consistent; who exercises control over his behavior; who escapes the debilitating effects of guilt; and who is oriented in a balanced way to both the present and the future. This composite, like any ideal, constitutes a standard for nonidealized human beings to press toward. Some always will get closer to it than others. Some will miss it almost completely.

In contrast to the mentally healthy person or mythical stereotype is his maladjusted opposite who, in varying ways, is escapist, neurotic, psychotic, or psychopathic. Eschewing such technical nomenclature, we describe him as one who moves opposite to, or tangentially away from, the positive outcomes previously identified. So conceived, he remains dependent throughout childhood and adulthood, leaning heavily, and often compulsively, on others for ego satisfactions and the solving of life's problems. He dislikes his self image. He projects blame on others for his futility. He escapes from reality into denial and rationalization, and even, at times, into phantasy. He is rigid and unbending. His behavior is characterized by compulsiveness. He is burdened with guilt. Life for him is a state of continuous uncertainty and anxiety.

When one projects the contrasting composites of the last two paragraphs on a world screen, these conclusions emerge as inescapable. The first is that a world made up of mentally healthy individuals would enable all groups and individuals to resolve their differences with respect and dispatch. Second, it would be a place where personality fulfillment and creativity would be attainable.

A third logical conclusion, but of a contrasting dimension, is that a world which continues to brush aside its mental-health problems probably is a world which inadvertently is effecting its own dissolution. Before science became monolithic and at a time when communication channels were relatively limited, the greater culture could survive the macabre existence of poor mental health. Even when psychopathic personalities attained positions of high office, their power to destroy or to blight remained within bounds. Today, in contrast, with science awesome in its power to destroy, and with communications media equally awesome in their power to influence minds, instability in high places makes the entirety of civilization insecure and vulnerable.

The School's Responsibility for Mental Health

With the greater society committed to a program of mental-health action, society's most powerful agency, education, cannot escape the same commitment. The issue, thus, is not whether education will get into the business of mental health, for it is already there; it is an issue of degree of the involvement.

Actually, from the time the first school master recognized the superiority of persuasion and motivation over force, the involvement began. Even though its purpose was exclusively to enhance the cause of cognition, it still provided a start. Then, with the passage of time, as education assumed ever more responsibility for the total welfare of the children whom it served, the alliance with mental health became firmer. The recent shift of emphasis has been from mental health as a servant of the intellect to mental health as a legitimate end in its own right. This shift is not complete yet; but it seems to be in the making.

Increasingly supportive of the mental-health position of education is school law. Interestingly, by its many declarations that a teacher stands in loco parentis, law commits education to just such a position. After all, if the society expects blood parents to be responsible for the well-rounded development of their children, schools, as legal extensions of presumably conscientious parents, cannot be held less responsible. If the home cannot be allowed to fragment or ignore important growth areas, neither can the school.

The recent Brown case adjudicated by the Supreme Court in 1954, although fundamentally concerned with racial equality, also espouses, both by implication and by direct statement, the mental-health position. Throughout, it underscores the importance of social learnings, alludes to the adverse effects of inferiority feelings by pupils, and postulates a need for educational breadth. Specifically, it states that education "is the very foundation of good citizenship. Today it is a principal instrument in awakening the child to cultural values, in preparing him for later professional training, and in helping him to adjust normally to his environment." This indeed is a broadly inclusive stand and one not far removed from a complete mental-health stand.

In spite of the society's growing support of mental health in the schools, the union is not yet intimate. Those educational efforts which stay close to the conventional norm are uncontroversial: for instance, the hiring of well-adjusted teachers, the maintenance of wholesome human relations in a school, and the providing of fringe counseling services. However, when more radical departures from normative practice take place, such as the hiring of a clinical psychologist and the associated dismissal of students from classes for purposes of counseling, the old guard inside and outside the ranks of education often becomes fitful and sometimes antagonistic.

The Total-Personality Position Is Requisite. Cognizant that the comfortable old understandably recoils from the threatening new, wise is the faculty which, when able to do so, relates the innovational to the existent. Thus it is logical procedure for any school to defend a projected or an on-going mental-health program on grounds of its possible contributions to the intellectual growth of students. The supporting thesis is that education serves the cause of intellectualism best when it treats learners holistically and organismicly. And this constitutes none other than the whole-man or the total-personality point of view.

Shoben states the point of view this way:

> Thus, the school is charged with the responsibility of attending not only to the "whole child" in a "child-centered situation," but to the creation in each child of a "healthy personality" comprising moral ideals, clear and realistic vocational goals, the necessary knowledges and skills for his social functioning, and the foundations of an emotional maturity that will protect him against the development of clinical symptoms.[12]

Specifically, the total-personality point of view makes the school responsible for the many facets of growth: emotional, esthetic, ethical, mental, physical, and social. Within this point of view, all are related; none is discrete. Within certain situations, however, the mental may need highlighting for the other qualities to appear palatable to the otherwise resistant critics.

The central theme of this total-personality position is that education must project a perspective in breadth if children and youth are to develop toward their potentials. The goal is the optimum of authenticated knowledge in the frame of wholesome attitudes and social responsibility. The desired escape is from the untrue, from provincialism in its many manifestations, and from neurotic distortion. Elementary schools, for the most part, have long since adopted this position; junior-high schools have been somewhat less enthusiastic; but senior-high schools have only half-heartedly fallen into line.

One reason for the high schools' reluctance is the long-lived dominance of university scholars over secondary education. Certain of these schol-

[12] Shoben, in Huebner, *Reassessment of Curriculum,* pp. 56–57.

ars, conceiving the cognitive as monistic, so thoroughly indoctrinate teacher trainees into that position that it accompanies them later into the classroom. A second reason is the tendency of many teacher-training institutions to accentuate child growth and development for the elementary-school teacher but to pass lightly over adolescent growth and development for the secondary-school teacher. A third reason is the assumption by many that growth along affective lines is a natural by-product of intellectual growth. The perennialists tend to make this assumption. And a fourth reason is the departmental arrangement characteristic of secondary education which, by the very weight of pupil numbers which it imposes, makes the affective outcomes difficult for teachers to accomplish. However, regardless of reasons for a counter arrangement, I categorically stand behind a broad learning base for the entire period of elementary and secondary education, and one which extends, although in a somewhat lesser way, even into professional specialization. I contend that the best in contemporary theory supports such a stand.

The Outward Limits of Education's Mental-Health Commitment. Demanding of answer at this point is the question: How deep and extensive is education's commitment to the cause of mental health? Should the schools make the same kind of frontal assault in areas other than the intellectual that they make in the area of the intellectual? A practical answer is that selected schools can do little more than selected local communities will permit them to do. This argument, while eliciting no counter, begs the philosophical issue. In regard to the latter, once more it is the author's conviction that emotional and physical health, esthetic sensitivity, social competency, and ethical values are important enough in themselves, apart from any contingent importance that they might have, to merit substantial attention from education. In a very vital sense, these are general-education outcomes that all who are to live the good life cannot do without. Furthermore, without these associated outcomes the single outcome of intellectualism, assuming that it can exist alone, stands remotely austere. Knowledge detached from overall personal well being and from overall social application can be sterile, at best, and destructive, at worst.

Returning to the question, now: How far should education's mental-health commitment go? We predict for the future that only public apathy will prevent its going at least as far as limited psychotherapy—psychological first aid, that is. Since education is for the good life, and since emotional maturity is essential to the good life, the case, from the point of view of logic, is already airtight. What is needed at the moment is time for the culture to accept it. Allinsmith and Goethals, addressing themselves to the same fundamental question, view formal education even now as entrusted with five responsibilities for mental health: detection, diagnosis and prognosis, psychological first aid, referral, and treatment short of depth methods.[13]

In this same connection, a sizeable minority of the nation's schools, mostly suburban and urban, have at present—and some have had for several decades—the services of one or more clinical psychologists or psychiatrists (or psychoanalysts) for purposes of limited psychotherapy. For instance, the Winnetka school system in Illinois, as long ago as the early twenties, had a psychiatrist on its staff for purposes both of prevention and correction. The community of Winnetka, being ahead of its time, realized that a maladjusted child is a fragmented child in need of more than just a hard core of academic learning. Schools with this orientation, however, are still in a minority. Most still accord firmer status to the cognitive component of the "whole-man" point of view than to the emotional component.

The School Needs to Be an Inviting Place. However much any school aspires to mental-health outcomes, its aspirations will fall short unless a school climate of warmth and receptiveness exists. In such a climate, adult authority will still need to establish standards and set limits, but in the process it will minimize its "power-over" position. In this way, the school becomes at once a businesslike place and an inviting place where human personality has premium value. Factors that make a school business-like are a sound curriculum and effective, scholarly teaching. Other factors that make it a healthy school are the mental health of the teachers, competition among pupils kept under careful control, and individualism accorded its rightful place of priority.

If mental-health outcomes in a school are to be achieved, the basic theory which underlies them must permeate every aspect of a school's program. As stated over two decades ago by Carl Rogers, mental health in a school "cannot be something extraneous to the educational structure, but must be an integral part of administrative and classroom policies and procedures . . ." He concluded that only the totality of a school's program can determine whether the mental health of children is being affected positively or adversely.[14]

A School Needs to Individualize Its Curriculum. A school climate as inviting as the one just described presupposes a curriculum that by its very nature meets each student where he is and then guides him progressively toward his potential. This outcome depends for consummation on the careful assessment of the needs of a student body preliminary to the tailoring of a curriculum to meet those needs. Such an approach goes counter to much existing practice which customarily starts with

[13] Wesley Allinsmith and George W. Goethals, *The Role of Schools in Mental Health* (New York: Basic Books Inc., 1962), pp. 42–91.
[14] Carl R. Rogers, "Mental Health Findings."

a fixed curriculum and expects pupils, ready or not, to rise to the fixed demands. Needed instead is the proper blending of general education, exploratory education, and specialized education into a unified curriculum totality that extends along the entire range of a student body's differences.

As stated earlier in the book, general education is that part of a curriculum that opens the door to meaning in life. It opens the door by giving to all a shared core of knowledge, understandings, skills, appreciations, and attitudes. Equipped with this core, individuals are better able to accomplish the goal of adaption while pressing toward the loftier goal of total development. The keys to general education are curriculum experiences balanced across the vast panorama of life, and these same experiences shared by the many. General education is a requisite of mental health in that it unites individuals with common bonds, enables them to relate better to each other, and lays a foundation for future growth. All of these are essential to a healthy emotional state.

Relatively uncontroversial in any program of general education are the basic academic skills; and the academic content areas of literature, the social sciences, the natural sciences, and mathematics. More controversial, especially at the high-school level, however, are the esthetic, the recreational, and the motor-manipulative areas. Yet no less an authority than William Menninger regards these as endowed with significant mental-health potentialities. He views them as opportunities for the acting out of aggressions, for the securing of social fulfillment, and for the satisfying of creative impulses. And because such activities are inherently therapeutic, he objects to their being doled out by authority figures as rewards for hard work or good behavior. His thesis is that the blowing off of steam on the athletic field releases tension; a creation in art or music fills a basic need; and group recreational activity leads to social fulfillment.[15] All of these are curriculum instrumentalities which aim, although not exclusively, at the desired outcomes of mental health.

And finally, general education is concerned with the attitudes that pupils develop toward other individuals, toward human differences, toward social purposes, and toward customs. When these attitudes are wholesome, the individual and society reap the benefit; when they are unwholesome or pathological, both are losers.

In addition to the general-education purpose of the curriculum, which is to form a common base of meaning for students, there exists the exploratory purpose which is to widen the range of a student's knowledge, skills, interests, and attitudes. This purpose is provided for at the ele-

[15] William C. Menninger, "Recreation and Mental Health," *Recreation*, 42 (November 1948), pp. 340–346.

mentary-school level by enriched offerings that go beyond the essentials; and at the junior- and senior-high grade levels primarily through the medium of curriculum electives, but also through the constants that are made deliberately exploratory. The recently popularized seventh, eighth, or ninth grade course in industrial arts is an exploratory course of this sort. It customarily provides a six-week unit block in each of the following areas: woods, metals, electricity, printing, mechanical drawing, and shop. A comparable exploratory course in art enables the individual student to explore such diversified art media as painting, plastics, copper enameling, and sculpturing.

General education and exploratory education, each in its own way, contributes to mental health. The first relates to both an individual and a cultural need, namely, the need of any individual to share a common bond with others while he makes an adjustment to his environment. The second relates to the mental-health need of an individual to open new vistas and to develop new interests on the way to greater personality fulfillment.

Supplementing the outcomes of general education and exploration in a curriculum is a third outcome of intensification that usually carries the label of specialization. This latter curriculum category, which is the almost exclusive property of the secondary school, has a definite place but needs to be controlled. Generally speaking, the schools should permit a reasonable amount of specialization but should discourage extremes. And under no circumstances, we are convinced, should students be allowed to escape a basic general education or elect themselves out of worthwhile exploratory experiences. For instance, it is to be decried when a student is allowed, as he would be in a number of secondary schools, to enroll for 2 Carnegie Units of credit in typing, 2 in shorthand, 1 in bookkeeping, 1 in business law, and 1 in business letter writing. In such a situation, his one commercial interest is allowed to become overly-dominant. To prevent this one-sidedness—whether in the commercial subjects, industrial-arts subjects, or academic subjects is immaterial—education needs to place a limit on specialization. In so doing, it would insure necessary breadth by preventing narrowly conceived, short-range curriculum choices.

It is also to be decried, however, when a high school regularly encourages overspecialization in the academic subjects. Conant's advocacy of an almost completely academic program for the gifted, to the extent of recommending that a fifth or sixth academic subject be added to the normal four, moves dangerously in such a direction. Fine art, music, and the practical arts have a message for the gifted as well as for the less gifted and the nongifted. Specialization in a specific area of life that completely excludes other significant areas must be regarded as running counter to the mental-health advocacy of breadth.

Students Need the Feeling of Success. Irrespective of the exact nature of the curriculum offerings of any given school, it must provide experiences wherein students can know success. This outcome is imperative for any curriculum with a mental-health orientation. And it is an outcome apparently ignored by a number of outspoken critics of recent vintage who have campaigned for "toughness" in the schools. Curriculum toughness used synonymously with curriculum challenge evokes no argument. But toughness conceived in terms of a fixed standard for all, regardless of individual differences, makes school an intolerable place for the have nots. Formal education admittedly has an obligation to play up to pupil strengths, but in the process it cannot ignore pupil limitations.

A curriculum which challenges all but which extends beyond the reach of none goes counter, however, to many existing school practices: for instance, competitive marking, honors conferred for firstness, failure of pupils who do their best, and teacher detachment from submiddle-class needs and expectations. The strongest case against these and related malpractices is built on the unfairness of differential recognition in a situation where the ability of individuals to compete is notoriously uneven. The usual rejoinder to this point of view is that because life is competitive, the schools must be competitive. The rejoinder is vulnerable, however, in that education's purpose is not to perpetuate a questionable status quo but to effect progressive change. The mental-health thesis is that the *what-is* is a forerunner to the *what should be.* And the latter finds its best validation in the humanistic values presented in Chapter 1, and in the goal of total-personality development espoused throughout the book.

The School Needs a Frontal Approach to Mental-Health Content. Within this structure of holistic humanism, schools need to inject into their curricula systematized content drawn from the several mental-hygiene orientations. Such content, at the moment, could not be regarded as constituting a discipline in the Bruner usage of the term because the content is still too dynamic and evolving. However, as indicated in Chapter 2, we do not consider this a deterrent, vague as most are about what a discipline exactly is.

The fundamental consideration, as far as we are concerned, is that mental hygiene does exist in a meaningful way as a more-or-less systemized body of postulates and concepts. That it exists in many academic fields: clinical psychology, psychoanalysis, sociology, and neuropsychiatry is not defeating. Nor are differences among, as well as within, any of these orientations any more defeating. Differences in the behavioral sciences are to be expected.

Regardless of differences, scholars from the several orientations need to lift from all of them a teachable body of meaningful content appropriate for incorporation into the schools' curricula. The problems we recognize: the rift between psychologists and psychiatrists; the resulting difficulty of diverse orientations in reaching agreement over appropriate content; the arduous task of schools' finding teachers qualified to handle the content sensitively; the inevitable backlash from parents; and the difficulties involved in a school's integrating new content into the various grade levels of an already crowded curriculum.

Yet, because the key to the future lies in man's understanding of himself, education is remiss not to consider seriously every avenue which might lead to that outcome. For centuries, it has looked to the academic disciplines to accomplish this purpose. More recently, it has turned to an amorphous, many-headed entity called guidance which is going in too many other directions—educational, vocational, and social—to do the job alone. These approaches undoubtedly have proved helpful, but not helpful enough, as the pathology in our society will testify. Thus the time may well be ripe for education to try out new approaches. One of these logically is the direct instructional approach to mental health.

The Teacher's Mental-Health Role in the Classroom

The emphasis of the preceding section was on selected mental-health responsibilities of the school as an organizational entity. The emphasis of this section will be on selected mental-health responsibilities of teachers in their roles as classroom leaders and guides of children and youth.

The Teacher Needs to Accept All Students.   The greatest single contribution any teacher can make to the cause of mental health is to accord every pupil acceptance. The mental-health mandate here is one and the same as the democratic mandate: human dignity must be respected. The ideal demands sincere warmth and total acceptance by every teacher of every pupil. The practical inevitably falls short of this ideal. The compromise calls for no less than operational neutrality before all, whether Christian or Jew, Negro or White, rich or poor, bright or dull, introvert or extrovert, child of physician or child of lathe operator, member of the middle class or of a submiddle class, resident of the Waldorf Astoria or of a trailer camp. Any of these may shed clinical light on a given personal or academic problem, but none can be allowed to obstruct receptiveness.

Acceptance Contributes to Pupil Self Worth.   An inherent reason why well adjusted teachers need to accept pupils with empathy is that by the very nature of their maturity they can do no less. But at the practical level, it is operationally essential that they act in this way. The reason is that pupils can attain gratifying heights of self-worth in no other climate.

The newborn appears in the world a bewildered, diffused personality who during the first few years of life constructs an entire subjective world around himself. Family and physical factors initially exist solely to serve him and his needs. Gradually he begins to relate outwardly: first to mother, then to father and siblings, and ultimately to an expanding personal and physical world.

A healthy progression is his to the extent that he moves from self, to family members, to a few outsiders, to the many, and finally to the cosmic all; and from a narrow physical world to an expanding universe. However, this progression stays healthy only when the maturing individual and his guiding super-ego figures are able collectively to remove or shove aside the inevitable roadblocks which thrust themselves periodically into the growth path. As each of these is removed or hurdled without undue loss of psychic energy to the individual, he retains ego strength to attack subsequent blockages.

What keeps this store of ego strength in adequate supply is, in great part, the acceptance accorded the individual by his associates. When this acceptance rises to great heights, the store remains almost untapped. When, however, this acceptance is denied, the store gets soon depleted. The communication to teachers here is clear: they are commissioned to accept each pupil with warmth, encourage others in a classroom or school to do the same, and through this combined effort to lay the groundwork for an ever improving pattern of ego development. With self-worth basic to all other psychic outcomes, this is none other than a reasonable expectation. The mental health of any pupil, in fact, may well depend on just such an approach.

Acceptance But Also Limits. Woven into the framework of acceptance is the associated need for the supporting structure of established limits. The child perplexed by such hard-to-explain phenomena as injustice, disease, pain, and death, although not expecting the impossible, looks to his world of authority for as much security as it can reasonably provide. Then when his world reveals to him that it has boundaries which set off right from wrong and limits which properly deter and restrict, he receives a measure of ego strength.

The concept of limits has been subjected to considerable experimentation in the field of psychiatry. For instance, in the psychiatric ward of the Michael Reese Hospital of Chicago (although certainly not exclusively there), certain types of neurotic, and occasionally a few mildly psychotic, patients are admitted to a family constellation of 15 to 20 individuals of varying ages. Communicated to a new arriver is the fact that any increase in his freedom in the future will depend upon his adjustment to established limits. He is told that if he carelessly and habitually invades the privacy of others, ignores schedules, or insists on other manifestations of rugged individualism, his freedom will remain limited; but if he demonstrates a growing ability to live within bounds, his freedom will be extended. The underlying theory is that established limits are essential to all of life and thus to therapy.

A primary task of the teacher, in this regard, is to establish a pattern of classroom expectation that will provide security for all without unduly restricting freedom for any. This pattern should never become immutable; rather it should expand and contract in response to group changes. When pupils demonstrate greater maturity, the teacher extends the limits of behavior; but when pupils demonstrate more infantilism, the teacher constricts the limits commensurately.

Power with, Not Power over.   Yet when a teacher exercises the authority inherent in his position, he needs to do so with restraint and trepidation. A satisfactory answer to each of the following questions might serve as a test of the propriety of his behavior. Was the amount of power superimposed on pupils held to a minimum? Was it imposed in a climate of emotional maturity? And was it imposed for ego-supporting needs of the teacher or as the best way to rectify a situation lying outside the framework of the teacher's ego?

The proper and judicious exercise of teacher authority is necessary if the classroom is not to become a battleground of the emotions. Compensation breeds compensation, and dominance breeds dominance. Thus the danger is ever present that the teacher who exercises power over pupils beyond the point of necessity will thereby give encouragement to a power-over relationship between and among students.

Unfortunately, the world of business and industry attests to the reality of this danger. By definition, the line and staff organization is characterized by position levels and power differences: the higher the position, the greater the power; the lower the position, the less the power. The existence of this power structure leads continually to such revealing questions as: Who is the top man? How many are under him? How much weight does he throw? Who is closest to the big boss? Even in Christendom, the power-structure trappings often adulterate what many sects purport to believe.

Unable to propose a practical substitute for universally-existing power structures, we accept them as inevitable. But in the process, we go on record that power should be increasingly employed by maturing individuals as an unavoidable evil, never as a deified value. A sharp distinction exists, for instance, between the individual who occupies a power position because he knows he has the qualifications to perform its duties in a competent way and his counterpart who manifestly is a glory seeker. Teachers particularly need to assess their attitudes toward power. Ideally, their strivings should be for power-with, not power-over roles. Their aim should be greater equality, not greater difference. They should guide more than demand, share more than allocate, and delight more in group success than in self success. The mental-health position actually gives teachers no choice but this power-with orientation.

Progress Should Be toward Independence. Within a classroom climate characterized by freedom in a framework of security and shared effort, independence looms as a cherished goal. After all, what is the ultimate of mental health but the optimum ability of an individual to use his resources for the good of himself and others? At one pole of any growth continuum, the infant stands out as completely dependent on others for his continuing existence. At the opposite end, the mature individual stands out as a person who has made maximum progress toward independence.

Actually, the movement of any individual toward independence is inevitably halting and uneven, characterized as much by regression as by overall progression. Fundamentally, independence is a function of chronological age, requiring teachers in the lower grades to sustain and to bolster more; those in the higher grades, to sustain and bolster less. But independence is likewise a function of pupil maturity irrespective of age. Accordingly, teachers of children of all ages must encourage it differentially. They can properly provide or withhold support only after assessing the personality needs of any individual at any given time.

Apart from factors within the maturing individual himself, the most important single conditioner of progress toward independence is the posture of authority that defines for others their operational roles and controls the patterns of action. When it is power-over authority, it demands allegiance to external standards of rightness and wrongness, rewarding the first and punishing the second. When it is power-with authority, it encourages allegiance to an ever evolving composite of internal standards with external criteria minimized. Under the shadow of the first, authenticity concedes to authority-pleasing behavior, to other-directedness, and to performance which tends to fall short of individual potential. Under the guiding influence of the second, the emerging individual becomes the locus of evaluation. To the extent that anyone's primary goal in life is conceived as pleasing authority figures and then being rewarded, dependence becomes the heritage. Conversely, to the extent that anyone's goal in life is selfhood with the attendant obligation to develop and adhere to lofty self-imposed standards, independence becomes the reward. It is interesting to note in this regard, although certainly not surprising in view of his orientation, that Carl Rogers translates this same point of view into the framework of counseling.

In almost every phase of our lives—at home, at school, at work—we find ourselves under the rewards and punishment of external judgments. "That's good"; "that's naughty." "That's worth an A"; "that's a failure." "That's good counseling;" "that's poor counseling." Such judgments are a part of our lives from infancy to old age. I believe they have a certain social usefulness to institutions and organizations such as schools and professions. Like everyone else I find myself all too often making such evaluations. But, in my experience, they do not make for personal growth, and hence I do not believe that they are a part of a helping relationship. Curiously enough a positive evaluation is as threatening in the long run as a negative one, since to inform someone that he is good implies that you also have the right to tell him he is bad. So I have come to feel that the more I can keep a relationship free of judgment and evaluation, the more this will permit the other person to reach the point where he recognizes that the locus of evaluation, the center of responsibility, lies within himself. The meaning and value of his experience is in the last analysis something which is up to him, and no amount of external judgment can alter this. So I should like to work toward a relationship in which I am not, even in my own feelings, evaluating him. This I believe can set him free to be a self-responsible person.[16]

The Teacher's Own Emotional Health

Operating as the catalyst of mental health in any school is the classroom teacher. And it is the quality of his own emotional adjustment that, in large part, crowns the school's program with success or condemns it to failure. To the extent that he has fought through to a satisfactory conclusion the many problems of self, he is better able to help his younger associates resolve theirs. By the same logic, however, to the extent that he has been unsuccessful in the battle of self, he is proportionately less qualified to assist others to overcome their conflicts.

The fundamental issue here is the feasibility of self-understanding and self-therapy, with these three questions demanding answers. First, is it possible for anyone to understand himself and then to administer self-therapy? Second, are the processes desirable? Third, if they are both possible and desirable, respectively, what are some recommended procedural steps?

Are self-understanding and self-therapy possible?   This most basic of the three questions would elicit some type of affirmative answer from most reputable therapists today, although it would be a qualified affirmative in almost all instances. A conservative few would predict the amount of insight achieved through self methods to range from negligible to

[16] Carl Rogers, "The Characteristics of a Helping Relationship," *Personnel and Guidance Journal* 37 (September 1958), p. 14.

little. The majority would predict the amount to be considerable. And a few would predict a highly gratifying outcome. One of the most sanguine and articulate of this last group is Karen Horney, theoretician and analyst practitioner. She directed an entire book at the defense of the self-help thesis.[17] An equally strong defense would be made by most neo-Freudians from Carl Jung to the present, by most existential psychiatrists and psychologists, and by most phenomenological psychologists.

The case for self analysis certainly has a firm base in logic. As I have asked elsewhere: "What is education but a means to self-growth and the associated change in personality structure? What is introspection but a means of peering into motivations and circumstances en route to better understanding? And what is therapy but self-analysis encouraged by a counselor?"[18]

Despite the logic of the case, however, it weakens when confronted with unconscious motivation. Is it possible that the unconscious mind might so distort any self-appraisal that authenticity would be impossible of attainment? Any answer here can rest only in relativity. To the degree than any individual is better adjusted and thus less susceptible to ego-escape temptations, he will be better able to face himself and effect needed change. But to the degree that he is more maladjusted and thus more susceptible to ego-escape temptations, he will be less able, or completely unable, to face himself and effect needed change. Yet for most, self-insight followed by self-effected change is as natural and inevitable as living. Living itself, in fact, encompasses just such a process.

Is introspection desirable? To this second question, we offer an unqualified "yes." The probing self-look is almost always revealing, sometimes may be disturbing, and occasionally may even be temporarily disruptive, but the overall positive is believed to outweigh the discordant. A negative to this same question is usually predicated on the alleged danger of an individual's exposure to the sordid before he is ready for its impact. Apropos of this point of view, an outspoken minority of a sample of psychiatrists and clinical psychologists recently voiced this fear in a research study of mine. However, two thirds to three fourths of the sample treated self-analysis as a natural process and thus not one to be feared.[19] Karen Horney's conjecture on this issue is an interesting one: it is that man has a built-in psychological valve that he unconsciously shuts off when about to uncover content that would be ego shattering.

My fear is less of people who engage in self-analysis than of those who do not. Like Carl Jung, I regard self-examination as a step "toward

[17] Karen Horney, *Self Analysis* (New York: W. W. Norton and Co., 1942).
[18] Gail M. Inlow, *Maturity in High School Teaching* (Englewood Cliffs, N.J.: Prentice-Hall, Inc., 1963), pp. 5–6.
[19] Gail M. Inlow, "Can the School Curriculum Make a Frontal Approach to Mental Health?" *Journal of Educational Research*, 36 (April 1963), pp. 395–402.

human dignity" and ultimately even toward international understanding.[20] Without self-examination, and the resulting clarity of vision, it is Jung's contention that all mankind conceivably may be doomed. In man's myopic state of psychological blindness toward others, he becomes easily victimized by unconscious hate, guilt, and delusions. Yet man looks on himself as harmless, hyper-intellectual, and holy, thereby concealing the sadism of deeds. The cure, says Jung, is self-criticism. "We can recognize our prejudices and illusions only when from a broader psychological knowledge of ourselves and others we begin to doubt the absolute rightness of our assumptions and compare them with objectivity."

How can insight be gained? This third question could well receive the capricious answer: "mature early, stay healthy, and live long." A straight answer is that although there are guiding principles, there is no fixed, absolute way. Insight is a lifetime assignment, and gains are always in relative terms. Yet within this framework of relativity, selected postulates are near the point of becoming truisms. Selected of these follow:

1. Physical health and insight are interdependent. With organic and functional conditions of the human body affecting the emotions, and with the emotions affecting insight, the three factors of the physical, the emotional, and self-understanding emerge as inseparable. Since physical health is basic to the other two, however, a teacher should give it unusually close attention.

2. Belief in the possibility of personality change is fundamental. Without contesting the influence of his biological and environmental inheritance, the teacher on the road to maturity should have absolute confidence in his ability to change his own personality for the better. The aphorism that says what the child is when he is six, he will be forever after, must be replaced by the conviction that personality is always changing, never static.

3. Change is a result of desire. And desire for change usually follows in the wake of dissatisfaction with self. Our admonition to the teacher, in this regard, is to motivate self-growth by avoiding complacency. When we advocate dissatisfaction, however, we have in mind only the degree of dissatisfaction necessary to motivate growth; not the excessive amount which would debilitate.

4. The teacher should always strive to increase his knowledge. Interrelated with most, if not all, significant personality change is the ever unfolding world of knowledge and understandings. The humanities help the individual to relate to himself; the social sciences help him to relate

[20] Carl G. Jung, "God, The Devil, And the Human Soul," *Atlantic Monthly,* **200** (November 1957), pp. 57–63.

to others; and the natural sciences help him to relate to the biological and physical world. And within the framework of all three, a growing sophistication in the area of symbolism helps him to refine his observations of himself and of life. Accordingly, education for the teacher, whether formal or informal in nature, should always be on the increase as he progresses toward his optimum of growth.

5. He should be fulfilled esthetically as well as intellectually. The good life cannot ever be disproportionately one-sided. Thus such experiences as contained in music, painting, sculpture, ceramics, the drama, the ballet, and other sources of beauty must ever be part of a growth pattern, because they serve to enrich personality.

6. Recreation relaxes and liberates. As indicated previously, recreational activities have therapeutic properties that bring reality into better focus. And as reality becomes sharper, insight invariably becomes clearer.

7. The outward-extension principle should be a beckoning guide. Maturity is described in various ways as progression from self to others, as progression from the narrow to the universal, or as altruism. All of these demand an outward extension of life until contact is made, at least at the hypothetical level, with the entire cosmos. Extension is from narrower to broader values, from few to many people, and from a body of restricted values to a world of expanding values.

As the teacher extends his knowledge horizons, esthetic horizons, recreational horizons, geographical horizons, social horizons, and time horizons, his life assessments will become more authentic. I make no effort to simplify the arduous process of insight and self-improvement, but neither do I consider it impossible to attain. Assuming good physical health, desire, conviction, and reasonable expectation, the teacher, within broad limits, con be his own therapist. Nor am I putting professional therapy out of business. Rather I am supplmenting it.

For Further Thought

1. Evaluate the twelve criteria of mental health listed in the early part of the chapter. Do you regard them all as valid? If not, give your reasons for rejecting any or all.

2. Evaluate your own mental health against the criteria that you regard as valid.

3. Assess your ability to take positive action on the shortcomings which your analysis uncovered. What specific action is indicated?

4. Do you agree with the author that competitive grading in education runs counter to a mental-health orientation? Defend your stand either way.

5. Will you be able to accept all students as likeable members of the human race? If not, what is the constructive compromise?

6. What relationship do you perceive between so-called goodness-badness theory and the more modern mental-health theory? Relate the latter to such concepts as sin, repentance, conversion, and forgiveness.

References

Abrahamsen, David, *The Road to Emotional Maturity*. Englewood Cliffs, N.J.: Prentice-Hall, Inc., 1958.

Allinsmith, Wesley and George W. Goethals, *The Role of Schools in Mental Health*. New York: Basic Books Inc., 1962.

Bonney, Merl E., *Mental Health in Education*. Boston: Allyn and Bacon, Inc., 1960.

Fromm, Erich, *The Sane Society*. New York: Holt, Rinehart, and Winston, 1955.

Hollingshead, August B. and Frederich C. Redlich, *Social Class and Mental Illness*. New York: John Wiley & Sons, 1958.

Horney, Karen, *Our Inner Conflicts*. New York: W. W. Norton and Co., 1945.

Horney, Karen, *Self Analysis*. New York: W. W. Norton and Co., 1942.

Hountras, Peter T. (ed.), *Mental Hygiene. A Text of Readings*. Columbus: Charles E. Merrill Books, Inc., 1961.

Inlow, Gail M., "Can the School Curriculum Make A Frontal Approach to Mental Health?" *Journal of Educational Research*, 56 (April 1963), pp. 395–402.

Inlow, Gail M., *Maturity in High School Teaching*. Englewood Cliffs, N.J.: Prentice-Hall, Inc., 1963, Ch. 1.

Jahoda, Marie, *Current Concepts of Positive Mental Health*. New York: Basic Books, Inc., 1959.

Jung, Carl G., "God, The Devil, and the Human Soul," *Atlantic Monthly*, (November 1957).

Maslow, Abraham S., *Motivation and Personality*. New York: Harper and Row, 1954.

Public Health Service, *The Teacher and Mental Health*, Publication No. 385. Washington, D.C.: U.S. Department of Health, Education and Welfare, 1962.

Redl, Fritz, and Wm. W. Wattenberg, *Mental Hygiene in Teaching*. New York: Harcourt, Brace & World, Inc., 1959.

Seidman, Jerome M. (ed.), *Educating for Mental Health: A Book of Readings*. New York: Thomas Y. Crowell Company, 1963.

Stevenson, George S. and Harry Milt, M.D., *Master Your Tensions and Enjoy Living Again*. Englewood Cliffs, N.J.: Prentice-Hall, Inc., 1959.

Torrance, E. Paul, *Constructive Behavior: Stress, Personality, and Mental Health*. Belmont, Calif.: Wadsworth Publishing Company, Inc., 1965.

Wall, W. D. (ed.), *Yearbook of Education, Education and Mental Health*. Geneva: UNESCO, 1958.

chapter 5

Creativity and Education

The mental-health theme of the past chapter flows logically into the creativity theme of the present one. Shortly, it will be developed that the two lie along the same dimension.[1]

Throughout the chapter, the term creativity will be used to connote the capacity of an individual to relate sensitively, to think divergently, and to perform imaginatively in his confrontations with people and ideas. The operational assumption is this: that creativity is a constellation of attributes that express themselves differently in any single individual depending on the specific talent under consideration. The rejected contrasting position is that creativity is a unitary component. Within the framework of our operational position, any individual predictably will be more creative in certain life areas than in others. He might, for instance, be more creative in biological research, less creative in chemical research; somewhat creative as a literary writer, not very creative as a literary critic; highly creative as a community citizen, almost totally uncreative as a business man. Creativity in any single person might reveal itself along several or many dimensions, in a single dimension only, or almost not at all along any dimension.

Furthermore, our operational thesis is that the individual himself constitutes his own standard of creativity. In other words, to the extent that he measures up to his own built-in creative potential, he is creative. Thus, rejected is the long-held assumption that creativity needs to rise to the heights of a Picasso in art, a Mahler in music, a Samuel Johnson in literature, or a Darwin in science. Each of these did no more or no

[1] This same position is taken, among others, by Catherine Patrick, *What Is Creative Thinking?* (New York: Philosophical Library, 1955); and by E. Paul Torrance, *Guiding Creative Talent* (Englewood Cliffs, N.J.: Prentice-Hall, Inc. 1962).

less than many less-gifted people of his own day might have done, or of the present might do, namely, reach their optimum potential.

Creativity translated into a school setting could well reveal itself as any of the following: a first-grader who makes a serious game of trying out new words; a fifth-grader who researches a case against the stereotyped perfectionism of George Washington; a tenth-grade "combo" group which develops a novel performance style; or a twelfth-grader who seeks practical uses for probability theory introduced by the new mathematics program. It could also reveal itself as a gifted student conceptualizing something novel in biochemistry, a social leader in a school conceiving a revision in the student-government organization, or a rebel attempting to change a foolish social convention. Each in his own way would be expressing a divergent interest in the individualistic and new, with imaginative overtones characterizing the process.

Selected Definitions

At this point, we project into the discussion selected definitions of other writers which, although differing in shadings, include one or more of the attributes of creativity previously identified. The respective name or names of those responsible for the definitions are included parenthetically after each.

1. "When a pupil gets insight into a relationship of facts which he never knew before, and he does this all by himself, he has been creative. This is true even though this relationship is quite well known to the teacher or to the whole adult world" (Leeper and Scofield).[2] This definition clearly postulates the individual as his own standard of creativity. However, it comes close to making creativity synonymous with such related processes as insight, understanding, and discovery.

2. "The creative process is the process of change, of development, of evolution, in the organization of subjective life" (Ghiselin).[3] This one highlights creativity as an evolving, never-ending process.

3. "Creativity is the ability to see (or to be aware) and to respond" (Fromm).[4] The emphasis here is on the ability of an individual to see the world authentically. Fromm's psychoanalytical orientation demonstrably shows through.

4. "Creativity is bringing something new into birth . . . a part of self actualization and the representation of the highest degree of emotional

[2] Robert R. Leeper and Robert W. Scofield, "The Creator Is Himself Created," *Educational Leadership*, **18** (October 1960), p. 5.
[3] Brewster Ghiselin, *The Creative Process* (Berkeley Calif.: University of California Press, 1952), p. 2.
[4] Erich Fromm, "The Creative Attitude," *Creativity and Its Cultivation*, edited by Harold H. Anderson (New York: Harper and Brothers, 1959), p. 44.

health" (May).[5] In this one, creativity is both allied to the processes of mental health and conceived as a culmination of those processes.

5. "It is the emergence in action of a novel relational product, growing out of the uniqueness of the individual on one hand, and the materials, events, people, or circumstances of his life on the other" (Rogers).[6] The key to this definition is the element of novelty.

6. Creativity is "a positive self-integrating force" (Andrews).[7] This definition places creativity in the strongest light possible, making it the catalyst of all psychic life.

The six definitions, when combined, portray creativity as a relative, evolving, integrative phenomenon which, by plumbing the wellsprings of the imaginative, leads to the novel and the new. And, what is highly important, the combined definitions reveal creativity as an individualized component attainable, under the proper circumstances, by all.

Creativity and Mental Health

As noted at the beginning of the chapter, creativity and mental health lie along the same affective dimension with both having psychic fulfillment or self-actualization as their goals. The only fundamental difference is that mental health has a base that reaches more broadly across all of life, whereas creativity, although also operating best from a broad base, is capable of operating from a narrower one. The two components have a circular relationship wherein mental health lights the spark and increases the flow of creativity which, in turn, feeds back into the mainstream of mental health. The two are reciprocal and thus inseparable, mutually dependent, mutually supportive.

With mental health and creativity this intimately related, the twelve attributes of the mentally-healthy person, enumerated in Chapter 4, apply equally here. Such a person, it is to be recalled, is relatively independent, is attuned to reality, stands behind his actions, accepts himself, is emergent, is flexible, is uncompartmentalized, relates well to others, is basically satisfied, is devoid of debilitating guilt, is both present- and future-oriented, and has a high tolerative level for frustration. An individual, so endowed, readily becomes the emergent, creative individual who constitutes the focal emphasis of this chapter.

Creativity and the Open Encounter

Throughout the centuries, man has searched diligently for the blueprint followed by creative personalities on their way to becoming cre-

---

[5] Rollo May, "The Nature of Creativity," *Creativity and its Cultivation*, cited in ref. 4. pp. 57–58.
[6] Carl Rogers, "Toward A Theory of Creativity," *Creativity and its Cultivation*, cited in ref. 4. p. 71.
[7] Michael F. Andrews (ed.), *Creativity and Psychological Health* (Syracuse: Syracuse University Press, 1961), p. vi.

ators, but the search has uncovered little. Man's efforts have been relatively fruitless for these two reasons. First, he has assumed naïvely that creativity is a single-patterned entity, which it is not. Second, he has also assumed that all creative individuals follow more-or-less identical paths, which they do not. Attempting to avoid these pitfalls, we postulate instead that creative individuals, while engaged in a multidimensioned pursuit of the imaginative, pursue it in widely different ways, yet share in the process certain common characteristics, which merit identification and analysis.

One of the most significant of these characteristics is the one of openness before their worlds. The truly creative, in the best traditions of the pioneer personality, consistently have lifted emerging horizons unafraid of what the new might bring. They are the ones who, aware of the stultifying possibilities of deduction, give induction every opportunity to make its voice heard. They are the ones who, not blinded by neurotic chimeras, are able to assess human behavior and ideational content authentically. They are the ones who contributed ultimately to man's disbelief in a flat earth, in a fire-and-brimstone hell, in "Galen sayeth," in chains to shackle the psychotic, in the American as God's special annointed, or in outer space as a phenomenon unable to respond to the rational processes.

Man has laid to rest these and other illusory figments, in part, because creative persons throughout history have remained as open before the seamy negative as before the more palatable positive. For instance, the social case worker in a big-city slum area has no illusions about the pathological complexities of the social conditions that confront him. He sees human misery, social unconcern, and callous neglect for what they are. He administers sociological first aid but realizes that only through the combined humanistic efforts of all appropriate societal agencies can slum conditions really be ameliorated. The germane consideration here is that he is able to face negative reality openly. His counterpart, not able or not willing to face negative reality as openly, opiates through rationalization or denial: "Slum dwellers," he avers, "really like it that way." "Things aren't really as bad as they seem." "There will always be the haves and the have nots." These provide him an escape from the unpalatable. This type of compartmentalization leads to partial viewing and, in turn, to false conclusions—in this instance, about slum etiology and social action needed to remedy primitive conditions. Both result from a state of psychological myopia before the negative in life. And both set back the cause of creativity.

Most writers on creativity, already cited in the chapter or to be cited, address themselves to this phenomenon of the open encounter. Rollo May, for instance, from his existentialist position, asserts that the encounter must be complete if the rewards are to be great; that it must be intense, absorbing the total individual into a keen awareness of the creative act.[8] The quality of the encounter, Schachtel says, is a function of the free and open play of attention, thought, feeling, and perception.[9] In a study of the reading interests of 1000 adolescents, Drew describes the encounter as leading to "an openness that fosters keen awareness of reality within and without themselves . . . characterized both by a passive receptivity and an active seeking."[10] Paul Tillich sees in the encounter the involvement of man in shaping "his world and himself, . . . according to the productive power given him."[11]

Requisite requirements of the open encounter are: minds cleansed of distortion and prejudice, minds knowledgeable and informed, and emotions capable of remaining integrated before truth. By way of applying these three attributes to a second concrete situation, we take the reader back to the Panama Canal crisis of January, 1964, recalling the following sequential events. (1) Around the turn of the century, the United States, through imperialistic methods, pre-empted land in a foreign country, built a canal, and assumed control over it. (2) The United States made a financial arrangement with Panama that gave it a share in the operational profits of the canal. (3) These financial arrangements were precursorily reviewed and slightly altered a time or two thereafter. (4) The United States established itself as autonomous in its operational role. (5) In 1959, Panama gained the right to fly its own flag side by side with the American flag. (6) In January of 1964, at a high school in Panama operated by the United States government for children of American Canal officials and employees, a few American students removed the Panamanian flag. This act precipitated a riot that led ultimately to a break in diplomatic relationships between the two countries.

Only minds educated to penetrate into the hard core of attitudes, as well as fact, could sustain an open encounter with the social-political situation just described. And those minds would have to be cleansed first of such affective adulterations as prejudice toward "foreigners," delusions of chauvinism, and spurious assumptions about material possession conveying a legal or moral right. Second, those minds would have to be well informed, not only regarding the affairs of Latin America but also regarding the affairs of the entire world. And finally, they would have to have the emotional strength and resilience to receive, recover from, and then act on, whatever disturbing messages truth had to send them.

[8] Rollo May, "The Nature of Creativity," pp. 58–61, cited ref 4
[9] Ernest G. Schachtel, *Metamorphosis* (New York: Basic Books, Inc. 1959), pp. 237–238.
[10] Elizabeth M. Drews, "Profile of Creativity", *N.E.A. Journal*, 52 (January 1963), p. 26.
[11] Paul Tillich, *The Courage To Be* (New Haven: Yale University Press, 1952), p. 104.

One of these messages might be that the United States was ethically and morally wrong in employing imperialistic tactics to annex territory and property outside its boundaries. A dimensionally different second message might be that rightness and wrongness are never irrevocably absolute but are always dependent on the circumstances at any given time and in any given era. A third message might be that regardless of what the United States did or did not do at the turn of the century, any resolution of the Panama issue today would have to take into account current as well as past circumstances: the present dangers from opportunistic world powers; the status of old treaties; Panama's ability to operate the Canal independently; and the social stake of other countries, large and small, in the Canal. The disquieting phenomenon here, as with most value considerations in life, is that absolute correctness or incorrectness does not stand out distinctly. However, to the degree that the encounter remained open, any final decision would be more proper and defensible; to the degree that the encounter underwent premature closure, the decision would be less proper and less defensible.

Creativity and Curiosity before the Unknown

The open encounter with life has a built-in attribute in the trait of curiosity before the unknown. As the creative person follows in the wake of his ever-emerging world, new vistas call to him to the extent that he is sincerely and spontaneously curious about the new which lies beyond—the new in people, places, events, and relationships. It is this characteristic of inquisitiveness that leads him to pursue and investigate the unexpected and the novel. Nor do such encounters with the unknown cause him undue concern.

This curiosity before the "not yet" Fromm identifies as the "capacity to be puzzled,"[12] which, he says, customarily precipitates an urge to remove the puzzlement. The mathematician Poincaré relatedly described it as the ability to wonder and to be surprised. This wonderment leads the creating individual, Rogers would say, "to toy with elements and concepts," to juggle them into "impossible juxtapositions."[13] It is this same wonderment that makes an investigator comfortable even in the presence of a wild idea or hypothesis, that makes him willing to take a flight of imaginative fancy either to rule out or to test out a vaguely credible thesis, and that makes him extend his exploratory range to the point of the seeming irrational. This quality of curiosity or wonderment often refuses to accept closure even in the face of seemingly conclusive authority, preferring instead to carry on the pursuit to a point of even greater certainty.

[12] Erich Fromm, in Anderson, Creativity and Its Cultivation, p. 44.
[13] Carl Rogers, "Toward a Theory of Creativity," p. 76.

Creativity and the Posture of Agnosticism

The genuinely creative person is one who is curious not only in the face of the unknown, but who also is agnostic before the alleged known. And he projects his agnostic posture across life's total range. He questions almost everything and spares almost nothing. His is the personality that is unconvinced by the tenuous, that looks for and finds biases in authority sources, and that is ever suspect of the existent. To him, even time-honored dogma, including religious dogma, has no right of exemption from the probing, questioning mind.

This is not to imply that the creative person delights in debunking popularly held opinion and belief. Not at all! Rather, the creative individual, because of his dedication to the authentic, has no choice but to remain agnostic before all sources of possible sophistry, before the status quo, and before the seductiveness of introjection. Within this framework, he affronts personality as little as possible, ever directing the spotlight away from the person to the idea. When a personality slight is unavoidable, he regrets it but, at the same time, regards it as the purchase price of a compensatory value. Although in one sense the creative person is a rebel, his rebelliousness has as its purpose the unseating of the false and the enthroning of the true.

A requisite for the creative person who assumes a questioning posture before life is that he first become well informed about life. In this connection, one who questions from a foundation of reasonably complete evidence operates from a defensible base. In contrast, another who despite being uninformed persists in questioning should better hold his peace. For instance, a competent artist operating in the field of his specialty has every right to evaluate a given art work. The man in the street turned critic, however, has no comparable right. When he insists on exercising it regardless, his ignorance usually shows through to a point of obviousness.

From Divergence to Convergence

To this point, it has been established that the posture of the creative person before his world should be open and receptive, curious, and agnostic. He addresses himself to all of life, he withdraws from none of it, and he remains unfragmented and uncompartmentalized before it. But once the act of creation begins to engulf him, by the very nature of the creative process itself, his focus narrows before the newly imposed restrictions. At one and the same time, he retains the perspective that only openness can provide while he converges on the newly assumed creative task at hand. He becomes selective of ideas, selective of materials, and selective of environmental setting. Then, equipped with these assets, he engages in a disciplined pursuit of the task, making maximum employment of his working materials and natural endowments.[14]

It is in this quality of discipline that the more creative individuals stand out from the less creative. The former are more likely to reveal tenacity of purpose and effort even in the face of aloneness, anxiety, and failure.[15] The very depth of their commitment seems to exercise a sustaining power over their actions. Like the existentialist prototype, they accept their responsibilities with intensity. In so doing, they look for only a minimum of outside help and make great sacrifice, if necessary, to achieve their creative goals.

From Convergence to Closure

What still awaits, however, is the act of closure. This involves knowing when and where to stop, a decision that is strictly personal and arbitrary: yet not completely arbitrary, because "creative people stop when their criteria are met."[16] The end-product might be a welter of apparently unsymmetrical art flourishes by a first-grader, a new insight into a geo-metrical relationship by a tenth-grader, or a new social conviction by a twelfth-grader. The point of closure in each instance would be when the individual pupil independently decided that he had accomplished his goals. Whether the accomplishment met, or did not meet, outside standards would be immaterial. Wallas[17] and Patrick,[18] in this connection, assert that closure follows a set sequence of preparation, incubation, il-lumination, and verification. We tend to be skeptical of any pattern this mechanical because it goes counter to creativity's individualistic nature.

The Distorted Genius Issue

Marshaled against the position that creativity resides in the mental-health camp is the counter position that creativity is uniquely at home around emotional distortion. Strangely, in this regard, popular opinion of every generation always has endorsed this counter point of view. Con-sistently paraded in support are those gifted of the past and present who, even though neurotic or psychotic misfits, made or are making creative contributions to scholarship and the arts. Illustrative are Blake, Poe,

[14] Arthur Foshay, "The Creative Process," in Alice Miel (ed.), *Creativity in Teach-ing* (Belmont, Calif.: Wadsworth Publishing Company, 1961), pp. 29–36.
[15] Carl Rogers, "Toward a Theory of Creativity," pp. 76–77.
[16] Arthur Foshay, in Miel, *Creativity in Teaching*, p. 39.
[17] G. Wallas, *The Art of Thought* (New York: Harcourt, Brace & Co., 1926), p. 10.
[18] Cathrine Patrick, *What is Creative Thinking?* (New York: Philosophical Library, 1955), pp. 4–46.

Gide, Nietzsche, Paganini, Nijinski, and Van Gogh, just to name a selected few.

Aligned against the position of this patent falsity, a growing number of individuals, most of them psychologically oriented such as Fromm, Hilgard, Moustakas, and Rogers offer a rebuttal which goes essentially as follows:

1. For every Blake, Poe, Gide, or Strindberg in literature, for every Nietzsche in philosophy, for every Nijinski in the ballet, for every Paganini in music, and for every Van Gogh in art, scores of others, more normal and of comparable talent, have made equally commendable contributions.

2. Quite conceivably, the genius of such individuals expressed itself despite their aberrations, not because of them.

3. Assuming that the aberrations had a significant influence on their artistry, a reasonable conclusion is that they affected the nature of the artistic content, not the nature of the intrinsic artistry itself.

4. Finally, assuming an improvement in the emotional stability of such geniuses, it is possible, even probable, that their artistic contributions might have been of even greater import.

Education's Role in Creativity

Although open before the distorted-genius point of view, most writers on the subject pass it off lightly. They regard creativity instead as a possession primarily of the well-adjusted, only incidentally as a possession of the maladjusted. And with creativity related thus to the positive, education has no choice but to play an active supportive role. It is to selected specifics of this role that we direct attention in the remainder of this section.

A Permissive School Climate Is Essential. What creativity needs from education more than anything else is a climate of permissiveness and encouragement. In essence, such a climate is one characterized by the positive. It is one which has the built-in features of creativity itself: sensitiveness, tolerance, openness. Only in such a climate can creativity flower. If, for instance, as stated in the opening paragraph of this chapter, creativity connotes "the capacity of an individual to relate sensitively," he can aspire to that capacity only in a sensitive environment. If he is to think and act divergently, he needs a divergent environment in which to accomplish these ends. Sensitivity breeds sensitivity, tolerance breeds tolerance, and openness breeds openness. And their opposites breed more of the same.

Fundamental to a creative learning climate is mature leadership. This latter is a component that has premium status in all organized aspects of any democratic culture: governmental, business, civic, educational. However, it is even more essential to formal education than to other cultural enterprises because education bears the responsibility for leadership development. One writer goes so far as to assert that "Creative leadership is needed if our present civilization is to survive."[19]

Any thoughtful consideration of the dynamics of creative leadership almost begins and ends with the "power-with" approach discussed in Chapter 4. This approach, by minimizing status levels, reduces fear of authority figures. The resulting outcome invariably is increased psychic output—a product of sincere cooperative endeavor. Power-with leadership in any school should extend from the so-called top to every member of a student body. The more comprehensive the projected leadership posture, the more productive the climate of creativity.

Leadership thus conceived remains true to the conventions of humanism by relying for results on respect for personal dignity, on friendly encouragement, and on service. Minimized in the process are artificial status distinctions which, by their divisiveness, tend to defeat the very purposes of true leadership, and, correspondingly, of creativity.

Permissiveness Acts to Reduce Unnecessary Conformity. It is only in a framework of permissiveness that certain creative acts, which in a less favorable climate might be forbidden, are permitted expression. Where else would pupils feel free to defend openly the bizarre in art or music, to pursue a narrow interest in natural science, to defend an idea that on the surface appears to be idiosyncratic, or to uphold a position that runs counter to accepted convention? The irony here is that the creative often have had to struggle against great odds for the rights of nonconformity in a culture that itself is grounded in these same principles of nonconformity. When this irony is confined to the uninformed, it has no great significance. However, when it permeates formal education, it constitutes a phenomenon to be feared and consequently one to be opposed. In this latter instance, education has an obligation to make practice conform to value theory.

The general setting for counteraction should be one where individualism has the most dominant status possible in a school program which is as flexible as possible. Such program characteristics as the following would be congenial in this setting: a curriculum sufficiently balanced and diversified to meet the needs of all; materials of instruction that are rich and varied; methods of instruction that are in tune with the needs of the learners and with the learning situation; time schedules with elastic properties; memory goals that do not pre-empt reflective-thinking goals; teachers who measure up to mental-health specifications; admin-

[19] Roger M. Bellows, *Creative Leadership* (Englewood Cliffs, N.J.: Prentice-Hall, Inc., 1959), p. ix.

istrators who know what true leadership is and who mirror it; and an interest by all in continuous experimentation.

The case against education's dalliance with conformity is growing as the voice of protest increases almost by the day. Friedenberg, for instance, avers that today's adults destroy the very selfhood of adolescents by expecting only adult-pleasing behavior of them.[20] Dow similarly sees spontaneity and creativity in pupils sacrificed to classroom conformity. "All day long," says he, "they sit in school with social rightness being forced into their systems. Unless they are in athletics, which calls upon their ingenuity, they end the day completely out of balance, and one can hardly blame them for grabbing the hotrod and tearing up the road."[21] Ralph Ojemann, wrestling with the same problem, asserts that: "If schools and universities give more credit to conformity than they do to originality, new ideas, unusual sensitivities, or insights, then creativity and mental health are incompatible."[22] Leeper and Scofield, in similar vein, admonish teachers not "to consider rote memorization or imitation of text book thinking as good learning."[23] Kubie forthrightly refers to the encouraging of unreasonable repetitive learning as the "kernel of neuroticism."[24] And Taylor, thinking in the same dimension, warns teachers against "over-programming" students and thus "fencing them in."[25]

The clear-toned message here is that individualism in general, and creativity as one of its crowning attributes, can experience release only in an atmosphere of permissiveness. The mandate to education is to break down all unnecessary barriers. Otherwise, with pupils unduly restricted by unreasonable adult barriers, creativity will die before it is born.

Creativity Allows Doubt and Error. Despite the fact that the creative way is the rewarding way, the journey to it inevitably is characterized, in part, by the negative as well as, in greater part, by the positive. The negative enters the picture because individualism that entertains doubt is individualism that encourages uncertainty; because learning that employs discovery is learning that is willing to tolerate error.

[20] Edgar Z. Friedenberg, *The Vanishing Adolescent* (New York: Beacon House, 1959).

[21] Allen B. Dow, "An Architect's Views on Creativity," in *Creativity and Its Cultivation*, p. 36.

[22] Ralph H. Ojemann, "Are Creativity and Mental Health Compitable," in *Creativity and Its Cultivation*, p. 34.

[23] Robert R. Leeper and Robert W. Scofield, "The Creator is Himself Created," p. 49.

[24] Lawrence Kubie, *Neurotic Distortion of the Creative Process* (Laurence, Kans.: University of Kansas Press, 1958), p. 122.

[25] Calvin W. Taylor, "Effects of Instructional Media on Creativity," *Educational Leadership*, 19 (April 1962), p. 455.

History witnesses many times to events that unfold in the following sequential manner. Certain individuals born into, what was to them, an unsatisfactory status quo became skeptical of it. In acting to change it, their efforts met with disapproval from authority figures. This disapproval customarily precipitated a conflict that forced the dissenters either to develop their convictions openly or to go underground to develop them. Whichever the elected method, the dissenters dared to doubt the existent and to test out their beliefs. In the process, they knew error, but often, because of it, they ultimately achieved the positive. In dreaming their dreams, in having their visions, in persevering toward their goals through error as well as through success, they channeled the course of history.

The message here for education is that learning which is built on doubt, which remains nonplussed before investigative error, which does not always insist on repetitive correctness may well be learning that most nearly meets creativity's specifications. If pupils are to grow imaginatively, they will need to explore their worlds; in the process, they inevitably will make mistakes; then if they can learn from their mistakes, education will be on sounder ground than when continually demanding mechanical correctness in the sterility of the unimaginative. Creation though tinged with error is superior to errorless imitation that never rises above the prosaic.

From Curriculum Extensity to Intensity.   Education which aspires to the imaginative is regularly faced with the age-old curriculum question: Is the educated mind a product of the *how well* or of the *how much?* Ideally, it should be both. Yet such an outcome looms as impractical when the vast store of knowledge is juxtaposed against the brevity of learning time. Our decided preference, in this regard, is for a deeper vertical penetration by students into fewer curriculum areas in lieu of a superficial coverage by these same students of more areas. The thesis is that education should transmit enough of the culture to enable the growing organism to adapt to life, after which the how-well criterion should assume control. It is the qualitative way more than the quantitative way that makes possible such sophisticated outcomes in education as reflective thinking, creativity, and selfhood. These rely for accomplishment on time for contemplation and on depth involvement, neither of which is an ingredient of the how-much approach.

A current school practice that may be operating against curriculum quality is one of adding to the course loads of the gifted on the ground that they can cover more territory than can the average and slow. A better solution, we contend, is intensification within the framework of the more normative curriculum dimensions.

The Issue of Competition and Creativity.   In a permissive school environment that in support of creativity encourages nonconformity, that is at home around skepticism, and that stresses the qualitative, education still has its age-old problem of assessing the effect of competition on learning. The question is whether students rise to greater heights of creative accomplishment when competing against external standards or when competing against their own abilities and potentials. Laden as this issue is with subjectivity, anything even resembling concrete evidence, one way or the other, is nonexistent. Thus we go to our mental-health orientation in making subjective reply. The reply is that external competition and creativity are discordant elements. The former is an other-directed value which, by definition, reaches outside the individual himself for direction. Creativity, in contrast, is an inner-directed value that charges the individual to release his own storehouse of creative energy. The operational answer is that to the extent any person is less mature, he may have to look outside creativity's sphere for stimulation; to the extent he is more mature, he will be able to draw commensurately on his own psychic powers for stimulation.

Schools, for the most part, ignoring the values within which creativity is comfortable, employ external factors as their primary motivators. These factors customarily are the teacher, the student body, and college expectancy. Schools thus pay allegiance to creativity but make it vie for survival in a program featuring such questionable mental-health practices as relative marking, honors only for the fortunate "haves," regimented class schedules, fixed curriculum content, and the shunting of slow learners into a manipulative-type of curriculum. Rogers develops the theme that education is more interested in sterotyping, regimenting, comparing, and mechanizing than in developing creators.[26] Leeper and Scofield specifically castigate formal education for employing marks and marking to punish the slow.[27] The issue in this latter regard is clear cut: if slow learners are to rise to their creative potentials, education cannot continue to compare them invidiously with their more gifted associates. No wonder slow learners leave school in droves at the earliest permissible time. No wonder they fall short of their creative potentials.

Creative Teachers Are of the Essence. Emerging unmistakably from the discussion to date is the unstated but implied truism that if education is to win the cause of creativity, creative teachers will have to be in the front ranks. Emotional stability and scholarship are the two fundamental requisites of this outcome. Any teacher possessed of these is able thereby to relate more maturely to himself; to others, especially to pupils; and to the substance of a curriculum.

Along with these general attributes of stability and scholarliness, however, he must have clear vision of the creative process in operation and

[26] Carl Rogers, "Toward a Theory of Creativity," pp. 69–78.
[27] Robert R. Leeper and Robert W. Scofield, "The Creator is Himself Created," p. 5.

of the creative individual at work. Etched into that vision will need to be the specific essentials of the creative process itself: openness to the new, tolerance before agnosticism and skepticism, comfortableness in the presence of experimental error, and a keen sensitivity to individualism in all its many expressions. So equipped, he cannot help viewing the entire process of education in a new light. The academic skills will no longer appear as ends but will emerge as means of enabling pupils both to relate intimately to life and to mature across the total personality spectrum of life. Similarly, knowledge will stand out as an essential to interpretation. And the latter will constitute a mandate for action aimed at individual and social change.

The message to education channels through unmistakably. It is that teachers need to be scholarly in a broad frame of reference to include the attributes of creativity previously identified and discussed. Just for them "to know" and to be able to impart what they know is not enough. More fundamentally and comprehensively, they need to be able to employ their scholarliness in pursuit of creative outcomes.

A Classroom Synthesis

From the previous discussion, a creative classroom composite emerges with some or most of these features. Above all else, the classroom is under the leadership of a permissive teacher who has solved enough of his own personal problems to be effective in helping others solve theirs. This teacher believes education's purpose to be one of helping elementary and secondary school children to reach fulfillment in all important areas of development. He conceives the end result of such development to be the creative individual.

Being a realist, however, and thus knowing that creativity pursued to its optimum must be imbedded in the hard rock of skill, knowledge, and technique, he is ever the advocate of thoroughness and competency. Yet, within this framework, he regards these attributes relatively realizing that some creating individuals, because of their environmental and genetic attributes, will be more thorough and competent; others will be less so.

While conceding that creativity rests more comfortably on a complete foundation, the teacher of the mythical classroom under discussion does not compel creativity to await the completion of the foundation. Rather, whether a teacher of pre-school children, of high-school students, or of pupils in between, he conceives the creative process or processes as permeating all educational levels and almost all educational activities. Reading, to him, is at once a skill and an avenue to critical thinking. Numbers do not stop with arithmetical manipulations but are made to follow through to interpretation and application. Knowledge is not regarded as something just to be memorized but as substance to be thought about, questioned, and related broadly to a developing world of problems and issues. Realizing that growth is a result of honest mistakes as well as successes, he remains unperturbed and unjudgmental when pupils err, insisting, however, that they analyze the reasons for their errors and that they profit from them.

The essential features of this mythical classroom are not how much but how well, not imitation but assessment, not external judgment but internal motivation, not just enough to get by but complete closure. Education's goal in this classroom is truth. The individual pupil's goal is to become his potential, to measure up to his imaginative best. Before these outcomes, the false educational gods of memory, docility, imitation, and most other ultra-traditional values and practices yield.

Intelligence Testing and Creativity

Highlighting education's interest in and concern for creativity and the creative process is the current debate being staged over intelligence testing and its relationship to creativity. The heart of the issue is reached by these questions: (1) Does intelligence exist apart from creativity, or are the two mutually related and even inseparable? (2) In either event, do intelligence tests currently in use assess too narrowly in the areas of memory and imitation, and consequently too little in the area of the imaginative?

It is to the task of answering these questions that a number of researchers recently have dedicated themselves. Two of these latter whose research investigations have generated the most heated reactions are Jacob Getzels and Philip Jackson. In this connection, as recently as 1962, their efforts were opened to public view in a book-length treatment captioned *Creativity and Intelligence*, and in a condensed coverage of the same data published as a monograph. Their stated purpose was "to differentiate two types of giftedness: . . . to discover variables differentiating the creative from the intelligent person."[28]

The experimental design involved two matched groups of pre-adolescents and adolescents, with the variables of intelligence and creativity allegedly controlled. The two groups purportedly were drawn from a population sample of 449 pupils, grades 6 through 12, in attendance at the University of Chicago Laboratory School. The mean intelligence quotient of the 449 pupils was 132. Selected other data pertaining to the two experimental groups were as follows: *The High Intelligence Group* numbered 28, consisting of 17 boys and 11 girls. When compared with others

[28] Jacob W. Getzels and Philip W. Jackson, "The Study of Giftedness," *The Gifted Student, Cooperative Research Monograph* No. 2, United States Office of Education (Washington, D.C.: U.S. Printing Office, 1962), p. 6.

of the same age and sex, all were in the top 20 per cent of the total sample on the factor of I.Q., but were below the top 20 per cent, however, on the creativity measures employed. Their mean I.Q. was 150. *The High Creativity Group* numbered 26, consisting of 15 boys and 11 girls. When compared with others of the same age and sex, all were in the top 20 per cent of the total sample on the creativity measures employed, but were below the top 20 per cent on the factor of I.Q. Their mean I.Q. was 127.[29]

The testing instruments employed to measure intelligence were one or more of the following three: the Stanford Binet, the WISC, or the Henmon Nelson. The creative measures were five in number: some original, some adapted from Guilford and Cattell. They had as their central motifs: (1)*Word Association:* The students were asked to define given words in as many possible ways as they could. (2) *Uses For Things:* the students were given stimulus words and asked to assign to them as many functional uses as they could. (3) *Hidden Shapes:* the students were assigned the task of discovering obscure shapes in given geometrical conformations. (4) *Fables:* the students were asked to supply endings to truncated fables. (5) *Make-up Problems:* the students were asked to construct as many mathematical problems as they could from a verbally described situation.

When the two groups, the High Intelligence and the High Creative, were compared on selected factors, the following selected differences resulted:

1. With motivational factors allegedly held constant, the High Creative Group, despite a lower Mean I.Q. of 23 points (127 to 150), did slightly better in school achievement than the contrasted group. The difference was not statistically significant, however.[30]

2. Teachers were more favorably disposed toward the High Intelligence than toward the High Creative students. Two possible reasons for this outcome were postulated: the halo effect of the I.Q. and the greater conformity of the High-Intelligence Group members.

3. The Creative-Group members revealed in their open-ended completions of stimulus situations a greater tendency toward phantasy, novel endings, humor, incongruity, capriciousness, and also violence.[31]

4. The two groups agreed in their respective understandings regarding what constitutes vocational success, but their value judgments toward it differed radically. The High Creative were critical and nonconformist; the High Intelligence were supportive and conformist.

[29] Jacob W. Getzels and Philip W. Jackson, *Creativity and Intelligence* (New York: John Wiley & Sons, 1962), pp. 15–24.
[30] *Ibid.*, pp. 28–29.
[31] *Ibid.*, p. 38.

5. The High Creative Group members revealed a wider range of future vocational choices and also choices that were more unconventional, for example, entertainer and dancer.[32]

The final major conclusions of Getzels and Jackson were these: that the typical intelligence test fails to evaluate satisfactorily the factor of creativeness; furthermore, that the creative person, because of his individualistic and often imaginative tendencies, fits less comfortably into a school or nonschool culture than his less creative counterpart; finally, that whatever the qualities are that the creative person possesses, they do not prevent him from competing favorably in a school milieu with others who have equal or higher I.Q.'s.

Lest the impression be left that Getzels and Jackson were the primary researchers or writers to address themselves to the issue of creativity versus intelligence, we hasten to state that they are just two of many. The contributions from this larger group appear, among other places, in the April, 1962, issue of *Education*, with Paul Witty, the guest editor, providing an excellent summary of the existing research. One of this larger group, Calvin Taylor, anticipated the later findings of Getzels and Jackson, announcing in 1960 that intelligence tests were too narrowly restrictive in the scope of their coverage.[33] Ellis Torrance, another writer and researcher who has become associated with the creativity movement, has reported recently in the same vein.[34]

A number of this larger group, although generally supportive of the major thesis of Getzels and Jackson's study—namely that many facets of creativity exist outside the areas covered by intelligence tests—challenge certain aspects of the study itself. Kaufman, for example, joined what is now a growing chorus to question the representativeness of the population from which the two researchers drew their sample. A student body with a mean I.Q. of 132 is scarcely typical. He also raised questions regarding the small size of the two groups studied (28 and 26). Furthermore, he criticized Getzels and Jackson for not reporting correlations between each or all of the five criteria of creativity on one hand, and the intelligence tests employed on the other, as a means of establishing discreteness of the contrasted measures or of discovering the extent of inbreeding between them.[35]

Probably the most caustic of the recent criticisms levied against Getzels and Jackson's controversial research has come from De Mille

[32] *Ibid.* pp. 56–61.
[33] Calvin W. Taylor, "The Creative Individual," *Educational Leadership,* 18 (October 1960), pp. 7–8.
[34] Ellis Paul Torrance, *Guiding Creative Talent* (Englewood Cliffs, N.J.: Prentice Hall, Inc., 1962).
[35] William E. Coffman, "Convergent and Divergent Excellence," *Contemporary Psychology,* 8 (March 1963), pp. 125–126.

and Merrifield. The opening statement of their book review sets the tone: "Despite the enthusiasm of the publisher and the quick acceptance of this book [Creativity and Intelligence], a rather discouraging evaluation of it must be made in a journal devoted to measurement problems." The critics then proceed to identify and discuss a number of alleged shortcomings of the research, several of which follow:

1. The so-called creative group of Getzels and Jackson was too loosely categorized by type apart from the specific traits that led to the classification.

2. The significance of inbreeding between and among the various instruments was not sufficiently taken into account.

3. The employment by Getzels and Jackson of the two different percentage ranges of 20 and 80 are subject to question.

4. The researchers failed to reveal the relative place of any of the sample members in either the 20 or 80 per cent category.

5. Those students who were both highly intellectual and highly creative were completely ignored.

6. The criteria used in selecting some, and rejecting others, from either the 20 to 80 per cent category were not given.[36]

In the last analysis, despite a number of probable cracks in their research design, Getzels and Jackson should receive credit for focusing widespread attention on the issue of creativity's relationship to intelligence testing and vice versa. To Guilford should go the major credit for pioneer research and the development of important instrumentation in the field of creativity. To Taylor and Torrance should go extensive credit for their follow up and refinement of earlier efforts. To Getzels and Jackson should go credit for catapulting one aspect of the total creativity issue into a position of prominence. In regard to the conclusions announced by Getzels and Jackson, we too believe that intelligence tests currently in use weight memory information and imitative outcomes too heavily. Rare indeed, in fact, is the test that calls for extensive application of, or for the imaginative extension of, what is known. Yet the reason for our point of view, in this regard, relies more on subjective observation and logical inference than on the research of these two investigators. Future research in the same problem area should involve students who are more typical; instruments that are more demonstrably discrete; and criteria of creativity that are more complete and convincing. Until such research is completed and reported, the announced findings of Getzels and Jackson should be looked on as just one link, albeit a significant

[36] Richard De Mille and Phillip R. Merrifield, "Creativity and Intelligence," *Educational and Psychological Measurements*, **22** (Winter 1962), pp. 803–808.

one, in a needed chain. Under no circumstances, in our opinion, however, should the findings lead to closed generalizations.

A Final Word

No topic is of greater interest in educational circles today than creativity: what it is, how it reveals itself, how it can be detected, and how it can be developed? Recent conferences have adopted it as their central motif. Articles and books in increasing number are being written about it. Its goal is self-fulfillment judged against individual personality potential, with the imaginative and the novel expected from each individual to the extent of his ability to attain the same. The enemies are the status quo, imitation, and conformity—society's flourishing commodities. However, with the attention currently being accorded creativity, a break with traditional educational practices may well be imminent with individualism reaping the benefits. Education of the future, short of condoning ego-oriented rebellion in students, will need to encourage more rebels in search of the imaginative. Education of the future will need to enlarge its component of teachers who not only remain composed before, but who actually become excited by, the unusual. If the nation is vulnerable to physical extinction by the lethal weapons of science, it is just as vulnerable to psychological extinction by the opiating weapons of conformity. With individualism the prize, education becomes accountable if it falters in the pursuit of creativity.

Suggested Readings

For those who wish to probe into the topic of creativity more intensively than this treatment permits, we recommend readings from the following selected recent publications. These are not repeated in the unannotated bibliography at the Chapter's end:

Anderson, Harold H. (ed.), *Creativity and Its Cultivation*. New York: Harper and Brothers, 1959. A symposium of excellent articles on creativity by Eyring, Dow, Sinnott, Fromm, May, Rogers, and others. This is one of the best.

Andrews, Michael F. (ed.), *Creativity and Psychological Health*. Syracuse, N.Y.: Syracuse Universtiy Press, 1961. This is a symposium, including, among others, articles by Sorokin, a sociologist; Fliegler, a clinical psychologist: Ojemann, a mental hygenist; Virtue, a philosopher; and Lowenfeld, the late head of the department of Art at Pennsylvania State University.

De Mille, Richard and Philip Merrifield, "Creativity and Intelligence." *Educational and Psychological Measurement*. Vol. 22. No. 4, Winter, 1962. pp.

803–808. This article somewhat acidly enjoins the issue dramatized by Getzels and Jackson, raising a number of thought-provoking questions about the researchers' experimental design, research methods, and conclusions.

Getzels, Jacob W. and Philip W. Jackson, *Creativity and Intelligence.* New York: Wiley and Sons, 1962. Attacks the issue of the ability of existing intelligence tests to evaluate creativity. Because of its timeliness, it is "must" reading.

Kubie, Lawrence, *Neurotic Distortion of the Creative Process.* Lawrence, Kansas: University of Kansas, 1958. Takes a firm stand against the specious reasoning that emotional distortion and creativity are allied.

Miel, Alice (ed.), *Creativity in Teaching.* Belmont, Calif.: Wadsworth Publishing Company, 1961. Another symposium containing a particularly excellent article by Arthur Foshay entitled, "The Creative Process Described." This relates best to elementary education.

Taylor, Calvin W., *Creativity: Resumé and Outlook.* New York: McGraw-Hill Book Co., 1963. Draws heavily on the findings of the research conferences held at the University of Utah in 1955, 1957, and 1959, but branches out abstractly also.

Torrance, E. Paul, *Creativity: What Research Says to the Teacher.* No. 28. Wash. D.C.: National Education Association, 1963. Title is properly descriptive.

For Further Thought

1. To what degree are mental health and creativity related concepts? Is it possible to have one without the other?

2. React to Kubie's strong assertion that conformity and repetitive school practices carry the kernels of neuroticism.

3. Which of the definitions of creativity provided do you prefer? Why? Can you offer an even more acceptable one?

4. Do you accept the assumption that all people, regardless of ability or personality levels, are creative? Defend your stand.

5. Assume a creative school philosophy that leads to the recommendation of psychological treatment of a student by a competent school therapist with the parents objecting. Who emerges the winner, the school or the parent? Do you agree with this outcome?

6. Define "openness" in creativity and relate it to convergence.

7. If Edgar Allen Poe had been given psychotherapy and "cured" of his illness, would he have lost his genius? Defend your stand.

8. Should a creative person be given the right to question even his religion?

9. What if "truthful reporting" reveals certain school practices as open to question? Should the creative teacher suppress such information?

10. How do you react to the issue of the I.Q. test and its relationship to creativity? Is the latter covered adequately in the former?

References

Cortright, Rupert, L., *Creative Discussion*. New York: The Macmillan Company, 1959.

Ghiselin, Brewster, *The Creative Process*. Berkeley, Calif.: University of California Press, 1952.

Haefele, John W., *Creativity and Innovation*. New York: Reinhold, 1962.

Hammer, Emanuel F., *Creativity*. New York: Random House, 1961.

Kneller, George F., *The Art and Science of Creativity*. New York: Holt, Rinehart and Winston, Inc., 1965.

Lowenfeld, Viktor and W. Lambert Brittain, *Creative and Mental Growth*. New York: The Macmillan Company, 1964.

Marksberry, Mary Lee, *Foundation of Creativity*. New York: Harper and Row, 1963.

Moustakas, Clark, (ed.), *The Self*. New York: Harper and Brothers, 1956.

Peet, Harriet E., *The Creative Individual*. New York: Ronald Press, 1960.

Rugg, Harold, *Imagination*. New York: Harper and Row, 1963.

Schachtel, Ernest G., *Metamorphosis*. New York: Basic Books, Inc., 1959.

Shumsky, Abraham, *Creative Teaching in the Elementary School*. New York: Appleton-Century-Crofts, 1965.

Smith, Paul (ed.), *Creativity: An Examination of the Creative Process*. New York: Hastings House, 1959.

Stein, Morris Isaac and Shirley J. Heinze, *Creativity and the Individual; Summaries of Selected Literature in Psychology and Psychiatry*. Glencoe, Ill., Free Press, 1960.

Taylor, Calvin W. (ed.), *Creativity: Progress and Potential*. New York: McGraw-Hill Book Co., 1964.

Torrance, Ellis P., *Guiding Creative Talent*. Englewood Cliffs, N.J.: Prentice-Hall, Inc., 1962.

chapter 6

Problem Solving and Education

The postulate of Chapter 4 was that mental health, the wellspring of psychic energy, determines in large part how far anyone can progress toward his potential. The sequel to this postulate, in Chapter 5, was that forward movement featured by the divergent, the curious, and the imaginative denotes progress of the highest type. Such movement is creative movement which, while relating first and foremost to the quality of any individual's encounter with life, constitutes at the same time the capstone of mental health. The postulate of the present chapter is that the method employed by anyone in the encounter determines, once more in large part, how complete and creative the encounter will be. And of the many ways of approaching and investigating life, one of the most comprehensive, yet penetrating, is the method of problem solving.

Before finally deciding on the title of this chapter, I engaged in considerable self-debate. My uncertainty stemmed from the fine semantic shadings that exist among three widely used terms: problem solving, reflective thinking, and critical thinking. Burton, Kimball, and Wing, for instance, openly declare that "the terms reflective thought, critical thought, and problem solving are used by different authors to mean about the same thing."[1] Dewey consistently employs critical thinking and problem solving as synonymous terms. And Thorndike employs reflective thinking and problem solving as synonymous terms.

All three share the idea of the reasoning faculty of the mind as a

[1] William H. Burton, Roland B. Kimball, and Richard L. Wing, *Education for Effective Thinking* (New York: Appleton-Century-Crofts, Inc., 1960), p. 17.

common element, but they differ over the amount of overt action implied. Two of the three, reflective thinking and critical thinking, like the analogous term "reason" in the traditions of philosophy, seem to connote almost exclusively the process of mental contemplation. The third term, problem solving, while also conveying the idea of contemplation, connotes as well the possible additional attribute of overt action. For reason of its greater comprehensiveness, therefore, "Problem Solving" became the title of this chapter.

The Thinking Dimension

Whether problem solving culminates or does not culminate in some kind of physical action, however, is not of primary importance. The major consideration is that problem solving from start to finish is a thinking process, and an active process at that—active in the sense that the thinking organism is always expending some form of energy. Even between the levels of passive meditation on one hand, and the more taxing process of critical thinking on the other hand, the difference in the mental activity expended is merely one of degree. Yet this is not to deny that as problem solving increases in complexity, activity in critical thinking has to keep pace. Neither, however, is it to say that thinking must be painful to be effective. Rather, thinking is a process that makes more-or-less challenging demands on those who think.

Because thinking exists at various levels, I propose a taxonomy, confessing to subjectivity in ranking. The purpose is more to acquaint readers with the existence of the several levels than to effect agreement over the ordered arrangement of the levels. In the taxonomy, the planes of thinking most detached from conscious reality appear first, followed in ascending order by those which make increasing contact with conscious reality.

1. *Pathological thinking*—thinking that is diseased and therefore characteristic of the mentally disturbed, particularly the psychotic. For instance, with the schizophrenic, the paranoid, or the manic-depressive, pathological thinking appears in the form of hallucination or delusion. With the neurotic, although usually more reality oriented, it increases in distortion the nearer it approaches the elements of the neurosis.

2. *Daydreaming or autism*—a phenomenon of the escapist who employs this method to enter into and enjoy for temporary periods the pleasures of an unreal world. Daydreaming is normal when engaged in incidentally and when not removed unduly from the conscious control of the individual; it is pathological when constituting a fundamental way of mental life and when not responsive to control by the individual.

3. *Sentiencing*—an unorganized and formless kind of thought meandering, which, in the illustration of Hullfish and Smith, aptly describes

the mental activity of an individual who, cozy and warm by a fireside, lets his mind wander aimlessly and at will.[2] Sentiencing is different from daydreaming in that the person's thoughts are detached extensions of, rather than escapes from, reality. The process is one of idle meditation in pursuance of cognitive goals charted by the moment. And because everyone is entitled to his occasional "vacant and pensive mood," sentiencing passes the reality test.

4. *Dream thinking*—obviously the type of thinking that goes on in the dream world. Many mental-health therapists of widely different orientations regard the dream as part of a never ending cognitive chain that reaches, in one form or the other, around the clock. Psychoanalysts, for the most part, project the dream directly into the stream of reality, differentiating it only in terms of its distinctive symbolism and its presumed detachment from conscious censoring. Because of the controversial and postulative nature of dream thinking, however, we assign it only moderately high place on this rank order listing. Many, we realize, would assign it no place whatsoever. A few would accord it a higher rank.

5. *Rote thinking*—a category of mental behavior wherein the individual introjects from his environment without giving critical thought to what he introjects. He learns without questioning and may repeat without understanding.

6. *Simple perceptualizing*—an elementary stage of thinking wherein the growing organism attaches meanings to sensory stimuli. When the infant recognizes the sound of his mother's voice, this represents an elementary level of thinking. When the three-year-old hears thunder and knows it to be thunder, this is thinking at a simple perceptual level.

7. *Thinking in simple concepts*—a process whereby the learner perceives and then transforms a number of his perceptions into a simple conceptual whole. The infant perceives a mother figure early, but only later does he relate to the abstract concept of motherhood.

8. *Thinking in more complex concepts*—an extension upward of 7 whereby the learner advances along the conceptual scale. In the process, he establishes relationships between and among more aspects of his environment, transfers in a more sophisticated way from one situation to another, and generalizes increasingly from a background of greater experience. Such concepts as democracy, altruism, or unconscious motivation characterize this level.

9. *Reflective thinking*— a level of thinking that runs the gamut of the entire cognitive apparatus. At this level, the learner moves from the simple to the complex, is highly selective of cognitive content, honestly ques-

[2] H. Gordon Hullfish and Philip G. Smith, *Reflective Thinking, The Method of Education* (New York: Dodd, Mead and Company, 1961), p. 33.

tions or doubts, at times is unashamedly skeptical, always assesses, and ultimately arrives at a decision or conclusion that he can defend. Its ultimate reaches the ultimate of creativity attained only by a selected few.

Reflective Thinking. At the top, thus, of the afore-presented taxonomy of thinking is reflective thinking. What gives it status is its totality of involvement. Above all else, it demands the thinking organism to inventory what he knows, to integrate it into a unified whole, and to conclude from it. Reflective thinking commits the organism to address himself to life, to keep in tune with life's messages, to code the messages accurately, and then to act on the interpreted meanings. Unlike information received by rote, reflective thinking puts responsibility for debate and decision on the individual. In the words of Dewey, reflective thinking consists of "active, persistent, and careful consideration of any belief or supposed form of knowledge in the light of the grounds that support it and the further conclusions to which it tends . . ."[3] Or as stated by Glaser, a psychologist-educator, it consists of "(1) an attitude of being disposed to consider in a thoughtful way the problems and subjects that come within the range of one's experiences, (2) knowledge of the methods of logical inquiry and reasoning, and (3) some skill in applying these methods."[4]

Reflective thinking, like creativity, depends for its consummation on life's being opened to full view. To the extent that the encounter is less open, such outcomes as breadth of perspective, unclouded meaning, and maturity of understanding are less likely to be accomplished.

Reflective thinking, again like creativity, depends on the mental health of the "thinker" to bring life into tune with reality. Only the mentally healthy are able to view people and events openly and objectively. Their counterparts, in contrast, invariably are so blocked by ego distortions that life becomes what it is not. For such individuals, understanding and experience find an outlet only in narrow channels; or they remain sealed off in the sterile abstract; or they even, at times, may appear as bizarre imitations of the real thing.

The authentic observer, at one and the same time, relates to life intimately while, as a critic, he stands apart from it. Both the close and the detached views are essential to the evaluative process. The observer of a cubist painting, for instance, projects his art knowledge into a painting but, while engaged in assessment, remains removed from the painting. Another observer listens to a cantata or a hootenanny, reads a contro-

[3] John Dewey, *How We Think* (Washington, D.C.: D. C. Heath and Company, 1933), p. 9.

[4] Edward M. Glaser, *An Experiment in the Development of Critical Thinking* (New York: Teachers College Press, Columbia University, 1941), pp. 5–6.

versial literary work, or participates in an affair of state. In each instance, he assumes the role of surrogate performer while backing off to assay the performance. In the latter role, he takes the hard look, reflects objectively on what he sees, and then concludes maturely in the best traditions of critical evaluation.

Germane to the topic of reflective thinking in formal education is the issue of time: when in a school program should reflective thinking begin? Two extremes are possible. One is for education to postpone the process until students have a fairly good foundation of basic learning. Hutchins, for one, appears to have taken this point of view. He and other advocates of postponement imply or state that for analytical thought to have stability, it needs first a supportive foundation of knowledge and understanding. At the surface level, this stand possesses enough prima facie logic to pass as convincing. However, to the extent that it fails to answer (as it customarily does) the following questions, it remains vulnerable. For instance, how large should the supportive foundation be? Is it a foundation of identical size and makeup for all, or does it exist as a function of human differences? If the latter, in what way? How can critical thinking catch spark in young adulthood if forced to remain dormant throughout childhood and youth? And, especially fundamental, do authority figures have the ethical right (assuming it is humanly possible for them to do so) to suppress critical thinking when it gives every appearance of being a fundamental aspect of developmental growth?

The opposite pole involves a learning arrangement wherein critical thinking begins when formal education begins and intermingles with the substance of knowledge at all grade levels. Supporters of this second position include most educational theorists, most dynamic psychologists, and probably the majority of practicing school teachers and administrators. Admittedly, however, many of the latter are more enthusiastic when verbally espousing this operational arrangement than when giving it practical application. The problem, in this connection, is that when teachers allow critical thinking to hold sway in a classroom, or administrators allow it to hold sway in a school, they subject their beliefs and practices—in fact, their very authority—to the cutting edge of the critical thinking process. Only the secure are comfortable before such a confrontation. On the other hand, for teachers and school administrators to place the school off-limits to critical thinking defeats the process before it can get into operation.

Regardless of the problems created, the rationale behind this second arrangement is that the human organism is dynamic; that it is also exploratory; and that although it learns by imitation, it also needs to learn by questioning. The questioning process, it is conceded, increases in complexity as the organism matures, but the process itself is a normal part of growth and development at almost all levels. Reflective thinking conceived this second way is thus an inseparable part of the total learning process, not a frosting which should await the graduation of a student into the thinking elite.

The Action Dimension

In problem solving, as indicated previously, action which accompanies reflective thinking manifests itself along dimensions both of the mental and the physical. When of the mental variety, it finds expression in personal debate over issues which, in the opinion of the debating individual, require decision. It was this type of action that Horace Mann had in mind when he postulated education's most important goal to be "a generation of men capable of taking up . . . complex questions . . . , of turning all sides of them toward the sun, and of examining them by the white light of reason, and not under the false colors which sophistry may throw upon them."[5] This same type of cognitive action is engaged in by an individual who, after careful preparation and analysis, concludes that racial equality is the right way, that possession by might is the wrong way, or that crusading is the controversial way—often right, often wrong, depending on circumstances.

However, once any individual has reached a conclusion on an issue, his next step is to select a course of action, and then to act. The manner and extent of the action consistently are functions of the situation and the individual himself. Some situations call for no more than a bit of routine searching followed by a commonplace act of closure. For example, suppose a teacher of English "blanks out" on the name of a leading figure in linguistics, Noam Chomsky, and then takes steps to rediscover the name in a library resource. This simple search is all that would be required.

On the other hand, conclusions reached on weightier issues such as two of the three identified in the last paragraph, namely, racial equality and dominance via might, would necessitate thought and commitment of substantial proportions. The range might well be from a low-pressure decision not to act at all, which even then would constitute a type of action, to a high-pressure decision for a crusade. In the second instance, needless to state, the physical would play a dominant role. However, barring a mob kind of emotionalized reaction, the mental still would be actively supportive. In either event, action would have taken over from passivity.

[5] Cited in J. E. Morgan, *Horace Mann, His Ideas and Ideals* (Washington D.C.: Washington National Home Library Foundation, 1936), pp. 93–94.

Steps in Problem Solving

We have depicted problem solving, to this point, as an overall process of discovering correct response to situations that mildly or tenaciously resist explanation or solution, and then of acting on those correct responses. Developing the topic further, we now reduce problem solving to its component parts—or, at least, alleged component parts—to the end of more specific analysis and a hoped-for greater understanding. It is postulated that any individual who engages in the problem-solving process moves more or less along the following sequence. He

A. Identifies a problem that needs solution.
B. Becomes interested in solving the problem.
C. Addresses himself to the problem carefully and thoughtfully.
D. Possesses appropriate knowledge, skills, and personality attributes on which he can draw as needed in solving the problem—or he acts to gain these.
E. Conceives what appears to him to be the best plan of attack.
F. Makes the attack.
G. Evaluates the success of his efforts.
H. When dissatisfied, looks for and discovers the reasons for the unsatisfactory first effort; and then, with new insight, readdresses himself to the problem.

In the same frame of reference, John Dewey's steps of problem solving, paraphrased in the following, are probably the most widely recognized and quoted.

A. A difficulty is felt.
B. It is intellectualized and defined.
C. A hypothesis about a possible solution is formulated.
D. The hypothesis is developed and evaluated.
E. The hypothesis is implemented and tested.[6]

In similar vein, Bingham, treating of the problem-solving process at the elementary-school level, lists and discusses these steps:

A. A problem is identified.
B. The problem is clarified.
C. Information germane to it is collected.
D. This information is organized and focused on the problem.
E. Possible satisfactory solutions are postulated.

[6] John Dewey, *How We Think* (New York: D. C. Heath and Company, 1933), p. 107.

F. The best, from these, is selected.
G. The solution is put into operation.
H. The case is closed if the individual is satisfied; if not, he pursues it further.[7]

As a final example, Hodnet, although writing for business and industry, not for education, espouses essentially the same sequence.

A. A problem is identified.
B. The problem is stated articulately.
C. The problem is analyzed.
D. Questions about the problem are raised.
E. The known facts about the problem are ascertained.
F. Basic assumptions are formulated.
G. An attack on the problem is made.[8]

These and other similar formulations highlight a pattern of thought and behavior that unfolds somewhat as in the ensuing.

First, an individual becomes dissatisfied with the status quo and wishes to change it. This desire for change might occur abruptly as a result of some event that motivates acutely at the time, or it might lie dormant in the unconscious for a short or long period before finally erupting into a more turbulent state. Regardless, the desire for change confronts the individual with a problem to be faced and resolved in some way.

Second, an individual balances a desire for change against his ability to do something about the problem. If possessed of the needed resources, he can proceed to the attack. If not so possessed, assuming capability and desire, he acquires the resources of knowledge, skills, or attitudes necessary to attack and solve the problem. The young child, for instance, hits a ball over a high fence, and, unable to reach the latch on the gate, or to make his voice heard, is prevented from recovering the ball. Under these circumstances, a new behavioral posture has to emerge if he is to surmount the difficulty. Or, again, an adolescent becomes worried over nonacceptance by his peer associates. He has a need—perhaps even a near desperate need—to belong, but most of his overtures meet with rejection. In each of the two instances, the focus is on a problem that old habits and understandings do not solve.

Third, a person with a problem that he desires to solve and is able to solve casts about for plausible solutions. In the illustration of the boy, the ball, and the high fence, the youngster conceivably would begin

[7] Alma Bingham, *Improving Children's Facility in Problem Solving* (New York: Teachers College, Columbia University, 1958), pp. 13–14.
[8] Paraphrased from Edward Hodnett, *Problem Solving* (New York: Harper and Row, 1955). He devotes chapter-length treatments to each of the seven.

to identify possibilities for future action. He might debate the choices of asking a larger person to open the gate, of standing on a box that would enable him to climb the fence, or of awaiting help from a member of the household—any or all of these could facilitate the return of the ball.

In the illustration of the adolescent needing "to belong," the unhappy teen-ager might make a negative response: either by withdrawing more and more into a social shell or by lashing out aggressively at those who denied him acceptance. At the constructive level, he might make a careful inventory of his personality and associated behavior in an attempt, on one hand, to eliminate his offensive mannerisms, and, on the other hand, to capitalize more effectively on his pleasing ones. Regardless of the exact pattern followed, he first would cast about for possible solutions to his problem, and then would select from the available alternatives the plan of action that, all factors considered, seemed to be most feasible.

Fourth, once an individual settles on a solution, he puts it into operation. The youngster who lost the ball might well ask help from the first adult who happened along. The ignored teen-ager, to the extent that his unconscious motivations would permit him to get better acquainted with his conscious ones, plausibly would set about to repair selected personality defects to the end of removing the resulting social blockages. The important point here is that problem solving has to move from the process of debate into the processes of decision making, and finally, as warranted, into follow-up action.

Fifth, an individual with a problem assesses the effectiveness of his efforts to solve it, passing judgment on whether his problem is being solved satisfactorily through the method, or methods, that he is employing. If his efforts are rewarding, he no longer has a problem. If they are unproductive, he either accepts defeat, or, if desirous of a better solution, he sets aside the original problem-solving approach and selects another that he proceeds to put into action. The order of events, although rarely as neatly sequential as we have presented it, inevitably culminates in some type of closure. Even the admission of futility and defeat is a type of closure.

Thus problem solving ideally moves from perplexity to its elimination, or, at least, to its mitigation; from a blockage to its removal; from old thinking to new thinking. In any event, the interacting organism faces life forthrightly and attempts to do something about the roadblocks which characterize it. And, as anyone can attest, the day that does not bring numerous problems in its wake is a rare day. For one person, a tardy alarm presents an immediate problem when he first arises. For another person, minor car trouble on the way to work poses a forced choice among alternatives. Should he wait for the car to be repaired or leave it in a garage and use some other means of transportation? Or should he go home and wait for the new day? The typical mother and housewife has perpetual problems pertaining to child care, menus, housekeeping, and the demands of a spouse. Problems are inescapable in living, but fortunately most of them are small enough, or routine enough, for most people to resolve them either through habitual response or without excessive conscious effort. A few problems, admittedly, however, are more consciously taxing.

Can Problem Solving Be Taught?

Any process as much a part of daily living as problem solving demands answer to the important question: To what extent is it a process that one can teach another? And because thinking permeates every facet of problem solving, this is really another way of asking to what extent is thinking itself capable of being taught. Addressing ourselves to this latter question and slanting it to the teacher-learner relationship at any level, we conclude that thinking may be taught in these three ways: (1) by a teacher's removing the blockages which stand in the way of learning, (2) by a teacher's stimulating an environment of learning, and (3) by a teacher's helping a learner to proceduralize his thinking.

The first of these, although in one form or another as old as man himself, constitutes, as has been stated several times already, a modern tenet of psychoanalysis. The thesis is that the psychic energy of a physically healthy individual will flow into productive channels unless detoured into unproductive channels by the negative aspects of an environment. To the extent that this thesis is sound, thinking as a vital positive life force will function properly when released from environmental inhibitions. In talking to this point, Kubie asserts "that thinking processes actually are automatic, swift, and spontaneous when allowed to proceed undisturbed by other influences. Therefore, what we need is to be educated in how not to interfere with the inherent capacity of the human mind to think."[9] Stated in a slightly different way by another analyst, "the organism has a given quantity of energy at its disposal. The distribution of these energies may be the decisive factors as to whether or not certain psychic activities gain access to motility and consciousness."[10] Thus thinking, viewed in this frame of reference, is a quality to be released, not one to be injected into a learning organism.

[9] Lawrence S. Kubie, *Neurotic Distortion of the Creative Process* (Lawrence, Kansas: University of Kansas Press, 1958), pp. 104–105.
[10] Ralph R. Greenson, "The Classic Psychoanalytic Approach," *American Handbook of Psychiatry*, Part II (ed. Silvano Ariete) (New York: Basic Books, Inc., 1959), p. 1402.

In effecting this outcome of psychic release, an effective teacher quite naturally utilizes the second listed method of teaching pupils how to think, namely, by stimulating the learning environment. In the process, he engages in practices such as the following: makes the classroom an attractive place for pupils to think in, makes available to them a rich variety of learning materials, makes learning a multisensory phenomenon, makes learning active, relates a curriculum to each individual, structures only to the extent necessary to preserve freedom for all, and utilizes his personality assets to an optimum—and these are just selected instances. In the last analysis, what are methods or approaches such as these but ways of helping pupils to think?

The third approach to the teaching of thinking is via the direct method of instruction. This method is most defensible when thinking is conceived as capable of reduction into one or more operational steps that may be "taught" in some degree of isolation. For example, if thinking is contingent on a learner's ability to identify the central theme of a verbal passage, then to the extent that an instructional figure can help him to develop or refine this ability, he is teaching the learner to think. In this connection, when I attended the Command and General Staff School at Fort Leavenworth during World War II, whenever an officer-student pursued a tangent in responding to an examination item, he was brought up short with the marginal symbol: R.T.P. (Read the Problem!). To the extent that this technique prevented irrelevancies of response, it constituted a method of direct teaching in how to think. By the same logic, when one individual helps another to generalize only from adequate data, to hold most conclusions as tentative, or to question the reliability of sources of information—and he accomplishes these didactically or by example—he is actually, in a direct way, teaching another how to think?

Specifically, to the extent that Dewey and the many others, who have reduced problem solving to fixed steps are correct in their assumptions, they give support to the feasibility of the frontal approach. Help which one can give to another in problem identification, in problem articulation, in the postulation of a solution, in the implementation of a possible solution, and in the evaluation of an attempted solution—such help, in effect, constitutes direct teaching in how to think.

Does Problem Solving as a Learning Process Transfer?

On the assumption that the methods (or techniques, or approaches, or steps) of problem solving work successfully in one situation, a crucial learning and research consideration is whether the methods will transfer to other problem-solving situations. And if so, to what extent and in what way? Thorndike's near lifetime of research on this phenomenon undoubtedly provides the best single, even though the most oversimplified, answer: to the degree that any two situations are similar, more transfer will take place; to the degree that they are not similar, less transfer will take place. Such current investigators as Carl Duncan[11] and Earnest Hilgard,[12] an experimentalist and a dynamicist, respectively, have taken a more diagnostic look at the issue, raising and responding to the following questions:

1. Is problem solving a single or multiple component? Our position, in this regard, has consistently been dynamic and organismic, whether in relation to problem solving, to creativity, or to mental health. Thus, to us, problem solving is a constellation of many parts with none discrete and all needing to operate as a whole. The goal of this totality is clarity of meaning and depth of understanding which, as indicated by Hilgard and other dynamicists, constitute the only legitimate basis for transfer from one problem-solving situation to another.

2. To what extent is problem solving predominantly cognitive? For anyone who espouses the dynamic point of view, as we do, the cognitive is never separated from the affective or the psycho-motor.

3. What is the place of mental set in problem solving and transfer? Again, from our dynamic point of view, we conceive set as being at the same dimensional level as the related qualities of flexibility, open mindedness, and poise before the unknown. Set is in contrast to what Hilgard calls functional fixedness, which is a near synonym for such blocks to problem-solving as unbending attitudes, hard-to-break habits, and other manifestations of rigidity. These mitigate equally against both problem solving and transfer.

4. Does problem-solving efficiency increase as knowledge about a problem increases? In general, it does, although not in a one-to-one ratio. Knowledge, however, that increases understanding and insight both improves problem-solving efficiency and increases the likelihood of transfer.

With problem-solving effort thus conceived as a function of the total person, dependent on insightful understanding, demanding of flexibility, and related to the totality of any situation, the phenomenon of transfer assumes new perspective. Unquestionably any individual engaged in the problem-solving process can profit from transferring certain tried and true procedural steps previously learned. Yet the process, far from being routinely mechanical, is above all dynamic. For this reason, future research on the transfer of problem-solving efforts, we predict, will deal

[11] Carl P. Duncan, "Recent Research on Human Problem Solving," *Psychological Bulletin,* **56** (November 1959), pp. 397–429. An outstanding review and analysis of approximately 100 research studies.
[12] Ernest Hilgard, "Creativity and Problem Solving," *Creativity and Its Cultivation* (ed. Harold B. Anderson) (New York: Harper and Row, 1959). An articulate defense of the dynamic point of view.

more with such factors as personality variables and thoroughness of cognitive understanding than with the learning and pursuance of fragmented procedural steps, important though these latter may be. The transfer of a consciously felt need for competency, or of a consciously felt need to persist to a point of closure, may, in the last analysis, be the most important outcome of the problem-solving process. However, that these and related complex outcomes will continue to elude exact assessment, only the uninformed would deny.

In summary, consensus exists that the transfer of problem-solving components can and does take place. Still vague, and consequently a research task of the future, is precisely how the process takes place and exactly what elements, under what conditions, lend themselves to transfer.

Problem Solving and the School

Employing the foregoing treatment for background purposes, we now turn to the role of education in problem solving. And the assumption at the start is that education must not neglect its role in view of the rich learning legacy involved. Thus this question is timely: What steps should the schools take to make students reflective thinkers and/or problem solvers, and to get them to act on the products of their thinking?

Schools Need a Clear Understanding of the Problem-Solving Process. A requirement more fundamental than any other is for schools to acquire a clear-cut understanding of the goals of problem solving and a vision to grasp the demands that the goals make on school personnel and facilities. The sought-after outcomes, in brief, are a curious and well informed mind, a keen desire for truth, independence in the search for truth, thoroughness in investigation, persistent effort toward closure, and courage to act on conclusions. These goals, when attained even in part, are so monumental as to have a dramatic impact on schools that attain them. And because of the almost cosmic nature of the goals, only certain types of teachers and administrators are comfortable in their presence. Also, only such facilities as are tailored to their uniqueness are functional.

Mature Professionalism Is Essential. Whether, as previously stipulated, the teaching of problem solving involves a process of psychic liberation, of environmental enrichment, or of direct instruction, a vital requisite is educational leaders who can rise to the intricate demands. Personality traits such as the eleven to be listed shortly are essential. At one and the same time, these traits should characterize teacher personalities, while serving also as goals for problem-solving learners.

1. Willingness to engage in and sustain the process of thinking even when it perplexes and disturbs.

2. An openness before knowledge and situations, with a readiness to accept the novel.

3. An increasing emancipation from the need of absolutism and unsubstantiated dogma.

4. Patience to engage in long-range as well as short-term projects.

5. Ability and willingness to suspend judgment and delay closure for long periods.

6. Thoroughness in fact finding.

7. Facility in the process of organizing, synthesizing, and concluding from data.

8. Objectivity and accuracy in assessing data and sources of data.

9. Doubt or skepticism before unsupported data.

10. Courage to defend with conviction against untruth—as a scholar, however, outside the framework of ego involvement.

11. Composure in the face of honest mistakes of judgment and performance.

Needless to say, students, teachers, and administrators will measure up to any or all of these only relatively, with individual differences along the entire spectrum of development determining the degree. At a modest level, movement of pupils toward some of these should begin as early as kindergarten; increasingly observable movement toward all of these should take place as pupils advance through the elementary and secondary-school grades. In the ranks of instructional personnel, progress should reveal itself as substantial throughout.

It is particularly necessary for teachers and administrators to demonstrate the tenets of reflective thinking that they expect students to demonstrate. If the open encounter is a cherished outcome for students engaged in the problem-solving process, it is an even greater necessity for professional adults in their many personal relationships. Teachers like their younger counterparts should have the right to question and should exercise that right; they should have the right of honest skepticism regarding the occasional policy inconsistency in a school; and they should have the right to press for change where change seems to be called for. By definition, professionalism can operate only outside the framework of a tight power structure; cannot be supine before authority and authority figures; when threatened, must stand up to be counted and must act.

Lying at the root of all professionalism is the requirement that schools accept every student at high premium value and thus lay the humanistic-social foundation essential to the healthy release of human energy. Actually, this is a reiteration once more of the thesis that psychic energy will flow positively into life's activities if not made by adverse influence to flow negatively. It follows, accordingly, that the school which converts this thesis into an operating principle is the one which accepts each pupil as he is and helps him to develop into what his potential will enable him to become. This is simply another way of saying that such a school needs to provide a climate of mental health as a means of releasing into constructive channels the psychic energy, collectively and individually, of its student body. This outcome is usually possible for children and youth only when adults make is possible. Education's need, accordingly, is for teachers and administrators who are mature enough to help others mature; who are secure enough to be challenged without counter challenging; and who are more comfortable when guiding than when ordering.

Problem Solving Properly Rests in Knowledge.   Under the professional leadership of mature individuals such as these, problem solving, in a most fundamental way, relies for results on the scholarly attributes and preparation of learners. In and of itself, problem solving is no more or no less than a planned posture before a life situation. It demands that investigators identify and articulate problems, collect and classify data, formulate and try out solutions, and assess the effectiveness of such solutions. But, without saying, it also implies that these same investigators will accomplish all these functions at a higher level of efficiency when bringing a richer background of knowledge and understanding to the process.

There are no magic properties, per se, in the method itself. Problem solving does not enable the ignorant to make sophisticated discoveries, the unprepared to postulate at a high level, or the inept and uninformed to conclude maturely. Such an expectation would be naïve as well as specious. The more customary outcome, instead, is for learning content and the problem-solving process to reinforce one another. The more extensive the background of preparation, the more refined the process of problem identification, postulation, application, and evaluation. Conversely, the more effective the utilization of the problem-solving process, the more extensive the ultimate store of knowledge and its meaning.

In essence, what we are saying here is that education in pursuit of problem-solving outcomes cannot neglect the curriculum skills, the hard core of content, or social attitudes anymore than it could do so if another method were being employed. If anything, the emphasis needs to be greater in recognition of the broader base of the problem-solving process. Yet, in the last analysis, the difference is more in how pupils have learned previously than in how much they have learned. When pupils, who have experience only in rote-learning methods, arrive at the brink of a problem-solving situation, the exact amount of the storehouse of rote knowledge is not the vital issue. Rather, it is whether or not these students have the ability to convert to a more sophisticated level what they learned at a lower level. Obvious to state, they would not transform suddenly from memorizers to discoverers.

On the other hand, within the framework of the problem-solving method itself, pupils who have learned more by that method will rise above those who have learned less by the same method. Thus we make this concluding statement: because problem solving is a scholarly process, it can reach fulfillment only in the presence of true scholarship, which is a process of discovery as well as of rote memory.

Facilities and Materials Are Essential to Problem-Solving Activity. The school with the vision of problem solving's potential and with the professional staff to convert that vision into reality needs next to bring the materials and facilities of instruction into line with the new purposes. Unfortunately for the taxpayer, these latter are usually more broadly dimensioned and therefore somewhat more expensive than their more traditional counterparts. Here are some of the basic essentials: more classrooms which can be partitioned off for small group or individual work; school libraries that seat more than the customary 5 per cent of a total school population; more use of several textbooks rather than just one; more emphasis on primary and less on secondary references; more opportunity for pupils to work in the school building at the end of the school day; and a greater utilization of community facilities. As for the professional staff, more teachers are customarily required as pupil effort becomes more individualized.

The School Needs to Capitalize on Problem-Solving Situations in the School. Any school with problem solving as a curriculum purpose usually needs to look no further than the school environment itself for problems which pupils can address themselves to and solve. Appropriate, in this connection, is John Dewey's often quoted statement, here paraphrased, that the school is not essentially a stepping stone toward the future but rather a miniature society in which pupils actually participate in the process of living. In effect, the school becomes a place where pupils, because they have citizenship, assume increasing responsibility both for their own development and for the welfare of the total school organization. In this kind of setting, situations such as the following lend themselves conveniently to problem-solving effort by pupils: organizing for leadership in a classroom, homeroom, or school; streamlining classroom-management procedures; preventing the violation of school rules; rethinking episodes and events of literature, the social scene, or the sciences; and facing the emotional and academic issues of the self. Wise is the teacher who utilizes natural situations such as these for problem-solving purposes.

Problem solving in a school is as much a part of the hard core of an academic curriculum as it is part of the social-civic processes of school living. However, in the former context when the spontaneous source of problems fails, teacher should unapologetically create problems for pupils to solve. Thorndike states this almost verbatim: "the school is as much concerned with creating problems as with solving them."[13] Teachers create problems, for instance, by translating an arithmetical concept into a practical problem situation, by having pupils explain what they have read, by encouraging agnosticism in the face of unsupported concepts, by encouraging specialized projects in a science class, or by having a pupil work his way out of an inconsistency in any type of class. Each of these deliberately channels learning from the imitative rote into the problem-solving dimension.

Language Is an Essential to Problem Solving.   Problem-solving activity that is other than primarily motor in character relies heavily on language facility for successful accomplishment. Symbols open the door to meaning, which, in turn, increasingly opens the door to the higher processes of thinking. Viewed in this light, the problem solver rarely is more successful than is his ability to extrapolate clear meaning from communications symbols and then to translate such meaning into the dynamics of the problem-solving process itself.

Thus education should never undersell and unquestionably can never afford to ignore the significance of this relationship between language and thinking. And one vital aspect of the relationship is a realization that language should always grow out of the context of human experience—because it exists only there. Word and mathematical symbols are nothing more and nothing less than a convenient condensation of life itself. As a result, they convey exactness of meaning only to the extent that they describe accurately the concretions they symbolize.

With language constituting one key to problem solving, then, the semantics of any problem situation are as essential to the situation as the more manifest externals. Within this framework, an effective instructional leader regularly ascertains throughout the process that pupils are eliciting accurate meanings from language. When they are not, he interprets, refines, suggests rereading, or even at times engages in direct teaching of the language skills.

We conclude this section with a statement of Hullfish and Smith from their excellent chapter on Meaning and Language: "Finally, as the daily work of the classroom progresses, teachers should ever remember that in using symbols both to denote with specificity and to help young people sprout the wings of their imaginations they are contributing directly to gains which, as these are later organized within the lives of individual students, will advance their reflective capabilities and tendencies."[14]

[13] Robert L. Thorndike, "How Children Learn the Principles and Techniques of Problem Solving," *Forty-Ninth Yearbook, National Society for the Study of Education* (Chicago: University of Chicago Press, 1950), pp. 211–212.
[14] Hullfish and Smith, *Reflective Thinking*, p. 28.

Problem Solving Is Not Just Cold Logic. In closing, we take issue with the sterotype of problem solving as a coldly logical process in which the emotions are out of place. To the contrary, a normal play of emotions is always congenial to, never in opposition to, the processes of reflective thinking and problem solving. Even hunches have a justifiable place despite their failure to meet the test of cold logic. In fact, we go so far as to accord status, at times, to the patently illogical, inasmuch as the logical of today not infrequently was the illogical of yesterday. Without deprecating the methodical and the scientific, we contend that reflective thinking and problem solving should make welcome the intangibles of feeling, the educated guess, and the intuitive. In brief, we propose a problem-solving laboratory characterized by reasonableness wherein children and young people can be their naturally reacting selves.

Recommended Readings

Finally, we submit the following annotated list of books and periodical articles for those who wish to pursue further the themes of reflective thinking and problem solving. These are not repeated in the bibliography at the end of the chapter.

Ausubel, David P., "Learning by Discovery: Rationale and Mystique," *The Bulletin of the National Association of Secondary School Principals,* **45** (December 1961), pp. 18–58. A frontal assault on the alleged trend in education to run pell-mell into the arms of problem solving without deciding first how much can be learned more productively by other methods. The article is thought-provoking even when not eliciting agreement.

Bingham, Alma, *Improving Children's Facility in Problem Solving,* edited by Alice Miel (New York: Teachers College, Columbia University, 1958). Geared to the elementary-school program and classroom, it has a sound theoretical base and offers helpful suggestions.

Black, Max, *Critical Thinking* (New York: Prentice-Hall, Inc., 1954). A scholarly treatment of logic and its many manifestations. Along with the book's scholarliness, it also has appeal for the nonspecialist in the behavioral sciences.

Duncan, Carl, P., "Recent Research on Human Problem Solving," *Psychological Bulletin,* **56** (November 1959), pp. 397–429. A review and critical analysis, by an experimental psychologist, of over 100 research and theoretical studies of problem solving, dealing most penetratingly with the issue of transfer of learned problem-solving techniques and approaches. The content, however, is more appropriate for the research specialist in learning theory than for the classroom teacher or school administrator.

Glaser, Edward M., *An Experiment in the Development of Critical Thinking* (New York: Teachers College, Columbia University, 1941). A doctoral study, quoted widely, which reports an experiment on transfer of problem-solving instructional content and devices. The study is categorical in support of the assumption that problem solving can be taught—not, however, as a discrete entity.

Harvard Educational Review, 29 (Spring 1959). In this, Kenneth W. Spence, a psychological behaviorist of the contemporary school, and Arthur W. Melton, primarily an eclectic, make a frank and modest appraisal of the limitations of psychology's research contributions to the issue of transfer. Spence states that the specificity of psychological research on the subject mitigates against its transfer to the classroom. Melton, recognizing the dynamic nature of education as a behavioral science, concedes that education cannot wait while psychology catches up, but also recommends greater research cooperation in the future between psychology and education.

Hilgard, Ernest, "Creativity and Problem Solving," in *Creativity and Its Cultivation,* edited by Harold Anderson (New York: Harper and Row, 1959). The author treats both the topics of creativity and problem solving. The chapter paints a lucid, condensed picture of problem solving as conceived by the associationist, the gestaltist, and the dynamic theorist. The author himself conceives transfer as a function of insight.

Hullfish, H. Gordon, and Phillip G. Smith, *Reflective Thinking, the Method of Education* (New York: Dodd, Mead, and Company, 1961). An excellent contribution to educational thinking, probing, in a scholarly way, into beliefs, fallacies, concepts, and semantics—all in terms of their relationship to reflective thinking.

Thorndike, Robert L., "How Children Learn the Principles and Techniques of Problem Solving," *Forty-Ninth Yearbook, National Society for the Study of Education* (Chicago: University of Chicago Press, 1950). Even though a bit dated, this is probably the best single article that we have seen on the topic of problem solving, although it is not as research oriented as are the treatments by Duncan, Spence, and Melton. It is a well organized and thought-provoking chapter.

For Further Thought

1. What problem-solving activity have you engaged in during the past several days or weeks? Did you use any of the patterned approaches discussed in this chapter? Should you have?

2. Do you agree that education, as it customarily operates, is more comfortable around imitative behavior than reflective thinking? If you agree, explain the reason why?

3. As a present administrator, teacher, or teacher-to-be, envision a class of thirty reflective thinkers. Would mass education force many regrettable curbs on you and them? What might some of these be?

4. Read one of the publications listed under "Recommended Readings" and analyze it critically.

5. Do you believe that problem-solving methods and techniques are of a general nature and thus subject only to diffused development; or are they specifically identifiable and teachable? Defend your stand.

6. At what age do you think reflective thinking should begin? Provide a few concrete illustrations of how it would then manifest itself.

7. In your field of greatest academic interest, identify selected problems that you could "create" and thereby convert into a problem-solving situation.

References

Bloom, Benjamin Samuel, *Problem-Solving Processes of College Students*, Chicago: University of Chicago Press, 1950.

Burton, Wm. H., Roland B. Kimball and Richard L. Wing, *Education for Effective Thinking*. New York: Appleton-Century-Crofts, Inc., 1960.

Burtt, E. A., *Right Thinking*, 3rd ed. New York: Harper and Brothers, 1946.

DeVault, M. Vere, "Problem Solving Ability of Junior High School Students," *The Bulletin of the National Association of Secondary-School Principals*, **46**, No. 274, May 1962, pp. 60–67.

Dewey, John, *How We Think*. Boston: D. C. Heath and Company, 1933.

Emm, Eloise, *A Factorial Study of the Problem-Solving Ability of Fifth-Grade Boys*. Wash., D.C.: Catholic University of America Press, 1959.

John, Erwin, Roy, *Contributions to the Study of the Problem-Solving Process*, Wash., D.C.: American Psychological Association, 1958.

Johnson, Donald M., *The Psychology of Thought and Judgment*. New York: Harper and Row, 1955.

Martin, Barclay, "The Assessment of Anxiety by Physiological Behavioral Measures," *Psychological Bulletin*. **58**, No. 3, May, 1961, pp. 234–255.

McKellar, Peter, *Imagination and Thinking*. London: Cohen and West, 1957.

Russell, David H., *Children's Thinking*. Boston: Ginn and Company, 1956.

Schultz, Rudolph W., "Problem Solving Behavior and Transfer," *Harvard Educational Review*. 30, No. 1, 1960, pp. 61–77.

Schwartz, George & Philip W. Bishop, (eds.) *Moments of Discovery: The Origins of Science*, Vols. 1 and 11. New York: Basic Books Inc., 1958.

Tyler, Louise L., "Can We Really Teach Children to Think?" *Chicago Public Schools Journal*, **43**, No. 3, Dec., 1961, pp. 128–130.

Wellington, C. Burleigh and Jean, *Teaching for Critical Thinking*. New York: McGraw-Hill Book Company, Inc., 1960.

part *III*

Current Experimentation in Content and Method

chapter 7

Current Large-Scale Subject-Matter Projects

Our focus to this point has been on the responsibility of education to the cherished outcome of individualism. This responsibility, as developed in the past three chapters, finds mature expression in such laudable causes as mental health, creativity, and problem solving. All three of these look to optimum growth as an ideal. All, dedicated as they are to an open encounter with life, regard uncertainty not with fear but with zest. And because of their imperturbability before the unknown, they constitute individually, or in the composite, a uniquely appropriate position from which education can face the present age of social unrest, electronic complexity, and widespread anxiety.

In this and the next two chapters, our attention turns to selected curriculum experimentation that has characterized education since the mid or late 1950's, and which still characterizes it. Public interest in this experimentation has been intense. In fact, not since the surcharged era of progressive education in the 1930's has educational investigation attracted more universal notice. In both periods, society's dissatisfaction with the educational status quo set in motion a concerted effort aimed at change. Similarly, in both periods, America came face to face with complacency in the presence of educational mediocrity, and went on the attack. That the attack has been more potent in the natural sciences than in the humanities, the local sciences, and the applied arts is regrettable.

The Scope of Experimentation Is Broadening

An innovational characteristic of educational experimentation in the past decade has been the broadening of its base and scope. Traditionally, such large-scale research as the Commonwealth Study of Charters and Waples, or the Eight-Year Study of Aiken has been the exception rather than the rule. More customarily, educational research has been of modest proportions, usually taking place at the local level under the aegis of one or of not more than several individuals from a school system or college. Once completed, it was usually written up, often published in a professional organ, and then implemented not at all, a little, or a lot, depending on its significance and practicality.

Today, the counter tendency is toward large-scale research with responsibility and leadership shifting from a local to a greater geographical, social, or professional level. As Goodlad stated in this connection, "The updating of curriculum content and materials is now following a new route. Committees of specialists and teachers . . . supported by substantial foundation grants, are developing and testing revised content, teaching procedures, and instructional materials. Their products are then produced and distributed by commercial publishers."[1] He goes on to state that much of this research, detached as it often is from the objectives of any local situation, may only approximate the needs of a given school or school system.

The Federal Government.   One of the most active agencies currently in support of large-scale educational research and experimentation is the Federal Government itself. The anomaly, in this connection, is that after almost two centuries of relative detachment from the operational vitals of the educational enterprise, the Federal Government at mid-century embarked on what shortly was to become an aggressive operational role. Historically, it had made its presence felt through educational legislation accompanied by a modicum of control. The Northwest Ordinances, the Land Grant Acts, the Smith-Hughes Act, and Public Law 316 are cases in point. Its role recently has become increasingly operational—a phenomenon that may well redound as one of the more significant of the present century.

In our opinion, the reasons for this new front are twofold. The first one is national defense. Because wars are won and defenses molded as much in a school's curriculum as on a battlefield, the Federal Government cannot stay detached from education's purposes and activities. The second reason in socio-economic. As automation increases, job opportunities for the unskilled decrease. Thus if the government is realistic about achieving universal employment, it must support education as a means to this end. Whatever the exact reasons, our considered conclusion is that the Federal Government now is operationally active in the business of education, and probably will remain active indefinitely.

[1] John I. Goodlad, *Planning and Organizing for Teaching* (Washington, D.C.: National Education Association, 1963), p. 48.

In specific reference to educational research and experimentation, the government's influence is felt in several ways: through the money it appropriates, through the causes that the appropriations advance, and through the agencies that advance the causes.

Federal expenditures for research and development of all kinds in all areas amounted to 7.7 billion dollars in 1960.[2] During the two-year period 1959–1961, in the field just of the sciences, federal expenditures for research alone, apart from development, increased 65 per cent, or from 1.39 billion to 2.3 billion dollars.[3] And as the financial support of experimentation by government has increased, the support by industry and education has proportionately decreased.

One piece of federal legislation that probably has had as much influence on education as any in the nation's history is Public Law 85-864, the National Defense Education Act, passed in 1958 and re-enacted yearly since. It begins with the ringing pronouncement:

The Congress hereby finds and declares that the security of the Nation requires the fullest development of the mental resources and technical skills of its young men and women. The present emergency demands that additional and more adequate educational opportunities be made available. The defense of this nation depends upon the mastery of modern techniques developed from complex scientific principles. It depends as well upon discovery and development of new principles, new techniques, and new knowledge.

We must increase our efforts to identify and educate more of the talent of our Nation. This requires programs that will give assurance that no student of ability will be denied an opportunity for higher education because of financial need, ...[4]

The law as originally enacted, and amended since, provides substantial support for the subject fields of science, mathematics, modern foreign languages, and guidance. In the past several years, it has accorded very modest support to the humanities and the social sciences. In addition, it makes provisions for loans and fellowships to students, training institutes for teachers, research in electronic teaching methods, and improvements in graduate programs of institutions of higher learning. Its allocations for 1965 totaled approximately $270 million. Amounts earmarked for selected purposes were as follows: student loans, $135 million; fellowships,

[2] U.S. Department of Health, Education and Welfare, *Health, Education and Welfare Trends* (Washington, D.C.: 1961), p. 5.
[3] Jennings Randolph, "The Role of Government in Education" in *Modern Viewpoints in the Curriculum* (edited by Paul C. Rosenbloom) (New York: McGraw-Hill Book Company, 1964), p. 233.
[4] Subcommittee on Education of the Committee on Labor and Public Welfare United States Senate, *Selected Education Acts of 1963*, p. 42.

around $20 million; science and mathematics curriculum, $75 million; guidance, $17.5 million; foreign languages, $13 million; and electronic devices, $5 million. For each of the years 1963 through 1965, approximately 70,000 needy students received college loans.[5]

A second law, 88-210, which presages important effects on the society is the Vocational Education Act of 1963. This legislation attacks the problem of unemployment, authorizing "vocational education programs for persons in high school, for those out of high school available for full-time study, for persons who are unemployed or underemployed, and for persons who have academic or socio-economic handicaps that prevent them from succeeding in the regular vocational education program."[6] This law was born in the travail that electronics precipitated in the job market. Vanishing are the days when the individual who is both uneducated and unskilled can anticipate ready employment. The need instead is for workers who either possess certain essential skills or have enough formal education to learn these same skills on the job. Public Law 88-210, in this connection, is an attempt by the government to bridge the gap between the unskilled masses, particularly of teenage school dropouts and slow learners, on one hand, and the skilled positions waiting to be filled in the world of electronics, on the other hand.

Despite their many merits, the two laws need to be evaluated for what they are: utilitarian measures conceived in the exigencies of the times. The National Defense Education Act, or NDEA as it is commonly called, is concerned with the Nation's defense posture. The Vocational Education Act is concerned with an immediate economic situation. Each, however, is an expedient and neither takes a hard look at the complete product that the society should be developing. In this regard, as indicated in Chapter 2, education is culpable if it neglects breadth for the sake of narrow specialization. In our considered opinion, the primary fallacy of NDEA is that it underemphasizes the humanities, the social sciences, and the applied arts by overemphasizing the natural sciences. Furthermore, it underwrites a program of guidance that is narrowly centered in education for the gifted. The shortcoming of the Vocational Education Act is that it is readying youth for the here and now, but not comparably for fulfillment in the future.

A third piece of federal legislation, The Elementary and Secondary Education Act of 1965, is too recent for us to evaluate at this time.

Turning now from legislation to organization, we single out for special analysis two of the most important Federal educational agencies that are active in research and experimentation. The first is the United States Office of Education, an affiliate of the U.S. Department of Health,

[5] *Ibid.*, p. 89.
[6] *Ibid.*, p. 86.

Education, and Welfare. The second is the National Science Foundation, an independent agency under the aegis of the executive branch.

The United States Office of Education is to the Federal Goverment what the National Education Association is to the teaching profession. Each provides leadership: sometimes by working independently, but most often by working with and through affiliates. The functions of the United States Office are as follows:

1. Approves through the office of the Commissioner selected educational projects in research and development for which federal monies have been allocated and are to be spent. For instance, from 1957 to 1961, a specialized segment of the United States Office—The Cooperative Research Program—alone approved 34 projects ranging from the retarded to the gifted child, from reading to science, and from the elementary school to higher education.[7] Many of the projects approved under NDEA fall under the province of the United States Office.

2. Approves the establishment of curriculum centers such as Project English, Project Social Studies, and Modern Language Materials and Development Center—all of which will be discussed later.

3. Extends its services in a consultant capacity to various professional groups and agencies.

4. Acts as a catalyst in bringing together qualified and interested professional personnel and agencies to focus on educational problems of national concern. The President's Council on Physical Fitness is an example.

5. Supports the field testing of theoretical constructs.

6. Publishes monographs and other written materials on pertinent educational topics such as *Social Studies in the Elementary School Program* and the Research Monographs.

7. Acts in cooperative liaison with other related government agencies.[8]

A second important educational agency of the Federal Government, actively engaged since its inception in research and experimentation, is the National Science Foundation. Legally created by Congress in 1950, it was commissioned "to initiate and support . . . programs to strengthen scientific research potential in the mathematical, physical, medical, biological, engineering, and other sciences . . . " The National Science Foundation is an agency of the executive branch and has organizational responsibility solely to the President of the United States.

[7] These are listed in Rosenbloom, *Modern Viewpoints in the Curriculum*, pp. 246–249.
[8] For two excellent treatments of the functions of the United States Office of Education, see David L. Clark's and J. Boyer Davis' excellent chapters in Rosenbloom, *Modern Viewpoints in the Curriculum*, pp. 206–211, and 216–222, respectively.

The National Science Foundation (NSF) pursues its mission in these ways: by supporting worthwhile science projects in business, industry, and education; by conducting training conferences for scientists and teachers of science who desire to update themselves; by underwriting the training costs of individuals who attend these conferences or institutes; by maintaining up-to-date registers of scientists and the science projects that they pursue; and by preparing technical books and publications. The cost of NSF's total mission amounted to a staggering 194 million dollars in 1963 alone: $117 million for research grants, $53 million for facilities, $14.5 million for national research centers, and $9.5 million "for special projects."[9] As of 1964, the National Science Foundation was the financial underwriter of 22 large-scale science and mathematics experiments throughout the country.[10] These cut across the spectrum of the many sciences and extended in organizational scope from kindergarten through grade 16.

The NSF performs its function of teacher improvement primarily through the media of institutes and of fellowships for those who attend them. Most of the institutes are conducted during the summer period, although a selected few are also held during the academic year. Their growth has been phenomenal, increasing in number from an experimental 2 in 1953 to 900 in 1963; and increasing in attendance from a handfull in 1953 to 42,000 in 1963. Of the 42,000 who attended in 1963, 3,300 were from colleges and universities; 36,300 were from secondary schools, grades 7 through 12; and 2,400 were from elementary schools.[11] Of this total, 5,092 received fellowship awards; the remainder, tuition only.[12]

The National Education Association.   We turn now from government to the profession itself, looking initially to the National Education Association for significant curriculum experimentation in which it has been, or is currently, engaged. In keeping with the innovational theme of the book, we focus attention here on the NEA Project on Instruction. Although not research in the technical sense of the word, it constitutes the effort of selected educators to chart the educational path of the future: curriculum goals, content, and methods of implementing both. Initiated in 1959, the Project reached fulfillment in 1963 with the publication of four significant issuances: *Schools for the Sixties, Educa-*

<hr/>

[9] National Science Foundation, *13th Annual Report 1963* (Wash., D.C.: U.S. Government Printing Office, 1963), p. 73.
[10] American Association for the Advancement of Science and the Science Teaching Center, University of Maryland, *Second Report of the Information Clearinghouse On New Science Curricula,* 1964, pp. iv–v.
[11] *Ibid.,* pp. 95–96.
[12] *Ibid.,* p. 110.

tion in a Changing Society, Deciding What To Teach, and *Planning and Organizing for Teaching.*

Ole Sand of Wayne State University, the director, was assisted in the experimental project by an advisory committee of fourteen members. In addition, literally hundreds of teachers, administrators, and university professors assumed *ad hoc* responsibilities as consultants, seminar deliberators, and writers. The Project participants, in gathering data on goals, content, and methodology reached into five sources: social forces and trends; the many behavioral disciplines; learning theory; growth and development; and current educational practice. The accent throughout the Project was on the need for curriculum balance during a period of intensive scientific activity and preoccupation; also on the need for education to retain its local nature without disregarding the wealth of enrichment available outside any given locale.[13]

Rather than review the four publications previously listed, we urge instead that any reader serious about the curriculum of the nation's schools read them in their entirety. They are thought provoking, forward looking, and challenging. We specially commend the following individuals as writers of the reports: Dorothy Fraser, John Goodlad, Robert J. Havighurst, Richard I. Miller, Dorothy Neubauer, Ole Sand, and Margery Thomson.[14]

Selected other experimentation in which the National Education Association is currently engaged includes the Project on Educational Implications of Automation, Project on School Dropouts, and the Technological Development Project.

Association for Supervision and Curriculum Development. One of the more important subsidiaries of the National Education Association is the Association for Supervision and Curriculum Development, or ASCD. In actual practice, it operates more or less autonomously. In the field of curriculum experimentation, ASCD contributes through: (1) publications consisting of the yearbook, the monthly periodical, *Educational Leadership,* the booklet-length treatments on timely educational issues; (2) annual meetings wherein small interest groups deliberate for two to three days on common curriculum concerns; and (3) continuing committees that meet intermittently through any year, or longer period, on specialized curriculum interests. One of these latter committees, in a booklet entitled *Using Current Curriculum Developments,* has contributed what is, in our opinion, an unusually valuable summary of cur-

---

[13] See Ole Sand, "NEA Project on Instruction," NEA Journal, **50** (May, 1961), pp. 53–54.
[14] The names of the individuals who participated in the many phases of any one of the four subprojects are listed in the appendix of each report.

rent educational research and experimentation on curriculum content. Prepared under the chairmanship of Robert S. Gilchrist and published in 1963, it devotes chapter-length treatments to current projects in the respective fields of the arts, English, foreign languages, health and physical education, mathematics, science, social studies, vocational education, and teaching method. Condensed into 115 pages, it constitutes a handy and useful reference for the student of education who seeks an overview of the more recent in curriculum content.

The Subject-Matter Professional Organizations.   Year in and year out, the agencies which—sometimes directly, sometimes indirectly—give the most consistent support to the innovational in curriculum are the professional organizations of the various subject-matter fields. For instance, the Music Educators National Conference recently engaged in a research project on creative music in the schools, receiving support for it from the Ford Foundation.[15] The National Council of Teachers of English is currently collaborating respectively with the College Entrance Examination Board, the United States Office of Education, and the NEA on specific research endeavor. And, as a third example, the American Association for Health, Physical Education, and Recreation, under a foundation grant, recently studied "the strengths and weaknesses of school-health instruction programs in public schools (including) an exploratory testing phase in which evaluation instruments have been administered to a sample group of students in grades 6, 9, and 12 to determine their levels of knowledge and understandings of health. The duration of the project is September 1961 to September 1963."[16]

Other Professional Organizations and Agencies Active in Experimentation.   In addition to the National Education Association, its many general affiliates, and its specific subject-matter affiliates, selected other professional groups also active in educational research and experimentation are the following:

1. The American Association of Colleges for Teacher Education. This is a voluntary organization with a membership of over 600 colleges and universities. Its purpose is improved programs of teacher education. It pursues its mission via large nation-wide conferences held annually, and via continuing committee work performed throughout the year. The AACTE and the schools influence one another: change in teacher education has an effect in the schools, and change in the schools necessitates change in teacher education.

[15] Commission on Current Curriculum Developments, *Using Current Curriculum Developments* (Washington, D.C.: Association for Supervision and Curriculum Development, 1963), p. 14.
[16] *Ibid.*, pp. 42–43.

2. The Department of Elementary School Principals. To advance curriculum change, this agency utilizes the media of conferences and its monthly periodical, *The National Elementary Principal*, published six times yearly.

3. The National Association of Secondary School Principals. Through formal and informal conferences and the *Bulletin*, this organization encourages and disseminates news of the new and experimental in secondary education.

4. The American Educational Research Association. Organized in 1930 as an affiliate of NEA, this association has as its purpose improvement in educational research and increase in the dissemination of research findings. AERA is best known for its annual February meetings and its three most significant publications: *Encyclopedia of Educational Research, Review of Educational Research*, and *What Research Says to the Teacher*.

5. The College Entrance Examination Board and The Advanced Placement Program. Each of these organizations, independently and in collaboration with other agencies, carries on an almost continuing program of research and experimentation. Both operate primarily at the secondary-school level in the individual departmental fields. They will receive more detailed attention in the book's final chapter.

The Private Foundations. Last to receive comment here are the private philanthropic foundations which, in addition to other functions, actively support educational experimentation. Approximately 12,000 such foundations are in existence with their expenditures for research totaling from 600 to 700 million dollars yearly. Of the approximate 12,000, 129 have assets of $10 million or more, and 10 have assets of $100 million or more. These 10 in descending order of size are: Ford, Rockefeller, Duke, Hartford, Carnegie, Kellogg, Sloan, Lilly, Commonwealth, and Danforth.[17] And unlike most other organizations that underwrite research, the private foundations support more projects in the behavioral sciences and the humanities than in the physical sciences.

Selected Curriculum Experimentation

Against this background of organizations and agencies that currently support research and experimentation in education, we project selected studies that are now in progress or just recently have been completed in the various curriculum areas. Because they are too numerous, by far, for us to cover all of them in a general treatment such as this, we have

---

[17] Russell Sage Foundation, *The Foundation Directory* (New York: Russell Sage Foundation, 1960), p. xv.

elected the alternative of identifying (whenever available) key sources of information pertaining to each of the major curriculum areas and then describing briefly selected studies in each area.

Science: An Introductory Statement. In the field of natural science, including mathematics, curriculum experimentation is particularly widespread and many-dimensioned. In addition to the 22 projects underwritten, as previously stated, by the NSF in 1964, 12 other significant ones, supported in some other manner, were likewise in progress in the same year. Approximately 80 per cent of the total were in sciences other than mathematics, and the remainder were exclusively in mathematics. And of the 80 per cent, somewhat less than half had to do with science in the elementary school. During the decade 1951–1960, curriculum experimentation took place primarily in the secondary-school grades. During the decade beginning with 1961, it has reached down, in almost but not quite equal amounts, into the elementary-school grades.

Because research in science is as dynamic as science itself, scientific writers and publishers have difficulty keeping up to date. Therefore, the problem of listing references that précis the more recent experimental efforts in the several sciences is a difficult one. All we can be reasonably certain of is that in this final draft of the chapter, the resources recommended are fairly current at the time of the writing.

One source rises above all others: it is the Second Report of The Information Clearinghouse On New-Science Curricula, 1964. Based on questionnaire returns from 350 key individuals in 50 states, the Report contains: "Information on projects receiving National Science Foundation support; information on projects receiving other than National Science Foundation support; and, a listing by states of the science curriculum materials received by the Information Clearinghouse in addition to that received from the two projects listed in the other two sections."[18] A second source almost as helpful but not quite as up to date, is "Science" by Paul E. Blackwood in *Using Current Curriculum Developments* 1963, pp. 59–70. A third source which concentrates, in chapter length treatments, on the major research projects in physics, biology, and chemistry is *New Curricula* by Robert W. Heath (ed.) New York: Harper and Row, 1964. Respective contributors in these three areas are J. Stanley Marshal, Bentley Glass, and J. A. Campbell.

A précis of selected of the major research projects in science follows:

Science: Physical Science Study Committee. In 1956, motivated by the interest of two physics professors of the Massachusetts Institute of Technology, Jerrold R. Zacharias and Francis L. Friedman, the Physical

[18] American Association for the Advancement of Science, et. al., p. ii.

Science Study Committee consisting of physics teachers and researchers embarked on a revision of the physics curriculum in the nation's schools. Organizations which underwrote the project were the National Science Foundation, the Ford Foundation, and the Sloan Foundation. The overarching goal of the project was a physics curriculum conceived not as a body of facts but "as a continuing process by which men seek to understand the nature of the physical world."[19] In the summer of 1957, selected scholars in the physical sciences first prepared preliminary curriculum materials, and then, during the ensuing academic year, arranged with selected teachers to try the materials out in the schools. After revising the materials following each dry-run, the Committee repeated the try-out process during each of the two successive years: reaching 12,500 pupils in 300 schools in 1958, and 25,000 pupils in 600 schools in 1959. The final outcome was the textbook *Physics*, along with a supplementary laboratory guide, a set of "new and inexpensive apparatus," several appropriate films, and paper-back books related to individual segments of the revised course.[20]

The Committee set its sights on two curriculum outcomes. One was greater pupil mastery within the framework of fewer conceptualizations rather than less pupil mastery, or no mastery at all, within the framework of a greater number of conceptualizations. The textbook moves toward this outcome by concentrating in four major areas: The Universe, Optics and Waves, Mechanics, and Electricity and Atomic structure. The second sought-after curriculum outcome was learning not from didactic instruction, but from discovery in a context of curriculum open-endedness. This second goal is straight from the traditions of problem solving and creativity.

A weakness of the PSCS program is that, like its traditional physics predecessor, it is strictly for the talented student, that is, for the upper 25 per cent of most school populations. Excluded in the process are the many less-talented pupils who, as future consumer scientists, could engage with profit in a physical-science sequence that goes beyond the customary general-science coverage.

Science: Biological Sciences Curriculum Study. In 1959, with Bentley Glass of Johns Hopkins University and Arnold Grobman of the University of Colorado, Boulder, as Chairman and Director, respectively, the Biological Sciences Curriculum Study got under way. The sponsor was the American Institute of Biological Sciences; the financial supporter was the NSF. Both organizations gave lavish support. AIBS, with a membership of approximately 85,000 biological researchers and teachers, gave

---

[19] Physical Science Study Committee, *Physics* (Boston: D. C. Heath and Company, 1960), p. v.
[20] *Ibid.*

unstinting leadership; and NSF, as of October 1, 1962, had made grants to the project in excess of 4 million dollars.[21]

The stated goal of the project BSCS was "to seek the improvement of biology education" in the secondary-school grades. In the last analysis, what really propelled the project into being was the inadequacy of conventional science teaching that for decades had stressed the organism and tissue but had failed to keep abreast of developments in the fields of ecology and the molecular. With science knowledge allegedly increasing five times with each new generation, as conjectured in the soon-to-be-discussed Blue Version, it was postulated that change had to come about, and fast.

Early meetings of the project participants resulted in agreement on these tenets: (1) Science needs to be unified. An organism is historical, structural, ecological, and contingent. Thus operationally, biology, chemistry, physics, and the other sciences must assume greater collective unity than in the past. (2) Attention must rest more on discovered information and data than on handed-down fact. (3) With science rooted in the method of discovery, the process of discovery in the classroom needs to receive greater attention. (This also is reminiscent of the content of the previous two chapters.) (4) Science teaching has to be kept current. The new, particularly in the ecological and molecular, cannot be longer ignored. (5) Teachers and researchers need to combine their efforts for the benefit of both.

After considerable deliberation, the participants elected to divide into three investigative groups, each operating from a distinctive biological orientation. Furthermore, each group agreed to prepare on an independent basis appropriate teaching materials, to try them out in selected schools, to revise them as often as deemed necessary, and finally, to make them available in published form to interested schools. By 1963, all three groups had completed basal textbooks: the Blue, Yellow, and Green versions, respectively. In addition, each had available for dissemination a teachers' handbook, a test manual, and a film series. The three groups shared an AIBS newsletter.

The Blue Version, *Biological Science: Molecules to Man* (Boston: Houghton Mifflin Company, 1963), focuses on the genetic and the molecular. First assembled in the Summer of 1960 by 70 researchers and teachers, it was tried out the ensuing academic year in approximately 100 schools; and again revised and tried out during each of the successive two academic years and summers. By the end of the preliminary period, approximately 1000 teachers and 150,000 students had become involved. Its final date of publication was 1963. Geared primarily to the sophisti-

[21] Biological Sciences Curriculum Study, *Newsletter No. 17*, (March 1963) p. 7.

cated learner, it, more nearly than the other two, brings the several sciences into unity.

The Yellow Version, entitled *Biological Science: An Inquiry Into Life* (New York: Harcourt Brace & World, 1963), emphasizes the cellular, with the developmental-evolutionary playing an important role. The Yellow Version is most like the conventional science text; however, it pays more attention to the cell, more to ecology, and less to organ and tissue. Its greatest appeal is to the average, or somewhat above, average learner. It came into being in the manner of the Blue Version.

The Green Version, entitled *High School Biology, BSCS Green Version* (Chicago: Rand McNally and Company, 1963), emphasizes the ecological, that is, the organism in a community of life and action. This version has been used most often with slow learners. It came into being in the same manner as did the other two.

The increased number of research participants and the greater diversity of effort made possible by the three-way approach constitute one of the project's greatest strengths. On the other hand, the detachment of each approach from the other two and its resulting discreteness constitute a serious weakness. A second weakness is the lack of close articulation of any of the 3 programs with the science curriculum in the elementary and junior high school. However, this last shortcoming may soon be remedied, at least in part, by a junior-high-school course in biology that is now on the planning board.

Science: The Chemical Bond Approach Project.   In 1957, the Chemical Bond Approach Project had its inception at a conference held at Reed College, Portland, Oregon. Later, the headquarters for the project shifted to Earlham College, Richmond, Indiana, where, in 1959, five college professors of science formally organized the project. The five professors were L. E. Strong (Earlham), L. B. Clapp (Brown), A. H. Livermore (Reed), H. A. Neidig (Lebanon Valley), and M. K. Wilson (Tufts). Later the five-man staff of directors was enlarged to eight including the addition of a sixth college professor and two high-school teachers of chemistry. The sponsor of the project throughout was the National Science Foundation.

As with the other experimental science programs, CBA pursued a sequence starting with the initial writing of course materials, followed by field testing, then by rewriting, then by retesting, and finally, by commercial publication of a basic textbook, *Chemistry CBAC* (New York: McGraw-Hill Book Co., 1963). Other publications included a laboratory guide and notebook, supplementary readings, testing instruments, a teacher's guide, and assorted visual aids.

Although the nonspecialist reader who wished to understand the CBA project in detail would need to spend extensive time studying it, a few selected abstractions that would clarify the program for him, at least a little, are these. First of all, it is built around three chemical bonds: covalent, ionic, and metallic. Substances have covalent bonds when, for instance, they boil at low temperatures, become liquids in short intervals, are transparent, and are nonconductors of electricity. Substances have ionic bonds when they boil at high temperatures, become liquids only around fairly intense heat on the order of 500 degrees centigrade, and are transparent. Substances have metallic bonds when they boil at high temperatures, become liquids only around very intense heat, and are opaque.[22]

The emphasis throughout the course is on atomic and molecular structure with the greatest stress possible—true to the traditions of problem solving—consistently placed on knowledge gained by investigation and laboratory exploration. As stated in a CBA Newsletter, "The laboratory program, then, is designed to develop the ability of the student to identify a problem, to design an experiment which will shed light on this problem, to carry out the technical operations of the experiment, and to arrive at a conclusion through an analysis of his own data. Initially, the student is provided with assistance in all these areas. Such assistance is withdrawn gradually until finally the student is asked to perform all these steps independently, employing ideas and techniques accumulated in the process of investigating other problems."[23] The CBA program, probably more than any other in the schools, employs the open encounter—in the opinion of many, perhaps too much of the time. Yet only extensive evaluation in the future will tell. As with the other experimental science programs, NSF has financed institutes to get teachers ready for the innovational in CBA.

Science: The Chemical Education Materials Study.   A second experimental program in Chemistry, also underwritten by NSF, is the so-called CHEM Study project which had its inception in 1959 at the Ohio State University. Under the leadership of J. Arthur Campbell of Harvey Mudd College, Claremont, California, and Glenn T. Seaborg of the University of California, Berkeley, the project got under way actively in 1960 with the preparation of the usual dry-run materials. It then proceeded through various tryouts to the outcome of commercial publication in 1963. The basic textbook is *Chemistry: An Experimental Science*, edited by George C. Pimentel, and published by W. H. Freeman and Co., San Francisco. In addition to the text, there are the customary laboratory and teacher manuals, aids, and other supplementary materials.

Like CBA, CHEM Study also places high premium on knowledge gained by discovery, but it structures somewhat more. In CHEM Study, laboratory endeavor is more formally related to the content of the text-

---

[22] Science Service Incorporated, *Chemistry*, 33 (February 1960), pp. 5–6.
[23] Earle S. Scott, "The Necessity for Variety," *CBA Newsletter*, 13 (May 1962), p. 1.

book. It tends to be somewhat more assertive also, particularly in the first part of the course. The emphasis is less on chemical bonds than on dynamical chemical processes and reactions.

To the apparently logical question: Why don't the two projects join hands? the answer usually comes out this way. Two experimental programs should yield more information than one. Strength lies in variety. And last, more experimentation and evaluation are necessary before any kind of fusion in the future could be seriously considered. Despite the logic of this answer, the facts might well reveal that either group knows so little about its counterpart's activities that fusion is impossible. While respecting the virtues of variety, we regret the detachment that variety in this instance has carried in its wake.

Science: Other Experimentation. The four science projects just described are the most encompassing, but a number of others, even though not as attention getting at the national level, are significant. Selected of these are the Elementary School Science Project, University of California; Elementary School Science Project, University of Illinois; Project on Science Instruction in Elementary and Junior High Schools, Commission on Science Instruction in Elementary and Junior High Schools; The Science Curriculum: K-12 Approach; and the Science Curriculum Program of the Science Manpower Project, Teachers College, Columbia University.

Science: A Summary Statement. The unleashing of Sputnik in 1957 triggered a world-wide chain reaction of seemingly endless dimensions. The United States interpreted this historically significant feat as a mandate first for it to inventory the nation's assets and liabilities and then to eliminate the more serious liabilities exposed by the inventory. One of these liabilities was America's notoriously dated programs of science in the areas of business, industry, and education. In regard to the last of these three, the science curriculum in the schools proved to be woefully behind the times, characterized often by half-truth and error. Almost immediately the society moved to set its scientific house in order. The accomplishments have been little short of phenomenal, for which the American people should be eternally grateful. What is needed now is for the humanities, the social sciences, and the applied arts to undergo commensurate updating. Without such counteraction, we may realize too late that victory over the physical is a costly one if the price is sacrifice of affective values.[24]

Mathematics: An Introductory Statement. Like the other sciences, mathematics too is in a state of upheaval and assessment in the schools. Nor is this a surprising turn of events with the mathematical such an

[24] I take this opportunity to thank my friend and colleague, Dr. Edward Victor, for the generous assistance he has given me throughout the preparation of this section.

inseparable part of the current wide-spread electronics revolution. The latter, because it runs counter to precedent, confronts with new challenges and demands. The curriculum of mathematics in the schools has responded to the confrontation both by updating the old (for the most part), and by adding the new (in smaller part). In regard to the latter, much of what may appear to certain parents and other uninformed observers as new in the mathematics curriculum is actually a resurrection of the old. For instance, the concept of set now introduced in one of the junior-high grades, usually the ninth, in centuries old. And as a second instance, computation from a binary or ternary base instead of from a decimal base has centuries of respectability to support it.

Readers who are not mathematics majors but who desire a broader look at the new than this section can provide might profit by consulting one or more of the following works:

1. American Association for the Advancement of Science and the Science Teaching Center, University of Maryland. *Second Report of the Information Clearinghouse on New Science Curricula,* 1964, pp. 7–14.

2. Fraser, Dorothy M., *Current Curriculum Studies in Academic Subjects.* Washington, D.C.: National Education Association, 1962, pp. 27–52.

Henderson, Kenneth B., "Mathematics" in Robert S. Gilchrist, *Using Current Curriculum Developments.* Washington, D.C.: Association for Supervision and Curriculum Development, 1963, pp. 49–58.

4. Moise, Edwin, "The New Mathematics Programs," in Paul C. Rosenbloom (ed.), *Modern Viewpoints in the Curriculum.* New York; McGraw Hill Book Company, 1964, pp. 73–87.

Mathematics: The School Mathematics Study Group. In 1958, with the support of NSF, the School Mathematics Study Group got its start at Yale University under the directorship of E. G. Begle, now of Stanford University. The Group is an instrument of the American Mathematical Society, with CEEB as a collaborator. Its initial purpose was improved materials and an overall improved program of mathematics for the more capable pupil in grades 7 through 12. However, on occasions it has prepared selected materials for the less capable pupil as well.

The program evolved in the manner of the science programs, as previously described: first work materials, then tryouts, then revisions followed by other tryouts, and ultimately commercially published textbooks, teacher guides, and other teaching aids. Publications for the junior-high grades are built around units, developed to assist teachers whom the authors assume to be less specialized than their higher-grade counterparts. In general, the curriculum content tends to be more sophisticated than what it replaces.

The curriculum of grades 7 and 8 usually includes the following: algebra, introduced through the various number systems; geometry, introduced primarily in the concrete; coordinates and simple equations; and the place of mathematics in the other sciences. The curriculum of grade 9 is basically algebraic including quadratic equations. In addition, it usually includes sets and descriptive statistics. The curriculum of grade 10 consists primarily of the traditional plane-geometry course, updated, with solid geometry appearing at the end. The curriculum of grade 11 consists of a combination of advanced algebra, trigonometry, and analytic geometry. The curriculum of grade 12 is the most innovational, including functions required for later calculus, introductory matrix algebra, the polynomial theorem, logarithms, and probability.[25] The titles of selected of the materials, now available for teachers of these courses, are listed by Henderson, p. 53.

Mathematics: University of Illinois Committee on School Mathematics. The goal of this project is for students both to understand and to apply mathematical knowledge. Under the directorship of Max Beberman, and with the financial support of three organizations: the Sloan Foundation, NSF, and the University of Illinois, this project has its focus on elementary-school mathematics, grades K through 6. The emphasis throughout is on pupil discovery, with arithmetical manipulation subordinated to the role of a tool. The first publications, by David Page, appeared in 1961: *Number Lines, Functions, and Fundamental Topics.*[26]

Mathematics: Studies from Stanford University's Institute for Mathematical Studies in the Social Sciences. In 1960, under the leadership of Patrick Suppes, and with the financial support of three agencies: NSF, the Carnegie Foundation, and the U.S. Office of Education, Stanford University embarked on two K-through-6 mathematics projects. The first dealt with set and number theory for pupils of all ability levels; the second, "Mathematical Logic For the Schools," was developed for gifted children only. Textbooks, teacher guides, and selected films are available for the two programs.

Mathematics: Other Projects. With the National Defense Education Act insuring generous financial support, an extensive number of mathematics projects, other than the three just covered, either are currently underway throughout the country or have been completed. Selected of these are as follows:

---

[25] A detailed discussion of the SMSG may be found in the following: Edwin Moise, "The New Mathematics Programs," *The School Review,* **70** (Spring 1962), pp. 82–101.
[26] David A. Page, in American Association for the Advancement of Science, *Science Education News* (December 1961), p. 8.

1. The Commission on Mathematics, College Entrance Examination Board. This project, starting with extensive experimentation in 1959, culminated in a recommended high-school program designed to enable students to begin calculus at the time of their college enrollment.

2. University of Maryland Mathematics Project. Conceived in 1957, this has been a cooperative study of mathematics for grades 7 and 8, participated in by the college departments of mathematics, education, psychology, and engineering. The result is a program that increases the difficulty of the customary junior-high-school mathematics sequence. Woven into the new program are deductive reasoning, selected abstract algebraic and geometrical concepts, number theory, logic, and simple statistical processes.

3. Ball State Teachers College Experimental Program. This is another example of a program designed to upgrade and update mathematics for the secondary-school grades.

4. Boston College Mathematics Institute's Program. This experiment, started as long ago as 1953, has been another attempt by curriculum makers to modernize mathematics in the high school and to prepare teachers for the "new look."

5. Geometry Project of Stanford University. This program attempts to discover whether a nonspecialist teacher can make Euclidean geometry a worthwhile experience for elementary-grade children.

6. The Syracuse University—Webster College Madison project. This program has as its goal student learning of mathematics by the process of discovery, with understanding substituting for memorization. Designed for grades 3 through 10, the program includes the usual printed and other materials.

Modern Foreign Languages. Shifting now from the field of the sciences to the field of the foreign languages, we present a status-quo picture in lieu of the separate experiments themselves. Selected of the latter, however, for those who desire them, can be found, among other places, in the following:

1. Birkmaier, Edna M., "Foreign Languages," in Robert S. Gilchrist *Using Current Curriculum Developments.* Washington, D.C.: Association for Supervision and Curriculum Development, 1963, pp. 25–39.

2. Gaarder, A. Bruce, "Current Experimentation in Foreign Languages," in Paul C. Rosenbloom, *Modern Viewpoints in the Curriculum.* New York: McGraw-Hill Book Company, 1964, pp. 49–56.

3. Fraser, Dorothy M., *Current Curriculum Studies in Academic Subjects.* Washington, D.C.: National Education Association, 1962, pp. 54–71.

An historical overview of foreign-language instruction in the schools reveals initially an exclusive preoccupation by education with the classical languages, followed next by an allegiance divided between the classical and the modern languages, and more recently by a primary allegiance to the modern languages. During most of this century, however, curriculum effort, whether in the classical or the modern tradition, has never been as noteworthy in the United States as in most other countries. America, in its own characteristically provincial way, consistently has favored a second language for pupils of other countries without approving a like pattern for pupils in its own schools. The nation's same lack of enthusiasm has further revealed itself in the inadequate preparation of foreign-language teachers: approximately half of them, even today, are teaching with less than a major in the specific language taught.

Dissatisfied with this unflattering picture of educational lassitude and mediocrity, the Modern Language Association reacted in 1952 by initiating its Foreign Language Study Program. Since that time, the Association's efforts have become increasingly multifaceted and experimental. Moving slowly until 1958, the MLA dramatically accelerated its research pace in that year, thanks to NDEA support. Five years later, the Association had become involved in 224 projects.[27]

Section 602, Title VI of the National Defense Education Act commissions the U.S. Office of Education "directly or by contract, to make studies and surveys to determine the need for increased or improved instruction in modern foreign languages and other fields needed to provide a full understanding of the areas, regions, or countries in which such languages are commonly used, to conduct research on more effective methods of teaching such languages . . . and to develop specialized materials for use in such training, or in training teachers of such languages . . . ." Under NDEA support, the MLA established two research centers: the Foreign Language Program Research Center in New York, and the Center for Applied Linguistics in Washington, D.C. The latter "serves as a clearing house for information about teaching neglected languages, mostly Asian and African, about teaching English as a second language, and about applying classroom-instruction findings in the field of descriptive linguistics."[28]

The Foreign Language Study Program has included extensive experimentation in the following areas: in the audio-lingual or aural-oral method of teaching a foreign language, in the learning value of the language laboratory and other electronic-methods devices, in the program of foreign travel for the language teacher, in the merit of a school's

[27] U.S. Department of Health, Education and Welfare, *National Defense Language Developmental Program*, OE. 12016, 1963, p. 1.
[28] Fraser, p. 57.

introducing foreign-language instruction in the elementary grades, and in the general field of teacher preparation.[29] The most controversial of these are the audio-lingual method of instruction and the appropriateness of foreign-language instruction in the elementary school. The various experiments now in progress are generally supportive of both.

A growing conviction within educational ranks is that a goal of no less than language mastery should characterize the foreign-language program of any school system. Mindful of this goal, the Materials Development Center in New York City is preparing or refining six-year programs in each of the more popularly spoken modern languages. These programs provide for a two-year pupil experience with a language in the elementary-school grades, followed by a subsequent four-year experience with the same language in the high school.

Regarding foreign-language teaching in the elementary school, the major questions are these: (1) How early should instruction begin? (2) Should it be spaced more lightly throughout a number of grades or concentrated more heavily into a few—particularly in grades 7 and 8? (3) If foreign-language instruction moves in, what existing curriculum components will have to move out? (4) Will language specialists without adequate training in elementary education be able to integrate their efforts with other faculty members who are specially trained for that level? (5) If not, what will constitute a balanced program of teacher preparation for language teachers? And (6) will elementary and secondary-school teachers be able to articulate a six-year program effectively? These and related issues are begging for resolution today, with ony the superficial pretending to have conclusive answers.

English: An Introductory Statement.   Leaving the three fields of the sciences, mathematics, and the modern languages, which since 1958 have been underwritten almost unstintingly by the NDEA, we turn now to the field of the English-Language arts. And, with few exceptions, the shift carries with it a marked decrease in large-scale experimentation. The research efforts currently in evidence are taking place, for the most part, under the aegis of the National Council of Teachers of English (NCTE), of individual school systems, of NDEA on a modest basis, or of individual researchers. And the substance of the research, it is interesting to note, reveals composition and linguistics along with reading to be the areas of most widespread experimentation.

Despite the admitted paucity of large-scale research in the English-language-arts field, three experiments of modest proportions, supported

[29] An indication of the growth of the foreign-language movement in elementary education is attested to by Elizabeth Keesee's 49-page booklet of references and materials: *References on Foreign Languages in the Elementary School* (Washington, D.C.: U.S. Department of Health, Education and Welfare, 1963).

by the U.S. Office of Education, the College Entrance Examination Board, and the National Education Association, respectively, are in operation at the moment. These we shall treat briefly.

English: Project English. Regarding the first, the Congress, in September of 1961, appropriated "limited expenditures for improvement of English instruction . . . [to be] administered by the Cooperative Research Branch, Office of Education." This appropriation set in motion what came to be known as Project English. With J. N. Hook as coordinator, Curriculum Centers were established initially in three universities, and in the latter part of 1962, in three additional universities. The names of the universities, the themes of the research, the grade levels at which the research was to be directed, and the size and duration of the grants are as indicated, respectively, in the following list:[30]

1. Carnegie Institute of Technology: English for the able college-bound student, grades 10 to 12, $220,000, four years.

2. Northwestern University: composition, grades 7 through 14, $250,000, five years.

3. University of Nebraska: composition, grades K through 13, $250,000, five years.

4. Hunter College: English materials in reading, speaking and listening for the urban deprived, grades 6 through 11, $249,802, five years.

5. University of Minnesota: history, structure, and characteristics of language, grades 7 through 12, $242,949, five years.

6. University of Oregon: bringing curriculum into harmony with what is known about language, writing, speech, literature, and reading, grades 7–12, $250,000, five years.

In addition to the Centers', ten specific, but lesser, university research projects were approved in 1961 and ten more in 1962. Grants for the latter ten totaled to a sum of $319,167. Four dealt with linguistics, three with reading, two with college composition, and one with spelling. Under Project English, the U.S. Office of Education published in 1962 *The Language of Elementary School Children: Its Relationship to the Language of Reading Textbooks and the Quality of Reading of Selected Children.*

English: Commission on English of the College Entrance Examination Board. Regarding the second English project, the College Entrance Examination Board, in 1959, established the Commission on English to evaluate how adequately the English curriculum in grades 9 through

[30] These data were secured from the following: U.S. Department of Health, Education, and Welfare, *English Project Newsletter* No. 1, May 1962; and No. 2, September 1962.

12 was preparing students for college. Following a period of study, it sanctioned the following emphases:

1. Language—attention to spelling, vocabulary enrichment, systematic study of word derivations and change in word meanings, and modern English grammar and usage.
2. Literature—chiefly English and American literature, with specific masterpieces allocated to each year to be studied in unabridged versions.
3. Composition—to be a part of each week's work, with exposition rather than creative writing stressed, and subjects to be derived for the most part from concurrent study of language and literature.[31]

Two years later in 1961, as a step in following through on its recommendations, the Commission conducted a curriculum-planning institute at the University of Michigan. "Sixty persons, representing twenty selected universities, met in three separate groups of twenty each to explore trends and needs and prepare sample syllabuses in the fields of literature, composition, and language."[32] In the summer of 1962, each of the afore-mentioned twenty universities conducted local institutes designed to train selected secondary-school teachers to use the curriculum guides in their classrooms. This led to an assessment of the guides the following summer.

English: NEA English Composition Project. Under the leadership of Arno Jewett, the NEA Project, the third and last to be discussed in this section, got underway in 1961 with these stated purposes: "to improve the ability of secondary school students to write compositions (exposition, description, and narration); to raise teacher effectiveness through the employment of theme readers and by elimination of nonprofessional duties; to develop and to test new methods and materials for teaching writing; to establish demonstration centers for visiting teachers to observe promising writing programs; to evaluate and to compare effectiveness of different programs; and to publicize effective techniques and programs."[33] In deference to its comprehensiveness, we submit this statement of purpose without elaboration.

Social Studies: An Introductory Statement. In the field of the social studies, as in English, there is a dearth of large-scale research and experimentation. Also, as in the field of English, most of the present experimentation is under the leadership of professional organizations, of school systems, or of individuals. Thus, relatively speaking, the extent of most of the experimental projects is quite limited, and the financial backing

[31] Fraser, in Current Curriculum Studies in Academic Subjects, p. 49.
[32] Harold B. Allen, "Current Progress in English," in Rosenbloom, *Modern Viewpoints in Curriculum,* p. 92.
[33] Max Bogart, "English," in Gilchrist, *Using Current Curriculum Developments,* pp. 21–22.

is commensurately modest. Yet the interest of schools in social-studies experimentation runs high, as attested to by this statement of the United States Commissioner of Education, Francis Keppel, when engaged in appropriations hearings before a congressional subcommittee in 1963: "Last fall, the Office of Education announced that cooperative research funds were available for the development of improved curriculums in the social studies. Within 3 months, more than 700 requests for information were received . . . In the social studies, we are now receiving 10 applications for every project we have funds to support."[34]

At the national level, the leading benefactor of the social studies is the Cooperative Research Program of the U.S. Office of Education, brought into being in 1954 by Public Law 83-531. Appropriations to support its overall program were increased from $11,500,000 for 1954 to $17,000,000 for 1964. Somewhat less than 10 per cent of this latter total was earmarked for social-studies research and development.

Social Studies: Project Social Studies.   One of the projects of the Cooperative Research Program is Project Social Studies, initiated in the fall of 1962. The program is four-faceted, consisting of the following components.

1. *Curriculum Centers.*   By the end of 1963, seven of these Centers were in operation in the institutions named. The focal concerns of the projects, the grade levels at which the concerns were to be directed, and the length of the projects are as indicated in the following list:

(*a*) Carnegie Institute of Technology: Reading material for able students, grades 9 through 12, 4 years.

(*b*) University of Minnesota: Identification by an interdisciplinary team of the structure of each of the social studies, K through 14, 5 years.

(*c*) Syracuse University: Identification of basic social studies concepts and the preparation of related materials, 3 grades unspecified, 5 years.

(*d*) Harvard University: Planning a social-studies curriculum based on an analysis of public issues, grades 8 through 10, 5 years.

(*e*) Northwestern University: Elimination of duplication in the social studies and preparation of related materials, grades 5, 8, 11, 5 years.

(*f*) University of Illinois: Planning a 5 year sequence of social studies for the secondary school, including 3 new courses, grades 8 through 12, 5 years.

(*g*) Ohio State University: Economics at the 9th grade level including preparation of related materials, grade 9, 3 years.

[34] Contained in *Hearings Before the Subcommittee on Appropriations, House of Representatives* (Washington D.C.: U.S. Printing Office, 1963).

Each of the seven institutions received an initial grant up to $25,000 for the first year, and will receive or has received up to $50,000 for each of the subsequent years of the Center's duration.

2. *Research Projects.*   By April of 1963, eleven research projects had been approved. These were to be of lesser proportions than those contracted for with the Centers. Rutgers University, for instance, had as its research theme the Social and Cultural Factors in School Achievement.

3. *Developmental Activities.*   Workshop seminars of a developmental type with follow-up conferences were approved for Stanford and Syracuse Universities. These seminars entailed synthesized program planning by leading social-studies educators and teachers.

4. *Small-Scale Research.*   A grant up to $7,500 was approved for individual researchers, especially doctoral candidates, who wished to engage in an approved project.[35]

Social Studies: Other Projects.   For other projects in the social-studies field, all of which are less comprehensive than Project Social Studies, we refer the reader to John U. Michaelis' Chapter 8, in Gilchrist, *Using Current Curriculum Developments,* pp. 71–85.

Additional Curriculum Areas.   Other than in the five fields of the sciences, mathematics, foreign languages, English, and the social studies, research and experimentation are being conducted by individual school systems or by individuals mostly at local levels. Projects in other than these five fields with national or near national dimensions are few and far between, and are of limited scope. For instance, the late President Kennedy's Commission on Youth Fitness spent for that specialized project only $5,460 of U.S. Office monies. Undoubtedly a tremendous research lag exists in the fine arts and the practical arts. Some of the slack is being taken up by the private foundations in the fine arts, but much room for improvement in both these areas still remains.

A Final Statement

It is the strong conviction of the author that the National Defense Education Act has thrown and is still throwing curriculum research and experimentation out of balance. The sciences, mathematics, and the modern languages are receiving the lion's share of Federal attention and support. English and the social studies are being helped, but not enough. And the fine and applied arts along with the classical languages are being almost totally neglected. The private philanthropic foundations are helping the cause of the English Language Arts, the classical languages,

[35] These data came from Gerald R. Smith, "Project Social Studies—A Report" *School Life,* **45** (July 1963), pp. 25–27.

and the fine arts—but insufficiently to compensate for the Government's dilatory efforts.

Education today is definitely heading toward the cognitive, in general, and toward the sciences, in particular. To the extent that this trend is to correct obvious shortcomings of the past, it is commendable—provided in the process it does not sidetrack for too long other important outcomes. To the extent, however, that the trend establishes a pattern, social-humanistic values will suffer. The fundamental need in education today is for a curriculum that, through perspective and balance, will eschew expediency and lead the way broadly to the good life. Education's present onesidedness may not be serious enough as yet to create panic; but it is serious enough, in our opinion, to warrant a high degree of concern.

For Further Thought

1. In your opinion, were the sciences, mathematics, and modern languages so much further behind other subjects in the fifties that they warranted the extra attention they have been receiving? Support your answer.

2. The possibility of a national curriculum in certain subjects may be in the making. Debate the pros and cons of such an eventuality.

3. Do you want to see large-scale curriculum experimentation extended, curtailed, or kept as is? Give your reasons.

4. Do you accept or reject the allegation of many educators that Federal control does not accompany Federal support? Explain.

5. If one leads to the other, and you regard this as a dangerous outcome, what countermeasures do you recommend?

6. What reasons do you postulate for current research being more extensive in secondary than in elementary education? How do you regard this imbalance: with favor or disfavor? Why?

7. Evaluate the merits of each of the following alleged reasons for the current rash of educational experimentation.

(a) To make the nation stronger for political and military reasons.

(b) To make its citizenry happier.

(c) To make its citizenry more sensitive to human values.

(d) To make its citizenry more intellectual.

(e) To make the schools' curricula more difficult.

(f) To improve the nation's mental health.

References

American Association for the Advancement of Science, *Science Education News*, December, 1961.

American Institute of Biological Sciences, *The Biological Sciences Curriculum Study Newsletter*. All issues.

Fast, Kenneth V., "The Role of Laboratory Experiences in the CHEM Study Program," *School Science and Mathematics*. **63**, February 1963, pp. 147–156.

Fraser, Dorothy M., *Current Curriculum Studies in Academic Subjects*. Washington, D.C.: National Education Association, 1962.

Fraser, Dorothy M., *Deciding What to Teach*. Washington, D.C.: National Education Association, 1963.

Gilchrist, Robert S. (chairman), *Using Current Curriculum Developments*. Washington, D.C.: Association for Supervision and Curriculum Development, 1963.

Goodlad, John I., *Planning and Organizing for Teaching*. Washington, D.C.: National Education Association, 1963.

Goodlad, John I., *School Curriculum Reform*. New York: Fund for the Advancement of Education, 1964.

Guernsey, Lee, "Programs Supporting Science Research," *The Teachers College Journal*. 33, March 1962, pp. 112–115.

Heath, Robert W. (ed.), *New Curricula*. New York: Harper and Row, 1964.

Keesee, Elizabeth, *References on Foreign Languages in the Elementary School*. Washington, D.C.: Department of Health, Education, and Welfare, 1963.

Mallinsen, George G., "The Summer Institute Program of the National Science Foundation," *School Science and Mathematics*. 63, February 1963 pp. 95–104.

Merrill, Richard J., "Chemistry: An Experimental Science," *The Science Teacher*. 30, April 1963, pp. 26–31.

Miller, Richard I., *Education In A Changing Society*. Washington, D.C.: National Education Association, 1963.

Moise, Edwin, "The New Mathematics Programs," *The School Review*, 70, Spring 1962, pp. 82–101.

National Science Foundation, *Programs for Education in the Sciences*, SPE-63-A-2, 1963.

President's Council on Youth Fitness, *Youth Physical Fitness—Suggested Elements of a School-Centered Program*. Washington, D.C.: Supt. of Documents, 1961.

Rosenbloom, Paul C. (ed.), *Modern Viewpoints in the Curriculum*. New York: McGraw Hill Book Company, 1964.

Seaborg, Glenn T., "The Story of CHEM Study," *Chemical Education Materials Study Newsletter*, March 1962.

Smith, Gerald, "Project Social Studies—A Report," *School Life*. 45, July 1963, pp. 25–27.

U.S. Department of Health, Education, and Welfare, *National Defense Graduate Fellowships, Graduate Programs 1964–65*. Washington, D.C.

U.S. Department of Health, Education, and Welfare, *National Defense Language Development Program*, Test No. 3, O.E. 12016-63, 1963.

U.S. Department of Health, Education, and Welfare, *Project English Newsletter*. Any issue.

U.S. Department of Health, Education, and Welfare, *The Language Development Program*, O.E.-50026, Washington, D.C.: 1962.

Vandeventer, W. C., "BSCS Biology," *School Science and Mathematics*. 63, February 1963, pp. 89–94.

chapter 8

Education by Television

On a November day of 1963, an assassin's bullet killed a president. Throughout the long weekend that followed, television became the bereaved society's talking mirror: it exposed, it narrated, it interpreted.

In the process, television revealed itself as a resource possessed of telling power; one whose talents formal education had only superficially tapped, one whose potentials education was just beginning to perceive. In this chapter, we intend to identify and analyze selected of those talents and potentials which, with the passing of time, are stirring education progressively more and more.

In the course of televisions's brief history, it has served selected purposes of education through these three organizational media: (1) commercial television (CTV), (2) educational television (ETV), and (3) closed-circuit television (CCTV). Each, while sharing common features with the other two, possesses certain unique characteristics. In regard to the similarities, we shall examine selected claims that have been made about the educational value of the three media, the issues they share in common, the principles they share in common, and the educational advantages and disadvantages they share in common.

Claims Regarding Television as an Educational Medium

The many observers who, in the past two decades, have studied television as an instructional resource have differed extensively in their critical appraisals of it. At one extreme, at least a selected few, without equivocation, have labeled it an instrument of harm. One of the earlier doleful prophets called it the Pied Piper "disguised as a television transmitter."[1] At an opposite extreme, others have made claims about it that

[1] Robert L. Shayon, *Television And Our Children* (New York: Longmans, Green and Company, 1951), p. 17.

challenge the limits of credulity. For instance, Thomas Pollack of New York University has recently described it as offering "the greatest opportunity for advancement in education since the introduction of movable type."[2] Burns, in similar vein, calls it "the most powerful teaching tool since the invention of the printing press five hundred years ago."[3] These are sweeping claims.

As television has matured, fortunately so have the critics. As a consequence, the extremes of critical opinion have narrowed in range during the past decade. Most observers today believe that television when employed discerningly can be a highly valuable educational medium; at its worst, that it is probably (a few would still differ here) more devoid of educational value than actually harmful to viewers. The basic question still in the minds of many, however, is whether television viewed excessively might make learners passive receptors and imitators rather than active doers and creators.

An emerging consensus today is that television constitutes a synthesis of previously existent technique, but in itself does not constitute a new one; is an instrument that holds promise for learning refinement but that can be no more effective than the learning context is adequate. One source aptly and dispassionately describes it this matter of factly: "No matter how complex its electronic processes may be, television is simply another medium of communication, like a book or a human voice. Communication begins with intelligible transmission and ends with intelligible reception."[4] Another source, with comparable conservatism, asserts: "Only if the classroom teacher uses the medium, or resource, with *a purpose* in terms of the needs and problems of learners—and knows when to use it and when not to use it—is it likely to have a maximum effectiveness."[5] Restrained appraisals such as these increasingly are replacing the more unbridled ones of a decade, or so, ago.

Issues Inherent in Instructional Television

During this period of modest hopes and expectancies for instructional television—whether commercial, educational, or closed-circuit—an important task of education is to decide what specific curriculum goals the medium can most efficiently contribute to. In this regard, four important questions particularly need satisfactory answers: (1) What aspects of learning theory can help to identify television's true place in

[2] Quoted from Philip Lewis, *Educational Television Guidebook* (New York: McGraw Hill Book Company, 1961), p. 4.
[3] John L. Burns, "The Promise of Classroom Television," *Parent-Teacher*, **55** (November 1960), p. 81.
[4] The Subcommittee on Television, *The Uses of Television in Education* (North Central Association of Colleges and Universities, 1961), p. 7.
[5] Harold E. Wigren, "The Role and Importance of Instructional Media in Improving Learning." Unpublished address made at the Turkey Run Conference of the National Education Association (DAVI and ASCD), October 1, 1962.

a curriculum? (2) To what extent is television instruction effective in accomplishing the intangibles of learning? (3) Might television, in time, divert education from local purposes and programming and channel it into purposes and programming primarily regional or national in scope? And (4) To what extent, if at all, should instructional television be made the responsibility of professional performers rather than classroom teachers?

Learning Theory and Instructional Television.   In answer to the first of these four questions, learning theory is every bit as fundamental to television instruction as it is to teaching by other media. Learning theory provides these imperatives for television instruction: Decide what curriculum purposes are to be served. Decide whether, and how effectively, television employs the methods which will contribute to those purposes. And, above all else, be definitive about the specific way in which instructional television is to be employed: whether as a total replacement for a given teacher, whether as a supplement to other teaching methods of a given teacher, or whether as a team-teaching device for a number of teachers.

Fundamentally, television is not a teaching method *per se* but a conveyor of method. Thus the key question is: What teaching methods does it convey most successfully? The answer goes something like this. Television performs best as a learning resource when telling and showing are the media. It follows, then, that it does its best job with the lecture and the demonstration. This is not to deprecate television by calling it a passive medium, for the act of thinking which follows listening and viewing is never passive. Furthermore, certain programs that start by telling and showing end by asking viewers to perform given motor responses, which, by their very nature, are active. The message of learning theory here is for television to do what it does best.

Television and the Curriculum Intangibles.   Within the framework of the lecture and the demonstration, to what extent does television lead to developmental growth in the intangibles of education? As mentioned in Chapters 4 through 6, many such intangibles involve the concepts of mental health. They find specific expression in such outcomes as self-fulfillment, happiness, altruism, ethical behavior, and creativity. A valid answer is that television instruction undoubtedly contributes both indirectly and directly to these important outcomes. In this connection, who is to say that the lecture and demonstration—the specialties of television—cannot and do not shape and refine human values?

The real issue, however, is whether these methods perform efficiently and economically in the area of the affective. Our conclusion is that on a relative basis they do not, in view of their greater preoccupation with the transmission of factual material. To the degree that this conclusion is valid, education is unwise in using television for purposes that such methods as the clinical interview, the class discussion, the pupil committee, and other methods can achieve better. If employed where it is most likely to succeed, television can be extremely effective. This effectiveness is not diminished because television is less successful in other areas.

Instructional Television's Threat to Local Autonomy.   A third issue, rooted both in curriculum theory and tradition, concerns the potential threat of instructional television to local educational autonomy. Education, although a state function legally, is usually a local function operationally. Thus individual school systems, and oftentimes individual teachers in those same systems, have a wide latitude of decision-making powers in the areas of curriculum planning and implementation. To the extent that television delimits these decision-making powers, it stands as a threat to local autonomy.

Fundamentally, a curriculum is adequate in proportion to its relevance to the needs of a given educational level: a school system, a particular school, a particular classroom, or an individual student. And the relevance of a curriculum generally increases in inverse relation to the size of an intended learning group: the smaller the group the more relevant the curriculum; the larger the group, the less relevant the curriculum. Furthermore, educational programming removed from a local situation tends to relate more to statistical abstractions than to "live" students, more to group averages than to individuals per se. Ever conscious of this danger of television's possible detachment from learners, schools should employ the criterion of curriculum germaneness before going overboard for the medium. A foreknowledge of what is to be projected is one essential. And a right of curriculum veto, at least on occasions, is another.

Training for Television Instruction.   A fourth and final issue here has to do with the amount and quality of training needed by teachers who participate in television instruction. A growing conviction, in this regard, is that a school which rushes into television without readying the participants for their tasks is more zealous than wise. Even when commercial television is the medium, some prior in-service "give and take" among teachers usually proves beneficial. Learning customarily improves to the degree that teachers promote a given program effectively, prepare a class adequately for its projection, and evaluate it acceptably.[6]

When the medium is closed-circuit television, the in-service program might well include such concerns as these: methods of cooperative teacher planning and sharing; practice on camera, emphasizing voice and personality projection; and ways of integrating large-group and small-group instruction. When the medium is educational television, even

---

[6] Neil Postman, *Television And The Teaching Of English* (New York: Appleton-Century-Crofts, Inc., 1961), pp. 78–88.

greater care should be taken in presentation because the programs are seen by a more diverse audience.

Other methods helpful in readying teachers for the advent of instructional television are these: visitations by teachers to schools and studios to observe television practices at work elsewhere, seeking advice from expert consultants, informal exchanges among planned participants, trial performances of planned participants followed by mutual evaluations, preparation of television guide books, employing tape recordings for practice purposes, and careful study of the mechanical gadgets that are a part of televison.

In general, any school unwilling to invest extensive time preparing for television education should not engage in it. Preventable mistakes perpetrated on a small, much less on a large, student audience seek in vain for justification.

Principles Underlying the Employment of Instructional Television

From education's trial-and-error experiences with television as an instructional medium, the following operational principles have emerged. They are basic to any curriculum that includes television in its constellation of teaching methods.

1. Television, like any other teaching method, cannot remain separate from educational purpose. Purpose is a determiner of method, not vice versa.

2. In and of itself, television produces nothing. It is an item of equipment that comes alive only with the human touch. Thus it is only as effective as the professional participants are knowledgeable and competent.

3. All professional participants in television instruction should be accorded equal status; for behind-the-scene participants to have scarcely any status at all operates adversely against motivation and performance spontaneity.

4. Instructional television should fit into an ensemble of teaching method; scarcely ever should it be dominant.

5. Instructional television, to be effective, usually should pursue a long, slow course that starts with methodical planning and that terminates with thoughtful evaluation. As stated by one writer, it should never begin or end with the simple turning of a dial.

6. The primary emphasis in television education should always be more on the process of education than on the processes of television. Teaching viewed in this manner is more than polished telling; and performance is more than slickness.

7. Instructional television should incorporate open-ended as well as close-ended learning situations. The performer's final word is less important than the observers' follow through.

8. Pupil-viewers like teacher-performers need to be trained for their roles.

Advantages of Television Instruction

From its many experiences with instructional television, education is near consensus in assessing the following uses and outcomes as worthy of acclaim. I enumerate them at the risk of an occasional re-echoing of early parts of the chapter.

1. Television excells as a medium for the oral presentation of facts and ideas. Thus it lends itself admirably to such teaching methods as the lecture, the symposium, the round table, or the interview.

2. Television excels equally as a music medium. In fact, in this area it knows almost no limitations.

3. Television excels comparably as a visual medium. In this area too it knows few bounds, possessing a range that extends from the close-up view to the distant image, from events of the immediate locale to those of a far off place, and from the intimate to the detached.

4. From the composite of these first three advantages, television may be viewed as constituting a powerful instrument for multidimensioned spectacles: for instance, real-life events of significance, drama, and the opera.

5. When the use of television is carefully spaced and integrated with the rest of the curriculum, television comprises a noteworthy motivational device.

6. When television is employed by a teaching team, the first medium complements the second. Television usually appeals most to those teachers who perform best on camera; small-group and one-to-one situations usually appeal most to the remainder of the team.

7. With its success dependent on the quality of on-camera performance, television tends to impose sharp controls over teaching method and personality projection.

8. Instructional television serves as an effective in-service growth medium, demanding that teachers think through the goals of learning more, plan more carefully, and integrate their efforts more professionally.

Disadvantages of Instructional Television

Although not yet at a point of consensus, educators are aware of a number of possible disadvantages of instructional television. Real or alleged, these disadvantages include the following. The reader may assess their validity as he relates them to the remaining content of the chapter.

1. It is fundamentally an authority-centered medium leading more to repetitive-type outcomes of a memory nature than to discovery-type outcomes of a reflective-thinking nature.

2. Assuming point 1 above to be valid, the medium fails the test of open-ended creativeness.

3. Because of its accent on observation and listening, it is a more-or-less passive learning resource.

4. As the size of its audience multiplies, it becomes increasingly less effective in adapting to the learning needs of individuals.

5. Being most at home in the cognitive, it is unable to contribute, except in small part, to the affective outcomes of education.

6. Being essentially a team medium, it depends for success on the cooperative endeavor of many participating individuals.

CTV as an Instructional Medium

As indicated earlier, commercial television (CTV), educational television (ETV), and closed-circuit television (CCTV) all have the potential to make significant contributions to education. Initially we examine CTV, which is both the oldest and the most widely employed of the three. For purposes of orientation, we delineate a few selected facts and figures pertaining to its growth history.

In 1934, as radio was growing rapidly and television was on the horizon, the Federal Communications Commission was established. It is made up of seven members regularly appointed by the President of The United States. In the early 1940's, this agency set aside 12 Very High Frequency (VHF) channels, 2 to 13, to serve Commercial Television's purposes. These VHF channels have extensive range, with transmission little affected by unfavorable terrain. In 1952, the government also set aside 70 Ultra High Frequency channels to share the transmission burden with the 12 VHF channels. Transmission over UHF bands, however, has two distinct drawbacks: the range is limited, with uneven terrain affecting reception adversely; and reception is possible only when a receiving set has a special electronic reception device. Because of these limitations, of the 527 CTV stations in existence in 1961, only 76 operated on a UHF band.[7] Despite a number of transmission obstacles, however, CTV has grown in an almost unbelievable way during the past two decades. In 1948, one hundred thousand viewing sets existed throughout the nation; by 1959, the total had reached fifty million. In 1950, 1 family in 15 had a set; in 1959, 7 in 8 had sets.[8]

With nearly the entire nation constituting CTV's audience, the educa-

[7] *Ibid.*, p. 19.
[8] Wilbur Schramm, Jack Lyle, and Edwin B. Parker, *Television in the Lives of Our Children* (Stanford: Stanford University Press, 1961), p. 11.

tional possiblities of the medium are tremendous. Unfortunately for education, however, entertainment is CTV's major purpose; education is only an incidental, or, at best, a secondary purpose. Yet even with this essentially noneducational emphasis, CTV has had moments of educational greatness. During these moments, it has brought into the American home social, literary, and artistic events of note; and it has advanced the cause of science. Formal education has capitalized on selected of these occasions by transmitting programs directly into the classroom, or by assigning television-viewing homework for out-of-school projects. Most often, however, the capriciousness of chance rather than careful curriculum planning has decided who will view given commercially sponsored programs of educational merit.

Within this framework of incidental educational viewing and accidental educational value, we now turn to the nature of CTV's overall appeal to children and youth, the different characteristics of the youthful viewers, the types of programs with greatest appeal, and the effects of the programs, if any, on the young viewers.

CTV's Appeal. A number of studies have had as their focal concern the appeal of CTV to children and youth. Three British researchers, in 1958, conducted one of the more monumental of these. Their sample consisted of 1854 matched pairs of viewers and nonviewers, who ranged in age from 10 to 14, and who lived in London, Portsmouth, Bristol, and Sunderland. The sample members identified the appeal of CTV to be: (1) security and reassurance, (2) excitement, (3) escape, (4) the magnetism of colorful personalities, and (5) the opportunity which CTV affords observers to broaden their people, place, and time horizons.[9] Schramm and Associates, in a series of significant studies, reaffirm (1) through (5) above, and add a sixth, social utility, to the list.[10] Shayon, speaking not from research but from purely subjective opinion, contributes these three others: the rebellion of children against parental restrictions, compensation by children for a lack of love and affection, and the need of children for status identification.[11]

Viewers and Selected Characteristics. Assuming CTV's appeal to be essentially as depicted in the preceding enumeration, we next analyze the differential characteristics of the viewing audience.

The television habit customarily begins early in life and ends only with death. In one study of a San Francisco sample, 14 per cent of the two-year-olds were characterized as more-or-less regular viewers.[12] The amount of viewing time, as reported by most researchers, increases

[9] Hilde Himmelweit, A. N. Oppenheim, and Pamela Vince, *Television And The Child* (London: Oxford Press, 1958), p. 15.
[10] Schramm, Lyle, and Parker, *Television in the Lives of Our Children*, pp. 57–59.
[11] Shayon, *Op. Cit.*, pp. 26–36.
[12] Schramm, Lyle, and Parker, *Television in the Lives of Our Children*, p. 27.

after infancy to a peak period in preadolescence, and then declines during the period of adolescence. Witty, Kinsella, and Coomer, in a study of a Chicago-area sample, report that in 1963, second graders spent an average of 17 hours weekly in television viewing; sixth-graders, 28 hours; and seventh- and eighth-graders, 18 hours.[13] Schramm and Associates report 2.2 hours of daily viewing time by second-graders, 2.9 hours by sixth-graders, and 2.3 hours by twelfth-graders.[14]

For the early school years, a positive correlation exists between mental age and amount of viewing time. A plausible explanation for this relationship is that intelligent children tend to do more of almost everything in their formative years. Beginning, however, with preadolescence, an inverse correlation between brightness and viewing begins to develop, which increases in significance with age.[15]

In addition to age and brightness, two other factors relate to television viewing. The first of these is the education of parents, which correlates inversely with the amount of viewing time engaged in by their children. The second of these is the viewing habits of parents, which correlate positively with the viewing habits of their children.[16]

When the heavy-viewing addicts—that is, those children who consistently rank highest on the viewing scale—are compared with their lighter-viewing counterparts, these differences stand out. The heavy viewers are more shy, are less secure emotionally, have less initiative, escape more into adventure, are more dependent and thus more fearful of striking out for themselves, and read more comic books. They also rank lower on intelligence, have fewer outside interests, read fewer books—other than comics—and are less social. And the younger ones, in particular, tend to come from lower socio-economic levels.[17]

Types of Programs Viewed. The next consideration is the kinds of programs children view. In this regard, the titles of specific offerings change from year to year, but the tastes of the viewing audience, within any age bracket, tend to be repetitive. In general, young children incline toward animal stories and fairy tales. Children from the middle elementary grades into high school incline toward adventure programs, variety programs, westerns, and science fiction. Older elementary-age children and adolescents incline, in addition, toward situation comedies, crime movies, and popular music or variety programs. When Witty and associ-

[13] Paul A. Witty, Paul Kinsella, and Anne Coomer, "A Summary of Yearly Studies of Televiewing," *Elementary English* 30 (October 1963) p. 590.
[14] Schramm, Lyle, and Parker, *Television in the Lives of Our Children*, pp. 169–170.
[15] *Ibid.*, p. 34.
[16] *Ibid.*, pp. 35–48.
[17] Himmelweit, Oppenheim, and Vince, *Television and the Child*, pp. 29–30, and p. 394; also Schramm, Lyle, and Parker, *Television in the Lives of Our Children*, p. 121.

ates asked the elementary age children of their sample what programs they would like to see more often, the second- and third-graders responded with "Space, Science, Movies, War, Mystery"; the fourth-through six-graders, with "Comedies, War, Movies, Horror, Mystery."[18]

Most analyses of the research on the various media of escape reveal these two thought-provoking phenomena. The first is that children and youth search outlets which conform more to their already existent tastes than for outlets which are likely to change their tastes. Thus if they like adventure, they seek vicarious adventure-program outlets regardless of the medium: whether a book, a movie, or a television program. Himmelweit and her associates uncovered this phenomenon in an indirect way. They noted that children who had access to only one transmission channel tended to watch whatever program the channel happened to be featuring at the moment; but when given access to a second channel, they "shopped" more for a program that conformed to their tastes.

A second phenomenon is that despite the existence of programs labeled "children's," the majority of young viewers, even during the so-called children's time from 4 to 9 P.M., watch adult programs.[19] Before becoming alarmed at this result, however, the more concerned should first examine the quality of children's programs. When Schramm and his associates analyzed 100 hours of "children's programs," they reported the transmission of 12 murders, 16 major gun fights, one case of stabbing with a butcher knife, and 4 attempted suicides of which 3 were successful.[20] Adult programs could well be preferable.

The Effect of CTV Viewing. The basic issue of what kind of substantive and psychological content is proper for children's CTV programs may be answered, in part, by a study of the effect on children and young people of presently existing content. A composite from such a study reveals a pattern essentially as follows:

A. Learning Effects of Television on:

1. *Amount of reading.* Negatively correlated in the early elementary years; positively correlated in the later elementary years. In general, television viewing tends to increase the amount of reading.

2. *Size of vocabulary.* Positively correlated in a significant way; gains total up to a year of additional progress.

3. *Overall knowledge.* Correlates at a low order (to a slight degree). Children, however, accumulate more facts earlier.

4. *School performance.* Correlates positively for the slow, negatively for the fast—particularly in case of the bright older students.

[18] Witty, Kinsella, and Coomer, *Elementary English,* p. 594.
[19] Himmelweit, Oppenheim, and Vince, *Television and the Child,* p. 13.
[20] Schramm, Lyle, and Parker, *Television in the Lives of Our Children,* p. 139.

B. Psychological Effects of Television on:

5. *Emotional stability.*   Sadistic realism frightens the younger; seems to have little effect on the older.

6. *Aggressive personalities.*   Television sadism may possibly reinforce existing aggressive personality tendencies, although this is supposition; but it has not been shown to develop aggressive personality patterns from nonaggressive ones.

7. *Passivity.*   Apparently has no influence because too many other influences ostensibly are at work. (A verbal minority of the critics take exception here.)

C. Physical Effects of Television on:

8. *Eyesight.*   Contrary to earlier opinion, probably has no effect.

9. *Night's rest.*   Makes a child lose not more than from 10 to 20 minutes of sleep per night.

10. *Overall health.*   Has no effect.

D. Social Effects of Television on:

11. *Acquaintances.*   Correlates negatively at a low order—probably decreases the number of casual acquaintances.

12. *Friendships.*   Correlates no lower than zero, and may correlate positively in that it provides a social meeting ground for children and teen-agers.

13. *Family life.*   Has no provable effect—does not bind families more closely together; neither does it separate them more.

E. Interest-Building Effects of Television on:

14. *Hobbies.*   Probably has no effect.

A Concluding Statement Regarding CTV.   A personal conclusion reached from an analysis of pertinent research is that CTV, even when uncontrolled, is basically a positive force; only incidentally or occasionally, a negative force. Fundamentally, CTV mirrors more than it molds. As such, it appeals to developmental tastes more than trying to change them. But in the process of this developmental appeal, it broadens and enriches. As would be expected, the more creative and independent among children and youth shun it for more imaginative endeavor. The less creative and independent adhere to it more slavishly.

A concern expressed by some, a few of them psychotherapists, is that sadism on CTV will transfer to sadistic behavior in real life. This is a logical inference, but to date it lacks solid proof. Yet even as a tentative hypothesis, it should give society pause. A precautionary antidote is for parents to set up sensible controls over programs that vent the more primitive emotions. However, these controls cannot become inflexibly rigid without blocking normal outlets for aggressiveness—masculine aggressiveness, in particular, which will escape in one avenue if dammed up in another. Phantasy, it should be remembered, is a developmental preliminary to realism. Thus the need is for balanced control over sadism in television, not complete truncation.

Selected Readings on CTV

The following constitute recommended readings on the topic of Commercial Television and education. All three have appeared several times in the chapter's footnotes.

Himmelweit, Hilde, A. N. Oppenheim, and Pamela Vince, *Television and the Child*. London: Oxford Press, 1958. An extensive study of 1854 matched pairs of British children, ages 10 to 14. A digest of the research appears first, followed by detailed research data. This study is scholarly and informative.

Schramm, Wilbur, Jack Lyle, and Edwin B. Parker, *Television in the Lives of Our Children*. Stanford: Stanford University Press, 1961. A more extensive study than the one above with samples from San Francisco, Denver, Canada, and other urban and nonurban areas, totaling eleven in all. This publication has made a deep imprint on scholarship pertaining to television and education. I recommend it highly.

Witty, Paul A., Paul Kinsella, and Anne Coomer, "A Summary of Yearly Studies of Televiewing, 1949–1963," *Elementary English*, 30 (October 1963), pp. 590–597. An excellent digest in all respects. Witty for a decade and a half has been one of the more prolific commentators on television and its relationship to the elementary-school child.

ETV as an Instructional Medium

The amusement interests of the society, as established in the previous section, has constituted television's primary focus during its early growth years. Nor should this prove upsetting. What should disturb, however, is the extreme one-sidedness of the focus. As a counter to this recognized distortion, educational television (ETV) came into being with the intended purpose not to amuse but to instruct and to enlighten. The extent to which it has performed its didactic function comprises the theme of this section.

As early as from 1932 to 1934, three institutions of higher learning: the University of Iowa, Purdue University, and Kansas State College made limited exploratory ventures into the field of television education. Two years later, in 1936, New York University and NBC cooperatively transmitted a selected few educational programs. Then, following a hiatus caused by World War II, research in educational television experienced a revival in the late 1940's. The first real breakthrough occurred in 1950, when a commercially operated station was leased, for educational purposes, to Iowa State College at Ames. Four other institutions of higher learning achieved comparable status from 1953 to 1957.[21] However, the first out-and-out ETV Station was licensed by the FCC to the University of Houston in 1953, followed by the licensing of 7 more in 1954, and 2 more in 1955.[22]

As of 1963, there were 79 ETV stations in operation in 32 states and the District of Columbia. Of this total, 71 had reserved channels and 8, unreserved channels. See the accompanying tabular breakdown by state of the 79 stations. The first numeral after the state name indicates the total number of stations for the year 1963. The second single-underlined numeral, if any, indicates the total of stations, by state, which were affiliates of institutions of higher learning. The third double-underlined numeral, if any, indicates the total of stations, by state, which were affiliates of public school agencies: local, county, or state.

ETV Stations, 1963[23]

State	Total	Higher Learning	Public School
Alabama	4		
Arizona	2	2	
California	3		1
Colorado	1		1
Connecticut	1		
District of Columbia	1		
Florida	6	2	2
Georgia	3	1	2
Illinois	3	2	
Iowa	2	1	1
Kentucky	1		
Louisiana	2		1
Maine	1		
Massachusetts	1		
Michigan	2	1	
Minnesota	1		
Missouri	3	1	1
Nebraska	1	1	
New Hampshire	1	1	
New Mexico	1	1	
New York	4		
North Carolina	1	1	
Ohio	6	3	1
Oklahoma	3		1
Oregon	2	2	
Pennsylvania	3		
South Dakota	1	1	
Tennessee	2		1
Texas	5	2	1
Utah	3	1	2
Virginia	1		
Washington	5	2	3
Wisconsin	3	1	2
Totals	79	26	20

[21] Donald G. Tarbet, *Television and Our Schools* (New York: The Ronald Press, 1961), pp. 3–4.
[22] *Ibid.*, p. 5.
[23] Gertrude G. Broderick, *Educational AM and FM Radio and Educational Television Stations by State and City* (Washington, D.C.: U.S. Department of Health, Education and Welfare, 1963), pp. 20–27.

As revealed by the table, 26 of the 79 ETV stations were licensed to institutions of higher learning or to state boards in control of such institutions, and 20 to public educational institutions at the local, county, or state level. The remaining 33 were licensed to other public agencies or to civic groups.

Some General Characteristics.   By definition, ETV's basic function is to educate. It accomplishes this function both through formal instruction and through noncommercial broadcasting of an educational nature. In instances where ETV is under the control of an educational institution or agency, the method of formal instruction usually dominates. But in instances where it is under the control of a noneducational organization, noncommercial programs outside the framework of formal instruction usually dominate.

Significant factual data pertaining to ETV appear in the following quotation:

> ETV stations are on the air, on the average, less than half as long as commercial stations; they use only about half as much national network programming (and even this is not network programming in the real sense), they produce about three times as much live programming proportionate to their total programming, over three times as much informational programming but less than half as much news, their audiences are minuscule compared to audiences of commercial stations.[24]

The average broadcast time of ETV is 8 hours and 42 minutes daily, with a range of from 4 to 15 hours.[25]

The Audience.   The size of ETV's over-all audience, according to Schramm, is 20 million, with 8.5 million fairly regular viewers, and 2.5 million viewers during any single week. The obvious implication here is that the vast majority of the 20 million view on only incidental occasions. The adult audience habitually is a select one, characterized by middle- and upper-middle-class status, participation in civic affairs, and by educational attainment higher than that of the average person.[26] In general, the audience has a wide variety of cultural interests.

The Programs.   As previously stated, the two formats for ETV programs are formal course instruction and noncommercial educational broadcasting. In 1959, the proportion of each, as reported by Schramm, was as follows: 40.9 per cent of broadcast time went into formal course offerings; the remaining 59.1 per cent went into noncommercial broad-

---

[24] Sidney W. Head, "A Friendly Critic on ETV Programs," in *Television The Next Ten Years* (Stanford: The Institute for Communication Research, 1962), p. 125.
[25] Wilbur Schramm, *The Impact of Educational Television* (Urbana: University of Illinois, 1960), p. 4.
[26] *Ibid.*, pp. 23–29.

casting with 46.2 per cent devoted to adult programs and 12.9 per cent to children's programs. Verbal methods characterize ETV just as they do CTV, with the lecture, discussion, formal address, drama, and documentary leading the way.[27] As would be expected, programs devoted to sports, to phantasy, and to other types of light amusement are almost totally absent. Within the framework of formal educational content, programs divide quite evenly among the natural sciences, the literary, the social sciences, and the fine arts; and they give short shrift to the applied arts. Approximately three-fourths of the programs originate locally; one-fourth come from networks.

Midwest Program on Airborne Television Instruction. One of the more significant of the recent network attempts in the Midwest Program on Airborne Television Instruction experiment, which, with Ford Foundation support, came into being in 1959. With headquarters at Purdue University, MPATI's broadcasting station is an airplane which, while flying at an altitude of 23,000 feet, telecasts to schools within a radius of approximately 200 miles. The broadcasts reach into six midwestern states: Illinois, Indiana, Kentucky, Michigan, Ohio, and Wisconsin. The network among stations and schools is made possible by microwave and cable connections.

By means of video tape, the MPATI curriculum, as of 1961–1962, was telecast on UHF channels 72 and 76, four days per week, to grades 1 to 12.

The respective offerings on channel 76 for Monday of the Fall Semester of 1961–1962, for example, were as follows: Advanced High School Biology; Music, grades 1 through 3; American History, senior high school; Science, grades 5 through 6; Mathematics for Gifted Children, grades 5 through 6; French, grades 3 through 6; General Science, junior high school; Arithmetic, grade 6; English Language Arts, grades 3 to 4; and Music, grades 1 through 3.[28] The offerings of MPATI's curriculum have grown by the year. To date, the program has been moderately successful, the chief criticism being the frequent lack of coordination between MPATI and the teacher consumers. And with curriculum content fundamental, MPATI fails its educational purposes when it does not announce content well in advance of a telecast or when it communicates it in too little detail to enable teachers to effect proper integration.

The 1965 through 1966 curriculum, for broadcast over 4 channels, consists of the following: 34 different offerings in 10 content areas for grades 1 through 6; 7 different offerings in 4 content areas for grades 7 through

[27] *Ibid.*, pp. 6–7.
[28] From the Broadcast Schedule published by MPATI, dated August 25, 1961.

8; and 19 different offerings in 14 content areas for grades 9 through 12.[29]

Problems of ETV.   The growth of ETV has been noteworthy, but so have its problems. One of the major ones has grown out of its tendency to vascillate somewhat aimlessly between formal-course instruction and noncommercial cultural broadcasts, with the public left confused about its true function. My opinion on this issue, although somewhat overstated, is that stations operated by colleges and public schools should do what they can do best: bring to the viewing public programs that draw on the best talents of the cooperating faculty. Direct course instruction, the formal address, the musical event, the art demonstration, and institutional spectacles fit into this category. By the same logic, stations operated by agencies other than educational should also capitalize on their strengths, which more often than not lie outside the frame of the more formal educational approaches. The pros and cons of a community issue, the significant event of local interest, or a long-term orientation to community affairs are illustrative here. The important need is for each station to develop a style that reflects the image of what it stands for. Better for ETV to operate from a position of confident strength than to dissipate its resources superficially and uncertainly in too many diverse directions.

A second problem of ETV relates to its posture before the controversial. My point of view on this issue is that ETV, although committed by its very nature to challenge viewers rather than to opiate them, accomplishes this purpose best when avoiding extreme positions on heated controversial matters. A balanced posture is important for these two reasons: first, it is the approach of openness; and second, when the approach is devoid of manifest editorial bias, the issues themselves stand out more clearly. In contrast, the exclusively polar position, even with truth on its side, tends to ostracize by nature of its one-sidedness. The balanced approach is particularly essential in view of the sophisticated nature of most ETV audiences.

Selected other problems of ETV are these: (1) A number of stations have too little program time to create and sustain audience interest. (2) The customary absence of performer competition makes for a diminution of performance quality. (3) The shortage of funds also mitigates against program quality. The need here may be for more governmental financial support. (4) The range of UHF bands is too limited. (5) Until the range is increased, the need will remain for more cooperative network and syndicated endeavor. (6) Without pressing for slickness, ETV needs to acquire more polish.

[29] Midwest Program on Airborne Television Instruction, Inc., *Blueprint for Airborne '65,* n.d.

Selected Readings on ETV

1. Broderick, Gertrude G., *Educational AM and FM Radio and Educational Television Stations by State and City*. Washington, D.C.: U.S. Department of Health, Education, and Welfare, 1963. A valuable booklet that lists all the ETV stations in the country by location, call number, and license.

2. Lewis, Philip. *Educational Television Guidebook*. New York: McGraw-Hill Book Company, 1961. Although covering all phases of instructional television, this publication, from pages 21 to 47, specifically treats of ETV and MPATI.

3. Minow, Newton, "Our Common Goal: A Nationwide ETV System," *The Education Digest*, 27 (May 1962), pp. 12–14. A plea to electronics engineers and persons interested in education to bestir themselves to the end of achieving the goal of a country-wide network of ETV stations. The intended purpose would be to improve programs via a more effective utilization of all existing networks.

4. Schramm, Wilbur (ed.), *The Impact of Educational Television*. Urbana: University of Illinois Press, 1960. Another excellent publication by this author, particularly useful for anyone interested in analyzing the programs of ETV and the viewing audience. Research constitutes the basis of most of the data provided and the opinions expressed.

5. Tarbet, Donald G., *Television and Our Schools*. New York: The Ronald Press, 1961. One of the better overall treatments of instructional television in its many manifestations. Chapter 11 presents an effective overview of ETV.

6. The Institute for Communication Research, *Educational Television The Next Ten Years*. Palo Alto: Stanford University, 1962. Of all the publications listed, this is the broadest in coverage of the many issues germane to ETV. As an anthology, it draws on the opinions of many experts who analyze the strengths and weaknesses of ETV. Furthermore, it analyzes ETV's projected growth into 1971. This constitutes "must" reading.

CCTV as an Instructional Medium

Paralleling the efforts of CTV and ETV as electronic instructional media is closed-circuit television (or CCTV). By far the least complex of the three methods, CCTV depends for its existence on three constituent components: a place of origin for programming purposes, a transmission system of coaxial cables, and a place of reception including television sets and other necessary equipment. Ideally, all the major facilities including a master-antenna system should be built into a school or school system at the time of its initial construction.

Several years ago, the writer of a section such as this would have felt obligated to list the educational institutions that employed CCTV. Today, the medium constitutes a part of the curriculum of so many institutions that any list would prove meaningless. Since the breakthrough at Hagerstown, Maryland, in 1956, the expansion of CCTV has been nothing short of phenomenal.

The Uses of CCTV.   Contributing immeasurably to the rapid growth of CCTV has been its intimacy with, and consequently its considerable adaptability to, the viewing audience. Unlike CTV and ETV, CCTV customarily transmits to an audience that possess known characteristics, that is modestly homogenous in nature, and that is reasonably limited in size. Favored with these endowments, it is able to focus on the identifiable needs of a local group of learners, thereby avoiding diffusion. Another asset which it customarily possesses is the presence of performers who fit into its purposes. Even though the majority of these individuals, as classroom teachers, are not necessarily highly skilled in the on-camera role, they compensate for this lack by their close relatedness to a school's curriculum and its aims.

Selected of CCTV's more common uses are these:

1. As substitutes for teachers in school systems which, because of financial restrictions, unfortunate locations, or size limitations are unable to hire live teachers for essential curriculum purposes. CCTV can do, for instance, what the Harvey White films currently are doing in many high schools: bring a specific course to a given classroom. Either of the two media would take the place of a nonexistent teacher. In this connection, while rejecting the forced choice between the "either-or" alternatives, we see the logic of Costello and Gordon's question: "Which is better, a physics class taught over television (even by a 'merely adequate' teacher) or *no* physics class? What is superior for college freshmen, a living lecture on Melville by a neophyte graduate student . . . or a televised talk by the greatest Melville scholar alive?"[30]

2. For curriculum enrichment when employed exclusively by the classroom teacher himself or by the classroom teacher as part of a team-teaching arrangement. Such employment adds a new methods medium without necessarily detracting from the personalized relationship of a teacher with his pupils.

3. For in-service-education purposes whereby teachers have the opportunity to grow professionally by observing their colleagues perform.

4. For large-group or all-school programs: for example, a creative dramatics activity projected to middle-grade pupils, careers-day presentations transmitted to all senior homerooms, or a guest speaker brought to an entire school.

5. As an intercom for purposes of announcements.

6. As a seeing-eye in school corridors or in study halls.

[30] Lawrence F. Costello and George N. Gordon, *Teach With Television* (New York: Hasting House, 1961), p. 14.

7. For observation and demonstration purposes enabling individuals and groups, such as college education majors, to view a school activity without disturbing by their physical presence.

Responsibilities of CCTV Teachers.   When CCTV is employed on a team basis as a teaching instrument, it usually knows success to the degree that personnel adhere to certain important preliminaries. One of these is the close coordination of effort on the part of all professional participants: administrators, teachers, and electronic specialists. When such coordination is achieved, the result almost habitually is greater curriculum continuity, a smoother and more graciously accepted division of labor, and better learning results. Close coordination is particularly essential between on-camera personnel and classroom-based teachers.

When all have identified and accepted their respective roles, the on-camera teacher can then devote his energies more efficiently to the performance role itself. One of his many responsibilities, in this connection, in the absence of an electronics specialist, is the care of cameras, props, screens, and other items of physical equipment. Once he has set the physical stage, the more professional aspects of his performance role will demand attention, with questions such as these requiring answers. Should he impart a closed body of information, stimulate by open inquiry, or do both? Encourage viewers to talk back (when technically possible), or have them listen and observe only? Lecture only, or lecture and demonstrate? Provide immediate closure or delay closure pursuant to pupil follow-up activities? These and other issues regularly require answers.

Responsibilities of CCTV Teachers Who Are Not On-Camera.   Although problems arise for the on-camera performer, they arise equally for other members of the television team. Included in this latter category are classroom teachers who, although not on-camera, are vital members of the team arrangement. They are particularly vital in an organizational scheme wherein CCTV transmits a program to a number of pupil groups manned in each instance by a classroom teacher. In such a scheme, the most fundamental need of the teachers is to know exactly what roles they are to play. Should they orient in advance, or not? Should they follow up, or not? And if expected to do either, what format should they follow and how long should they take?

Irrespective of their exact roles, they usually have these routine responsibilities: to establish context for the TV performance; to encourage pupils to relate maturely to the performance; to assure the physical readiness of the room including TV sets, lighting, and seating; to assure the presence of necessary learning materials such as pens, notebooks, maps, microscopes, or mimeographed material; to supervise during the demonstration; and finally, to provide a transition to the curriculum activity to follow. Even though these may appear routine, CCTV's success is dependent on their efficient implementation.

A Point of View.   After the several media of television undergo thorough evaluation in the not too distant future, I am convinced that of the three, CCTV will emerge as the most effective for educational purposes. Unlike the other two, it is blessed with the attributes of adaptability and flexibility. Thus, it can fit into the *what is* rather than having to create the *what is to be.* And because the two attributes are inseparable from the nation's traditions of individualism, CCTV, we predict, will maintain its preferred position.

Selected Readings on CCTV

1. Costello, Lawrence F. and George N. Gordon, *Teach With Television.* New York: Hasting House, 1961. Although a general treatment of all forms of television teaching, this does a particularly good job on the mechanical features of studio and classroom layout and utilization for CCTV purposes.

2. Board of Education, Hagerstown, Maryland, *Closed-Circuit Television,* 1959. An unpublished pamphlet that describes many of the problems encountered by the Washington County schools in their mammoth, historically significant CCTV venture; also an evaluation of the many attempts at solution of these problems.

3. Lewis, Philip, *Educational Television Guidebook.* New York: McGraw-Hill Book Company, 1961. Another general treatment, this makes a penetrating analysis of CCTV as a specific medium. It describes the Hagerstown experiment in detail, and does a good job of describing and discussing the many possible uses of CCTV.

4. Tarbet, Donald G., *Television and Our Schools.* New York: The Ronald Press Company, 1961. Another good general overview with effective coverage of CCTV as a specific medium.

5. The Institute for Communication Research, *Educational Television The Next Ten Years.* Stanford: Stanford University, 1962. Although primarily preoccupied with ETV, this book interweaves much meaningful information pertaining to CCTV.

6. The Sub-committee on Television, *The Uses of Television in Education.* North Central Association of Colleges and Secondary Schools, 1961. Provides a detailed listing of pros and cons, usages, and other data pertaining to television in the classroom.

Administrative Responsibilities in Television Instruction

Whatever the outlet for television in the educational process—whether CTV, ETV or CCTV—the medium can perform to its optimum only with the strong support and imaginative leadership of a school administration. These qualities, as evidenced by past and current practice, can properly manifest themselves in the following ways.

One way is organizational. In this connection, a major contribution that an administration can make in behalf of television instruction is to ready a faculty and appropriate elements of the greater community for the decision-making process. Curriculum itself is fundamentally a faculty, not an administrative, concern. Thus whether television is to be adopted or not is a decision that only a faculty ultimately should make. If the decision, in contrast, is made unilaterally, the resulting program will probably experience failure, or, at best, will achieve less than satisfactory success. Likewise, because television education invariably involves the greater community, appropriate representatives of the non-school public should also have a voice in decisions falling within the province of their knowledge and interests. Apropos here, Washington County, Maryland, early in the formulation of its television program, established "a steering committee whose membership was drawn from the Board of Education, county staff, principals, teachers, State Department of Education, State Teachers College, and P.T.A."[31] I believe that initial decisions should be made by a faculty working closely with an administration. Only later should a steering committee with both in-school and out-of-school membership assume a leadership role.

A second important administrative responsibility has to do with the business and financial aspects of the program. Selected specifics of this responsibility relate to the selection of electronic firms, the installation of necessary electronic equipment, the selection and purchase of projection equipment, making space available for program development and projection, and ruling on financial matters.

This sobering array leads logically to a third major responsibility, namely, the need for an administration to determine who will staff a planned program. Selections, in this regard, have to be made both from the ranks of electronic specialists and from the ranks of teacher and professional performing personnel.

Once these choices have been made, there remains yet a fourth requirement, namely, the need for an administration to establish and support a training program designed to ready the participants for their new responsibilities. Depending on local and organizational circumstances, such a program might consist of a summer workshop, in-service conferences spaced throughout an academic year, visits to studios or selected schools, or more than one of these. Whatever the exact nature of the program, the success of the entire electronic venture would depend, in great part, on the professional adequacy of the in-service program.

[31] Quoted by William Benjamin in an unpublished paper entitled: "Educational Television: A Background Report For the Peabody-Public School Cooperative Program" circa 1960.

An Evaluation of Televised Instruction

Two last fundamental questions regarding television instruction are these: Does it work? And if it does, how well? In this connection, these questions are recurring ones that probably were asked centuries ago of Commenius about his *Orbis Pictus;* more recently in the early thirties they were asked about the motion picture; and in the late thirties, they were asked about the radio. Television, like other learning media, conveys a message, conveys it by a messenger, and conveys it to a learner. Thus it is capable of teaching. The "how well" question is more of a conundrum.

Certainly the slanted claims of television zealots have added to the confusion. So have the claims of some researchers, many of them from the various foundations, who, definitely biased from the start, purport to evaluate objectively. Harry Skornia reacts scathingly to such practices. "Most research," says he, "is being done by the wrong people . . . TV, radio, and film researchers—each saddled with the same old myopias they've always had . . . The project designer is the operator, is the evaluator, is the critic, is the reporter, and so on. Even in industry we realize the value of separate quality control testing. A man who 'puts it in here' and then runs around to see it 'come out there' is likely to be slightly prejudiced."[32] Edgar Dale similarly faults evaluation done by the inaugurators, a practice which, he says, logically leads to a suspicion of the Hawthorne-effect.[33] Yet, if unbridled emotionalism distorts evaluative accuracy, so does overrestrained conservatism. Each is biased in its own way.

In an attempt at objectivity, Schramm, without completely ruling out the possibility of bias, assembled "393 cases in which instructional television . . . was compared with classroom teaching, and 14 cases in which military instruction by television . . . was compared with face-to-face teaching, with what seemed to be adequate design, controls, and statistics." The results reported were that television instruction excelled in 21 per cent of the studies, face-to-face instruction in 14 per cent, and neither method in 65 per cent.[34]

However, within the framework of these results, television instruction gives evidence of becoming less effective and appealing as children progress from elementary school through high school. Of children in grades

[32] Harry J. Skornia, "Aspects of Educational Television That Need Investigation." Unpublished address made at the Turkey Run Conference, National Education Association (DAVI and ASCD), October 1, 1962.
[33] Edgar Dale, "The Effect of Television on Teachers and Learners, same as 32 above.
[34] Wilbur Schramm, "What We Know About Learning From Instructional Television," in *The Institute for Communication Research, Educational Television The Next Ten Years.* Stanford: Stanford University, 1962, p. 54.

3 to 9, 33 per cent thought it to be more effective; of high school children, 13 per cent thought it to be more effective; and of college students, only 3 per cent thought it to be more effective.[35]

Like Schramm, Kumata reports that when the factor of information gain is the criterion, "most of the studies report no significant differences . . . between students taught by TV and students taught under face-to-face conditions." And quoting P. D. Holmes, Kumata further reports that of 281 studies analyzed, 246 revealed no significant differences in results.[36]

However, along with the factor of grade placement mentioned earlier, the factor of subject matter also seems to produce differential results when TV and non-TV teaching are compared. The subject areas of mathematics, science, and social studies usually respond very successfully to TV instruction; the humanities, particularly literature, very unsuccessfully. For further differential analyses, we refer the reader to Schramm's excellent Chapter, pp. 52–71, in *Educational Television, The Next Ten Years,* 1962.

As important as, probably even more important than, research regarding educational television's effectiveness is common sense evaluation of it. As indicated by William Brish, Superintendent of Schools at Hagerstown, Maryland, educational television is first and foremost a resource. It does not take the place of anyone, and its use somewhat resembles that of a textbook. Furthermore, in the last analysis, face-to-face relationships, with or without television, will continue to dominate education.[37] Television cannot conduct a seminar, cannot give intensive personal help, and cannot contribute much to the very specialized outcomes of individualism and creativity.

As an imparter of information; as a demonstrator of things and activities; in general, for many situations involving telling and showing, it has unquestioned merit. But the emotional, social, ethical and esthetic intangibles will continue to resist it either completely or in great part. Television performs best in a more-or-less formal learning situation that rests in the cognitive. It reaches out effectively to a larger than class-sized audience. But it is no more than a single medium, albeit an important medium, in the total methods ensemble.

For Further Thought

1. What curriculum problems does television instruction, particularly CCTV, bring to education that are dimensionally different from those already imposed by the motion picture?

[35] *Ibid.*
[36] Hideya Kumata, "A Decade of Teaching By Television," in Schramm, *The Impact of Educational Television,* pp. 178–179.
[37] William Brish, "Testimony By William Brish" in *The Institute for Communication Research,* p. 77.

2. Analyze yourself as an actual or potential on-camera television teacher. What do you believe to be your strengths and shortcomings?

3. What changes do you believe teacher-education institutions should make in their programs in an attempt to ready students more adequately for the new TV dimension?

4. Which of the three television media promises most for educational purposes? Defend your stand.

5. What are some possible artifactual reasons for television's excellent teaching record?

References

American Council on Education, *Teaching by Closed-Circuit Television*. Washington, D.C.: 1956.

Diamond, Robert (ed.), *A Guide To Instructional Television*. New York: McGraw-Hill Book Company, Inc., 1964.

Dunham, Franklin, Ronald Lowdermilk, and Gertrude Broderick, *Television in Education*. Washington, D.C.: United States Department of Health, Education, and Welfare, Office of Education, 1957.

Educational Policies Commission, *Mass Communication and Education*. Washington, D.C.: National Education Association, 1958.

Ford Foundation, *Teaching by Television*. New York: 1961.

Instructional Television Library Project, *A Guide To Films, Kinescopes, and Video-Tapes Available for Televised Use*. Lincoln, Nebraska: 1962.

Midwest Program on Airborne Television Instruction, Mary H. Smith, ed., *Using Television in the Classroom*. New York: McGraw-Hill Book Co., Inc., 1961.

National Association of Educational Broadcasters, *Educational Television Bulletin*. Published monthly by the National Education Television and Radio Center.

National Association of Secondary School Principals, *Bulletin*. Jan. 1958, 1959, 1960, 1961, 1962.

Postman, Neil, *Television and the Teaching of English*. New York: Appleton-Century-Crofts, Inc., 1961.

Schramm, Wilbur, *The People Look At Educational Television*. Palo Alto: University of Stanford Press, 1963.

Steeves, Frank L., *Fundamentals of Teaching in Secondary Schools*. New York: The Odyssey Press, Inc., 1962, Chapter 10.

The Subcommittee on Television, *The Uses of Television in Education*. North Central Association of Colleges and Secondary Schools, 1961.

Trump, J. Lloyd, and Dorsey Baynham, *Guide to Better Schools,* Focus on Change. Chicago: Rand, McNally and Co., 1961.

Witty, Paul, Paul Kinnella, and Anne Coomer, "A Summary of Yearly Studies of Televiewing 1949–1963," *Elementary English*, **30.** (October 1963), pp. 590–597.

chapter 9

Programmed Instruction and Teaching Machines

Continuing with the prevailing theme of this section, experimentation in curriculum, we analyze next the highly innovative and controversial area of programmed instruction and teaching machines. It is appropriate to state at the beginning that Professor Pressey struck a spark in the mid 1920's which took a third of a century to ignite fully, but which once ignited has become a small but significant flame. How much the flame will grow, only the future will reveal. My prediction is that growth of the new movement, although considerable, will fall short of the expectations of its more ardent proponents.

Events to date, however, should prove heartening to these same proponents. As of 1962, curriculum specialists had readied 122 courses for use in elementary, secondary, and college education. By 1963, this total had increased to 352, with over-all quantitative gains taking place despite relative losses in selected content fields. A detailed breakdown of these totals appears in the tabular listing shown on page 164.

The vast majority of these programs were, and most continue to be, conceived and designed for the elementary- and secondary-school grades, with a small minority, only, comparably conceived and designed for the college grades. One source reports programs in 1962 to have been available, by grade level, as follows (the numbers are transposed into percentages): for K through 3, 7.4 per cent of all programs; for grades 4 through 6, 21.7 per cent; for grades 7 through 8, 22.5 per cent; for grades 9 through 12, 35.6 per cent; for grades 13 and higher, 9.7 per cent;

	1962		1963	
Subject	per cent	number	per cent	number
Mathematics	43	(52)	35	(123)
Science	20	(24)	20	(69)
Grammar and spelling	13	(16)	7	(25)
Modern languages	8	(10)	6	(21)
Social studies	6	(7)	5	(16)
Business and economics	3	(4)	6	(22)
Language arts	4	(5)	7	(26)
Miscellaneous	3	(4)	14	(50)
Totals	100	(122)	100	(352)
	(122 programs)		(352 programs)[a]	

[a] Lincoln F. Hanson, *Programs, '63: A Guide to Programed Instructional Materials Available to Educators by September 1963* (Washington, D.C.: The Center for Programmed Instruction, Inc., in cooperation with the U.S. Department of Health, Education, and Welfare, 1963), p. vi.

and for mental retardates at various grade levels, 3.1 per cent.[2] Thus, if we combine the percentages for nonretarded children, 29.1 per cent were for elementary-school pupils; 58.1 per cent, for secondary-school pupils; and 9.7 per cent, for college pupils.

Although the elementary and secondary schools throughout the country constitute important operational bases for programmed learning, they concede to the universities, to commercial agencies, and to the defense establishments as research and development centers. For instance, as one writer disclosed in 1961, only 11 of 160 research projects in programmed learning were sponsored by public or private schools.[3] Schools thus find themselves not infrequently in the untenable position of serving as experimental laboratories without possessing the necessary research controls. This state of affairs removes curriculum responsibility from its most important source—the schools themselves.

From this position of detachment from the mainstream of education, a number of programmed-learning advocates have indulged in profligate claims about the merits of the new medium. Some make it appear as an educational panacea. One such writer describes the content of programming as "the first prose ever constructed especially for the purpose of education."[4] B. F. Skinner, along a somewhat different dimension,

[2] Information Division, The Center for Programed Instruction, Inc., *Programs, '62: A Guide to Programed Instructional Materials Available to Educators by September 1962* (Washington, D. C.: Government Printing Office, 1962), p. xvi.
[3] Charles I. Foltz, The World of Teaching Machines (Washington, D.C.: Electronic Teaching Laboratories, 1961), pp. 93–116.
[4] Cited by Wilbur Schramm, *Programed Instruction Today and Tomorrow* (Washington, D.C.: Fund for the Advancement of Education, 1962), p. 18.

casts the teacher in a role of "a purely mechanical reinforcing mechanism." And Benjamin Fine, speaking contrary to much existing data, declares: "I have observed that 85 to 90 per cent of the students prefer teaching machines."[5] Claims such as these, founded as they are more on subjective opinion than on researched fact, do a disservice to the new movement. Programmed learning in the future will be the winner to the extent that this inclination toward overstatement is curbed in favor of more objective assessment.

As injurious as positive hyperbole to the new movement is the sweeping, unsupported destructive statement. The machine, more than the program, has been the target of the negative cliché mongers. These latter have dubbed the machine a disease, a monster, a Frankenstein. One has called it a mechanical page, turner. A few have advised, in effect: If you have one, get rid of it before it contaminates the whole curriculum.

Even frustrated poets write limericks about it. Benjamin Fine and I are respectively to blame for the following:

> The latest word from the Dean
> Has come down on the teaching machine
> It's that Oedipus Rex
> Could have learned about sex
> Without even disturbing the Queen.[6]
> and
> The machine has impishly purred
> To give live teachers the word
> With the program the locus
> And knob turning the focus,
> To work is simply absurd.

The Program

To facilitate the reader's recovery from an understandable literary hangover, we elect to move hurriedly now to the safety of descriptive analysis, with the program aspect of programmed instruction receiving first attention. And, in this connection, I state forthrightly at the start that the program is fundamental to the new movement; the machine is not. Silberman, for example, in 1962 reported that of 80 programs in existence during the previous three-year period, 55 per cent were of the book variety, whereas only 45 per cent were of the machine variety.[7]

[5] Benjamin Fine, *Teaching Machines* (New York: Sterling Publishing Co., Inc., 1962), p. 83.
[6] *Ibid.*, p. 26.
[7] Harry F. Silberman, "Characteristics of Some Recent Studies of Instructional Methods," in John E. Coulson (ed.), *Programmed Learning and Computer-Based Instruction* (New York: John Wiley & Sons, Inc., 1962), p. 15.

Constituent Parts of a Program.   Whether designed for employment with or without a machine, a program consists of learning content detailed into a series of small steps. These are designed with the intent of leading a student sequentially to a predetermined learning outcome. Most programs develop along the lines of the following sequence.

The Determination of Objectives.   Programmed instruction, like any other legitimate medium of learning, needs properly to originate in, and then to continue to revolve around, educational objectives or purposes. In effect, the programmer's first task thus is to establish intent: that is, to decide in advance what learning outcomes he hopes to achieve; or, stated differently, to identify the behavioral changes that he hopes will take place in the learner. The objectives might reside in the areas of cognitive content to be acquired, attitudes to be changed, or skills to be learned—any or all of these.[8]

The Selection of Teaching Methods.   Having decided on learning outcomes, the programmer next searches for teaching methods which seem to have the greatest likelihood of achieving the predetermined end results. Assuming that programmed-learning methods give evidence of this likelihood, the programmer proceeds to develop a program.

The Preparation of Stimuli or Frames.   A program, by definition, consists of a series of interlocking learning steps, the intent of which is always the steady progression of learners to the intended goal or goals. A step is referred to in the literature interchangeably as a stimulus, a frame, a display, or an item. One such step in a program in arithmetic might be this: "The expression 9×3 represents the number which is obtained when the *whole number* 9 is multiplied by the (_____) 3." Or, "In a communist society the means of production are owned and controlled by the state; in a democratic society the means of production are usually owned and controlled by private (ind____ls)."

Content between and among Frames Must Be Closely Knit.   By this covering statement, I mean that the content of a program should be so closely interlocked that one frame will flow naturally into another without undue difficulty to the pupil. A sequel to the first illustration of the preceding paragraph might well be this: "Thus when the two (_____) 9×3 are multiplied, the resulting product is (___)." In general, the process of cueing effects a well-knit sequence. Two methods of cueing already introduced have been the verbal plant and the partial answer. Other methods are opposites, analogies, repetition, and vanishing stimuli. Whatever the exact method, the obvious intent of a program is for the learner to be right most often and wrong very seldom. A percentage of error exceeding 10 to 15 usually leads to revision of a program. Pupil

[8] Robert F. Mager does an excellent job on this topic of objectives in *Preparing Objectives for Programmed Instruction* (San Francisco: Fearon Publishers, 1961).

error in programmed learning customarily is attributed more to a deficiency in the program than to a shortcoming in the learner. This conclusion, however, as will be developed later, relates more to the Skinner than to the Crowder method of programming.

The Student Keeps Active by Continuous Participation. Because persistent student involvement is basic, program developers consistently attempt to weave into curriculum designs an optimum of student-action possibilities. The primary means to this end is via the inclusion of a steady sequence of thought-provoking stimuli in any given program. The general assumption is that, within reason, the more numerous the frames, the easier the transition from learning step to learning step. In this con-nection, some have likened programmed learning to the Socratic method wherein the teacher by probing with many questions compels the learner to respond with many answers. This individualistic feature of pro-grammed learning sets it apart from a normative classroom situation where a teacher has to divide his efforts among 20 to 40 pupils. In such a situation, all usually cannot be creatively active at one and the same time. This shortcoming, allege the proponents of electronic teaching, is not comparably a characteristic of programmed learning.

The Student Is Kept Informed of Learning Results. After a pupil has responded to a stimulus item, the program informs him, by one means or another, whether he has answered correctly or incorrectly. In the Skinner method, this information is supplied immediately; in the Crowder method, it is often delayed, although usually not for very long. In either system, the operational postulate is that future responses are more likely to be correct when past correct responses have been rein-forced through the process of feedback recognition. By the same logic, it is claimed that incorrect responses are discouraged when their incor-rectness is exposed and when the reasons for their incorrectness are ex-plained by indirect or direct means.

Programs Underscore Individual Pacing. With few exceptions, pro-grams allow students to move sequentially, and at their own pace, from beginning to end. The only exception is that some programs pace the frames for the students. With this one exception, the speed of movement through a program is a function of the individual learner. The slow reader or the retardate can and does slow up the pace of movement; the fast reader or the fast learner (or both) can and does speed up the pace. In the long run, this provision for self pacing may prove to be programmed learning's greatest asset.

Two Major Program Formats

Programs customarily appear in one of two formats: as books to be used independently; or as rolls, tapes, slides, discs, or film-strips to be used in connection with designated teaching machines. The only fundamental difference between the two is that the latter can be made completely cheat proof; the former, in contrast, cannot prevent the learner from "peeking" at correct responses. Skinner considers this to be a making-or-breaking difference. However, most others, including myself, would not attach such great importance to it. In a programmed text, the correct answers usually appear either on the right side of the page, in which event the learner is told to cover them; or on a different page (usually the succeeding one), in which event they are still easily accessible to the learner for evaluative purposes.

Heated debate over the relative merits of the two formats is taking place today in a number of places, with the final word yet to be spoken. The book program offers more flexibility for the learner; the machine program restricts him more. The choice between the two actually depends more on theoretical assumptions regarding certain niceties of the learning process than on any yet demonstrated superiority of either approach.

Two Major Program Patterns.   Regardless of the exact format employed, programming customarily proceeds along one of two learning patterns: the linear of the branching (scrambled) patterns. These we shall discuss and illustrate in the order named.

The Linear Pattern.   Characteristic of the linear pattern is a logical flow of program content that all learners are required to follow in a prescribed sequential order. Whether the content appears on frames as in a machine program or on a page as in a book program, the identifying feature is the straight line flow of the content, and consequently of the learning sequence. All learners, whether slow or fast, move along the same progressive path. The pace may differ but the sequential order does not.

Below is an illustration of the linear pattern. Although prepared with the machine format in mind, it could just as readily fit into book format. The only distinction would be that the answers in the latter format would appear in a different organizational arrangement.

The Linear Pattern

Frame 1

S. (Stimulus) Of the several patterns of programming employed, two stand out above all others: the <u>linear</u> and the <u>scrambled</u>. We shall analyze them in the order named. First, we discuss the l_____ pattern.

R. (Response) <u>linear</u> ⎧This would be written in by the student in⎫
                            ⎨the appropriate place provided by the teaching⎬
                            ⎩machine.⎭

Frame 2

S. The linear pattern breaks learning content into small segments, thus requiring the student to make frequent re   s.

R. responses

Frame 3

S. The term linear implies that all students will respond to the same frames in the same sequence. This straight-line progression is the reason the pattern is called _____.

R. linear

Frame 4

S. If all students respond to the same frames in the same sequence, the sequence has to be identical for both the slow reader and the fast reader, for the slow learner and the fast learner. This statement is [true or false]? _____.

R. True

Frame 5

S. By way of review, keep in mind that we have been talking about the (1) _____ pattern of programming which, because it breaks learning down into small segments, requires the student to make many short (2) _____s.

R. (1) linear

(2) responses

In essence, a program is linear to the degree that it meets the following specifications:

1. It moves sequentially from stimulus to stimulus in a straight-line flow.

2. The psychological distance between learning steps is small. The aim of any program is to teach, not to discriminate. Thus, if a pupil errs (at least, very often), it is assumed that the program, not the learner, is at fault.

3. As stated earlier, a failure rate on any step of 10 to 15 per cent is high; a failure rate of not over 5 per cent is a desired goal.

4. With steps small, pupils have to make frequent responses. This keeps them actively involved in the learning process.

5. Most responses in linear programs are of the constructed (written-in answer) type. Skinner is particularly adamant on this requirement; some of his colleagues, however, do not regard this as an absolute essential.

6. The linear pattern demands learning reinforcement at the end of every step.

The branching (or scrambled) pattern.   What most distinguishes the branching from the linear pattern is the feature of learners pursuing not necessarily identical paths to the same instructional outcomes. Each individual makes an initial response to a stimulus item; then, depending on the exact nature of the response, he proceeds, upon direction, along one of several learning paths. The following illustration draws on branching itself for content.

Frame 1

We now direct attention to branching as a second pattern of programming. The major assumption behind branching is that learning responses, whether correct or incorrect, react positively to verbal elaboration. A branched program customarily includes a number of stimulus items (such as this one), with each followed by multiple-choice answers. Now, from three ensuing multiple-choice answers, select the one which is most accurate. (Press the proper button).

(1) Correctness or incorrectness of a response is less important than the learning process itself. (*This selection takes him to Frame 2*).

(2) It is essential that a learning response of any kind be followed by some kind of elaboration. (*This selection takes him to Frame 3*).

(3) Branching and multiple-choice testing are practically synonymous. (*This selection takes him to Frame 4*).

Frame 2

So you have decided on your own initiative that the process of learning is more important than a learner's being correct or incorrect. Without questioning the validity of your decision, we deny its relatedness to the context of the present issue. Now press the button for Frame 1 and, after rereading the statement, select another answer.

Frame 3

Yes, you read and answered correctly. Congratulations!

One assumption of branching proponents would be that the word "Congratulations" here is not enough; instead, that elaboration of some kind would be called for. Crowder and others contend that true psychological reinforcement (reward for a correct response) must involve a certain amount of verbal explanation. The purpose of this paragraph, thus, is to highlight in your mind the value of verbal explanation as a reinforcing agent of correctness. Verbal elaboration, we again note, is a distinctive feature of the branching pattern.

(Now move on to Frame 5)

Frame 4

The fact that branching and testing both may employ multiple-choice methods of eliciting responses does not make the two operations "practically synonomous." It looks as if you *did not read the problem* carefully enough. Go back and try it again. (Now press the button for Frame 1 and, after re-reading the problem, select another answer).

The branching pattern of programming, with Crowder its leading advocate and spokesman, possesses these identifying attributes.

1. It provides a variety of learning paths, with any single response determining the nature of the subsequent path.

2. The psychological distance between any two steps is usually greater than in the linear pattern. The student led less protectively, and thus is placed on his own more.

3. An incorrect response is not necessarily corrected immediately. The rationale is that an explanation of wrongness that delays the discovery of correctness makes for better learning than a too-easy path to correctness which avoids verbal elaboration.

4. Branching relies on multiple-choice rather than on written-in responses. The former gives the programmer complete control and permits him, in advance, to program in the light of each anticipated response.

5. When a pupil errs, the pupil, more than the program, is blamed. The penalty is regression in the program and a reapplication to the learning stimulus.

6. The frames in a given branching pattern are usually more demanding of sustained thought than their counterparts in a linear pattern. Thus more reading, in general, and more complex learning, in particular, are involved.

7. Branching usually leads to longer programs.

8. Branching is alleged by many to be more effective than the linear in the teaching of concepts.

From this enumeration of differences between the linear and the branching types, a pronouncement of superiority of one type over the other would give tidy closure to this section. Such a pronouncement, however, is not possible in view of the ambivalence of the available research evidence. Investigations by the followers of Skinner, obvious to sate, claim superiority for the linear pattern; those by the Crowder supporters, equally obvious to state, claim superiority for the branching pattern. And the limited remaining research by groups or individuals who are unaffiliated with either camp reveals few significant differences between the two. My personal point of view is that too much time and effort have already been spent on the Skinner-Crowder, linear-branching controversy; also, for that matter, on the teaching machine—program book argument. What is needed by program developers and critics of the future is a forward look toward the evolving new. The old has dominated for too long already.

The Machine

Unlike the program, which is a learning medium, the teaching machine is no more than an inert mechanical device. It can become a living thing when responsive to a program, but in and of itself it is nothing. In this area of programmed learning, however, the machine not infrequently receives the limelight, and programming, only desultory attention. An inversion such as this, according higher priority to learning gagetry than to learning vitals, is naïve, at best, and downright detrimental to learning, at worst.

The basic role of the machine is as servant—servant to learning and to a programmer responsible for learning. And in this subservient role, it mirrors decisions that the programmer has made, a priori, on issues such as the following:

1. Whether a program is to be linear, branched, or a combination of both.
2. Whether a program is to be "cheat-proof" or not.
3. Whether a teacher, for diagnostic purposes, wishes to have pupil responses recorded, or not.
4. Whether pupils are to respond to stimuli by using constructed or multiple-choice responses.
5. Whether stimuli are to be visual, or audial, or both.
6. Whether machines are to be used in a stationary place or are to be carried from place to place—for instance, to and from home.

Irrespective of these issues, a machine for classroom use (not for school-to-home use) ideally should possess the following mechanical attributes. It should be:

1. Small enough and light enough to be functional.
2. Close to a conveniently located service agency.
3. Equally comfortable for use by left-handed and right-handed students.
4. Securely mounted.
5. Simple to operate.
6. Relatively quiet when operating.

7. Relatively easy to load or unload programs.
8. Fairly large in program capacity.
9. Capable of being locked.
10. Easy on programs as regards wear and tear.

In the final analysis, a teaching machine should be adopted or avoided in terms of the number and quality of the programs available for it to project. A machine without adequate programs is as useless as a car chassis without a motor, book covers without content, or a school without a curriculum. Whether the machine adapts to rolls, tape, film slides, film-strips, discs, or some other mechanical learning medium, it can be no better than the quality of the learning content contained in each. The importance of this priority—the program first and only then the machine—we can scarcely overstress. Only in this way will attention remain focused in the proper place; on the substance of learning itself.

Teaching machines differ greatly on almost every identifiable dimension. In terms of cost, for example, Grolier, the largest Commercial Company, sold its simple Min-Max machine in 1963 for $20.00 and its more complex Wyckoff Film Tutor for $445.00. Some machines can project both verbally and visually; most, only visually. Some elicit answers via constructed responses; others, via multiple-choice responses. Some have knobs to turn, others have buttons to push, and a few have handles to crank. However, our primary interest in this chapter is in the contributions which machines generally can, and do, make to learning: it is not in the specifics of the machines themselves. Thus we leave to others the task of describing the technical features of the many machines currently in use. Finn, Galanter, Hughes, Ross and others, listed at the chapter's end, do a commendable job on this topic. Their coverages include pictures, descriptions, and evaluations.

"Pros" of Programmed Learning

Programmed learning whatever the exact pattern of its implementation, has attracted a militant number to its following. These advocates read into the method the following values.[9]

1. It is first and foremost a self-pacing device that allows each learner to progress at his own individual rate. In a typical classroom situation, where pupils differ widely in ability and in other significant learning traits, the instructor who "teaches" the whole group at any one time can never relate equally to all. If he reaches the bright, he excludes

[9] Claude Mathis presents one of the better listings of programmed learning assets and debits in "Programmed Instruction In University Education," *Journal of Dental Education*, 28 (March 1964), pp. 82–89. I am also indebted to him for making his library available to me while I was researching this chapter.

the slow; if he reaches the slow, he bores the bright; if he appeals to the average, he slights both the slow and the bright, although for contrasting reasons. With a self-pacing, individualistic device such as a program, however, each pupil, in contrast, is able to progress down learning's path at his own rate unaffected by the differing learning rates of his associates.

2. When a pupil works individually on his own program at his own rate, his mistakes do not evoke ridicule from his peer group, nor do they evoke possible disapproval from instructional authority figures—at least not to the degree that they otherwise might in a more conventional classroom arrangement.

3. One of the most often-stated advantages is that programmed learning keeps all pupils, at one and the same time, active in the learning process. The supporting rationale is that each pupil has his own program; each pupil thus is able to progress at his own pace; therefore, each pupil is more likely to stay active. These are results, so it is alleged, of the individualistic nature of programmed learning. This same outcome, the thesis goes, is less likely in a more conventional learning situation, where the few customarily exclude the many from the scene of action. However, we are not as categorical on this issue as is one advocate of programmed learning who avers without equivocation that the average student is "engaged or interested in classroom activity only 20 per cent of the time."[10] This appears to be one more instance of a somewhat slanted evaluator's building up one side of an issue by unduly deprecating the other side.

4. Because of pin-pointed goals and methodically structured sequences, programs result in more efficient learning than do the less highly structured classroom arrangements. This justification has more validity when the specialized outcomes of a given program are the sole criterion, less validity when the diverse goals of education constitute the combined criteria.

5. Programmed learning, unlike its less structured curriculum counterparts, offers a controlled laboratory situation. It predetermines learning content, it neutralizes teacher variability, and it assures learning results that are measurable.

6. Programmed learning, particularly when designed for machine presentation, can, and usually does, maintain a record of pupil performance. Thus, with a minimum of teacher effort, it makes diagnosis readily attainable.

7. Furthermore, because of the demonstrated affinity of programmed learning for the methodical in any curriculum, many allege that it will increasingly take over the drill processes of learning, releasing teachers,

[10] Charles I. Foltz, *The World of Teaching Machines* (Washington, D.C.: Electronic Teaching Laboratories, 1961), p. 7.

as a result, to move more purposefully toward the higher outcomes of mental health, problem solving, and creativity.

8. A final often-stated advantage of programmed learning—only, however, when designed for projection in a teaching machine—is that it neutralizes cheating.

"Cons" of Programmed Learning

As would be expected, these positive claims of the advocates of programmed learning do not go unchallenged by the counter claims of the critics, and, to a lesser extent, of the wait-and-see neutrals. Selected of these counterclaims are as follows:

1. First and foremost, programmed learning is a didactic medium, completely at home only in the area of the cognitive.

2. In the area of the cognitive, it deals most effectively with factual content and simple concepts; it deals least effectively with sophisticated concepts.

3. Being oriented to the cognitive, it contributes only in an indirect way to the personality-fulfilling outcomes of emotional health, social development, and creativity.

4. Habitually relying on the written symbol as its instructional medium, programmed learning makes prohibitive demands on the slow reader.

5. Relatedly, even with the fast reader, this single-dimensioned methods emphasis may lead in time to a sub-standard level of student interest and motivation.

6. Programmed learning retards the progress of pupils toward independence by keeping them closely tied to predetermined structure of outside authority.

7. Programmed learning's insistence on the importance of reinforcement via externally imposed rewards may well result in this same outcome of pupil dependence. Rogers and Hilgard, among others, hold to this point of view. In this regard, pupils who are overprotected from their mistakes may be pupils who will be unable to learn from such mistakes.

8. So long as commercial agencies continue as prime movers in programmed learning, just that long will programs tend to fall short of the criterion of curriculum relevance. Programs that serve educational purposes must be programs that mesh into the planned mosaic of any school's curriculum.

9. The factor of cost, identified by many as a shortcoming, I shall pass over lightly. In the first place, the cost of materials may be considerable at times, but it will rarely be prohibitive. Furthermore, mass production will soon lead to reduced costs. And finally, most communities

have long demonstrated a willingness to underwrite anything in education that, even though somewhat costly, appears to be eminently worthwhile.

An Overall Evaluation

With opinion divided about the merits of programmed learning, research ideally should cast the deciding vote. Research, unfortunately, is too inconclusive at the moment to play such a decisive role. A disproportionate amount of it, as indicated previously, relates more to the less significant than to the fundamental. While not belittling the importance of such issues as those involving the linear format versus the branching format, the constructed response versus the multiple-choice response, the programmed book versus the program in a machine, and immediate reinforcement versus delayed reinforcement, we are convinced that research should go beyond these issues.[11]

A major shortcoming of many investigators is their tendency to overgeneralize conclusions from limited evidence. Apropos here, one such investigator (with a sound research reputation) aroused the educational world in 1959 with an eye-lifting pronouncement that in the teaching of spelling, the programmed-learning method negates the influence of intelligence. Specifically, he avowed the absence of any significant relationship between intelligence and the performance of second and sixth graders on a machine program of spelling. The exact reason for this patently erroneous conclusion, we do not know. What we do know, however, is that research by Silberman, Shay, and others—as well as common sense—kept the conclusion from spreading.[12] The fundamental point here is that education which abandons time-honored and time-validated evidence for less authentic new evidence stretches or breaks the bonds of credulity.

Too frequently, current and past research on programmed learning evaluates the amount of retention just moments after its initial acquisition. Very few studies, in contrast, evaluate the extent of retention after a protracted time lapse. Furthermore, practically none of the studies evaluates the learning results which follow an extended exposure by pupils to the new learning method. Until such studies are forthcoming, the Hawthorne effect as a possible cause of any improvement in learning cannot be ruled out. By this we mean that the sheer newness of a program book or the novelty of a teaching machine might in and of itself constitute cause enough to motivate a pupil to work more conscientiously

[11] One of the better treatments, brief and to the point, on this topic of evaluation is by Wilbur Schramm, *Programmed Instruction*, pp. 11–15.
[12] Edward Fry, *Teaching Machines and Programmed Instruction* (New York: McGraw-Hill Book Company, 1963), pp. 84–85.

at a given learning task. What change might take place in this new found source of motivational energy once the new paraphernalia became humdrum, only continued experimentation will reveal.

Even though many research studies oversell the case for programmed learning, there is no denying the fact that programs do teach—and teach effectively, at that—under the proper conditions. As stated by Schramm:

A great deal of learning seems to take place, regardless of the kind of program or the kind of students. Even a bad program is a pretty good teacher. Programs have been used successfully at all levels of ability from slow learners to the very best students, and to teach a great variety of academic subject matter and verbal and manual skills.[13]

This is a statement by one who himself is far from sold on many aspects of the medium.

When convinced that programs can be effective learning instruments, curriculum planners have the following responsibilities. First, they need to decide what kinds of outcomes programmed learning seems most capable of achieving. Second, they need to analyze the curriculum to discover which parts seem to lend themselves best to a programmed format. Third, they need to analyze any given program under consideration to assure themselves of its specialized curriculum relevance. Only following these preliminaries, should curriculum planners recommend a program for classroom implementation.

Curriculum planners can never afford to become so lost in curriculum specifics that they lose sight of overall curriculum purposes—purposes which we discussed earlier in Chapters 4 through 6. In brief, the viewpoint expressed was this: that a curriculum to be effective must be mental-health oriented, must be creativity oriented, and must be problem-solving oriented. It must stimulate growth not only in the cognitive area but in the emotional, social, ethical, and physical areas, as well. And even in the cognitive area, per se, it needs to regard factual content and the learning skills as merely preliminary to the higher mental processes of understanding, transfer, and practical application.

This point of view about curriculum leads to the logical question: Which of the curriculum outcomes above can programmed learning accomplish more effectively than the more conventional and traditional teaching methods? While conceding that only the ubiquitous could answer this question with any degree of accuracy and completeness, ordinary mortals, with educational theory to guide, might answer it essentially as follows.

[13] Wilbur Schramm, *Programmed Instruction* pp. 11–12.

Programmed learning unquestionably is able to make a substantial contribution in the teaching of facts and concepts; in fact, it has demonstrated such an ability many times. At Roanoke, for instance, Allen Calvin, in a program experiment dealing with algebra, professed to reduce the learning time of eighth-graders by as much as 30 to 50 per cent. At Hamilton College, John Blyth, in a program experiment dealing with freshman logic, was so optimistic as to state: "We found many advantages and no disadvantages." He reported the more significant advantages to be these: the instructors regularly knew what had, and what had not, been learned; with this diagnostic insight, their lectures thus could be directed more pointedly; the range of individual differences was lessened, with several slow students doing much better than expected; and interest in the course increased.[14]

A theoretical analysis of programmed instruction, apart from any controlled experimentation, seems to indicate that programs can teach almost any learning content that needs to be memorized. Illustrative are vocabulary, names and dates of places and events, names of classified parts or objects, speeches, and documents. What is not known, however, is how long information learned by this method will be retained; and how much can be learned before satiation sets in. Analysis likewise seems to indicate that when programs in certain areas are carefully designed, they can bridge, at least partially, the distance between rote memory and understanding, between rote memory and the less complex levels of conceptualization, and between rote memory and certain aspects of transfer. Selected existing programs in mathematics, logic, and science are illustrative of the above.

Yet I, along with many others, am convinced that programmed learning becomes less appropriate the further it operates from the simple cognitive processes. A given pupil, for instance, from a given program in English grammar can learn that a nonrestrictive clause is to be set off from the remainder of a sentence by a comma; he can even apply this rule to examples contained in a program; but true transfer can be assured only when he directly applies the principle to his own writing. This he can do only outside the province of a program.

Social learning likewise has to look elsewhere for fulfillment. A program by the sheer nature of its individualistic properties cannot compete for social outcomes with a student committee, a panel, a symposium, a cocurricular activity, or any other shared group effort. Neither can it compete with a discussion group whose goal is social interaction directed at an idea, a principle, or a controversial issue. A program can present these

---

[14] John W. Blyth, "Teaching Machines and Human Beings," in A. A. Lumsdaine and Robert Glaser, *Teaching Machines and Programmed Learning* (Washington, D.C.: National Education Association, 1960), pp. 404–406.

latter in the intellectualized abstract; it can even present them from several points of view. But irrespective of cognitive completeness, it still would fall short of social outcomes such as respect for the conflicting opinions of others, sensitivity to personality differences, and tolerance for occasional downright illogic. If these latter are essential to healthy social living—as they unquestionably are—education needs to deal with them in an adequate way. Programmed learning does not constitute that adequate way.

If programmed learning fails the test of social development, it is no more successful in its confrontation with mental health and creativity. For example, it is powerless to give needed help to the inflexible, to the pathologically fearful, to the guilt-ridden, to the easily discouraged, or to the compartmentalized individual. And how can programmed learning foster creativity when it insists on a slavish adherence to predetermined logic? Also, where, if at all, does it allow for the free play of imagination? We answer these questions, as previously indicated, to the effect that programmed instruction is most suitable to fundamental cognitive learnings; it is not at all suitable for the social, the personal, and the creative. Thus an important task of education in the future is to assign to programmed learning the role that it can play best, assuring in the process that it be made to avoid the role, or roles, in which it is destined to fail or, at best, to know too limited success.

Final Conclusions

Based on our background of theoretical and practical experiences with programmed learning, we have arrived at the following conclusions.

1. Programmed learning in the future will find its place as part of a multifaceted ensemble of teaching methods. Within that ensemble, it will play a significant, but not a dominant, role.

2. The issue of whether or not a machine can, or will, replace a teacher should be laid to rest. Electronic devices of all kinds merely recast the roles of human beings; they do not eliminate the need for human beings.

3. To the extent that quality programs can "teach" the basic facts and the learning skills, the effective teacher will be able to spend commensurately more time on such more complex outcomes as those related to mental health, creativity, and problem solving.

4. The relatedness of programs to the mainstream of curriculum will determine, in great part, the extent of their future employment in education. To date, too many programs have been conceived and prepared in the psychological laboratories of universities or of commercial organizations. In the future, teachers and school administrators will play an

increasingly active role in programming, with the classroom serving more and more as an experimental laboratory.

5. Programs of the future will be more closely tailored to predetermined educational goals or purposes.

6. Learning theorists will become more active in seeking answers to such important questions as these: In any curriculum, what elements should programmed instruction replace and what elements should it supplement? In what grade levels will the new approaches be most effective? What will be the long-term effects of programmed instruction on motivation? If sound programs are conceived, are machines actually necessary? What can well designed programs do that well designed textbooks cannot do?

7. Programs of the future will become more specialized to serve the differential needs of individuals and groups: for example, the slow and fast learners; the slow and fast readers; and those who seek knowledge in depth in contrast to others who are capable only of less penetrating insights.

8. The self-pacing feature of programs and machines may well prove to be one of their most significant attributes. Individual differences loom as less foreboding when each student is able to pace himself via a given program. Large group instruction does not afford a comparable opportunity.

9. Because the programmed book or machine provides the reticent or slow with asylum from teacher or peer ridicule, it will lessen in the future the debilitating and defeating effect of adverse emotions on learning.

10. The methodical organization of programs may become more and more a feature of textbooks and lectures.

11. Programmed learning in the future should emphasize programming more and should split hairs about the mechanics of implementation less.

12. Finally, programmed learning in the future should be more concerned with long-term retention than with immediate acquisition. The reverse has typified the past decade of experimentation.

A Final Word

The new in education, like the new anywhere else, comes into being unevenly and uncertainly. The unfolding world of programmed learning certainly has constituted no exception to this rule. Not infrequently, the greatest friends of the new movement, by their highly exaggerated and clearly unsubstantiated claims, have proved to be worst enemies of the movement. By the same logic, the closed-minded critics who never have been able to get beyond the question "Will the machine replace the teacher?" have indirectly befriended the cause by their reverse brand of extremism. What is needed now is a moratorium on visceral judgment, during which the issues of programmed learning will be researched carefully and completely. Only in this way will authentic assessments eventuate.

With Lysaught and Williams, we agree that programs and teaching machines are not visual aids, are not tests, are not panaceas, and are not answers to the teacher shortage.[15] And with Stolurow, we agree that they are fixture, not fad.[16] But exactly what they are, it is too early for anyone to say. More conclusive answers need to await future investigations. Only then will education know under what conditions programs and teaching machines will play their most effective roles.

Recommended Readings

For those who wish to probe more deeply into programmed learning than this chapter permits, we recommend the following selections:

Audiovisual Instruction. A monthly periodical published by the Department of Audiovisual Instruction, National Education Association. Contains selected sections on programmed learning.

Coulson, John E. (ed.), *Programmed Learning and Computer-Based Instruction.* New York: John Wiley & Sons, Inc., 1962. A collection of chapter-length treatments by various theoreticians and practitioners: Carter, Silberman, Crowder, and others.

Cram, David, *Explaining Teaching Machines and Programming.* San Francisco: Fearon Publishers, Inc., 1961. Employs the several program methods to explain the programs themselves. For the reader still in doubt about the linear and branching methods, we recommend this highly.

De Cecco, John P. (ed.), *Educational Technology.* New York: Holt, Rinehart, and Winston, 1964. Another collection of treatments by such well-known specialists in the field as Glaser, Finn, Fry, and Stolurow.

Finn, James G. and Donald G. Perrin, *Teaching Machines and Programmed Learning: A Survey of the Industry.* Washington, D.C.: U.S. Department of Health, Education, and Welfare, 1962. An excellent historical and status study of the movement, with a particularly good pictorial presentation on pages 35–47 of the various teaching machines themselves.

Fry, Edward, *Teaching Machines and Programmed Instruction.* New York: McGraw-Hill Book Company, Inc., 1963. One of the most scholarly, constrained, and complete treatments on the list.

Galanter, Eugene (ed.) *Automatic Teaching: The State of the Art.* New York: John Wiley & Sons, Inc., 1959. Although a bit dated, it made a pioneer contribution at the time of its original publication.

[15] Jerome P. Lysaught and Clarence M. Williams, *A Guide to Programmed Instruction* (New York: John Wiley & Sons, Inc., 1963), pp. 19–21.
[16] Lawrence M. Stolurow, *Teaching by Machines,* Cooperative Research Monograph No. 6, OE 34010 (Washington, D.C.: U.S. Department of Health, Education, and Welfare, 1961), p. 150.

Hanson, Lincoln F. (ed.), *Programs '63: A Guide to Programmed Instructional Materials Available to Educators by September, 1963.* Washington, D.C.: U.S. Printing Office, 1963. One of the most complete collections of programs (sampled) in use throughout the country.

Hughes, J. L., *Programmed Instruction for Schools and Industry.* Chicago: Science Research Associates, Inc., 1962. An expository and pictorial presentation of the entire field of programmed learning.

Journal of Programmed Instruction. A periodical published by The Center for Programmed Instruction, Inc., New York. This is consistently timely and the work of careful scholars.

Lumsdaine, Arthur A. and Robert Glaser (eds.), *Teaching Machines and Programmed Learning: A Source Book.* Washington, D.C.: National Education Association, 1960. Although a bit dated, this is still a classic in the field.

Lysaught, Jerome P. and Clarence M. Williams, *A Guide to Programmed Instruction.* New York: John Wiley & Sons, Inc., 1963. One of the more recent, down-to-earth, complete treatments by two experienced theorists and practitioners.

Mager, Robert F., *Preparing Objectives for Programmed Instruction.* San Francisco: Fearon Publishers, 1961. Does an excellent job of bringing together educational objectives and programming.

Markle, Susan Meyer, *Good Frames and Bad: A Grammar of Frame Writing.* New York: John Wiley and Sons, Inc., 1965. Fundamental for anyone engaged in the preparation of a program.

Programmed Instruction. A periodical published by The Center for Programmed Instruction, New York. Keeps readers abreast of current happenings in the field.

Schramm, Wilbur, *Programmed Instruction Today and Tomorrow.* Washington, D.C.: Fund for the Advancement of Education, 1962. A balanced, thorough presentation and evaluation by a knowledgeable scholar.

Stolurow, Lawrence M., *Teaching by Machine*, Cooperative Research Monograph No. 6 OE-34010. Washington, D.C.: U.S. Department of Health, Education, and Welfare, 1961. At the time of publication, it was one of the better treatments of the programmed-learning field.

For Further Thought

We assign the reader just this one challenging task: Determine in what parts of a school curriculum programmed-learning methods should or should not be used. In the areas where you think they should be used, explain their superiority to the teaching methods that they would have to replace.

Other References

Aid: Auto-Instructional Devices for Education and Training. Lubbock, Texas: Institute of International Research and Development (a periodical).

Audio-Visual Communication Review. Department of Audio-Visual Instruction. National Education Association (a periodical).

Buchanan, Cynthia Dee and M. W. Sullivan, *Programmed Reading for Kindergarten or First Grade*. New York: McGraw-Hill Book Co., 1964.

Carpenter, Finley, *Teaching Machines and Programmed Instruction*. Syracuse: The Library of Education, Center for Applied Research in Education, Inc., 1963.

Deterline, William A., *An Introduction to Programmed Instruction*. Englewood Cliffs, N.J.: Prentice-Hall, Inc., 1962.

Epstein, Sam and Beryl, *The First Book of Teaching Machines*. New York: Franklin Watts, 1961.

Fine, Benjamin, *Teaching Machines*. New York: Sterling Publishing Co., Inc., 1962.

Foltz, Charles I., *The World of Teaching Machines*. Washington, D.C.: Electronic Teaching Laboratories, 1961.

Gagné, Robert M. (ed.), *Psychological Principles in System Development*. New York: Holt, Rinehart, and Winston, Inc., 1962.

Green, Edward J., *The Learning Process and Programmed Instruction*. New York: Holt, Rinehart, and Winston, Inc., 1962.

Holland, James G. and B. F. Skinner, *The Analysis of Behavior*. New York: McGraw-Hill Book Company, 1961.

Margulies, Stuart and Lewis D. Eigen (eds.), *Applied Program Instruction*. John Wiley & Sons, Inc., 1962.

Mathis, Claude, "Programmed Instruction in University Education." *Journal of Dental Education*, 28 (March 1964), pp. 82–89.

Ross, Wilbur L. and Others, *Teaching Machines: Industry, Survey and Buyers' Guide*. New York: The Center for Programmed Instruction, Inc., 1962.

Smith, Wendel I. and J. William Moore (eds.), *Programmed Learning*. New York: D. Van Nostrand Co., Inc., 1962.

Trow, William Clark, *Teacher and Technology*. New York: Appleton-Century-Crofts, 1963.

part **IV**

The Society and
the School

chapter 10

Society, the School, and Negroes

Turning somewhat abruptly from the impersonal content of the past three chapters, we turn now to the social and to the social-political in this and the next three chapters. And revealingly, in this regard, the social is competing currently with the scientific for major world attention. This question, if asked in 1955, "What is the outstanding phenomenon on the world scene?" predictably would have elicited one of the following answers: "The horror weapons of destruction; the industrial electronics revolution; or the struggle for dominance between capitalism and communism." The same question asked in 1965, although likely to have elicited one or more of the same three answers, just as conceivably might have brought forth the response: "the struggle of the 'have-nots' for the good life." The possibility of such a reply may well reveal a world, long burdened with the guilt of inconsistency, eager to bridge the hiatus between a humanistic philosophy verbalized on one hand, and considerably less than humanistic living practiced on the other.

Although the global struggle of the "have-nots" is a broad one, it channels into these specific needs and human rights: physical survival, an adequate standard of living, social equality, freedom from political exploitation, and educational opportunity. Because these are humanistic cornerstones, they properly should constitute, individually and collectively, the birthright of all people.

Before selecting the topic of this chapter, I seriously considered the alternate topic of the culturally-deprived child. A noteworthy feature of the latter is its greater breadth; yet, for this very reason, it was rejected. For too long, I believe, writers and researchers have lumped together children from such divergent parentage as the underprivileged Puerto Rican, the West Virginia mountaineer, the slum white, the

American Indian, and the American Negro. This is stretching the bonds of homogeneity too far. For this reason, I elected to focus on just one element of the country's underprivileged—the American Negro. Actually, the timeliness of the topic, its social significance, and its far-reaching dimensions are justification enough for the final decision.

For three and a half centuries, the Negro in the United States has been the victim of ignorance, of bigotry, of psychological projection, or of all of these. During most of this long period, he has relied for amelioration of his lot—through necessity, not choice—on the slow process of social evolution. More recently, however, chafing under the paucity of his gains, he has adopted a more aggressive posture in his struggle for status. And his efforts have projected him beyond the national into the international spotlight.

What he needs most from his strivings is to find a holistic psychological self, a self which mirrors worthwhileness and dignity. A requisite to this outcome is social acceptance, something that he has had too little of—even, at times, too little of it from fellow members of his own ethnic group. Denied social acceptance from without, and accorded it too sparingly from within, he has tended quite understandingly to downgrade himself and his entire race.

In the words of Stonequist, the American Negro is "poised in psychological uncertainty between two (or more) social worlds; reflecting in his soul the discords and harmonies, repulsions, and attractions of these worlds."[1] He no longer is an African, but neither does he yet have all the rights of an American. Forces around him lead him alternately to hope and to despair. Although on the threshold of self-discovery, he still looks to the future for realization of his potential. However, he is able to look more confidently with each passing day.

In actuality, the Negro problem, if it can be called that, stems from white society's refusal, or slowness, to implement with action what it has long avowed as a belief. The words freedom and equality ring out in the Constitution with silver-toned clarity, but the notes too frequently have been muted or have become discordant in practice. However, despite the inconsistency, society during the past several decades has made noteworthy progress in advancing the cause of Negroes. The courts have been particularly active in this movement; formal education, unfortunately, less so, influenced as it so often has been, and still is, by ill-conceived local attitudes and pressures.

Yet education, with its dedication to truth, cannot stand idly by while social problems "erupt into crises and violence."[2] Nor can it remain neu-

[1] Everett B. Stonequist, *The Marginal Man* (New York: Charles Scribner Sons, 1957), p. 8.
[2] Charlotte Epstein, "Introduction: Teaching Intergroup Relations," *The Journal of Intergroup Education* 111 (Summer 1962), pp. 198–202.

tral toward a "social order which breaks the spirit and trammels the selfhood of any segment of its population."[3] Instead, in the words of a third writer, it must "search for a consistent way of mediating a partially confused and chaotic culture in the process of transformation; a way, moreover, which is . . . compatible with the development of integrated personalities and acceptable to most, if not all, of the major social groups in our society."[4] Although this rings of the ideal, education can scarcely settle for a lesser goal.

Historical and Social Antecedents

To provide a context for the later treatment of Negroes in an educational setting, we proceed now to identify and examine selected tenets, historical landmarks, and unfounded opinions about them.

Fundamental Democratic Values.   A logical starting point for any serious investigation of American-Negro problems is the U.S. Constitution. This source, as even elementary-school children know, confers on him a status of equality with all mankind. Furthermore, it guarantees the freedom he needs to develop to the optimum of his capacities. This guarantee rises above such extraneous factors as race, color, nationality, religion, and political affiliation.

Second, it confers on him the right of legal redress when social practice conflicts with judicial dictum. However, it is realistic to note that courts at the various jurisdictional levels differ in the patterns of interpretations that they make. In this connection, local courts are more prone to absorb and then reflect provincial attitudes and prejudices; state and federal courts, to predicate their decisions more on broadly conceived social policy and values.

Third, even when the several courts agree on issues and on the decisions they render about them, social practice not infrequently lags behind legal dictum. This phenomenon usually is indicative of a smaller segment of society being out of step with another larger one. At the present moment, the South and many large cities of the North are illustrative.

Selected Historical Landmarks.   The saga of the Negroes' progress toward a better life finds tangible expression in the following social, political, and legal milestones.[5]

[3] Regina Goff, "Culture and Personality Development of Minority Peoples," *Negro Education in America*, edited by Virgil A. Clift, Archibald W. Anderson, and H. Gordon Hullfish (New York: Harper and Brothers, 1962), p. 146.

[4] William O. Stanley, *Education and Social Integration* (New York: Bureau of Publications, Teachers College Press, Columbia University, 1953), pp. 129–130.

[5] For an excellent chronology of historical events pertaining to the Negro, we recommend the reading of William W. Brickman, "Chronological Outline of Racial Segregation and Integration in U.S. Schools," in *The Countdown on Segregated Education*, eds. William W. Brickman and Stanley Lehrer (New York: Society for The Advancement of Education, 1960), pp. 152–165.

1. Slavery was brought to this country in 1619 when a group of African Negroes were shipped, against their will, to Jamestown.

2. The first Insurrection Laws were passed in 1680, and others periodically thereafter, prohibiting slaves to gather together in large assemblies. These laws constituted a tacit admission by the white man that the human spirit, when enslaved, is likely to erupt in rebellion against its oppressors.

3. Education of slaves was almost nil in the earliest colonial days but increased as religious and economic motives gained ascendance. In 1717, Cotton Mather made a formal assault on the problem by opening a school for both Negroes and Indians. The Quakers and other religious sects made comparably significant contributions to Negro education throughout the eighteenth and nineteenth centuries.[6]

4. As early as the eighteenth century, an occasional school admitted both races, but this practice was more often the result of convenience than of conviction.

5. In the first half of the nineteenth century, certain states: Virginia, Louisiana, and Georgia, among others, passed laws prohibiting the education of Negroes. Despite these laws, however, Negro education in those states and in others continued to increase.

6. When the Abolitionist Movement became intensified before the middle of the century, a number of Negro schools were burned or razed, for example, in Connecticut in 1838 and in Washington, D.C., in 1843.

7. In 1865, the Thirteenth Amendment abolished slavery, and in 1868, the Fourteenth extended equal protection of the laws to Negroes.

8. Following the Civil War, two extreme approaches to Negro education manifested themselves. One was an attempt by white reactionaries to circumvent law via prohibitive state legislation (most since has been declared unconstitutional). This legislation segregated Negroes educationally and gave them, at best, second rate opportunities. At the other extreme, the Federal Government via its Freedman's Bureau[7] and via philanthropic foundations (Carnegie, Peabody, and others) made aggressive attempts to expedite educational progress for Negroes.

9. A number of Negro universities came into being shortly after the Civil War: Fisk in 1866, Howard in 1867, Hampton in 1868, and the famous Tuskegee of Booker T. Washington in 1881.[8]

10. The separate-but-equal doctrine regarding Negro education became the accepted one for a century after the Civil War, with the Supreme Court giving it some legal dignity in 1896 in the Plessy v. Ferguson

[6] See George S. Brooks, Friend Anthony Benezet (Philadelphia: University of Pennsylvania Press, 1937).

[7] See Paul E. Pierce, The Freedman's Bureau (Iowa City: University of Iowa Press, 1904).

[8] See Booker T. Washington (ed.), Tuskegee And Its People: Their Ideals And Achievements (New York: Appleton-Century-Crofts, 1910).

case (163 U.S. 537). Ironically, this case involved the segregated seating of Negroes on trains but was transferred in principle to segregation in education.

11. Aided by the massive Julius Rosenwald fund established in 1911, Negro schools and colleges shortly thereafter entered a period of rapid expansion and improvement.

12. In school systems that practiced racial segregation, the separate-but-equal principle, until declared unconstitutional in 1954, resulted in a close adherence to the "separate" part of the principle, but in no more than lip service to the "equal" part. The latter constituted the axial issue in the following court cases:

A. *Pearson v. Murray,* 1936, Maryland.

B. *Gaines v. University of Missouri,* 1938, Missouri.

C. *Sipuel v. University of Oklahoma,* 1948, Oklahoma.

D. *Sweatt v. Painter,* 1950, Texas.

E. *McLaurin v. Oklahoma State Regents,* 1950, Oklahoma

In all of these, the plaintiff claimed that equal educational opportunity had been denied him: either when, because of discriminative legislation, he had to go out of state for professional or graduate training; or when in his own state he had to attend a Negro institution that did not offer the program he wanted or offered it at an inferior level.

These cases, more than merely pressing for greater educational equality of the races, actually looked beyond this important issue to a rejection of the separate-but-equal doctrine itself. These cases, along with several others like them, exposed the *Plessy v. Ferguson* decision of 1896 to legal scrutiny, pointing ahead to the historic pronouncement of the Supreme Court on May 17, 1954.[9] A major part of the decision in *Brown v. Board of Education* follows:

(*The Brown Case*)

The Text of the Court's Decision

SUPREME COURT OF THE UNITED STATES

(May 17, 1954)

Mr. Chief Justice Warren delivered the opinion of the Court.

These cases [Brown, Briggs, Davis, Gebhart] come to us from the States of Kansas, South Carolina, Virginia, and Delaware. They are premised on different facts and different local conditions, but a common legal question justifies their consideration together in this consolidated opinion.

[9] See James C. Paul. *Law and Government: The School Segregation Decision* (Chapel Hill: The University of North Carolina, 1954); or David Fellman, *The Supreme Court And Education* (New York: Teachers College Press, Columbia University, 1960), pp. 79–106.

In each of the cases, minors of the Negro race, through their legal representatives, seek the aid of the courts in obtaining admission to the public schools of their community on a nonsegregated basis. In each instance, they had been denied admission to schools attended by white children under laws requiring or permitting segregation according to race. This segregation was alleged to deprive the plaintiffs of the equal protection of the laws under the Fourteenth Amendment. In each of the cases other than the Delaware case, a three-judge federal district court denied relief to the plaintiffs on the so-called "separate-but-equal" doctrine announced by this Court in *Plessy versus Ferguson*, 163 U.S. 537. Under that doctrine, equality of treatment is accorded when the races are provided substantially equal facilities, even though these facilities be separate. In the Delaware case, the Supreme Court of Delaware adhered to that doctrine, but ordered that the plaintiffs be admitted to the white schools because of their superiority to the Negro schools.

The plaintiffs contend that segregated public schools are not "equal" and cannot be made "equal," and that hence they are deprived of the equal protection of the laws. Because of the obvious importance of the question presented, the Court took jurisdiction. Argument was heard in the 1952 Term, and reargument was heard this Term on certain questions propounded by the Court.

Reargument was largely devoted to the circumstances surrounding the adoption of the Fourteenth Amendment in 1868. It covered exhaustively consideration of the Amendment in Congress, ratification by the states, then existing practices in racial segregation, and the views of proponents and opponents of the Amendment. This discussion and our own investigation convince us that, although these sources cast some light, it is not enough to resolve the problem with which we are faced. At best, they are inconclusive. The most avid proponents of the post-War Amendments undoubtedly intended them to remove all legal distinctions among "all persons born or naturalized in the United States." Their opponents, just as certainly, were antagonistic to both the letter and the spirit of the Amendments and wished them to have the most limited effect. What others in Congress and the state legislatures had in mind cannot be determined with any degree of certainty. . . .

In the instant cases, . . . there are findings below that the Negro and white schools involved have been equalized, or are being equalized, with respect to buildings, curricula, qualifications and salaries of teachers, and other "tangible" factors. Our decision, therefore, cannot turn on merely a comparison of these tangible factors in the Negro and white schools involved in each of the cases. We must look instead to the effect of segregation itself on public education.

In approaching this problem, we cannot turn the clock back to 1868 when the Amendment was adopted, or even to 1896 when *Plessy versus Ferguson* was written. We must consider public education in the light of its full development and its present place in American life throughout the Nation. Only in this way can it be determined if segregation in public schools deprives these plaintiffs of the equal protection of the laws.

Today, education is perhaps the most important function of state and local governments. Compulsory school attendance laws and the great expenditures for education both demonstrate our recognition of the importance of education to our democratic society. It is required in the performance of our most basic public responsibilities, even service in the armed forces. It is the very foundation of good citizenship. Today it is a principal instrument in awakening the child to cultural values, in preparing him for later professional training, and in helping him to adjust normally to his environment. In these days, it is doubtful that any child may reasonably be expected to succeed in life if he is denied the opportunity of an education. Such an opportunity, where the state has undertaken to provide it, is a right which must be made available to all on equal terms.

We come then to the question presented: Does segregation of children in public schools solely on the basis of race, even though the physical facilities and other "tangible" factors may be equal, deprive the children of the minority group of equal educational opportunities? We believe that it does.

It is not overstatement to say that the *Brown versus Board of Education* decision of 1954, by the highest court of the land, is one of the most socially important that has ever been handed down. For Negroes, specifically, this decision ranks in significance just a notch below the Emancipation Proclamation itself. During the past decade, a number of states have questioned it, have fought it, and have attempted by various means to circumvent it, but legally it firmly stands. The job of the future is for the society to implement it, in the spirit of goodwill.

Selected Truisms. A major task of teachers, social workers, political leaders, or just plain citizens who address themselves to the plight of Negroes is to ferret from the welter of fiction about them a composite of reasonably authenticated fact. This latter emanates from postulates such as the following:

1. The Negro race cannot be and therefore should not be categorically stereotyped. It runs a gamut from brightness to slowness, from morality to immorality, from ambition to sloth, from conformity to rebellion, and from mental health to pathological states.

2. Negroes do less well on academic-aptitude tests than do whites. One reason for this phenomenon may well reside in the barrenness of the Negroes' environment. As stated cryptically by one writer: "The fact that there is a definite and measurable relationship between the scores which pupils obtain on intelligence tests and the social status or cultural background of their parents has been known since the time of Binet."[10]

A second possible reason is that with most items of an academic, apti-

---

[10] Kenneth Eels, "What Is The Problem?" in *Intelligence And Cultural Differences*, edited by Kenneth Eels, Allison Davis, et al (Chicago: University of Chicago Press, 1951), p. 3.

tude test almost habitually drawn from a middle-class culture, Negroes who come from a marginal culture are consequently disadvantaged.[11] This may be the reason why middle-class children, as Havighurst states, are known to "get more out of themselves in the ordinary school test situation than do lower-class children."[12]

A third possible reason, rejected by most (including me) but espoused by a few, is that there is an intrinsic difference between the two races. One of the more articulate devotees of this point of view is Audrey Shuey, Chairman of the Department of Psychology at Randolph Macon College. While rejecting her conclusion, we admit that her research raises a number of questions remaining yet to be conclusively answered.[13]

3. Negroes constitute approximately one tenth of the country's population, but they provide only one twentieth of the total college population—and eighty per cent of these students are in Negro colleges.[14] The obvious surface implication of this ratio disparity is that Negroes, regardless of cause, are educationally deprived. The deeper import is that society loses trained manpower as a result.

4. Society has forced Negroes into a posture of social servility, which is probably even more injurious to their intellectual development than is their disadvantaged status in formal education. Both self-concepts and the intellects suffer from such a posture.

5. An artificial posture characterized by servility and conformity cannot be sustained indefinitely. In fact, I agree with Adler, Horney, Fromm, and others, whose dynamic philosophies have strong social overtones, that unless Negroes are aroused from this artificially enforced passivity, it will lead them ultimately to pathological withdrawal or to pathological aggression. Both are manifesting themselves today.

6. Seen in proper perspective, the Negro-white problem has its basis more in attitudes than in substance. Consequently, any program of education directed at the problem needs, by necessity, to relate to the emotions as well as to the mind. And in view of the rigidity of attitudes, such a program, if realistic, while pressing toward the long-term goal of total change, should expect only limited affective gains during any short-term period.

Selected Unfounded Beliefs and Opinions about Negroes.   Existing side by side with supportable tenets regarding Negroes and their place

[11] Virgil E. Herrick, "What Is Already Known About the Relation of the I.Q. to Cultural Background," in *Eels, Intelligence And Cultural Differences,* p. 14.
[12] Robert J. Havighurst, "What Are the Cultural Differences Which May Affect Performance on Intelligence Tests? in *Intelligence and Cultural Differences,* p. 21.
[13] Audrey M. Shuey, *The Testing of Negro Intelligence* (Lynchburg, Virginia: J. P. Bell And Company, Inc., 1958), p. 318.
[14] Richard L. Plaut, "Closing The Educational Gap," *The Journal of Intergroup Education,* 111 (Spring 1962), p. 139.

in a white culture are many beliefs and opinions that have only a tenuous relation to fact. However, people do hold these beliefs and anyone thinking about the problems of Negroes must be ready to answer the following questions. Some pertain to minority groups in general; others, specifically to Negroes.

Is one race inherently inferior or superior to another? An affirmative answer has no basis in fact and is rejected by such writers as Benedict, Davis, Klineberg, Montague, Myrdal, Powdermaker, and Wellfish. All are convinced that because the various races originate from a common species, they do not divide logically into hard-and-fast categories. Even such classifications as Caucasian, Negroid, and Mongolian apply most generally to skin-color differences. These classifications are not respectors of blood chemistry, however, for each of the three divides similarly into the commonly-recognized blood types of A, B, and O. A summarizing statement here is that races differ primarily on unimportant externals, little or not at all on important fundamentals.[15]

Will integration make for racial impurity? An allegation to this effect would have to rest on a tenuous base for the simple reason that if all races are of a single species, as indicated in the preceding paragraph, racial impurity becomes a figment. Thus, often expressed fears of "mongrelization" through the loss of Anglo-Saxon, or other ethnic, characteristics are unfounded.

Are Negroes innately more immoral and less hygenic than white men? A valid answer to this question has to revolve around the word innately. Illegitimacy is undoubtedly higher, and personal hygiene probably lower, in the colored than in the white race, but both conditions are better explained environmentally than genetically. Negro fears of the future undoubtedly lead to closer alliance with the pleasure principle, which is keyed to the present, than to the reality principle, which is keyed to the future. This alliance, in turn, leads more often to an immediate than to a delayed gratification of instinctual desires. After all, the present is for the taking; the future may never come. Furthermore, such factors as illiteracy, crowded living conditions, and frequent migrations result both in increased immorality and in lower standards of sanitation. However, for anyone to relate the externals of Negro life and habits to genetic causation is like relating the unhygienic conditions of pioneer life in the early colonies to genetic factors. Such specious inferences have no justification in fact.

Will educational standards for whites be lowered when Negroes are desegregated? This often-talked-about outcome is probably more a

[15] Corinne Brown, "Anthropological and Sociological Factors in Race Relations," *Negro Education in America,* edited by Virgil A. Clift, Archibald W. Anderson, and H. Gordon Hullfish (New York: Harper and Brothers, 1962), pp. 99–104.

bugaboo than a realistic possibility. Specifically, when the school system of Washington, D.C. was desegregated, there allegedly was no decrease in overall academic achievement despite the considerable influx of Negroes into previously existing "white" schools.[16] A conservative conclusion here is that white students will do little, if any, worse in desegregated schools, and Negroes will probably do somewhat better.

Is strife inevitable when schools are desegregated?   The implied conclusion here, if nothing else, is too categorical. Strife may well result in certain instances, particularly at the beginning of desegregation when tensions run high, but strife is not necessarily an inevitable outcome. In Washington, D.C., once more, social events attended by the several races reportedly were "without incident."[17]

Will integration take away the white man's right of private selection?   This fear over the possible loss of private choice goes counter to existing democratic tenets and to common sense, as well. Integration or no integration, members of either race will continue to choose their friends, select their marriage partners, and, in general, keep company with individuals of their own choosing. And they likewise will continue to receive at least a modicum of protection from the law when their private rights are invaded.

What Are the Aspirations of Negroes?   In the previous discussion of selected unfounded opinions regarding Negroes, such terms as fact, tenable assumptions, and unfounded assumptions were employed—terms which, because of their controversial nature, were only as applicable as the author was objective in employing them. In this section, less editorial subjectivity will enter in because the ideas presented will be mostly those that Negroes themselves have expressed. Specifically, attention will be directed at the questions: Just what do Negroes want from society? And what are their aspirations and expectations?

First, they desire personal worth and social respect.   This aspiration rises above race and encompasses all mankind. It relates both to what any individual thinks about himself and to what society thinks about him. As expressed at the beginning of this chapter, Negroes are searching for satisfactory psychological self-acceptance. But this outcome, it must be remembered, is inseparably related to their acceptance by society. If Negroes are unable to achieve self-fulfillment in the larger culture, they may well search for it in radical groups, such as the Black Muslims,[18]

[16] Francis A. Gregory, Carl F. Hansen, and Irene C. Hypps, "From Desegregation to Integration in Education," *The Journal of Intergroup Education,* 4 (Winter 1962–1963), pp. 64–65.
[17] *Ibid.,* p. 65.
[18] Franklin Edwards, "The Changing Status and Self Image of Negroes in the District of Columbia," *The Journal of Intergroup Relations* 4 (Winter 1962–1963), p. 12.

which, despite their falsity, may be the only open avenue to self-respect and group identification.[19]

Second, they want the right of suffrage. For Negroes to feel worthy, the greater society needs to guarantee them their just rights and privileges, one of which is the vote. In the North, they have suffrage, but in parts of the South, at least at present, they are caught in the crossfire of federal edicts and opposing state practices. In this struggle, federal dictums are gradually achieving dominance although at the price of ill will of some whites, and at times at the price of the shed blood of both races.

Third, they crave optimum educational opportunity. Although law is the buttress of the good life, education constitutes the means of social implementation. Within its framework, Negroes, like whites, seek optimum development in the light of individual ability and potential.

Fourth, they desire equal vocational opportunity. In recognition of the social and ethical propriety of this aspiration, legislation directed toward the outcome of fair employment has become commonplace during the past several decades. Fundamentally, Negroes desire the right to compete fairly with all other citizens in the capricious world of the market place. And when a certain job or profession is denied them, they want the reason to be lack of qualification, not improper skin color.

Fifth, they want housing equality. Their goal, in this regard, is a right to live wherever economic circumstances permit. However, whether open-occupancy legislation is the answer is a debatable issue. If such legislation, in its admittedly laudable effort to provide better housing accommodations for Negroes, destroys more civil liberty than it creates, a hollow victory will have been won.

Sixth, they desire the unfettered right to public accommodations and services. Ready access to hotels, vending establishments, and public transportation facilities are among the former. Police services, legal redress, and medical attention are among the latter. In short, their goal is to have the rights and privileges of all free men in a democratic society.

The Negro Awakening. Negro social progress during the past two to three decades constitutes an amazing success story. As recently as 1943, Negroes were segregated in the armed services. As recently as 1950, they were segregated educationally almost as much as not. As recently as 1960, their right of access to public accommodations and services was more academic than actual. Today, a reversal in these and in related areas is evident throughout the country. Why the dramatic change?

One reason lies in mechanical farming which, by removing opportunities for Negroes to earn a living as farm workers in the South, drove

[19] *Ibid.,* p. 22.

them to the large cities of the North. In the early 1950's for instance, the Negro migration form southern farms was averaging 700,000 annually.[20] The comparable statistics for one city, Chicago, which became a major recipient of the migrants, are equally impressive. In 1900, Chicago had a Negro population of 30,000; in 1944, of 350,000;[21] in 1966, of almost a million.

Massive dislocations such as these, while having immediate deleterious effects on almost all concerned, often lead to long-term gains achieved more or less as follows. (1) Migrants move to large cities in the North, where their concentrated political influence eventually becomes a power to be reckoned with locally. (2) Sooner or later, local power becomes national power. (3) As minority concentrations increase, however, so do local conflict and violence, in disproportionate ratio to the numbers involved. (4) To the degree that local power converts into national power, concerns of a local nature become concerns of a national nature.[22] The result ultimately is a national effort to effect amelioration. Ironically, however, most cultures, including the American, are prone to let their social problems become acute before attending to them. The problems of Negroes are certainly no exception.

A second reason for the recent Negro awakening is the climate of world opinion. The international social revolution of the mid-century has pitted the have-not's against the have's, the enslaved against the free, the power of economic and mechanical might against humanitarian values. In this struggle, social injustice in one part of the world does not remain local; in fact, it almost regularly attracts the glare of world opinion. In this regard, the combination of an aroused international conscience and the far-reaching scope of mass-communications media constitute a potent weapon against nonhumanistic social practices anywhere in the world.

A third reason lies in the struggle between Communism and the Free World. With unrest and injustice in one of these power blocks feeding propaganda to the other, each is deeply concerned about keeping its house in order so as to project a more defensible image before the world.

A fourth reason lies in the recently achieved freedom of African nations. With the American Negro's genetic roots in Africa and his environmental roots in the United States, what happens in the one place cannot be kept separate from events in the other. Thus if freedom is on the march in Africa, it cannot remain at a stand still in the United States.

[20] Joseph W. Holley, *Education And the Segregation Issue* (New York: The William-Frederich Press, 1955), p. 17.
[21] St. Clair Drake and Horace R. Clayton, *Black Metropolis, A Study of Negro Life in a Northern City* (New York: Harcourt, Brace & Co., 1945), pp. 7–8.
[22] Robert B. Knapp, *Social Integration in Urban Communities* (New York: Teachers College Press, Columbia University, 1960), p. 70.

A fifth reason (postulated at least by some) is the immediately preceding three-to-four decades of increasingly strong federal leadership on behalf of Negroes' rights. Gregory, Hansen, and Hypps hold this point of view.[23] Vander Zanden, among others, points out that since the first inauguration of Franklin D. Roosevelt, the Democratic Party has increasingly supported the rights of Negroes and has become correspondingly less solicitous of the Southern white vote.[24]

A sixth and final reason is improved insight of people in key places. Most knowledgeable individuals admit that at the theoretical level, segregation is not workable; and at the practical level, it is not working.

From the beginning, the problem has been for the mind of man to relate what he knows to what he feels. This is a big order, as any therapist of dynamic orientation can testify. Yet, there are convincing signs that social common sense is winning out slowly over bias and prejudice. The victory is not at all clear cut—if it is a victory at all—but gains are increasingly manifest. As these multiply, the gap between the American Dream and its uncertain implementation will proportionately narrow.

Dangers to Be Avoided. As the Dream makes increasing contact with reality, both the Negroes and whites need to avoid the inevitable pit falls inherent in almost any movement for social betterment. The primary danger is extremism.

Extremism in Action. At the action level, Negroes, in moving with their while counterparts toward the legitimate end of equality, will experience defeat to the degree that they employ means out of character with their goals.[25]

Negroes and whites have recoiled, and continue to recoil, from the cross of the Klan. They recoil because the Klan ethic does violence to the democratic and the Judeo-Christian ethic to which both generally subscribe and which must ever be the star to guide their action. However, at a time when extremism by whites is undergoing increasingly careful scrutiny, extremism by Negroes should undergo equally careful scrutiny.

Conceivably as dangerous, in my opinion, as the outright radicals in the Negro movement today, are others, who under the guise of peaceful protest, advocate or condone law breaking. Such individuals also need to scrutinize their values carefully. When they guide children into mass

---

[23] James W. Vander Zanden, "Foundations of the Second Reconstruction" in Brickman and Lehrer, *The Countdown on Segregation Education*, p. 45.

[24] Gregory, Hansen, and Hypps, "From Desegregation to Integration in Education," Op. Cit., p. 58.

[25] We cite the following as at least one instance of a source that goes counter to the point of view expressed above. Adam Clayton Powell Jr., *Marching Blacks* (New York: Dial Press, 1945), pp. 19 and 214.

truancy from large-city schools, as many are doing today, they veer dangerously toward an advocacy of anarchy.

Overdependence on the Racial Reference Group.   Contributing to racism by effect, although not by design, is Negroes' sustained dependence on their own ethnic reference group. Kurt Lewin's opinion on this issue is that Negroes must hold tenaciously to their reference group or end psychologically anchorless. My point of view, which may differ from Lewin's more in degree than in direction, is that all individuals must learn to regard themselves first as members of the human race and only second as members of a man-named ethnic group. If Lewin is advocating strong racial affiliation as a supplement to, rather than as a substitute for, a greater cosmic allegiance, there is no argument. Such racial identification provides interim support in the time of emotional need. However, for racial identification to persist actively after a satisfactory measure of social integration has been attained is to lose the greater victory of equality. The danger of race identification continued beyond the point of need is that stereotypes, which originally may have been impugned from without, have a way of remaining to become perpetuated from within. For example, Negroes have been referred to so often as inferior that some of the race actually believe the allegation to be valid. Such beliefs can be laid to rest most effectively by successful participation in interracial relationships.

Education and Negroes

What initially must be stated about Negroes and education is that their presence, whether in an integrated or in a segregated school or classroom, does not alter at all the basic goals or design of American education. Regardless of the specific make-up of any group of children or youth in attendance at any school unit, the ultimate purpose of education remains the same: to help each child develop to his potential to the end of self and societal change. Programs may vary from place to place in response to individual differences, but purpose remains constant.

This viewpoint, interesting to note, runs counter to the premises which undergirded Negro education shortly before and shortly after the turn of the century. At that time, the opinions of the great Negro humanitarian and scholar, Booker T. Washington, were dominant. In accordance with the climate of social opinion then in existence, he deemed it best for the Negro to accept his status and to educate himself for those tasks such as farming and other manual pursuits that the social scheme had allocated to him. A state of affairs such as this, regardless of Mr. Washington's good intentions, constituted status quoism purely and simply. Furthermore, a society that restricted the Negro to such a narrow role was a society that denied him his inherent humanistic and educational right to grow. Washington's position was so far out of line with the country's traditions and values that understandably it was short-lived.

Selected Administrative Considerations.   Although educational purpose, regardless of the ethnic make up of any school population, remains constant, administrative problems in the presence of the Negro tend to heighten. Some of these problems are both social and educational; others are uniquely educational.

1. School zoning in cities is one that is both social and educational. The issue in the abstract, stated in question form, is this: Is it better for the society to preserve its traditionally held value of the neighborhood school at the price of segregation of minority groups; or to modify the concept of the neighborhood school for the reward of better integration of minority groups?

The issue in the concrete, however, is not this clear cut. Educational opportunity is at best uneven in many Negro neighborhoods. Negro schools customarily are more overcrowded than white schools; teachers are less well-trained; social learning suffers from racial and ethnic separation; facilities are less adequate; and at the high-school level, the curriculum tends to be less encompassing.[26]

A further complication is that certain school systems, through the process of gerrymandering, have made district lines conform more to racial population concentrations than to legitimate factors such as the distance of pupils from a school, the availability of transportation to schools, the adequacy of school facilities, and the appropriateness of curriculum offerings.

Unable to protect the ideal of the neighborhood school and, at the same time, to achieve educational parity for all the races, a number of large city systems have instituted, or are in the process of instituting, the following compromise. They have designated selected "permissive" areas wherein students may elect (*a*) a neighborhood school close by, usually segregated de facto because of the ethnic character of the community, or (*b*) a more distant school which is sometimes white, sometimes integrated, sometimes partially integrated.

The advantages of this plan are several-fold. Children who commute outside their school districts become part of racially mixed school populations where intercultural growth, without being assured, is more likely. Those who attend schools in their respective neighborhoods tend to have a more tolerant attitude toward the social authority that gave them the right of choice. Furthermore, this plan in the long run tends

[26] The Advisory Panel on Integration of the Public Schools, *Report to the Board of Education of Chicago*, March 31, 1964. (This is the so-called Hauser report.)

to upgrade schools in disadvantaged communities. One potent argument against it, however, is this: If race is a legitimate criterion for school attendance, why not religion, or politics, or ethnic preference? Thus our support of the plan is more in terms of present-day expediency than of defensible long-term policy.

2. Assuming the continuing existence of de facto segregation in many communities with children denied the right to attend schools outside their districts, what then? Will the culturally deprived children continue to be deprived? The answer of many school systems, including those of the Great Cities Project and of the Higher Horizons Project of New York City, in particular, is to transport such students, on frequent occasions, to outlying places of culture. Because this method has proved so highly successful wherever employed, we strongly underwrite it. The November, 1963, issue of *Phi Delta Kappan* is a condensed source of information on the two projects cited in this paragraph.

3. Yet another problem revolves around teaching faculties and race. Once again, ideally, the race of a teacher, irrespective of the characteristics of any school population, should be no consideration. However, at the practical level, it is a consideration. Thus a minimum requirement is for schools with interracial populations to have interracial teaching faculties, although not necessarily in comparable proportions.

4. The necessity for a school administration to work closely with representatives of selected other public agencies looms as a further task of the integrated school. As with many of the other problems identified in this section, this requirement is accentuated, not created, by the presence of Negroes. A cooperative liasion among such agencies as the school, the church, the local YMCA or YWCA, the chamber of commerce, and local political organizations often prevents problems by anticipating them, or at least ameliorates them once they have arisen[27]

5. Integration is frequently accompanied by a need for additional or more intensified services in such areas as testing, home visitation, job placement, personal-emotional counseling, and remedial teaching. Accepted phenomena are that many Negro students are less advanced academically, are less motivated, present a different cultural posture, and are more rebellious against authority than are white students of comparable age. All of these factors can be mitigated by a proper expansion of counseling services.

Riessman attributes the Negroes' academic retardation and low motivation to (*a*) lack of academic traditions in the home, (*b*) inadequate language skills, (*c*) unrealistic long-term goals, (*d*) resentment of middle-class standards, (*e*) poor health, (*f*) transient living conditions, (*g*)

---

[27] For the YWCA's experiences in integration, see Margaret Hiller, (ed.), *Toward Better Race Relations* (New York: The Woman's Press, 1949).

discrimination by white teachers, (*h*) lack of learning and testing know-how, and (*i*) enforced adaptation to strange academic environments.[28] All of these point to a need for the closest possible relationship between Negro parents and school personnel.

Yet such a relationship is frequently difficult to attain. A major obstacle is usually the cost of additional staff to provide the necessary additional services. Another obstacle is the psychological distance which, at least initially, tends to exist between a white-authority figure and a Negro, a distance which has to be eliminated if the relationship is to accomplish its purpose. The presence of at least a few Negro teachers on any school staff makes this much less of a problem.

When the school and the Negro home remain at separate poles, facts too frequently get lost in the cliché, the specific episode succumbs to the stereotype, and personal responsibility for behavior fades into scape-goating.[29] For this reason, Negroes, like other people, need to be helped to face themselves realistically and assume responsibility for the consequences of their actions. This outcome is more readily achieved when the school and the home work together and when teachers and specialized case workers are willing to work, and do work, diligently toward its accomplishment.

6. A part of the overall guidance problem is the necessity for small-size remedial classes in such academic areas as reading, speech, and arithmetic. These additional services inevitably pose a budget problem, which administrators and school boards have to resolve together.

7. How best to utilize a given school for community purposes is a seventh concern, particularly for administrators of schools located in deprived urban areas. Education, in this regard, has only begun to investigate the benefits of evening and Saturday school programs for deprived children and often, even more, for deprived adults. Such programs, although not unique to the underprivileged Negro community, are certainly germane to it.

8. A free-lunch program for the needy is another important administrative concern, usually requiring local school officials to solicit aid from governmental sources.

Basic Curriculum Issues.   In the integrated school, as in any type school, curriculum problems are at one and the same time both administrative and academic. One issue that definitely falls into both categories is that of the proper place in education of the Negro in literature. Certain Negro groups today are protesting the required reading in the schools

[28] Frank Riessman, *The Culturally Deprived Child* (New York: Harper and Row, 1962), pp. 4–6.
[29] For further development of the phenomenon of scapegoating, see Harry H. Giles, *The Integrated Classroom* (New York: Basic Books, Inc., 1959), pp. 84–85, and Riessman, *The Culturally Deprived Child,* p. 27.

of such literary works as *Huckleberry Finn, Little Black Sambo,* and "Othello." The issue can find adequate solution only in what anyone conceives the primary purposes of literature to be. If literature is to portray only the nobler virtues, many books would have to be banned not only on racial grounds but on other grounds as well. But if literature is to portray realism also, then censorship must tread more softly. Othello evokes a universal human emotion rather than specifically the emotions of a black Moor; Little Black Sambo is more an engaging *little* boy of phantasy than a *little black* boy of phantasy; and Mark Twain's Jim is more a part of mid-western provincialism than a Negro per se.

It is near a point of universal acceptance that literature's purpose is to challenge thought and analysis by involving a reader in all kinds of situations with all kinds of characters. Such characters can include a Fagan or a Pollyanna, a Bigger or an Uncle Tom, and a Mrs. Warren as well as a Mrs. Grundy. To emphasize the whiteness or the blackness of any of these is to miss the basic point. Each, whether adult villain or saccharin juvenile, whether tragic character or wooden stereotype, whether prostitute or prude, plays his part. If the races themselves rebel against being averaged out and leveled off, literature is no less rebellious.

A second issue which once again is both administrative and curricular has to do with the relationship between homogeneous grouping and Negroes. One predictable result of such grouping is the concentration of a disproportionately large number of Negroes in remedial sections and a disproportionately small number in so-called honors sections. The rightness or wrongness of this outcome looks to curriculum purpose for an answer. If it is exclusively cognitive, such an organizational arrangement has some justification in logic even though little justification in educational research. However, if curriculum purpose incorporates the additional outcome of emotional and social growth, the arrangement loses even the support of logic.

A compromise arrangement is the adoption by any school of some type of organizational pattern that permits both heterogeneous and homogeneous grouping practices to operate flexibly in the light of specific curriculum circumstances. Team teaching constitutes one such pattern. So does any other temporary grouping arrangement for remedial or enrichment purposes which escapes rigidity.

A third curriculum issue which the presence of Negroes magnifies, but does not create, relates to single-symbol marking practices. The facts of the case are these. Negroes in the typical highly verbal curriculum of most schools tend to be behind white students of the same age. Yet Negroes have to compete in this curriculum for external recognition. As a result, more often than not they suffer by comparison. When compared unfavorably for any long period, they become less motivated in academic matters and more rebellious in human relationships. Inevitably, they develop resentment against a social system that consistently casts them in this unfavorable light. In the elementary school, where evaluation adapts comfortably to parent conferences and written behavior descriptions, the issue is less acute. But in the high school, where evaluation predictably converts into single-symbol marking, the issue is of serious proportions.

While not having a pat answer to a problem this complex, I shall offer a few suggestions that fall within the framework of a single-symbol marking arrangement. This system, impossible to defend convincingly, bedevils because of its basic illogic. In general, teachers should avoid such unhealthy marking practices as posting grades publicly on bulletin boards, reading them aloud in class, publicizing honor-roll or honor-society membership, employing the mark as a reward, or employing the mark as punishment. Furthermore, teachers should do extensive soul-searching before assigning a failing mark to a pupil who is working up to capacity. Administratively, schools should determine eligibility for extra curricular participation on an evaluative base broader than marks alone.

All in all, we recommend that nonintegrated and integrated schools alike take a clinical approach, operating out of the following marking tenets:

> The clinical approach begins and ends with pupil uniqueness . . . As in mental health, the goal is optimum development . . . [The pupil] is a dynamic person expected to work with what he has and to develop it as much as circumstances permit . . . By this standard, the teacher's commission is to respect the worth of each student, understand him as best he can, discerningly help him to develop, and evaluate him separately from all others.[30]

A fourth curriculum requisite of the integrated school is materials of instruction that reach selectively into the cultures of both Negroes and whites. The "Look, Jane, look" brand of forced white middle-class sweetness may have a respectable place in some school arrangements, but in a typical integrated school situation, a little of it soon becomes excessive. The need instead is for primers, readers, and resource materials to reflect authentically the cultures of many races.

Rising above all other educational requirements, however, is the need for a curriculum to take each pupil—whether Negro, white, or of some other racial designation—as he is, and relate uniquely to him. Thus if he needs reading instruction of a remedial nature, the curriculum at all levels should provide it. If he is neurotically dispositioned against academic learning, the school, without shortchanging the academic program,

[30] Gail M. Inlow, *Maturity in High School Teaching* (Englewood Cliffs, N.J.: Prentice-Hall, Inc.,) p. 321.

should look to the non-academic program for balance: to the applied arts and to the extracurriculum in particular. Or if a pupil cannot read a textbook in a given subject, either he should receive one that he can read or the school should make other provisions for him. The keynote is curriculum flexibility. The enemy to growth is curriculum rigidity.

In the last part of this section on curriculum practices in the integrated school, I shall make additional suggestions in the form of imperatives to the teacher.

Encourage the intermingling of the races through random seating arrangements, through combined racial representation on committees, and through a combined racial sharing of classroom housekeeping tasks of various kinds. Both the prestigious and the menial assignments should be distributed more or less evenly between or among the races. Proximity and shared responsibility may not regularly break down barriers of misunderstanding and resistance, but without them such barriers tend to fade more slowly.

Face issues openly regardless of the racial makeup of any group. The teacher, with rare exception, should treat students first as human beings and only second as members of racial groups. Race, to the greatest extent possible, should be neutralized whether the issue is an infraction of a school rule, a discussion of Uncle Tom, or a realistic give-and-take on civil rights. Intellectual honesty provides the key here.[31]

When facing racial issues openly, be objective and empathic, but not emotional.

When tension does develop, look for common bonds as healers. Possible examples might be a group "show-and-tell" project in an early elementary grade, a shared science demonstration in an intermediate grade, a homeroom-committee activity in a junior high school, or any shared classroom project in a high school. In the process of group deliberations, tensions have a way of easing.

When the more subtle methods of easing tensions fail, take a firm stand, thereby establishing the fact that a public school is an educational sanctuary for all children, not just for one group. Education, which is civilization's institution of greatest enlightenment, must lead courageously here where lesser institutions might be fearful.

When punishment is in order, make no concession to race. A teacher of one race often veers toward leniency in punishing a student of a different race. Overly eager to avoid the very appearance of discrimination, he discriminates in reverse, to the detriment of the offender as well as to those who did not offend.

---

[31] See Cooper C. Clements, "Creating a Classroom Setting for Emotional Learning," *The Journal of Intergroup Relations*, **3** (Summer 1962), p. 213; also Riessman, *The Culturally Deprived Child*, p. 82.

Regard the I.Q. as just one index of a Negro's ability, and only an approximation, at that. The reasons, as indicated earlier, are that Negroes customarily come from an unenriched environment where they are not necessarily motivated; the test items are often slanted away from their culture; and Negroes usually compete in a white-dominated atmosphere. In view of these reasons for caution, the knowledgeable teacher does not regard the I.Q. as an exact indicator of ability. Instead, he maintains a posture of flexibility toward this or any other single index, looking for cues more broadly from many sources.

In any mixed group, eschew interracial competitiveness.

Resist the temptation to preclassify members of any group into fixed vocational categories. Regardless of central tendencies regarding the current vocational status of Negroes, or whites (or Jews or Gentiles, or Catholics or Protestants), a rightful goal is to break through the narrow cordon of tradition into a world of unfolding opportunity. Thus, guidance counselors at any level, while operating within the framework of reality, must let the cumulative information about any individual be the criterion of vocational planning, not a set of predetermined social conclusions. Overpersuading Negroes out of the professions and other more prestigious job outcomes is just as harmful as false optimism about opportunities for Negroes in them. The correct position is somewhere between the reality of today and the idealism of tomorrow.

Give Negro students, particularly those who come from deprived environments, needed help in how to take tests, how to study, how to read text books, and how to use the library. Assistance on such basic matters is often the crux of educational success, present and future.

Finally, prepare to deal in interview situations with adults and students who are hostile to you and your race. Although ready answers here fail, the following four suggestions are germane.

1. Be friendly regardless of hostile attitudes. Your warmth and acceptance will be better neutralizers of aggression than words.

2. Move slowly and unaggressively in establishing your points of view. Rapport needs to precede ideas.

3. Don't attempt to oversell another on your opinions. Explain but don't try to convert.

4. Be satisfied with slow progress.

Recommended Readings

For the reader who desires a more extensive acquaintanceship with the role of Negroes in American culture than this chapter has provided, I recommend the following publications. These are not duplicated in the rather lengthy bibliography at the end of the chapter. A few of the publications go beyond Negroes into minority problems in general or into racial problems in general.

Benedict, Ruth and Gene Weltfish, *The Races of Mankind*. New York: Public Affairs Committee, 1943. The motif here is fact and fiction about race differences.

Bloom, Benjamin S., Allison Davis, and Robert Hess, *Compensatory Education for Cultural Deprivation*. New York: Holt, Rinehart, and Winston, Inc., 1965. The basic theme in this is extra effort for the deprived.

Brickman, William C. and Stanley Lehrer, eds., *The Countdown on Segregated Education*. New York: Society For the Advancement of Education, 1960. An excellent series of articles relating to the history, foundations, and current status of Negroes. It also has a timely report by Superintendent Hansen on the Washington, D.C. integration story.

Brown, Robert R., *Bigger Than Little Rock*. Greenwich, Connecticut: The Seabury Press, 1958. A sensitive ethical-religious plea for racial understanding in this period of social crisis.

Clift, Virgil A., Archibald W. Anderson, and H. Gordon Hullfish, *Negro Education in America*. New York: Harper and Brothers, 1962. It is difficult to find enough good things to say about this book. The treatment is thorough, interesting, and forthright.

Drake, St. Clair and Horace R. Cayton, *Black Metropolis, A Study of Negro Life in a Northern City*. New York: Harcourt, Brace and Co., 1945. One of several books of the forties relating to the urban Negro problem. This specific one, with its setting in Chicago, is somber and disturbing.

Caldwell, Dista H., *The Education Of the Negro Child*. New York: Carlton Press, 1961. Included here to show that the Negro problem is multisided. Among other ideas, Caldwell advocates exclusive private Negro schools which will equate with the better private schools of the white man.

Du Bois, W. E. B., *The Negro*. New York: Holt, Rinehart, and Winston, 1915. Is included for its historical significance. Du Bois, a Negro, made the first extensive break away from Booker T. Washington's "agricultural" approach to education.

Eels, Kenneth, Allison Davis, Robert Havighurst, Virgil E. Herrick, and Ralph W. Tyler, *Intelligence and Cultural Difference*. Chicago: University of Chicago Press, 1951. An informative treatment of the I.Q. and cultural influences.

Giles, H. Harry, *The Integrated Classroom*. New York: Basic Books, Inc., 1959. A detailed and heavily documented presentation of the educational integration issue, with numerous excerpts included to increase authenticity.

Jewett, Arno, Joseph Mersand, and Doris V. Gunderson, (eds.), *Improving English Skills of Culturally Different Youth in Large Cities*. Washington, D.C.: U.S. Department of Health, Education, and Welfare, 1964. A bit idealized but forward looking.

Myrdal, Gunnar, *An American Dilemma*. New York: Harper and Brothers, 1944, 2 Vols. A literary classic on the problem of minorities and the cultural lag in their achieving status. It deals more with broad social, than with educational, issues, however.

Passow, A. Harry (ed.), *Education in Depressed Areas.* New York: Teachers College, Columbia University, 1963. One of the most meaningful and down-to-earth treatments in the entire list.

Powell, Adam Clayton, Jr., *Marching Blacks.* New York: Dial Press, 1945. We have included this one as an example of an outspoken and somewhat closed point of view by one who wants change "now."

Riessman, Frank, *The Culturally Deprived Child.* New York: Harper and Row, 1962. This one goes beyond Negroes to the deprived in any category, who, Riessman says, number 1 child in 3. It is a bit slanted and oversimplified in its proposals for education.

Shoemaker, Don., (ed.), *With All Deliberate Speed.* New York: Harper and Brothers, 1957. This is one of the "musts"—an anthology of the ideas of well-informed scholars.

The Journal of Intergroup Education, National Association of Intergroup Relations, 2027 Massachusetts Ave., N.W., Washington, 6, D.C.: A quality journal published quarterly. We recommend it highly ($6.00 per year).

The Journal of Negro Education, Howard University Press, Howard University, Washington, 1, D.C. Another excellent and timely quarterly journal ($4.00 per year).

The Journal of Negro History, 1538 Ninth Street, N.W., Washington, D.C. The title is self-explanatory ($5.00 per year).

Washington, Booker T., *Tuskegee and Its People: Their Ideas and Achievements.* New York: Appleton-Century-Crofts, 1910. This portrays Booker T. Washington in all his greatness—which lay in his empathic feeling for all people.

A Last Word

Only the blind optimist could fail to see the many problems that have to be faced and solved in the future before true educational integration can take place. Desegregation is an interim step but it is only a step. Legal enactments have been noteworthy, but they too are only beacons along the way. In actuality, attitudes change laws more than laws change attitudes. Thus education's abiding concern in the integration issue must be for changes in the intangibles of feeling as well as for changes in the province of the mind. Both are mutually dependent and supportive.

We conclude this chapter with three thought-provoking quotations.

However, it is not the fact of integration or disintegration which makes a society "free" or authoritarian; it is, rather, the conceptions of man, society, and human values that find institutional expression which determine the moral order.[32]

[32] Riessman, *The Culturally Deprived Child,* p. 21.

A real educator is a social and intellectual leader, and he begins to exercise his leadership when he recognizes the conditions of his society and brings to bear upon them the force of a humanitarian philosophy.[33]

If America is to be a leader in the world, "responsibility must reach out to meet moral obligation, humility must attend policies, and love must accompany its deeds . . . it is not what is said with the lips that convinces, it is what is believed in the heart and practiced in life . . . Diplomats can adorn their speeches with abstract words like 'liberty,' 'equality,' and 'fraternity,' but it will take America to show what the words really mean."[34]

For Further Thought

Here the reader should take time to state what he believes about racism, in general, and Negroes, in particular, and then decide whether his beliefs are based on fact or emotion.

References

Allport, Gordon, W. *The ABC's of Scapegoating.* New York: Anti-Defamation League of B'nai B'rith, 1948.

Anti-Defamation League, *Miracle of Social Adjustment: Desegregation in the Washington D.C. Schools.* New York: ADL, 1957.

Angell, Robert C., *The Integration of American Society.* New York: McGraw-Hill Book Co., 1941.

Aptheker, Herbert, *American Negro Slave Revolts.* New York: Columbia University Press, 1943.

Bartky, John A., *Social Issues in Public Education.* Boston: Houghton Mifflin Company, 1963, Chap. 19.

Boyd, William C., *Genetics and the Races of Man.* Boston: Little, Brown and Company, 1950.

Brooks, George S., *Friend Anthony Benezet.* Philadelphia: University of Pennsylvania Press, 1937.

Chandler, B. J., Lindley Stiles, and John Kitsuse, *Education in Urban Society.* Dodd-Mead & Co., 1962.

Conant, James B., *Slums and Suburbs.* New York: McGraw-Hill Book Co., 1962.

Davis, Allison, *Social-Class Influences Upon Learning.* Cambridge: Harvard University Press, 1948.

Dollard, John, *Caste and Class in a Southern Town.* Garden City, N.Y.: Doubleday Anchor, 1957.

Drucker, Peter F., *The New Society.* New York: Harper and Brothers, 1950.

Dunn, L. C., and T. Dobzhansky, *Heredity, Race and Society,* New York: Mentor Press, 1952.

[33] Ronald J. Rousseve, "Teachers of Culturally Disadvantaged American Youth," *The Journal of Negro Education,* 3 (Spring 1963), p. 115.
[34] Robert R. Brown, *Bigger Than Little Rock* (Greenwich, Connecticut: The Seabury Press, 1958), p. 142.

Goff, R. M., "Problems And Emotional Difficulties of Negro Children, Contributions to Education, N. 960." Doctoral dissertation, Teachers College, Columbia University, 1949.

Grambs, Jean D., *A Guide to School Integration*. Public Affairs Pamphlet No. 225. New York: Public Affairs Committee, 1957.

Harlan, Louis R., *Separate and Unequal*, Chapel Hill: The University of North Carolina Press, 1958.

Herskovits, Melville, J., *The Myth of the Negro Past*. New York: Harper and Brothers, 1961.

Hollingshead, August B. *Elmtown's Youth*. New York: John Wiley & Sons, 1949.

Klineberg, Otto, *Race Differences*. New York: Harper and Brothers, 1935.

Knapp, Robert B., *Social Integration in Urban Communities*, New York: Teachers College Press, Columbia University, 1960.

Lane, Howard and Mary Beauchamp, *Human Relations in Teaching: The Dynamics of Helping Children Grow*. New York: Prentice-Hall Inc., 1955.

Lewin, Kurt, *Resolving Social Conflicts*. New York: Harper and Brothers, 1948.

Logan, Rayford W., ed., *What the Negro Wants*. Chapel Hill: University of North Carolina Press, 1944.

Lynd, Robert S. and Helen M. Lynd, *Middletown*. New York: Harcourt, Brace & Co., 1925.

Lynd, Robert S. and Helen M. Lynd, *Middletown in Transition*. New York: Harcourt, Brace & Co., 1935.

Miller, Arthur S., *Racial Discrimination and Private Education*. Chapel Hill: The University of North Carolina Press, 1957.

Paul, James C. N., *Law and Government: The School Segregation Decision*. Chapel Hill: The University of North Carolina, 1954.

Pierce, Paul S., *The Freedmen's Bureau*. Iowa City: University of Iowa Press, 1904.

Pierce, Truman M., James B. Kincheloe, Edgar R. Moore, Galen N. Drewry, and Bennie F. Carmichael, *White and Negro Schools in the South: An Analysis of Biracial Education*. New York: Prentice-Hall, Inc., 1955.

Sexton, Patricia, *Education and Income*. New York: The Viking Press, Inc., 1961.

Shuey, Audrey M., *The Testing of Negro Intelligence*. Lynchburg, Virginia: J. P. Bell Company, Inc., 1958.

Stanley, William O., *Education and Social Integration*. New York: Teachers College Press, Columbia University, 1953.

Stonequist, Everett B., *The Marginal Man*. New York: Charles Scribner's Sons, 1957.

Sutton, Elizabeth, *Knowing and Teaching the Migrant Child*. Washington, D.C.: National Education Association, 1960.

The Advisory Panel on Integration of the Public Schools, *Integration of the Public Schools—Chicago*. Chicago: The Board of Education, City of Chicago, 1964.

Woodson, Carter G., *The Negro in Our History*. Washington, D.C.: Associated Publishers, 1945.

chapter 11

Sex Education and the Schools

The next topic of consideration is the controversial one of sex education. The most fundamental issue of all, in this regard, is whether sex education actually is a proper concern of the nation's schools. If it is not, this chapter and other comparable treatments have no reason for being. If it is a proper concern, as we are convinced that it is, questions such as the following require valid answers. What is the rightful place of sex education in a curriculum? What should be its goals? On what principles should it rest? And of what ingredients should a sound program consist?

Each of the three major purposes of education—the transmissive, the adaptive, and the developmental—testifies in its own persuasive way to the need for sex education to have a place in school curricula. The assumption behind the first is that selected information and attitudes about sex are transmissible. The assumption behind the second is that as a result of the transmission, individuals will adapt more appropriately to themselves and to their environments. The assumption behind the third is that by reason of the transmission and the better resulting adaptation, individuals will be able, more nearly, to attain their respective physical and emotional potentials. Any counterview either assumes sex to lie outside the reach of didactic instruction, or to conclude that some agency or agencies other than the institution of education are responsible.

Whatever the establishment of education—or, for that matter, of the family, of the church, of the community agency, or of the law—does or does not do about sex education, one outcome is certain: the sex drive will continue to produce social consequences. Some of these, such as participation in the approved rites of courtship and marriage, will have the society's sanction. Others, such as premarital intercourse, will not. In this latter regard, the number of recorded illegitimate births doubled during the fifteen-year period 1945 to 1960. Of 224,300 such births in 1960, approximately 40 per cent involved teen-age girls.[1] Both social conscience and common sense plead eloquently for the schools to act against this growing tide, but the response to date has been lethargic.

Like illicit sexual relationships and illegitimacy, the high rate of divorce in the society constitutes another crucial concern. And, once more, education is generally indifferent or detached. Dr. Bauer invades the traditions of tragi-comedy when he reveals in an unforgettable cartoon a hard-nosed little urchin, perched between his battling parents, announcing to the judge: "I don't want to live with either one. I'd like a completely fresh start."[2] Conceivably this is what education needs: a completely fresh start in dealing with the numerous issues of sex, including divorce as just one of the many.

My thesis is that sex is a natural and a wholesome phenomenon. Because it is natural, the young, being curious about it, are entitled to discover selected of its mysteries. Because sex is also wholesome, the young have a legitimate right to possess knowledge and insight about it—but at developmentally proper times, in approved ways, and in approved places. The thesis furthermore is that sex is both procreative and "recreative." With the two functions intimately related, the society through its most appropriate agencies needs to educate toward the outcome of social control, pending the time that it can sanction procreation itself.

Controversial Issues

Not surprisingly, the controversial topic of sex education is a divisive influence in many school systems and communities. One man's logic in this area not infrequently is another man's illogic. When differences solidify, opposing camps customarily form over the following issues.

The Question of Differential Responsibility. One of the most fundamental questions has to do with agency responsibility, with the home, the school, and the church often at odds over the relative status of their respective roles. Tradition generally supports the primacy of the home in matters of sex education. For one reason, the family as the primary reference group has many inherent rights that secondary agencies do not routinely possess. Sex education, from the beginning of time, has been regarded as one of those rights. Also, children usually spend more time in the home than at school or church.

The case for home primacy in matters of sex education weakens, how-

---

[1] Joan Beck, *The Chicago Tribune*, Magazine Section, Sunday, June 30, 1963.
[2] William W. Bauer, *Stop Annoying Your Children* (Bobbs-Merrill, Inc., 1947), Chapter 1.

ever, when instructional adequacy becomes the criterion. When parents do not possess sufficient knowledge about sex, have confused attitudes toward it, or have personality problems that prevent communication, they are ill-suited for their roles of sex leadership. Regarding the criterion of knowledge, one writer estimates that 98 per cent of all parents know too little about sex to impart authentic insights to their children.[3] Even if this estimate is far-fetched, a corrected one predictably would still be eye opening. Regarding the criterion of personality, many parents for reason of prudery fail to qualify as instructional leaders. Nor should this result be surprising in view of the society's long manifested defensiveness about sex. False modesty has long been an enemy of sex education.

Granted that the home has been relatively ineffective in preparing the young for the later demands of adult sexuality, the church and the synagogue, more often than not, have been even less effective. Some of the reasons are these. Certain ecclesiastical groups, believing sex education to be exclusively a family matter, deliberately remain detached from the problem. Other groups, while admitting a responsibility for the problem, remain so bogged down in theological dogma that their efforts in social action of all kinds, including sex education, rarely rise above the nominal. Still other groups, sincerely interested in doing something constructive about the problem, lack the specialized training, facilities, materials, and other resources essential to a successful implementation of their manifest interest.

The Roman Catholic Church is in a unique position, in this regard, in that for centuries it has engaged quite actively in the sex education of its membership young and old alike. How effective its efforts have been, however, is a moot question. At one extreme, the Kronhausens scathingly refer to it as a "parody of what sex education could or should be."[4] At a second polar extreme, the church fathers describe it glowingly. I believe that any program must be considered in terms of a specific set of circumstances. Thus the quality of Roman Catholic education is bound to vary from parish to parish, and from situation to situation within any given parish.

I admit, however, to reservations about a program of any ecclesiastical group where the educational leader is, at one and the same time, God's annointed and also counselor on sex matters. Clerical status and associated dogma many times tend to constrict rather than to open the encounter for the counselor. Relatedly, they tend to translate more often

[3] Benjamin C. Gruenberg, *How Can We Teach About Sex?* Public Affairs Pamphlet No. 122 (Wash., D.C.: Public Affairs Committee, 1946), p. 6.
[4] Phyllis and Eberhard Kronhausen, "Sex Education—More Avoided Than Neglected," *Teachers College Record,* **64** (January 1963), p. 322.

into a confessional-expiational exchange than into an uninhibited two-way consideration of specific behavior, specific ideas, and specific attitudes pertaining to sex. We do not share Kardiner's extreme position on this issue, but we understand his reasons for identifying theologians, moralists and Casanovas as unqualified for leadership in sex education.[5]

The church or the synagogue which includes sex education in its curriculum needs to meet these specifications. It needs to provide leaders who are clinically trained. It needs to establish a climate where frankness is a likely outcome. And it needs to avoid externally imposed judgment. An ecclestiastical body that sees a justification for meeting, and is able to meet, these high standards can perform an inestimable service to its constituents. If not cognizant, however, of a need for these high standards, or not able to meet them, it should make no pretense of having an organized program.

The establishment of education stands as a third social institution with a natural interest in and a justifiable concern for sex education. In actuality, any school which accepts responsibility for general-education outcomes can avoid, only by illogic or psychological compartmentalization, an associated responsibility for sex education. If general education encompasses that hard core of knowledge, skills, attitudes, and appreciations needed by all to relate to one another in a complex society, sex cannot be excluded from that hard core. Comparably, if general education constitutes a path to the good life for all, sex education lies along the path. Furthermore, any curriculum that includes courses in health and biology can scarcely avoid a confrontation with the problems of sex. Accordingly, the issue is not whether a school is responsible or is not responsible for sex education; the issue is when and how a school should accept the responsibility that rightfully belongs to it.

Interestingly, parents, rather than opposing an active role by the school in sex education, generally support the school's assuming such a role. Strain and Eggert underwrite this conclusion in their forthright declaration that: "Never, so far as we can discover, has there been a parent survey in the past fifty years that has not been in favor."[6] The American Association of School Administrators voices a similar opinion: "Parents are usually . . . anxious to have the school assume leadership."[7] Wetherill, a third source, goes so far as to assert that "parents of San

[5] Abram Kardiner, "New Attitudes Toward Sex," in *Personal Problems And Psychological Frontiers*, edited by Johnson E. Fairchild (New York: Sheridan House, 1957), p. 121.
[6] Frances B. Strain and Chester L. Eggert, *Framework for Family-Life Education: A Survey of Present-Day Activities in Sex Education* (Washington D.C.: American Association for Health, Physical Education, and Recreation, 1956), p. 16.
[7] American Association of School Administrators, *Health in Schools* (Washington, D.C.: A.A.S.A., 1942), p. 84.

Diego children who received sex education in the schools were behind it almost one hundred per cent."[8]

Probably the best solution to the issue of differential responsibility for sex education is for anyone to conclude that the home, the church, the school, and all other appropriate community agencies are collectively responsible but in differing ways and in differing degrees. The American Association of School Administrators has so concluded, averring that: "the school cannot do it alone, but working with the home and other community agencies, it can provide leadership and give direction to the program."[9] Wetherill, converting the concept into procedure, affirms that, "A committee representing teachers, school administrators, doctors, nurses, P.T.A., Council of Churches, Community Welfare Council, and other important segments of the community will not only help prepare the community for the program but will help decide and assume responsibility for the type of program best suited to schools."[10]

Although, as previously noted, most parents customarily align behind sex instruction in the schools, an occasional few here and there stand in opposition. What does a school do then? In anticipation of such an eventuality, many schools wisely secure in advance written authorization from parents for the enrollment of their offspring in a planned program. Through such a procedure, these schools, by making parents partners in the new enterprise, tend to ward off later criticism. In contrast, schools that, apart from parental approval, embark unilaterally on a project of sex instruction, need to ready themselves for possible friction and conflict that might easily have been prevented.

Agreement on Scope Is Essential. Regardless of the specific roles that school personnel and selected parents play in any program of sex education, the program's scope cannot exceed by much the limits of the beliefs, mores, and expectancies of a given local community. Elements of a curriculum, like the goals of education, can extend a given society's horizons a little but they cannot project those same horizons far into the uncharted unknown. Thus, in the curriculum area of sex, a school has to start basically where a given community is and proceed from there. Nor will a program conceived this narrowly necessarily run counter to the convictions of the greater social group, for, as stated by Duvall, "A sex code, based on the world today, has yet to be developed."[11]

Despite a lack of centrality, however, an approximation of a credo is beginning to take a form that should give any program, initially at

[8] G. G. Wetherill, "Sex Education in the Public Schools," *The Journal of School Health*, 31 (September 1961), p. 236.
[9] American Association of School Administrators, *Health in Schools*, p. 84.
[10] Wetherill, "Sex Education in the Public Schools," pp. 235–236.
[11] Evelyn M. Duvall, *Keeping Up With Teen-Agers*, Public Affairs Pamphlet No. 127 (New York: Public Affairs Committee, 1947), p. 26.

least, a semblance of direction. The evolving sex credo has its foundation, as would be expected, in civilization's acceptance of sex as a basic survival function. This position puts the topic in a natural setting. With the topic thus placed, a transition from sex projected as natural to sex practiced as pleasurable in the proper social setting is easy for instructional leaders to effect. Yet the ease of the transition does not lessen in the least the need for authority figures to safeguard against license. In fact, it might even heighten the need. As a result, the creed assigns this important task to each culture (and thus to a school): to formulate and make known those standards against which individuals are expected to assess the propriety of such sexual rites and practices as the following: marriage, monogamy, polygamy, divorce, body exposure, free love, premarital coitus, petting, homosexuality, lesbianism, and incest. And certain of these standards, it should be kept in mind, vary not only among cultures but among elements of almost any given culture.

The evolving credo casts sexual activity, when practiced under culturally approved standards, into a wholesome physical as well as psychic light. Although past generations intermittently have made the physical manifestations of love appear as unclean, unesthetic, and debased, at the moment a counter trend of overcorrection is unfolding. The mass media currently are fanning the flames of the physical so feverishly and in such a one-sided way that the psychic aspects of sex have become almost lost in the melodrama. Aware of this distortion, the school needs to place a counter emphasis on the psychic side of all wholesome affective relationships. This it can do without deprecating at all the natural beauty of the physical dimension.

Because sex attitudes are liberalizing by the year, most sex-education programs are able to maintain a fairly wholesome posture toward such topics as the names and functions of the intimate body parts, differences between the sexes, conception and birth, menstruation, masturbation, sexual curiosity, and sexual abberrations. However, liberalism cannot be allowed to ease into radicalism, regardless of a teacher's individual orientations. Such a teacher's days in a school would be numbered if he went so far as to advocate, for example, premarital coitus or the use of contraceptives. From a professional point of view, however, his days should be equally numbered if his sex ideas and values remained those of 1900. The trend quite properly is toward greater frankness, but frankness within the framework of moderation and reasonableness.

Will Sex Education Lead to Promiscuity? In any realistically-conceived program of sex education, an often expressed fear is that frankness in certain aspects of the curriculum may be construed by students as an invitation to license. This is a legitimate fear when individuals in leadership positions in the program are unqualified for their roles by reason of either inadequate knowledge of the content or personality deficiency. Weak leadership can be harmful to any venture. But by the same logic, when instructional leaders are well qualified for their roles, the fear is unfounded.

The choice more often, however, is between a fairly adequate program of sex education in a school, on one hand, and a counterpart hit-or-miss one of the streets, on the other. Only the narrow-minded could see a greater danger of promiscuity in the former than in the latter.

The Goals of a Program of Sex Education

Once a school resolves the controversial issues which inevitably arise prior to the implementation of a program of sex education, its next step is to formulate a body of major purposes. A composite from the many programs in operation throughout the country includes the following:

1. Communicate to the young factual knowledge about sex in its many manifestations: biological, psychological, and functional.

2. Instill in the young wholesome attitudes about sex in it many manifestations.

3. Combat misinformation and misunderstanding about the sexual anatomy and its functions.

4. Detect and treat, as early as possible, minor pathological conditions about sex that are in the process of developing.

5. Detect and refer to other agencies for treatment more serious pathological conditions about sex.

6. Relate sex to a broad context of character development.

7. Communicate the need for students to exercise premartial sex control.

8. Provide a mature understanding of sexual deviation in the culture and communicate to students both what their own and what the society's obligations should be in regard to it.

9. Reduce, by means of sex education, the incidence of neuroticism and borderline psychoticism in the school itself.

10. Improve home-school cooperation on sex matters.

11. Provide individual counseling services on sex which allow for greater personalization of problem discussion than a large-group approach permits.

Principles on Which a Program Should Rest

Goal formulation, which emanates in a listing such as the previous one, constitutes a major preliminary step in any program of sex education. Agreement on key operational principles constitutes a second major preliminary step. Curriculum formulation and staffing constitute the crowning third step. It is to the second step of principle formulation that we direct attention in this section. And, in general, we believe that the principles, without veering from social norms too far, should have a closer affinity to the liberalism of the psychoanalytical school than to the conservatism of the lavender-and-old-lace school. From a somewhat indefinable middle ground between these two extremes, the following principles, a few of which have been touched on before, emerge.

Sex Education Should Operate from a Climate of Naturalness. As already stated, sex is a natural phenomenon which, in an appropriate setting, is never sordid; only the distortions of a person or of a culture might make it appear that way. Physical attraction, emotional love, marriage, childbirth, and other sex-related processes are just as wholesome as they are vital. Thus any program of instruction that deals with them should cast them in a properly wholesome light and treat them in a wholesomely objective manner. Only in a climate such as this can a program extend appropriately beyond the cognitive into the crucial area of the affective. And without this transitional step, otherwise noteworthy outcomes will remain meaningless.

Sex Education Should Follow Developmental Lines. A second important principle of sex education is that it should follow as a controlling guide the developmental needs and interests of children and youth. Sex growth like any other aspect of physical and psychological growth is developmental. With this in mind, those responsible for a program of sex education should keep the curriculum consistently related to the physical and emotional growth patterns of the learning group and of individuals within it.

The sexual growth progression is one of stages. The infant's first interest, as would be expected, is in the act of feeding, with the oral thus having a place of primacy. The extent to which the oral act is gustatory only, or gustatory-sexual, is still very much open to conjecture. After a year or so of life, the infant, first in a casual way, later in a more intent way, develops an interest in his organs of elimination and reproduction. During this narcissistic period, he enjoys looking at, and making frequent explorations of, himself. For most, this period terminates at the age of 3 or 4; for the immature, it extends well beyond that point.

As the infant grows into early childhood, his interest in himself continues, although in an increasingly diffused way, while interest in others begins to compete. It is during this period that he develops a natural curiosity about the bodies of others, particularly about the bodies of members of the opposite sex. It is during this period also that he becomes understandably curious about where babies come from.

Subsequently, during the period of later childhood or latency, encompassing the years 6 or 7 to 12 or 13, the child's affective interests extend increasingly outward but along a homosexual progression. The boy identifies with male companions, including his father, and the girl identifies in the same homosexual way with her female counterparts. Irrespective of this homosexual phenomenon, however, children of both sexes remain curious about childbirth and become increasingly curious about members of the opposite sex.

With the coming first of puberty, then of adolescence, the normally developing youngster makes the transition from childhood to adulthood, and from homosexuality to heterosexuality. And with the transition, he gropes in all directions for standards to guide his behavior. Culturally he may still be a child, but biologically he is an adult.

This fundamental principle emerges from the previous discussion: namely, that any sound program of sex education has to keep pace with the developmental needs and interests of pupils. The key to the matter is pupil readiness. When pupils are ready to understand, and need to understand, a developmentally appropriate process related to sex, they should have the opportunity, under knowledgeable leadership, to achieve such understanding. Thus a proper explanation of where babies come from becomes a proper consideration for children aged 4 or 5 as well as for those who are older. Instruction of girls on menstrual matters becomes appropriate for 10-, 11-, or 12-year-olds. Instruction of both sexes on bodily sanitation becomes appropriate shortly before the sebaceous glands step up their activity just prior to puberty. And instruction on the topic of pregnancy becomes appropriate at a time when both sexes have matured to a point where this issue is a developmentally germane one.

Sex Education Should Deal with the Emotions as Well as Factual Substance.   Any program of sex education worthy of the title unquestionably needs to make a factual treatment of sex and sexuality. But more than this it likewise must penetrate into the emotions and attitudes of students. The memorization of selected facts is a proper starting point, provided it does not stop there. But the learning of facts reinforced by feelings and attitudes constitutes the ultimate.

Almost all writers concur in this point of view. Baruch states it simply: "In sound Sex Education Feelings come first."[12] Alden and Blanchard make almost the same word-for-word pronouncement.[13] Lawrence Frank embellishes the idea a bit: "We cannot expect to dispose of the child's

[12] Dorothy Baruch, *New Ways in Sex Education* (New York: McGraw-Hill Book Co., 1959) p. xiii.
[13] Carl B. Alden (M.D.) and Jane Blanchard (R.N.) "Experiences in Giving a course in Sex Education," The Journal of School Health, **32** (April 1962), p. 128.

curiosity and concern by purely biological explanations, since, as Otto Rank has pointed out, adults themselves are not satisfied with purely biological answers."[14] Kardiner extends the concept a step further by projecting sex into a framework of broad social relationships, declaring: "You cannot treat sex custom and sex education as a thing apart . . . or educate the sexual drive in isolation.[15] These and other writers concur that factual information is essential. But they likewise conclude that feelings of any individual toward this information, the relationship of this information to broader understandings, and society's attitudes toward it—all comparably demand careful consideration.

Scholarship Is an Essential.   Yet when we conclude that sex education should deal with the emotions as well as the intellect, we do not at all imply that instructional leadership can be devoid of scholarship. Far from it. In fact, a program of sex education may require even greater competency than in other fields in view of the importance of the content to all concerned, in view of its multifarious curriculum facets, and in view of its controversial nature. Several things we are convinced of in this connection. One is that biological understandings are not enough. A second is that kindly interest in the problems of others and a resulting willingness to help are not enough. A third is that marital status and fatherhood or motherhood are not enough. Beyond all these, the qualified instructional leader needs to posses a systematic understanding of the specialized area of sex and to have a sufficient enough background of clinical experience to enable him to relate what he knows to what others need to know, to what others need to feel, and to what others need to understand.

Emphasis Should Rest on the Positive.   A curriculum enriched by this kind of teacher leadership accomplishes its purposes best when depending principally on positive sources for needed motivation rather than on negativeness. The most sought-after outcomes, in this regard, are increased knowledge, improved understandings, and keener affective responses by pupils toward the entire constellation of sex phenomena. These, apart from any other outcomes, are their own excuses for being. These attack the negative by adding to the store of the positive.

In contrast, many programs become so mired in the "don'ts" of sex that the "do's" become obscured. Such programs rely on the fear of consequences to operate against premarital pregnancy, venereal disease, and resulting psychic scars. Our point here is not that the negative aspects of these and related phenomena should be talked down. The point is

[14] Lawrence K. Frank, "The Fundamental Needs of the Child," in *Readings for Educational Psychology*, eds., William A. Fullager, Hal G. Lewis, and Carroll F. Cimbee (New York: Thomas Y. Crowell Company, 1956), p. 131.
[15] Kardiner, "New Attitudes toward Sex," pp. 134–135.

rather that no program can succeed if fear and apprehension are the dominant motivators.

A Value System Is the Ultimate Goal.   This accent on the positive is consistent with our conceptualization of the ultimate in sex education as the development by each participant of his own value system. Actually, this constitutes the ultimate of education in any of its many phases. The framing thesis is that knowledge and understanding that, by necessity, initially reside in authority sources outside the individual will lead ultimately to insights that will find residence and receive justification within the individual.

Self control, standing at the focal center of this sought-after value system, finds vindication in moral, religious, and social explanations. The home usually operates from the combined moral and religious position; the church, from the religious position; and the school, from the combined moral and social position. The logic of the school's position is essentially this. Any significant affective relationship with sex as a base has physical, psychological, and social overtones and implications. It is never single dimensioned. Thus any individual who engages in sexual activity needs to look beyond his physical self to assess the compounded consequences. These latter might find expression in psychic effects on himself, on his sexual partner, or on others; or in social effects on possible offspring and the larger reference group of which he is a part. This approach relates sexual maturing to personal-emotional maturing, and both of these to social maturing. By the greater breadth of this approach, sex escapes isolation and becomes inseparable from social responsibility. Then when the church and the home, if so inclined, translate this approach into the specifically spiritual or moral, the case for self control and delay becomes all the stronger. But the significant consideration here is that the reason for deterrence comes from an internalized rather than from an imposed value system.

The Program Should Seek the Cooperation of Many Agencies and Individuals.   A final tenet on which all programs of sex education should rest is this: results will be only as successful as the program is successful in bringing all interested individuals together into what, by its very nature, has to be a cooperative venture. A more complete discussion of this point will appear in the ensuing section on programming.

Programming for Sex Instruction

Once a school system formulates a body of goals, conceivably including many or all of those described previously, and then postulates the principles on which a program of sex education is to rest, the next step is the formidable one of programming.

Securing Home and Community Support.   As lightly touched on previously in the discussion of controversial issues, wise indeed is the educational group that insures parental and community support before embarking on any ambitious venture into sex education. One sound preliminary step is the formulation of a steering committee of key community representatives to serve as an overall advisory body for the intended program. The recommended sources of membership are mental-health workers, physicians, clergymen, civic leaders, and educational personnel. Leadership, by choice and necessity, would remain in the school, as would professional and legal responsibility, but the council would serve as an important check-and-balance force.

The school's purposes in bringing such a group into existence would be four-fold: (1) to secure and incorporate into the planned program as many new ideas as possible, (2) to assure the attitudinal support of key community individuals and organizations, (3) to "short-stop" possible opposition within the community, and (4) to have council members available as spokesmen when the program needs defense. The council's function would be to advise, promote, and adjudicate. Such a group, being close to the masses, often can sell a program better than can the school alone.

However, no matter how effectively a steering committee performs its important functions, the day-in and day-out support of parents always remains crucial. A school starts in the right direction by eliciting written attendance approvals from the home. But this should be only the beginning of a long-range program of orientation. A rewarding second step, taken by many schools, consists of a written program description sent to the home or an oral description given at a PTA or comparable school gathering. Ultimately, any program of orientation conceivably should culminate in a parents' night at the school at which time the planned program is explained in detail with selected parts presented verbatim to parents. This last step informs and at the same time enlists good will.

The Need for Competent Instruction.   The securing of qualified instructional leadership constitutes a second (not necessarily *the* second) formidable task of any school engaged in programming for sex education. The greatest difficulty in staffing occurs when a sex-education program is diffused throughout a curriculum rather than concentrated specifically in one or more designated areas. The primary and early middle elementary grades are cases in point, as are, although less so, the academic areas of biology and health at the high-school level.

In this connection, we agree with the American Association of School Administrators that all teachers in a curriculum that incorporates the sex issue should have these characteristics: emotional maturity, a balanced attitude, sympathy with and understanding of pupils, good character, poise, and forthrightness.[16] But what are these but characteristics of effective teachers in any curriculum area? An additional requisite is for the teachers under discussion here to understand also those sex concerns which relate uniquely to the developmental needs of the children whom they are teaching. Even though "generalist" teachers cannot be, nor should anyone expect them to be, specialized sexologists, they at least should be relatively more specialized in the developmental areas for which they have primary responsibility.

In the early grades, from kindergarten through grade 5 or 6, the generalist classroom teacher should be as competent in the academic area of sex as he is in other curriculum areas for which mass education makes him responsible. Even beyond grades 5 or 6, when content relating to sex fuses causally into such other curriculum components as health and biology, the regularly assigned teacher should be able to demonstrate specialized competency. However, when a curriculum reaches out to include such particularly specialized topics as petting, masturbation, homosexuality, prostitution, and psychic preparation for marriage, a school needs to take a closer look at where these and related topics specifically should fit into a curriculum and who should "teach" them. Assuming, as we do, that these fit better into a curriculum of the school than into a curriculum of the streets, responsibility for their coverage can be placed only in the hands of highly knowledgeable, sensitive, skillful teachers. And the orientations and approaches of these latter have to be ethical, moral, and social, as well as biological.

For years, when sex education has appeared as a specialized curriculum segment, the vogue has been for schools to delegate responsibility for it to the school physician or school nurse. This practice we regard as an abdication of educational responsibility. First of all, the medical representative selected may know biology and physiology, but he may not necessarily be a behavioral scientist. Furthermore, neither will he customarily be a professionally trained teacher. We suspect middle-class prudishness and habit as the real reasons for this pattern of delegation.

Rejecting such a pattern, we recommend that every school have within the ranks of its own professional teaching staff one or more individuals able to instruct with scholarly proficiency, or to counsel students with clinical effectiveness, on sex problems. The need for such specialized individuals is particularly great at the junior- and the senior-high levels. It is at these levels that the sex problems of pupils usually becomes too critical to be entrusted completely to a generalist.

Our order of staffing preference is as follows: (1) a classroom teacher of an already existing course who is as qualified to deal with all related

[16] American Association of School Administrators, *Health in Schools*, p. 85.

issues of sex as with other issues of the course; (2) a specialist teacher who extends his services throughout a school or school system; (3) a school physician or nurse, or the counterpart from the community, who heads up and implements the program.

Regardless of the exact organizational pattern, the qualified teacher needs to meet the following specifications:

1. Scholarship in the field of sex education, including, but not limited to, factual knowledge and information.

2. Good mental health and sufficient personality integration to have worked out his own sexual problems before attempting to help others with theirs. Such a person invites and respects confidences, is not easily shocked, relates to sex without overemphasis, and removes from it the sham and other artificial trappings that often go with it.

3. Several years of teaching experience to enable him to relate the topic to the more inclusive world of children, the entire school curriculum, parents, and the greater community.

4. Skill as a counselor, as well as a teacher, to make him effective in face-to-face relationships.

Methods of Instruction and Curriculum Context. Once instructors, whether classroom teachers or specialized personnel, have assumed their assigned roles in a program of sex education, they next logically need to engage in those teaching methods that hold forth the promise of greatest success. These should be selected and adapted to a classroom atmosphere where (1) student readiness operates as the key factor, (2) curriculum context is utilized to the fullest, and (3) objectivity of treatment is associated with human warmth and understanding. In such an atmosphere, the following methods, if balanced properly, should enjoy varying degrees of success.

1. *Direct teaching.* One universally employed instructional approach to the diverse issues of sex education is oral explanation. This method unquestionably is effective for purposes of abstract learning. However, by very reason of its abstract nature, it always should be just one member, albeit an important member, of a greater constellation of method. Its particular forte is exposition and description in the presence of the verbally responsive. But, by the same logic, it fails its mission with the verbally inept. It likewise is moderately effective, at best, in relating to the attitudes and emotions of learners. Furthermore, it is generally less effective with younger than with older children.

2. *Textbooks.* A single technique of the direct verbal method is the textbook. And, in this regard, self-styled sexologists have been far more prolific in spawning love treatises to a gullible public than educators have been in writing textbooks on sex for the classroom. In fact, the

latter are scarce commodities at all grade levels. Whether this is necessarily good or bad is debatable. We regard it more as asset than debit,
forcing teachers, as it does, to make use of a wide variety of resource
materials.

3. *Resource materials.*   These latter should consist, as appropriate,
of extensive publications contained in classroom and school libraries, of
models, of films, of film strips, and of pictorials. These broaden the base
of learning by intermingling the informal with the formal, the individual
approach with the group approach, and the concrete visual with the abstract symbolic. It is particularly important for pupils to have ready
access to individual learning materials as an antidote to reticence, which
customarily is a characteristic of more formal classroom situations. For
instance, a student's curiosity about how a baby comes into the world
may be satisfied adequately when he can do free reading on the subject
or view authentic pictures in the privacy of a library. But his curiosity
may become stifled when exposed in a group situation.

4. *Individual conferences.*   There is an ever-present need in any
well-conceived program of sex education for the more strictly academic
to be supplemented by the clinical. The latter should take the form of
one-to-one conferences wherein pupils with problems of a more-or-less
intimate nature are able to discuss them with a knowledgeable and understanding counselor. These conferences should be on a voluntary basis
and should be scheduled in such a way as to protect individual privacy.
Only under such an arrangement will the timorous seek needed help.

5. *Student questionnaires.*   For a program of sex education to become
and remain functional, it should always relate to the needs and interests
of students, as well as to those of the organized society. Accordingly,
early in any program, authority figures should consult students, preferably via a questionnaire, regarding the problems and issues that they
wish to discuss or have discussed. Preferably, this questionnaire should
be unstructured, consisting of such a simple request as: "Please list the
topics pertaining to sex in any of its manifestations that you would like
to face either privately or in a group. Be completely frank. Please turn
this paper in unsigned. Our interest is in the topics themselves, not in
the individuals who list them." Paul Landis and others who have used
this questionnaire technique report a complete frankness of response.
What better basis is there on which to build a program than the expressed preferences of the pupils themselves?

6. *The utilization of plants and animals as a starting base.*   A comfortable and casual transition to the topic of human reproduction is invariably provided by the exposure of pupils, particularly at the elementary-school level, to live plants and animals in the classroom or science

laboratory. The vocabulary and the processes of plant and animal reproduction lead logically and naturally to their counterparts in human reproduction. Such terms as reproduction, genitalia, or homosexuality are less disturbing, even to the relatively inhibited, if pursued along a broad evolutionary sequence.

Curriculum Content. A school that in a program of sex education has taken the necessary steps of orientation, has staffed the program with qualified teaching personnel, and has assayed instructional methods has the remaining task of subject-matter selection. And the criteria that should guide the latter task can never be other than the developmental needs and interests of pupils evaluated against professional norms and against the expectancies of a given social group.

Many topics, as pupils progress through the respective grades, will appear spirally, receiving more thorough and analytical treatment with each new year. Selected of these topics are birth, sex differences, hygiene, social relationships between the sexes, and the processes of elimination. A second group of topics will relate more closely to specific developmental growth levels. Selected of these are menstruation, masturbation, dating habits, and nocturnal emissions. A third group of topics will need to await the social maturity of the later adolescent years. Selected of these are prostitution, pathological sex behavior, the dangers of aphrodisiacs, and the myth of the double-sex standard. Generally speaking, curriculum coverage from the earlier to the later grades will move from the specific concrete to the general abstract; from the simple to the complex; from individual needs, to group needs, and back again to individual needs; and from more normal sex concerns to the more pathologically abnormal concerns.

In this progression, the topic of birth in a kindergarten or early primary-grade setting conceivably would be treated in response to questions such as: "Where do I come from?" The question would receive a simple direct answer which would be kept within the developmentally appropriate confines of the age group. The treatment would be low-keyed, would be couched in a natural context of readiness, and would be factual but casual. Later in the junior and senior-high grades, however, the same topic would be treated in more graphic detail and projected into a broader social and ethical as well as a broader biological context. Hygiene, in similar fashion, would proceed progressively from routine cleanliness, to offending sebaceous glands, to deodorants, to menstruation. Under any circumstances, developmental readiness would dictate not only the nature of the content but the way it should be handled.

We recommend the following topics, by organizational level, to be part of any curriculum on sex education.

A. Kindergarten Through Grade 5 or 6 (Handled More Incidentally Than Directly)
  1. Birth.
  2. Sex differences—physical: body parts and functions.
  3. Avoidance of strangers.
  4. Self concept and self acceptance.
  5. A developing code of moral behavior.
  6. Personal cleanliness; making oneself attractive.
  7. Masturbation (individual treatment as required).
B. Grades 5 or 6 Through Grades 8 or 9 (Handled Both Directly and Incidentally)
  1. Same as I but at a higher level.
  2. Social-sexual growth progression: from self to others, from homosexuality to heterosexuality; from the heterosexual many, to the few, to the ultimate one; acceptance of one's sex role.
  3. Hygiene: sebaceous glands, deodorants.
  4. Menstruation (some group, some separate treatment as needed).
  5. Masturbation (mostly separate).
  6. Nocturnal emissions (some group, some separate treatment as needed).
  7. Drugs and alcohol.
  8. Dating standards.
  9. The need for sexual control.
  10. Correction of misconceptions regarding female fragility, female non-intellectualism, female intuition, male stoicism, and male superiority,
C. Grades 8 or 9 through Grade 12 (Handled Mostly Directly; Sometimes Indirectly)
  1. Same as I and II but at a more sophisticated level.
  2. Mate selection.
  3. Fallacy of the double sex standard.
  4. Marriage and family responsibilities.
  5. Grooming for attractiveness to the opposite sex.
  6. Venereal diseases.
  7. Prostitution.
  8. Homosexuality.
  9. Psychic aspects of love and sex.
  10. Aphrodisiacs.
  11. Pathological sexual behavior.

Not only should the program of sex education which includes these topics be graduated from less to more sophistication and from less to more direction, but it should also progress from more group instruction to more personal counseling as a means of relating to the specific needs of individuals. The hoped-for outcomes would be more extensive and more accurate knowledge, improved understandings, fewer fears and phobias, a sharpened code of social behavior, and generally better personality integration.

Significant References and Other Materials

To support a program such as the one just delineated, a rich variety of references and other supplementary curriculum materials would need to be readily accessible to the administrator, the teacher, the pupil, the parent, or anyone else professionally interested in the program. A rather extensive listing of these resources follows.

Publications

A. For the Teacher and Administrator

1. Generalized Treatments of Sex

American Association of School Administrators, *Health in Schools,* Washington, D.C.: A.A.S.A., 1942, pp. 82–85. This selection establishes sex instruction in a context of total personality and character growth. It emphasizes that knowledge alone is not enough.

Baruch, Dorothy W., *New Ways in Sex Education.* New York: McGraw-Hill Book Company, 1959. Although written for parents, teachers and administrators should read it. *New Ways* conceptualizes sex phenomena in a realistic, simple, matter-of-fact way. Perhaps its best feature is the group of illustrations on pages 236–239; the first series reveals the various stages of fetal growth, and the second shows a baby first emerging from the mother's vagina and then lying next to the mother with the umbilical cord still attached to both.

Bauer, William W., *Your Health Today.* New York: Harper and Brothers, 1955. A conservative approach to health in general and sex understandings in particular.

Bundeson, Herman, *Toward Manhood.* Philadelphia: J. B. Lippincott Company, 1951. A wholesome treatment of sex analyzed developmentally. It contains an excellent glossary of sex terminology and treats forthrightly such topics as nocturnal emissions and masturbation.

Davis, Maxine, *The Sexual Responsibility of Woman.* New York: Permabooks, 1959. Although too sophisticated for high-school students, this outstanding book needs to be read by all professional personnel who are engaged in sex-education activities. It is a frank revelation of woman's role in sex. For prospective brides it is particularly informative.

Ellis, Albert, *Sex Without Guilt.* New York: Hillman Periodicals, Inc., 1958. This book goes far in the direction of sexual permissiveness before marriage. It is a point of view to which, regardless of opinion differences, professional educators should be exposed. We have selected this book as just one of the many which veer toward such permissiveness.

Ellis, Albert and A. Abarbamel (eds.), *Encyclopedia of Sexual Knowledge.* New York: Hawthorn Books, (2 vols.) 1961. This is an all encompassing treatment of almost every imaginable phase of sex. Although, in certain instances, a shocker to the sheltered teacher, it should be a valuable source of hard-to-find sex information for most professional personnel. It is too onesided, however, in its treatment of the bizarre.

Gardner, George E., "Psychiatric Problems in Adolescents," in *Handbook of American Psychiatry,* Vol. 1, Sylvano Ariete, editor. New York: Basic Books, 1959, pp. 870–892. This is at its best when discussing the need for each person to ready himself to accept, and then to play, his destined sex role.

Kinsey, Alfred A., *Sexual Behavior in the Human Female.* Philadelphia: Saunders and Co., 1953. This and the next reference have received enough comment in popular publications to warrant the omission of added comment here.

Kinsey, Alfred A., *Sexual Behavior in the Human Male.* Philadelphia: Saunders and Co., 1948.

Museum of Science and Industry, *The Miracle of Growth.* Champaign, Illinois: University of Illinois Press, 1950. An excellent portrayal of human embryology, richly illustrated.

2. *Treatments Relating to School Programs*

Alden, Carl B., M.D. and Jane Blanchard, R.N., "Experiences in Giving A Course in Sex Education," *The Journal of School Health,* 32 (April 1962), pp. 127–132. A success story—with the authors enthusiastic.

Gannon, F. B., "Sex Education—Why, Where, and How?" *The Bulletin of the National Association of Secondary-School Principals,* 45 (September 1961), pp. 109–111. Gannon thinks the junior-high grades are the best for sex-education purposes.

Gruenberg, Benjamin C., *How Can We Teach About Sex, Public Affairs Pamphlet No. 122.* Public Affairs Committee, 1946. This is still one of the musts even though somewhat dated. It takes the multi-agency approach.

Marland, Sidney P., "Placing Sex Education in the Curriculum" *Phi Delta Kappan,* 43 (December 1961), pp. 132–134. A brief description of sex education in the Winnetka School system.

Maw, Wallace H., "Your School and Sex Education," *Education,* 83 (January 1963), pp. 298–301. Maw writes that schools have taken many diverse approaches to sex education, from silence, to fear, to personal and social development.

Strain, Frances B. and Chester L. Eggert, *Framework for Family-Life-Education: A Survey of Present-Day Activities in Sex Education.* Washington, D.C.: American Association for Health, Physical Education, and Recreation, 1956. This is probably the most comprehensive single treatment of school programs. It is a reprint of a 1955 *Bulletin* of N.A.S.S.P. It furnishes testimonials as well as including programs.

Wetherill, G. G., (M.D.), "Sex Education in the Public Schools," *The Journal of School Health,* 31 (September 1961), pp. 235–239. This article describes San Diego's twenty-three years of experience with sex education. It recommends a multi-agency approach.

In addition to these books and periodical articles, we recommend that interested school personnel contact the following agencies for appropriate pamphlet and other related materials.

(*a*) American Medical Association—the nearest large city office.

(*b*) American Social Hygiene Association, 1790 Broadway, New York 19, New York.

(*c*) Curriculum Laboratories of nearby universities.

(*d*) Departments of Health and Hygiene of state universities and of local and state governmental units.

(*e*) Family counseling service agencies.

(*f*) Family Life Publications, Box 6725, College Station, Durham, North Carolina.

(*g*) Local and state associations for mental health.

B. For the Pupil

De Schweinitz, Karl, Growing Up: *The Story of How We Became Alive, Are Born, and Grow Up,* 2nd. ed., New York: The Macmillan Co., 1947. Excellent supplementary reading for the intermediate or junior-high-school pupil who has a normal, but yet unsatisfied, curiosity about conception, birth, and growth. It could also be a useful textbook.

Duvall, Evelyn R., *Before You Marry.* New York: Association Press, 1949. Best for high-school juniors and seniors. The title is self explanatory.

Duvall, Evelyn R., *The Art of Dating.* New York: Association Press, 1958. A rather gentle treatment of the topic of dating—quite uncontroversial.

Gruenberg, Benjamin C., and Sidone M. Gruenberg, *Wonderful Story of You: Your Body—Your Mind—Your Feelings.* New York: Garden City Books, 1960. See the comment after De Schweinitz above.

Kirkendall, Lester A., *A Reading Study Guide for Students in Marriage and Family Relations.* This is not too sophisticated, we feel, for senior-high students in an elective course.

Levine, Milton J., and Jean S. Seligman, *A Baby Is Born, The Story of How Life Begins.* New York: Simon and Schuster, 1949. See comment after De Schweinitz above.

Louisiana Association for Mental Health, 1528 Jackson Ave., New Orleans 13, La. Send for the set of seven letters to teen-agers, four pages each, entitled, for instance, "Milestones to Maturity," "Love—or "Love?" and "When Are You Ready For Marriage?" We cite these as typical of what the many state and local mental-hygiene agencies are doing for schools and the general public.

Modess Personal Products, Inc., Director of Education, Box SS-A-I Milltown, New Jersey. This company furnishes, at no cost, several excellent pamphlets and films on menstruation, which are geared to fifth grade and older girls who are nearing puberty. Cellucotton products, 919, N. Michigan Ave. Chicago, offers similar services.

Parkhurst, Helen, *Growing Pains*. Doubleday and Company, Inc., 1962. The problem of sex is treated gently in this book. Because of its noncontroversial nature, it would be acceptable to all parents.

Suehsdorf, Adie, (ed.), *What To Tell Your Children About Sex*. New York: Arco Publishing Company, Inc., 1961. Although written primarily for the parent, we recommend its usage as a text in a marriage and family course in the upper high school grades. It is one of the best of the many listed in this section.

Also see 19 in the previous section.

C. For Parents

American Institute of Family Relations, *A Home Study Course In Sex Education for Parents*. Los Angeles: 1956. This provides parents with down-to-earth information of a very practical nature. We recommend it highly for parents of children up to and through the period of adolescence.

American Social Hygiene Association, *Your Child's Questions*, (For parents of children under 6), 1952. Title is self explanatory.

Bauer, William W., *Stop Annoying Your Children*. New York: Bobbs-Merrill, 1947. Contains a plea for more independence for children.

Bolles, Majorie M., *Sex Education for the Ten-Year Old* (Reprinted from Hygeia). New York: American Medical Association, 1953. Title is self explanatory.

Dunbar, Flanders, M.D., *Your Pre-teenager's Mind and Body*. New York: Hawthorn Books, Inc., 1962. Practical, readable, and informative; however it tends to talk down at times.

Dunbar, Flanders, M.D. *Your Teenager's Mind and Body*. New York: Hawthorn Books, Inc., 1962. A companion volume to the one above.

Landis, Paul H., *Understanding Teenagers*. New York: Appleton-Century-Crofts, 1955. A mature, comprehensive treatment.

Landis, Paul H., *Coming of Age: Problems of Teen-agers*. New York: Public Affairs Committee, 1956. A condensed, practical pamphlet, very well done.

New York State Department of Health, *The Gift of Life*, 1951. This little booklet is used by many schools as a parental icebreaker, preceding the opening of a program of sex education in the school. It sets the stage for future home-school relationships.

Sadler, William S., M.D., *A Doctor Talks To Teenagers*. St. Louis: The C. V. Mosby Company, 1948. This separates sexual fact from fiction in a commendatory way. It is written by a practicing psychiatrist.

Suehsdorf, Adie, (ed.), *What To Tell Your Children About Sex*. New York: Arco Publishing Company, Inc., 1961. See comment in Section B.

Wolf, Anna W. M., *Your Child's Emotional Health*. Public Affairs pamphlet No. 264. New York: Public Affairs Committee, 1958. A terse, well written document which treats of sex and other growth topics involving the emotions.

Films and Film Sources, for Varying Levels

Brown, E. C., Trust, Portland, Oregon. "Human Growth," 20 mins., intermed. and up; and "Human Beginnings," 22 mins., intermed. and up.

Churchill Films, 6671 Sunset Blvd., Los Angeles 28, California. "Boy to Man," 16 mins., jr. high.

International Cellucotton Products Co., 919 North Michigan, Chicago, Illinois. Walt Disney, "The Story of Menstruation, circa 20 mins., intermed. and up.

Mental Health Association of Oregon, 229 Park Bldg., Portland, Oregon. "Mental Health of Normal Adolescents," circa, 30 min., sr. high.

Modess Products Inc., Box SS-A-I, Milltown, New Jersey. "Molly Grows Up," circa 15 min., intermed. and up; and 'Confidence Because You Understand Men, circa 25 mins., jr. and sr. high.

University of Illinois, *Health-Physical Education-Sports.* Springfield: Audio Visual Aids Service, various dates. This and similar listings may be secured from most state universities and state departments of health. We recommend that you get on the mailing list. We have extracted from the list several films to indicate the available variety in this one state.

(*a*) "As Boys Grow," 17 mins., sr. high.
(*b*) "Dangerous Stranger (Molesters)," 11 min., intermed. and jr. high.
(*c*) "From Generation to Generation." 30 mins., sr. high.
(*d*) "Human Heredity," 20 mins., jr. high.
(*e*) "Human Reproduction," 22 mins., jr. high.
(*f*) "Name Unknown (Sex Criminals)," 10 mins., jr. high and up.
(*g*) "Human Beginnings," 20 mins., Grade I.
(*h*) "Age of Turmoil (Adolescence)," 20 mins., jr. and sr. high.

Tapes

University of Illinois, *Tapes for Teaching.* Springfield: Audio Visual Aids Service, various dates.

(*a*) "Growth process," 10 mins., intermed., and up.
(*b*) "Puberty—The Gang, the Hero," 15 mins., sr. high.
(*c*) "Sex Education (masturbation)," 15 mins., sr. high.

A Closing Word

Along with others interested in sex education, we realize that the basic and attendant issues cannot and should not be oversimplified. In this regard, as early as 1905, G. Stanley Hall cautioned against anyone's believing that sex understanding can be engendered "by means of flowers and their fertilization, and that mature years will bring insight enough to apply it to all human life."[17] In the same vein, two contemporaries aver that sex education is part of a total life experience of the maturing individual, not a subject to be "taught at some time in his later life."[18]

In one way of thinking, sex instruction may be conceived as lying exclusively within the province of the home. But cannot algebra, social

[17] G. Stanley Hall, *Adolescence* (New York: Appleton and Co., 1905), p. 469.
[18] Phyllis and Eberhard Kronhausen, "Sex Education More Avoided Than Neglected," (*Op. Cit.*), p. 323.

studies, and literature be similarly conceived? Obviously they can. However, all of these, including the topic of sex, logically come under the province of the school when it is accepted that: (1) the school can hire teachers, who, on the average, are better trained to do the job than are parents; (2) the school cannot logically exclude anything as basic as sex education from its overall responsibility for general education; and (3) the school with its social setting can better face the issues of sex education than can parents in a more individualized setting. Therefore, with Gannon, we regard it to be "the duty and obligation of the public schools to see that today's youth are not tomorrow's guilt laden adults."[19] But such a viewpoint commits education to do more in the future than it has done in the past about its curriculum responsibilities for sex education. The pressing need now is for better prepared teachers; for a greater availability of quality textbooks; for more supplementary references and audio-visual aids which conform to high standards; and for better orientation programs involving the home, the school, and other appropriate agencies.

With the society challenging education, the latter needs to meet the challenge with aplomb, conviction, and a well thought-out program.

For Further Thought

1. Do the school, the home, and the church have a commonly shared responsibility for sex education, or does each have a unique responsibility for some specific phase? Elaborate your stand.

2. How far should any single one, or all together, go in revealing the "facts of life" to the uninitiated? Should pictures, or statutes, or nudes be deliberately displayed? Should the sex organs of the male and female human being be frankly studied via models and films or filmstrips? Should coitus be a topic of discussion? Defend your stand.

3. Support the pro or con of: "A too frank extension of sex information will lead to promiscuity."

4. Answer each of the following, *true* or *false*, and explain the reason(s) for your choice.

(a) Sexual curiosity by children as young as 5 or 6 is abnormal.

(b) States should pass laws making sex education compulsory.

(c) Such practices as masturbation and homosexuality are too sordid to be part of a school's curriculum.

(d) Schools probably have to concede to the wishes of parents who object to their children's involvement in a sex-education program.

5. On what grounds would you justify the delay of sex intercourse prior to marriage?

[19] Gannon, F. B., "Sex Education—Why, Where and How," *The Bulletin of the National Association of Secondary-School Principals*, 45 (September 1961), p. 109.

chapter 12

Juvenile Delinquency, Society, and the Schools

A third social problem is juvenile delinquency and education's responsibility toward it. Delinquency is as old as man himself. It is a phenomenon which, in one form or another, every known society has had to contend with and resolve in some way. Cain in the Old Testament may well have been a juvenile delinquent before becoming an adult fratricide. And The Prodigal Son in the New Testament comparably may have been an early-adolescent menace before becoming a late-adolescent rake.

Throughout the ages, a few or many of every generation have viewed delinquency almost exclusively as a concern of law, very little as a concern of education. As a result of this narrowness, interest has remained focused more on law breaking, on legal ajudicating, on retaliatory recompence, and on the society's need for protection than on the delinquent himself. In fact, he, as often as not, has been more a stereotype or statistic than a human being in difficulty.

Others throughout the ages, whose numbers are growing with each new generation, have looked beyond symptoms and legalism to the delinquent as a person; likewise to the pathological conditions of his society which might have been responsible for the unsocial behavior in the first place. Viewing delinquency this divergently, they understandably have expected not one but many agencies—the home, the church, education, and neighborhood organizations, as well as the law—to attack the menace of deliquency across a broad front.[1]

[1] Starke R. Hathaway and Elio D. Monachesi, (eds.), *Analyzing and Predicting Juvenile Delinquency with the MMPI* (Minneapolis: University of Minnesota Press, 1953), p. 8.

The goals of this second group are more the understanding of offenders than the punishment of offenses, more the prevention of law breaking than its detection after the fact. And despite occasional differences, they agree on this one fundamental tenet: the delinquent is a troubled person who, for reasons outside as well as inside himself, has been unable to adapt to his social surroundings. He is more a personal and social misfit than he is a legal offender.

In the coming year, the police will apprehend over one million juveniles for offenses that range from speeding in automobiles to a hit-and-run accident, from assault to homicide, from molestation to rape, from inebriation to narcotics addiction, and from minor thievery to grand larceny. And this estimate of one million, which was made by the then Attorney General, Herbert Brownell, in 1953,[2] is undoubtedly an underestimate for today's greater population. Of all those apprehended, approximately 100,000 will be jailed and 40,000 will be committed to training schools.[3] The ratio of boys to girls, in most of these totals, will be 4 to 1.[4]

It is because of the vast misery-dealing propensities of delinquency, because of society's general lassitude toward it, and because of its need to be attacked early and often, that education should lead in the assault on it. Delinquency thus constitutes a logical inclusion for a curriculum book of this type.

Definitions of Juvenile Delinquency

To aid in establishing structure, which a topic as amorphous as juvenile delinquency badly needs, we invite attention to the following definitions.

1. *The legal base:* "A child is to be regarded as technically a delinquent when his antisocial tendencies appear so grave that he becomes, or ought to become, the subject of official action."[5]

(or)

A child is delinquent if "presumptively [he] has been guilty of offenses considered severe enough by law enforcement agencies to justify placing his name on the public records."[6]

---

[2] Benjamin Fine, *1,000,000 Delinquents* (Cleveland: The World Publishing Company, 1955), Foreward.

[3] Frank J. Cohen (ed.), *Youth And Crime* (New York: International Universities Press, Inc., 1957), p. xi.

[4] Joseph W. Eaton and Kenneth Polk, *Measuring Delinquency* (Pittsburgh: University of Pittsburgh Press, 1961), p. 19.

[5] Cyril Burt, *The Young Delinquent,* 4th Ed. (London: University of London Press, 1944), p. 17.

[6] Hathaway and Monachesi, *Analyzing and Predicting Juvenile Delinquency with the MMPI,* p. 7.

2. *The social base:* Delinquency represents "a way of life that has somehow become traditional among certain groups."[7]

3. *The dynamic base:* "Delinquency is . . . a dynamic expression; it can be attributed to the interplay of psychic forces which have created the distortion which we call dissocial behavior."[8]

(or)

Delinquency is maladaptive behavior representing "an emotional and conduct pattern that is often deeply anchored."[9]

4. *The age base:* "Juvenile delinquency constitutes any act which, if committed by an adult, would be a crime."[10]

These along with other definitions of juvenile delinquency share the common element of a law having been broken or of behavior having been engaged in which deviates from the beaten path of social propriety. The definitions differ, however, in their implications concerning, or in their explanations of, the causes of the maladaptive behavior. And most of the definitions skirt, completely or in part, the issue of how young or how old an individual has to be to hold title to the descriptive term juvenile. This vagueness is understandable in view of the fact that in some communities (or states) the top juvenile age is 14, in others 16, and in a few as high as 18. In this same general connection, an offense committed in most communities by a youngster not yet 12 or 13 is laid to the neglect of his parents. The same offense committed by an older adolescent usually results in the finger of legal and moral blame being pointed more at the culprit himself than at his parents.

Explanations of Delinquency

As already implied, society is far from reaching consensus on why children and youth become delinquent and what society should do about them once they have earned the label. Consensus is nonexistent because different groups approach delinquent behavior from diverse and often contradictory value positions. Four such are the religious orthodox, the sociological, the dynamic, and the eclectic.

The Religious Orthodox Position.   Built into Christian orthodoxy from its inception have been the following postulates: man is conceived in iniquity; he remains a sinner until he seeks and gains forgiveness;

[7] Albert K. Cohen, *Delinquent Boys* (Glencoe, Illinois: The Free Press, 1955), p. 13.
[8] August Aichhorn, *Wayward Youth* (New York: The Viking Press, 1936), p. 38.
[9] Sheldon and Eleanor Glueck, *Unraveling Juvenile Delinquency* (New York: The Commonwealth Fund, 1950), p. 4.
[10] Benjamin Fine, *1,000,000 Delinquents*, p. 31.

he has the free will to choose between right and wrong; thus when he sins, because he has chosen to do so deliberately, he justly deserves punishment. This position when analyzed from other than a religious setting is vulnerable on these grounds. (a) It de-emphasizes determinism, both genetic and environmental, assuming apparently that a psychotic has as much free will as does a mentally healthy person. (b) It focuses more on symptoms than on causes, assessing punishment usually in terms of the act rather than the "actor." (c) It stakes its case for correction more often on the physical than the psychological. And (d) it casts an aura of self-righteousness around nonoffenders, which conceivably may be as injurious to their personalities as are many of the so-called corrective measures applied to the offending culprits.

Anyone who subscribes to this orientation usually views himself as dedicated to seek out evil and to see that it is punished. The delinquent, in the process, tends to get lost somewhere between the crossfires of abstract goodness and badness. Furthermore, because of the stigma that most societies associate with arrests, court trials, houses of correction, jails, and juvenile authorities, once a juvenile is apprehended, guilt and resentment rather than true repentance tend to dominate his emotions, making his rehabilitation difficult, if not actually impossible.

As a counter to the falsity of this position, a social effort is mounting to rescue delinquency from the climate of sin, symptoms, and unnecessary sentencing. Some of the more charitable and optimistic start, as does Benjamin Fine, with the assumption that "There is no such thing as a 'born' bad boy. Every boy is born with equipment to be good."[11] Such individuals regard the delinquent more as troubled than as troubling, and more as a young person with problems than as a problem young person. This position made a mid-western juvenile court judge, at least so he averred, learn a new language—"social workese." Because sympathetic with the new attitudinal approach, he felt at liberty to quip about it. Said he, he had to learn to "make contact with," not arrest; "evaluate his problem, not have a hearing; . . . [and] interpret his need for protection from himself, not put him in jail."[12]

Needless to say, exponents of the newer approach have to guard against surface sentimentalism to escape attack by ultraconservatives.

The Sociological Position. The sociological position constitutes one of several orientations which views the etiology of delinquency as residing in conditions outside the individual himself. This particular position has roots in ecological determinism, holding that certain urban phe-

---

[11] *Ibid.*, p. 133.
[12] George Edwards, "Meeting the Challenge of a Juvenile Code," in Mathew Matlin (ed.) *1953 Yearbook of the National Probation and Parole Association* (New York: N.P.P.A., 1954), p. 96.

nomena make delinquency almost inevitable. It purports to discover in the evolution of a city a tendency for industry and commerce to invade residential living areas, ultimately leading to slum living and a so-called interstice of unsupervised space where law breaking becomes almost a routine. Shaw and McKay, for years, have held to this point of view, seeing justification for it in the fact that in large cities "the rates of delinquents have remained relatively constant in the areas adjacent to centers of commerce and heavy industry, despite successive changes in the nativity and nationality composition of the population." From such evidence, they conclude that "delinquency-producing factors are inherent in the community," not in the person.[13]

Inherent in the sociological position is the culture-conflict postulate that conceives the causes of misbehavior as residing in a conflict between two value systems: one of an underprivileged culture and the other of a middleclass dominant culture.

Two irreconcilable ways of life, so the theory goes, exist side by side with submarginal social groups expected to meet, but unable to meet, the standards of the controlling middle class. This state of affairs not only leads to misunderstanding, frustration, and conflict in any given generation but tends to transmit itself to each succeeding generation.

Irrespective of the sociological position itself, value differences between the two cultural levels are essentially as indicated in the following contrast.

Characteristics of the Typical Subculture	Characteristics of the Middle-Class Culture
1. Lives more for the moment than for the future; practices short-term hedonism true to the tradition of the pleasure principle.	1. Lives for the moment but plans for the future; is true to the traditions of the reality principle in terms of vocational, educational, and moral outcomes.
2. Is materialistic and, as indicated in 1 above, grasps for and finds satisfaction in the material substance of the immediate.	2. Is also materialistic, but is willing, if necessary, to sacrifice today's for tomorrow's materialistic outcomes.
3. Upward mobility, because long range, loses to the status quo of the immediate.	3. Upward mobility constitutes an accepted avenue of progress.
4. Resistance to law, other constituted authority, and associated authority figures constitutes a way of life.	4. Law, other constituted authority, and associated authority figures exist to be respected.

[13] Clifford R. Shaw and Henry D. McKay, *Juvenile Delinquency and Urban Areas* (Chicago: University of Chicago Press, 1942), p. 435.

Characteristics of the Typical Subculture	Characteristics of the Middle-Class Culture
5. Violence and force are acceptable means of achieving material goals.	5. Lawful effort is the approved medium of achieving material goals, but humanism as a value often loses to inhumane competition in the market place.
6. Education is not of vital importance. Accent instead is on cleverness and smartness.	6. Education is a major cultural value. Accent is on knowledge and understanding.
7. Homes for the most part are rented; property care and maintenance have low-priority status.	7. Home ownership is common; property care and maintenance have high-priority status.
8. Monogamy has relatively low value.	8. Monogamy constitutes a fundamental value.
9. Children achieve independence early, shifting for themselves often from childhood.	9. Children remain (are kept) dependent until well into adolescence, or beyond.
10. The female parent is usually dominant, providing the major family stability.	10. Parents of both sexes contribute more-or-less equally to family stability.

The foregoing value differences force submarginal groups into one of these three action alternatives: genuine acceptance of and adaptation to middle-class values; a facade of adaptation characterized by secretive circumvention; or open rebellion. When submarginal groups elect either of the latter two alternatives, they defend their actions, consciously or unconsciously, with a Robin Hood kind of logic. The *haves*, so their reasoning goes, are not any more deserving than we, the *have nots*; therefore, we have a moral and ethical right to repossess what is rightfully ours, even by force if necessary.

At times, the economic motive for asocial behavior becomes submerged in such dynamically related personality considerations as lack of status, inferiority feelings which result therefrom, and other ego-deflating influences. When these become dominant, reason effortlessly eases into projection, and projection into aggression. The resulting posture of defiance sometimes manifests itself in stealing for the sake of stealing, in vandalism, or in bodily harm to an outsider who unfortunately just happens to be close. In this acting-out process, aggression serves as the unconscious badge of masculinity. The male actor, as described in one source, swaggers, pillages, fights, and never "chickens out,"[14] engaging in actions, which, in the words of another source, are "nonutilitarian,

[14] Richard A. Cloward and Lloyd E. Ohlin, *Delinquency and Opportunity* (Glencoe, Illinois: The Free Press, 1961), p. 24.

malicious, and negativistic."[15] And the identity of the external objects of the aggression is completely lost sight of in the detachment of the actor's own emotions.

Some possible loopholes in the sociological position are these. (a) If interstitial areas breed delinquency, why do they breed selectivity, attracting most often only one of many siblings in a family, or only two or three individuals in a given neighborhood? If temptations are built into a culture, why are not all persons affected similarly by them? (b) Second, the position is urban-centered, thus failing to account for delinquency in nonurban locales. (c) Third, the position when carried to an extreme makes the individual a mechanistic victim of social forces, voiding free-will choice almost completely in the process.

The Dynamic Position.   A third position, the dynamic, has the individual person as its focus. Advocates of this position, although cognizant of the debilitating effects of an unfavorable social environment, postulate that persons can rise above the latter by coming to grips with their twisted emotions.[16] The key to such change is self-understanding. Descriptive terms and processes that characterize this third orientation are: the conscious and the unconscious minds, transference, ventilation of the emotions, self-acceptance, and altruism.

The fundamental postulate of the dynamic position is that social offenders basically are disturbed personalities, most of whom can be re-educated. The shortcomings of this position when applied to the complex problems of delinquency are these. (a) Depth therapy is a laborious process and thus too time consuming to reach other than a few of the needy many. (b) It is also too costly to reach other than a few of the many. (c) Therapists are in short supply, particularly those qualified to work with, and interested in working with, a clientele of delinquents. (d) Delinquents have to want help before they can be helped. (e) Therapy is usually available, if at all, only from middle-class professional persons—whom the sub-marginal delinquent can relate to, if at all, only with difficulty. And (f) when environmental change is indicated, the therapist needs assistance from the greater social order to supply the resources and pay the bills. This assistance rarely is available in sufficient quantity.

The Eclectic Position.   Selected theoreticians and practitioners who see merit in each of the sociological and dynamic positions but who view neither as adequate in itself combine the best features of both into an eclectic position. In this way, they are able to operate from a base

[15] Albert K. Cohen, *Youth and Crime*, p. 26.
[16] The following are two of the better book-length treatments of the dynamic position: *Wayward Youth* by August Aichhorn; and *The Psychoanalytical Approach to Juvenile Delinquency* by Kate Friedlander.

broad enough to encompass problems that are ecological without avoiding problems that are more specifically individual. This composite position is the one taken by the Gluecks, by Healy and Bronner, by Kvaraceus, and by Albert Cohen, to name just a few. The Gluecks sum up the case this way: "Anyone desiring to make more than a superficial study of the causes of human maladjustment must soon realize that there is no single divining rod and no simple path . . ."[17]

I subscribe to this eclectic position because breadth, flexibility and unity are its identifying characteristics. Not fragmenting either the society or the person, the eclectic position views both as an interlocking composite of influences and vectors. From this vantage point, the psychodynamist, in the words of Kvaraceus and Ulrich, cannot disregard "the generic aspects of delinquent behavior."[18] But neither can the sociologist disregard the dynamics of the person. The implications here for university training programs are clear. Medicine and psychology cannot continue to shortchange the social; and sociology may have to step up its emphasis on the psychological. Education should move more sure-footedly along both dimensions.

The eclectic position we view as resting on the following basic tenets:

1. A child at inception does not select his parents or his community.

2. Regardless of who his parents are or what his community is like, he, if normal, bears differing degrees of responsibility for his behavior.

3. Certain social classes have been more successful than others in giving needed love and affection to children and youth.

4. The child or young person who does not receive familial affection in sufficient quantity may develop personality characteristics that will lead to so-called juvenile delinquency—and later, conceivably, to adult crime.

5. The seriously deprived individual may need two kinds of help: (a) he may require therapeutic services; and (b) his living environment may need to undergo change.

6. While individuals are being helped after the fact of delinquency, society must engage in a relentless effort at delinquency prevention by providing troubled youth with: adequate housing, a balanced diet, decent sanitation, needed medical and dental services, recreational facilities, a nonjudgmental understanding of their serious psychological problems, and help in overcoming these problems.

For those who regard this position as too idealistic, the reason may be that the society for too long has been settling for too little. Humanism

---

[17] Sheldon and Eleanor Glueck, *Unraveling Juvenile Delinquency*, p. xi.
[18] William C. Kvaraceus and William E. Ulrich, *Delinquent Behavior: Principles and Practices* (Washington, D.C.: National Education Association, 1959), p. 19.

is the dominant characteristic of the American way of life, and these principles are definitely humanistic. The logical sequel, then, is for the society to take what it accepts as its theoretical ideal and convert it into a practical way of life. The eclectic position with its open-ended approach to people and communities presages hope for such a metamorphosis.

Correlates of Juvenile Delinquency

The logical approach to the study of juvenile delinquency ideally would be through its etiology—provided the latter were readily identifiable. With the etiology uncertain and elusive, however, the preferable approach is through those phenomena which go hand in hand with, but which are not necessarily causes of, delinquency. These phenomena, which bear the label of correlates, constitute the theme of this present section.

Correlates within the individual. First we look at the delinquents themselves for characteristics which seem to appear more frequently in them than in their nondelinquent opposites.

The Ego. One of the most noteworthy of these characteristics has to do with the delinquent's ego which, when exposed and analyzed, predictably reveals a narcissistic pattern. Emotional growth for the mentally healthy, while starting inevitably with the self, moves progressively toward an ever-expanding world of others. The end result is altruism which, admittedly, some achieve more completely than do others. Emotional growth for the pathological delinquent, although also moving toward others, usually stops with a small off-beat group of associates whose role, as conceived by the delinquent, is to serve his narrow ego needs. The social end result for the delinquent is never altruism. He relates to his small in-group in order that its members, in turn, will relate reciprocally to him. This constitutes self-centeredness, not altruism. It is the way of the neurotic, not of the well adjusted.

The Superego Dimension. To the degree that a delinquent is one-sidedly preoccupied with himself, he remains that much less susceptible to superego influences and broad cultural values. At a more general level, to the degree that any individual, by reason of a faulty human environment, fails to develop a wholesome value system, the more self-centered and delinquent-prone he is likely to remain. Environmental contributors to this negative outcome are material deprivation, psychological rejection, and a social order which remains calloused over both conditions.

Physical Correlates. Physical similarities between delinquents and nondelinquents are more the rule than the exception. Selected investigators, however, identify a few distinguishing characteristics. The

Gluecks, for example, although admitting their evidence to be inconclusive, suggest that delinquents are somewhat larger than their counterparts.[19] They and a second source[20] also report a higher incidence of neurological disorders, such as acne and tics, in delinquents than in their control opposites.

Intelligence. Until recently, many took it for granted that delinquency was almost the exclusive property of illiterates and mental retardates. Current research, however, tends to discredit the myth, usually revealing only a low-order correlation between delinquency and low intelligence.[21, 22] And one noteworthy study, although several decades old, reports a near zero correlation between the two factors. Eleven per cent of the sample of delinquents had IQ's of 110 or higher; only 9 per cent had IQ's of 80 or lower.[23]

Behavior Correlates. Delinquent juveniles in the composite characteristically engage in such socially unapproved acts as the following: drinking intoxicating beverages, smoking marihuana, commiting arson, thieving, absenting themselves periodically from home and school, frequenting pool halls, sneaking into places of amusement, and associating with unsavory older characters.[24] All of these share a common element of hostility to social convention and constituted authority. All likewise reveal the delinquent's inability to develop a set of acceptable social values, as well as the failure of his primary reference group to give him needed help in the process.

In recreation, the delinquents of one study appeared as more adventuresome but less competitive than their non-delinquent counterparts. Comparative percentages for hanging around street corners were 95.2 and 58.4; for remaining in their neighborhoods for recreation, 13.2 and 85.8; for gang membership, 56.0 and 0.6; for some leisure time voluntarily spent at home, 41.6 and 93.2; for inhabiting playgrounds 29.4 and 61.0; and for frequenting pool halls and other similarly frowned-on amusement places, 15.2 and 0.8 respectively.[25]

Correlates in School Performance. As individuals, juvenile delinquents vary greatly in their behavior and performance in school, but

---

[19] Sheldon and Eleanor Glueck, *Unraveling Juvenile Delinquency*, pp. 181–196.
[20] William McCord, Joan McCord, and Irving Zola, *Origins of Crime, A New Evaluation of the Cambridge-Somerville Youth Study* (New York: Columbia University Press, 1959), p. 167.
[21] Clara C. Cooper, *A Comparative Study of Delinquents and Non-Delinquents* (Portsmouth, Ohio: The psychological Service Center Press, 1960), p. 201.
[22] George B. Vold, *Theoretical Criminology* (New York: Oxford University Press, 1958), Chapter V.
[23] William Healy and Augusta F. Bronner, *New Lights On Delinquency And Its Treatment* (New Haven: Yale University Press, 1936), p. 52.
[24] Sheldon and Eleanor Glueck, *Unraveling Juvenile Delinquency*, p. 107.
[25] *Ibid.*, pp. 156–163.

collectively they form a reasonably predictable composite. Generally speaking, they do not adapt to a curriculum that depends solely on delayed benefits. Attuned essentially to the here and now, the delinquent reacts antagonistically or apathetically to content designed to ready him for future dividends that he thinks may never come. When compared with others, juvenile delinquents customarily get lower grades or fail more frequently, drop out of school earlier and in greater numbers, are less verbal, read at slower rates, do less well in arithmetic, move from school to school more often, and do better, relatively speaking, in a curriculum of the manual arts.[26] With schools notoriously passive, verbally oriented, and adult dominated, the delinquent who is just as notoriously active, nonverbally oriented, and resistant to adult domination predictably confronts education with a paradox. This topic will be developed later in the chapter.

Correlates in the Family. The family is a third, and highly important, source of possible clues to juvenile delinquency. Constituting as it does the primary reference group, it casts its influence on the child in ways too legion to mention. From birth through childhood for most, and from birth into adulthood for some, the young look to the family: for the physical necessities of life, for warmth and affection, and for value standards to live by. More than anything else, the family exists as the breeding ground for human relationships. Generally speaking, when these latter develop in a satisfactory way, delinquency characteristics do not come to light. It is when human relationships develop distortedly, however, that delinquency characteristics appear and often become pathological.

The question of causality rears its head once more at this point. In Healy and Bronner's sample of 153 delinquents, for instance, 91 per cent were reported as having "emotional-provoking relationships with others in the family."[27] But who knows whether 91 per cent of nondelinquents do not comparably have emotionally provoking relationships with others in the family.

Irrespective of this possibility, however, the family's contribution to the evolving value system of the growing child must be regarded as its most noteworthy function. When it fails this part of its mission, the superego of the child may well be the loser. Apropos here, although not conclusive, are selected research findings on the topic. Half of Eaton and Polk's sample of delinquents, for example, "came from homes broken by death or marital discord."[28] Weeks uncovered conflicting results, with the broken home factor significantly related to truancy and ungoverna-

---

[26] *Ibid.*, p. 153.
[27] Healy and Bronner, *New Lights on Delinquency and its Treatment*, p. 203.
[28] Eaton and Polk, *Measuring Delinquency*, p. 37.

bility, but only randomly related to property offenses and traffic violations.[29] However, some homes can be as much broken by internal friction as others can be by physical separation of the parents.[30]

Research customarily describes the "good home" as one in which the father and mother are warm, reasonably firm, and consistent.[31] Inadequacy in the male parent usually elicits such unflattering adjectives as transient, abusive, neglecting, inconsistent, erratic, and unaffectionate; in the female parent, such equally unflattering adjectives as passive, erratic, lax, inconsistent, and unloving. The male parent of both delinquents and nondelinquents arouses more antagonism than does his distaff counterpart, but the difference is more pronounced among delinquents.[32] Apparently, delinquents have more trouble resolving the Oedipal conflict than do nondelinquents.

Limited economic means, as another family characteristic, distinguishes the homes of delinquents. Kvaraceus categorically identifies this bond of poverty as the one which his sample most shared in common.[33]

In the Gluecks' sample, about half dwelt in "blighted tenement areas," and 65 to 70 per cent in "blighted or decaying tenement areas."[34] More were dependent on relief, and the families had fewer breadwinners.[35] Once more, however, we advise against any hasty conclusion about a cause-and-effect relationship here. It is highly possible that instead of poverty causing delinquency, some third factor or some composite underlying set of factors was responsible for both outcomes. Also, it is to be remembered that the vast majority of the poor do not become delinquent.

Two edditional characteristics of family life bear on delinquency: church attendance as one, has a significant inverse relationship; and education of parents, as the second, has a slight inverse relationship.[36]

Gang Membership.   As may be gleaned from one item in the preceding section, gang membership and gang participation are positively related to delinquency. As early as 1927, Frederic Thrasher made a study of 1313 gangs in Chicago, commenting that many more gangs existed

---

[29] H. Ashley Weeks, "Male and Female Broken-Home Roles by Type of Delinquency," *American Sociological Review*, 5 (August 1940), pp. 601–609.
[30] Benjamin Fine, *1,000,000 Delinquents*, p. 75.
[31] Maud A. Merrill, *Problems of Child Delinquency* (Boston: Houghton-Mifflin Company, 1947), pp. 72–73.
[32] *Ibid.*, pp. 27–28.
[33] William C. Kvaraceus, *Juvenile Delinquency and The School* (New York: World Book Co., 1945), p. 98.
[34] Sheldon and Eleanor Glueck, *Unraveling Juvenile Delinquency*, pp. 79–80.
[35] *Ibid.*, pp. 84–91.
[36] William and Joan McCord, and Irving K. Zola, *Origins of Crime*, p. 168.

that he hadn't studied. "Gangland," he says, "is a phenomenon of human ecology. As better residential districts recede before the encroachments of business and industry, the gang develops as one manifestation of the economic, moral, and cultural frontier which marks the interstice."[37] This is the sociologist speaking. The dynamicist would describe the gang as a substitute family with which an individual identifies and from which he receives psychological feed back. With gang members, he achieves fulfillment that most realize through the more normal channels of the family reference group.

Attitudes regarding the dynamic properties of gangs, like the descriptions of the gangs themselves, differ among writers and observers. For example, Thrasher regards them as mobile, engaging in predatory practices first here, then there. Block and Neiderhoffer, in contrast, view any single one as a fixed feature of a given neighborhood.[38] These same co-authors envision gang life as a "struggle for survival in a hostile world" of parents and peers—in fact of any and all antagonistic figures.[39] Albert Cohen, on the other hand, conceives gang life as a rebellion of the lower classes against the middle class.[40]

Although gangs differ somewhat in specific purposes, in the age of their members, and in their practices, there are a few features that most gangs, particularly the more sophisticated adolescent ones, have in common.

1. They are primarily masculine. As indicated by Cohen and others, girls rarely form gangs.[41] The activities, as well as the membership, of gangs are also basically masculine with aggressiveness, rebellion, and violence characteristic.

2. Ultimate authority resides in the gang itself. Thus the desires and dictums of gang-leadership usually take priority over the desires and dictums of parents, teachers, police, and other legitimate authority figures.

3. Toughness must be demonstrated. Even initiation into gang membership not infrequently demands acts of violence, such as theft or assault.

4. Incarceration by the law, if unpreventable and in conformity with gang-sanctioned standards, affords status.

5. Soft and gullible adults are held in contempt.

[37] Frederic M. Thrasher, *The Gang* (Chicago: The University of Chicago Press, 1927), p. 23.
[38] Herbert A. Block, and Arthur Neiderhoffer, *The Gang, A Study in Adolescent Behavior* (New York: Philosophical Library, 1958), p. 6.
[39] *Ibid.*, p. 176.
[40] Albert Cohen, *Youth and Crime*, p. 28.
[41] *Ibid.*, p. 47.

6. Sexual promiscuity is characteristic, with gang shagging (sexual intercourse of many gang members with one "bad" girl) often an approved practice.

7. The "good girls," however, are exempt from violence. A rule of the gang is for each member to respect another's prior rights with a female associate of virtue.[42]

In a sense, the well organized gang provides its own culture including human companionship, solidarity, rules, mores, and psychological sustenance of diverse kinds. As stated by Thrasher, "The gang, in short, is *life,* often rough and untamed, yet rich in elemental social processes significant to the student of society and human nature."[43]

Prevalent Countermeasures to Delinquency

To this point, we have painted a picture of juvenile delinquency that admittedly is stark and unpleasant. Its ugliness stands as a blight both on the affected individuals themselves and on the society whose preventive efforts most often are minimal and unimaginative. And if the efforts to prevent are inadequate, those to correct are equally so.

Society's most commonly practiced countermeasures are as follows: The first step customarily is apprehension by the police authority. Subsequent action, in instances of minor offenses committed by individuals with relatively clean records, consists of a didactic lecture followed by dismissal. In instances of repeated minor offenses or of major offenses, action consists of one of the following: incarceration of the offender in a public institution for juveniles, commitment of the offender to a foster home, or probation with certain accompanying demands made of the offender.

The effectiveness of none of these can be assayed apart from the etiology of the offenses in the first place and the desired ends of the social authority in the second place. Any method of correction is usually only as successful as is the ability of authority figures at any time to peer beneath symptoms into the pathology of an individual or of a neighborhood. If the goal is true personality change, corrective action needs always to include either some type of therapy for the offending person or social change within the environment.

The outcomes of corrective methods currently being employed elicit little optimism from knowledgeable observers. Hassler, once a jailed pacifist, cryptically states that attitudes "are not changed easily by coercive measures applied by the majority group."[44]

[42] See Block and Niederhoffer, *The Gang,* pp. 104 and 163–169 for a more elaborate treatment of gang practices.
[43] Frederic M. Thrasher, *The Gang,* p. 3.
[44] See Alfred Hassler, *The Diary of a Self-Made Convict* (Chicago: The Regnery Press, 1954).

Healy and Bronner assert just as feelingly "that processes of dealing with the delinquent by admonition, threat, compulsion, or punishment are almost bound . . . to be failures because such treatment is repressive in character rather than reconstructive."[45]

The McCords and Zola, in a review of incidental outpatient counseling of probationed delinquents, mostly juvenile, report a failure. They hold out hope, however, for intensive counseling practices. They also caustically aver that "Incarceration in reform school is about as effective in curing delinquency as is whipping a stubborn donkey to make him carry a load."[46]

Edwards, a judge, scoffs at the eulogizing of detention homes which, he says, are notoriously inadequate in facilities, and which are staffed with personnel who usually get paid $1000 per year less than do jailers.[47]

Herbert and Jarvis also express doubt over the effectiveness of current corrective practices, commenting editorially that: "The old fashioned didactic enunciation of moral precepts has been found insufficient in many ways, but there is varied opinion and some hesitation as to what is to take its place."[48]

And finally, Kvaraceus serves notice that the day of the birch rod is over and that scolding "has diminished in importance . . . Replacing them is reliance upon clinical services in the fields of psychology and psychiatry to explain why children misbehave."[49]

Needed Remediation and Prevention

From society's mounting dissatisfaction over the unprofessional and haphazard ways in which juvenile delinquents are being handled, opinion regarding proper remediation and prevention is beginning to solidify. Lying at its heart is the conviction, as indicated in the last section, that such after-the-fact methods as incarcerating, moralizing, and threatening neither remediate nor prevent. Removing a culprit from society may protect others, but it does little for the offender.

If dealing with symptoms is not the answer, treating causes must be. But the society recoils, and understandably so, from the magnitude of the problems that this point of view poses. Many of these problems are social: for instance, slums in urban areas, poverty in Southern bayous, and squalor of unbelievable proportions in the "Other America" of the

[45] Healy and Bronner, *New Lights on Delinquency*, p. 205.
[46] William and Joan McCord, and Irving K. Zola, *Origins of Crime*, p. 178.
[47] George Edwards, in Matlin, *1953 Yearbook of the National Probation and Parole Association*, p. 97.
[48] W. L. Herbert and F. V. Jarvis, *Dealing With Delinquents* (London: Methuen and Co., Ltd., 1961), p. 17.
[49] Kvaraceus, *Juvenile Delinquency and the School*, p. 3.

Appalachians. Yet, to the extent that juvenile or adult delinquency has a social basis, the cure needs to have a comparable basis.

The society just as understandably recoils from the magnitude of the task of providing extensive psychotherapy for those in need. As noted earlier in the chapter, psychotherapy is a slow process, it is an expensive process, and qualified therapists to administer it are in short supply. Juvenile authorities, at the moment, are trying to hurdle these obstacles by spreading counseling services superficially among the many. But the results of this forced compromise have been unsatisfactory, as attested to, in particular, by the Cambridge-Somerville experiment. The categorical conclusion of the experiment was this: when counseling personnel and facilities are limited, it is better that they be concentrated on the few than extended, with little predictable effect, to the many.[50]

The social goal of the future, however, must be adequate therapeutic help for all, not just for some, who need it. We realize full well the many implications of this statement, but we ask whether a humanistically oriented society can remain true to its nature and be willing to settle for less.

But unfortunately, for too long it has been all too willing to settle for less. The juvenile-court system came into being in 1899, when the first one received legal recognition in Cook County, Illinois;[51] but the qualifications of the professional personnel required to staff these courts have failed to keep pace with the latter's rapid rate of growth. As a result, untrained individuals too often have filled professional positions. Willingness, warmth, and general knowledge are not to be decried as requisites, but neither are they more than a start in the proper direction.

From the welter of disagreement over the posture that the society should assume toward delinquency, this consensus is emerging: delinquency is a society-wide problem. Accordingly, in any single community, it can be none other than a society-wide responsibility.

The School and Delinquency

Within the framework of delinquency viewed in this way, education has an important role to play. As a discrete agency of society, it handles its own everyday problems of delinquency as best it can. As a unit in a social network of many agencies, it has an obligation to cooperate in important shared endeavor.

Underlying Tenets and Practices.   In either role, education operates best when adhering to the following principles, or when engaging in the following practices.

[50] William and Joan McCord, and Irving Zola, *Origins of Crime*, p. 184.
[51] Milton L Barron, *The Juvenile in Delinquent Society* (New York: Alfred A. Knopf, 1954), p. 21.

The total-personality orientation is essential. Any school serious about the issue of delinquency needs a philosophy broad enough to accommodate it. Such a philosophy finds best expression in a total-personality orientation. A curriculum grounded in this orientation looks beyond the purely academic to such other developmentally essential components as the emotional, the social, and the physical. And it is only through all of these that a school can reach the typical delinquent whose fundamental problem is an inability to adjust adequately to a many-faceted social environment.

Personnel services are of the essence. A school which operates from this total-personality orientation invariably is one which has a well-organized and effective program of personnel services. Through it, the school is able to identify the delinquent or the incipient delinquent and to offer him needed help after the act of identification.

In the area of detection, these are some of the recognized danger signals.[52]

In the home: hostility or indifference by either parent; overstrictness by the father; inconsistency of supervision by the mother; in general, an unintegrated family situation.

In the person of the individual: adventuresomeness, stubborness, extroversion, suggestibility, detachment, and general emotional immaturity.

In the school: a pattern of rule violations often beginning as early as ages 6 to 7, underachievement, inconsistent performance, destructiveness of school property, frequent failure, below-average performance particularly in reading and arithmetic, boredom with school, chronic absenteeism, and resentfulness of and resistance to authority.

In the community: resentfulness of and resistance to authority, and gang membership.

Detection, however, is only one part of the guidance battle. A more important part is what the school does about the problems it detects. And action can be effective only when the community becomes ready to underwrite the costs and when the school arrives at a clear concept of the services needed. For purposes either of detection or treatment, schools need the services of clinically minded, mature, capable classroom teachers backed up by clinically trained, mature, capable personnel workers. The personnel workers perform best when proficient in psychometrics including the use of projective instruments, and when equally proficient in the clinical interview. Furthermore, they need to work

---

[52] For a more elaborate treatment of these and other manifestations of delinquency proneness we recommend the reading of: Sheldon and Eleanor Glueck, *Unraveling Juvenile Delinquency,* pp. 258–281; William C. Kvaraceus and William E. Ulrich, *Delinquent Behavior: Principles and Practices* (Washington, D.C.: National Education Association, 1959), pp. 34–121; and Hathaway and Monachesi, *Analyzing and Predicting Juvenile Delinquency with the MMPI,* pp. 34–85.

closely with professional individuals from other clinical agencies and interest groups to the end of a concerted attack on their common problem—the delinquent.

Schools with the most problem students should have the services of the best qualified teachers. Although certain aspects of delinquency can be handled only by highly-trained personnel workers, the classroom teacher remains central in the school life of each student. It is he in any school who has the most frequent contacts with pupils. It is he who can breathe vitality into a curriculum or let a curriculum degenerate into a thing of mechanical-like properties. It is he who can make the subtleties of human relationships a telling force for good or a debilitating force for ill.

Because of the unique position that the classroom teacher occupies, schools which have in their populations the highest incidences of delinquency should have on their faculties the greatest relative number of teachers equipped to deal with delinquent children and their problems. However, this problem of matching teachers and pupils resists easy solution. Unfortunately, schools with the highest delinquency rates exist in greatest numbers in deprived urban areas. Such areas are featured by excessive poverty, by substandard sanitation, by more than average vandalism, by above-average crime rates, and by other characteristics which are repellent to many middle-class teachers.

Because of these conditions, when experienced teachers have a placement choice, as they customarily do in most cities, they tend to gravitate away from schools in greatest need of their services toward other more favored schools that require their services commensurately less. Under an inverse arrangement such as this, the rich, figuratively speaking, get richer and the poor get poorer. Because the most experienced and better qualified teachers gravitate disproportionately toward the favored schools, the less experienced and also the less qualified teachers almost habitually receive assignments in the less favored schools. That education suffers as a result, is an understatement.

A preferable pattern, needless to say, is for the best qualified teachers, motivated by dedication alone, to volunteer for the most demanding assignments in submarginal communities. However, because such an idealized outcome is not practical in a far from ideal world, external incentives may have to provide the solution. These incentives might be any or all of the following: higher salaries, smaller classes, more specialized clinical assistance, better facilities, closer police protection, school-supplied transportation, and school-supplied financial assistance for necessary teacher training in colleges or universities.

Teachers who are clinically interested in, and who are clinically able to relate to, delinquent children are desperately needed in submarginal communities. These teachers should be secure, well-adjusted, unjudgmental, empathic individuals with backgrounds of broad professional training. Such individuals, in the technical meaning of the term, cannot be identification figures to all pupils, but they can relate warmly to all pupils.[53] It is through them that the "haves" can make a socially significant contribution to the needy "have-nots."

A well-conceived curriculum is a necessity. A curriculum for delinquents, not unlike one for any other type of group, should relate specifically to the individualism of the learners. Thus, to the degree that delinquents have relatively nonverbal abilities and interests, a curriculum for them cannot be too highly verbal. To the degree that they adhere to the pleasure principle, the reality principle if over-emphasized will prove an unsuccessful motivator. To the degree that male delinquents are typically active and aggressive, a passive, nonactivity oriented curriculum will aggravate more than educate. One conclusion is certain in this regard: a curriculum which (or a teacher who) goes down the straight and narrow path of the academic, unheedful of the specialized needs of the learners involved, will know failure. A curriculum does not have to turn completely away from accepted traditions, but neither can it remain unchanged in the midst of change.

A community centered curriculum is important. One logical direction for the curriculum to take is toward learning experiences that exist in the local community. The periodically planned field trip or the occasional speaker invited into the school from the community may fit in well with the delinquent's predictable interests in the practical, the familiar, and the present. Experiences thus provided likewise make more palatable the inevitable return to the theoretical-verbal, to events of the past, and to the world of the unfamiliar.

In this connection, a high-school program, whenever possible, should effect a close tie-in with business and industry for purposes of a cooperative work-study arrangement. This same proposal appears in Chapter 2. The City of Chicago, operating in this vein in the early 1960's, joined hands with business and industry to combat the dropout problem. The cooperative venture was reasonably successful. It transported delinquency-prone youth into the world of the practical without losing them to the world of the abstract theoretical.

The skills retain their importance. In this world of the abstract theoretical, the learning skills retain their status but have their locus in a more practical context. They may have an increased scope, particularly reading and arithmetic, extending beyond the elementary grades into the junior-high and senior-high-school grades. But it is essential that they

[53] Paul W. Tappan, *Juvenile Delinquency* (New York: McGraw-Hill Book Company, Inc., 1949), p. 501.

appear in a context of meaningful activity so that the abstract and the concrete will mutually reinforce.

Selected schools should be neighborhood centers.   In submarginal urban areas—areas which breed more than their share of delinquency —selected schools should remain open afternoons, evenings, and Saturdays. As similarly recommended in the chapter on Negroes, such schools would build their programs around the needs of local residents, young and old. For the young, many of whom also would be enrolled in school during the day, the program would highlight recreational activities. For the nonschool attenders, it would highlight the practical arts, the fine arts, the skills, and other subject areas that a diagnostic study would reveal as germane. For all, the program would include a wide variety of counseling services.

Education is the best equipped single agency of government to heal the disease of fragmentation in the society. The causes are ignorance, divisive attitudes that are perpetuated from generation to generation, and emotional pathology. With these the causes, enlightenment, altruistic attitudes, and emotional health need to constitute the cure. Although education cannot achieve these outcomes unilaterally, it can and should become the rallying center for the attack on them. And its success will increase to the degree that it reaches out to the minds and emotions not only of children and youth, but of adults as well.

A Multiagency Approach Is Needed

In the attack on delinquency by interested agencies of the society, including education, success will be theirs to the extent that they coordinate their efforts. The obstacles are well known: insecurity, organizational jealousy, political finagling, professional incompetency, administrative ineptitude, and social blindness to the values inherent in cooperation. Yet despite these roadblocks, cooperation even at this moment is possible with a little more effort and vision. It is possible anytime that institutional autonomy can lose a little of its rigidity, anytime that a few more people of good will and enlightenment hold key positions, and anytime that common sense converts a few more well-meaning individuals to the greater efficiency of the cooperative way.

It is only through close cooperation that agencies can have an open encounter with the problem. Suspicion and distrust close the encounter; trust opens it. When the encounter is open, the cooperating agencies exchange information more freely, express doubts more unhesitatingly, and admit error less defensively. In such a climate, juvenile authorities and the school exchange information and opinion to the mutual gain of both. Then as they widen the operational base to include such other organizations as the church, the Y.M.C.A., the community house, and the park district, even more noteworthy outcomes become possible.

One Community-wide Project

We turn now to the way that one community put into practice the theory just discussed. The community is Passaic, New Jersey, which as early as 1937 took the first step of organizational unity in meeting head-on the problem of juvenile delinquency. In that year, The Passaic Children's Bureau came into being. Three years later, it was placed, by public referendum, under the auspices of the School Board, a relationship which has continued to the present. From its origin, the purposes of the Bureau, in more or less this priority of importance, have been prevention; readjustment; protection; and, last of all, punishment.

As revealed by the first Director of the Bureau, William Kvaraceus,[54] the personnel of the Bureau initially consisted of a director, one psychologist, one psychological social worker, two attendance officers, four police officers—three male and one female—and associated clerical personnel. Since 1940, additions to the Bureau staff have been a second psychologist, a third attendance officer, three reading specialists, and a part-time psychiatrist.

The underlying reasons for the Bureau's becoming the organizational responsibility of the School Board were these: it was deemed important for juvenile offenders to receive continuous clinical attention throughout the period of their treatment; it was considered desirable for the Bureau to operate as far removed as possible from the stigma of police authority and the law; and it was believed that earlier detection of potential offenders would be possible if the school had primary organizational responsibility.

Essential features of the Bureau's *modus operandi* were, and still are, these. The police officers, called investigators, are under the auspices of the Bureau but are paid from nonschool funds. They are selected, by the School Board, because of their personal and professional qualifications. Any juvenile when first apprehended (for other than a serious crime) by any law officer at any level is turned over to one of the Bureau's investigators. The first step is a physical examination. The second step is a psychological examination through which "we find the school misfits, problems of failure, personality clashes and very often just everyday 'growing up' through adolescence."[55] A third step is a study

---

[54] For the early days of the experiment, we recommend the reading of Kvaraceus and Ulrich, *Delinquent Behavior;* for the more recent story, we recommend the reading of the pamphlet: John P. Gower, *What One Community Has Done for Its Children* (Passaic, New Jersey: Passaic Public Schools, 1961).

[55] John P. Gower, *Ibid.*, p. 5.

of the offender's environment. All who are not institutionalized receive a fourth step of treatment, namely, that of "continuing supervision."

Finally, in the words of the Director of the Bureau, Dr. John Gower,

> If a child is unhappy at school—
> If tensions are high at home—
> If the social climate of the community is low—
>   then the child needs help . . .

In solving problems rather than getting rid of them we have found tremendous satisfaction in a most challenging area of need.[56]

The Passaic approach is not for every community, because every community is not ready for it. However, the approach possesses these inviting features: (1) a number of agencies—the police force, the courts, the school, and the church—work together to fight juvenile delinquency; (2) the school is active on a broad front of personal and social as well as strictly intellectual pursuits; (3) the juvenile offender by being treated clinically often does not receive the stigma of a police record; (4) the police officers of the Bureau, being guidance oriented, are not punitively motivated; and (5) early detection and prevention have a status of higher priority than later correction and punishment.

A Closing Word

The attitude of education toward the delinquent and the problems that follow in his wake can be described only in reference to the philosophical position from which education operates. If a school conceives of its role as exclusively academic, it focuses on symptoms of delinquency but worries little about underlying causes. If, on the other hand, a school conceives its role as more broadly mental-health oriented, it properly becomes engulfed in the totality of the delinquency problem. In this latter instance, the issue becomes not one of what position the school should assume—for its philosophy has already decided that; the issue rather is what methods the school will employ to accomplish what it knows it needs to accomplish.

Because education is committed to a mental-health orientation, I believe it cannot avoid responsibility for socially maladaptive as well as for socially adaptive behavior. Thus education has to be increasingly on the search for teachers who are able to work clinically with individuals as well as academically with class-sized groups. Whether any school plays a leadership or a supportive role in delinquency is immaterial. What is very material, however, is for education, once its role has been determined, either to lead with enlightenment or to follow with equal enlightenment.

[56] *Ibid.*

We grant that the verbal, middle-class, reality-oriented pupil may be easier for education to reach; yet he is no more deserving of attention as a human being than is his sometimes pleasure-oriented, sometimes present-centered, sometimes less verbal, sometimes submarginal counterpart. And, if those vast human wastelands of "The Other America" are ever to become fertile, the more favored America of the "haves" will need to redouble its efforts toward improving the lot of the less favored "have nots." What agency should have a greater stake in this outcome then education?

Recommended Readings

For those who wish to read further, I recommend the following publications, selected because of their quality and the variety of the view points they represent.

Aichhorn, August, *Wayward Youth*. New York: The Viking Press, 1936. Typifies the psychoanalytical orientation, presenting case studies of a number of youths who, although placed in a detention home, were treated in such a way as to encourage transference, the unblocking of the unconscious, and finally, insight.

Block, Herbert A. and Arthur Neiderhoffer, *The Gang, A Study in Adolescent Behavior*. New York: Philosophical Library, 1958. A revealing exposé of gang life in the raw.

Cloward, Richard A. and Lloyd E. Ohlin, *Delinquency and Opportunity*. Glencoe, Illinois: The Free Press, 1961. Oriented to the culture-conflict point of view, this is interestingly descriptive of "criminal" and "retreatist" beatnik gangs.

Cohen, Albert K., *Delinquent Boys*. Glencoe, Illinois: The Free Press, 1955. One of the most widely quoted books on juvenile delinquency. Although an eclectic, Cohen ventilates selected of the more specific orientations.

Fine, Benjamin, *1,000,000 Delinquents*. Cleveland: The World Publishing Company, 1955. Because written for popular consumption, this is one of the most readable on the list.

Glueck, Sheldon and Eleanor Glueck, *Unraveling Juvenile Delinquency*. New York: The Commonwealth Fund, 1950. One of many by the Gluecks, this, like the others, makes a scholarly contribution. We highly recommend it.

Kvaraceus, William C., *Juvenile Delinquency and The School*. New York: World Book Co., 1945. Is "must" reading, dealing with the Passaic Project in detail.

Kvaraceus, William C., and William C. Ulrich, *Delinquent Behavior Principles and Practices*. Washington, D.C.: National Education Association, 1959. Its best feature is the descriptions of practices throughout the country relating to programs that have been designed to counter delinquent behavior. It is wordy and labors in spots, however.

McCord, William and Joan McCord, and Irving K. Zola, *Origins of Crime, A New Evaluation of the Cambridge-Somerville Youth Study.* New York: Columbia University Press, 1959. A sobering revelation of the ineffectiveness of incidental counseling of delinquents, but encouraging regarding depth-counseling.

Shaw, Clifford R. and Henry D. McKay, *Juvenile Delinquency and Urban Areas.* Chicago: University of Chicago Press, 1942. One of the most quoted treatises on the culture-conflict point of view.

Vold, George B., *Theoretical Criminology.* New York: Oxford University Press, 1958. An excellent treatment of juvenile delinquency with unflattering parallels made frequently to middle-class "legal" delinquency.

For Further Thought

1. Given a background of slum living with its attendant temptations, is delinquency-proneness a greater likelihood. Or do you believe that one's character, regardless, acts as an adequate buffer?

2. Does stealing represent the same degree of immorality for the underprivileged, hungry, poorly clothed person as for the affluent? Defend your stand.

3. If all the new born were placed, and provided for until adolescence, in a desirable neighborhood as determined by middle-class standards, do you believe that the tendencies toward delinquent behavior of the otherwise sub-middle-class individuals would be any different? Explain.

4. Is price-fixing in business more or less immoral than stealing outright? Defend your answer.

5. Are you a culture-conflict, dynamic, or eclectic proponent? Defend your chosen position.

6. Describe the best possible program you can think of to eliminate juvenile delinquency. Ignore the factor of cost. Might society ever be ready for it?

7. Assuming yourself to be a social worker, what methods might you use to "infiltrate" a gang, and what would you do once you had infiltrated?

8. For any single grade level, describe the curriculum that you would recommend for a slum-area class. How would it differ from a more typical class?

9. Should schools move toward the Passaic-type of school-leadership organization to handle delinquency or should they assist mostly from the sidelines? Explain your choice.

10. When the school and the law are organizationally independent, what should their relationship be when a school-enrolled child becomes, or is in the act of becoming, a delinquent?

References

Andry, Robert G., *Delinquency and Parental Pathology.* London: Methuen and Co., Ltd., 1960.

Barron, Milton L., *The Juvenile in Delinquent Society*. New York: Alfred A. Knopf, 1954.

Burt, Cyril, *The Young Delinquent*. New York: Appleton-Century and Co., 1925.

Cohen, Frank J., ed., *Youth and Crime*. New York: International Universities Press, Inc., 1957.

Cooper, Clara C., *A Comparative Study of Delinquents and Non-Delinquents*. Portsmouth, Ohio: The Psychological Service Center Press, 1960.

Eaton, Joseph W., and Kenneth Polk, *Measuring Delinquency*. Pittsburgh: University of Pittsburgh Press, 1961.

Friedlander, Kate, *The Psycho-Analytical Approach to Juvenile Delinquency*. New York: International Universities Press, 1947.

Glueck, Sheldon and Eleanor Glueck, *Predicting Delinquency and Crime*. Cambridge: Harvard University Press, 1959.

Hassler, Alfred, *The Diary of a Self-Made Convict*. Chicago: Regnery Press, 1954.

Hathaway, Starke R., and Elio D. Monachesi, eds., *Analyzing and Predicting Juvenile Delinquency with the MMPI*. Minneapolis: University of Minnesota Press, 1953.

Healy, William (M.D.) and Augusta F. Bronner, (Ph.D.), *New Lights on Delinquency and Its Treatment*. New Haven: Yale University Press, 1936.

Herbert, W. L. and F. V. Jarvis, *Dealing With Delinquents*. London: Methuen & Co. Ltd., 1961.

Kvaraceus, William C., Walter B. Miller and others, *Delinquent Behavior: Culture and the Individual*. Washington, D.C.: National Education Association, 1959.

National Probation and Parole Association, The various Yearbooks.

Merrill, Maud A., *Problems of Child Delinquency*. Boston: Houghton Mifflin, 1947.

Miller, Walter B., "Lower Class Culture as a Generating Milieu of Gang Delinquency," *Journal of Social Issues*, 14 (April 1959), pp. 5–19.

Tappan, Paul W., *Juvenile Delinquency*. New York: McGraw-Hill Book Company, Inc. 1949.

Thrasher, Frederic M., *The Gang*. Chicago: The University of Chicago Press, 1927.

chapter 13

Teaching about Communism

Still in pursuit of the innovational, we focus attention now on the topic of communism and the position that it should have in the curricula of the various schools throughout the nation. Needless to say, a theme as controversial as this has social and political, as well as strictly educational, implications.

It has personal implications also, which reveal themselves in differing ways to people of differing orientations. As one author put it: to the African colonial it means revolt against a white master; to the French worker it means defense against bourgeois exploitation; to the Western intellectual, it is Eutopian idealism "tarred by inhuman practices."[1] To these three we add three more. To certain Christians and Jews, it is godlessness with a political face. To the individualist, it a collectivist enemy. And to the entirety of the Western World, it is a militant competitor for the minds and the spirits of man. Communism truly is a phenomenon of many faces, but, for that matter, so was feudalism a millenium ago, and so is capitalism today. One thing is certain: whatever its implications, communism exists throughout the world as a very real social and political fact of life.

The attitude that education should assume toward the topic is the moot issue. From the more conservative, come position statements such as the following. The risks of inverse indoctrination are so great that the schools should avoid the topic as much as possible—and the greater the avoidance the better. When the schools do cover the topic, they should do so by revealing only the evils of the system. Time spent on the teaching about communism is time stolen from more worthwhile aspects of any curriculum.

[1] Alfred Meyer, *Communism* (New York: Random House, 1960), p. 1.

From the more liberal, come such position statements as these. Communism is too real and too stupendous for enlightened education in the Western World to ignore. Rather than avoid the topic, education should make a systematic coverage of it via the open encounter. Any school which, for the curriculum in general, espouses reflective thinking cannot settle for a lesser outcome when communism is the curriculum consideration. Numerous other positions fall somewhere in between these two extremes.

In one sense, Thomas Jefferson settled the issue a century and a half ago with his insightful conclusion that an ignorant nation cannot long remain free. At a practical level, however, Jefferson's conclusion, when applied to the issue of communism, has undergone frequent emasculation. I personally am gratified to note, none the less, that the translations are increasing in authenticity almost with each passing day.

As recently as the frenetic fifties, when Senator McCarthy was leading a self-styled crusade against communism, anyone in the schools brash enough to have proposed, much less to have taught, a unit on communism would have found life intolerable. Being impugned as a fellow traveler might have been one of the lesser outcomes. Today, in pleasant contrast, more and more individuals and groups in policy-making positions are favoring the exposure of communism to the bright light of truth. For instance, in 1962 the National Education Association and the American Legion collaborated on a publication pertaining to teaching about communism.[2] Such a project in 1950 or 1955 would have been inconceivable.

Even law, probably the most slow-to-change of all American public institutions, has given statutory sanction in most states for schools to teach about communism. A survey published by Gray in 1964 revealed this status picture: 8 states required schools to teach about communism; 14 states had prepared courses or units of study on the subject of communism which were available to schools for the asking; 16 additional states were in the process of preparing such courses or units of study; and 3 states had statutory policy legislation pertaining to the teaching about communism but had no curriculum materials. Thus, within the 50 states, some kind of positive legal action had been taken by at least 41 (3 did not answer the questionnaire).[3]

Admittedly, however, much existing legislation pertaining to teaching about communism is slanted more toward an exposure of the "evils" of its ideology than toward an open encounter with all its ideology. As

[2] Joint Committee of the National Education Association And the American Legion, *Teaching About Communism: Guidelines for Junior And Senior High School Teachers* (Indianapolis: The American Legion, 1962).
[3] Roland F. Gray, "Teaching About Communism: A Survey of Objectives," *Social Education,* 28 (February 1964), p. 71

Gray states, "Few states indeed seem willing to permit a completely rational and unbiased analysis of the subject."[4] By way of illustration, the state legislature of Florida, while conceding that "The use of Communist materials . . . should not be excluded from the instructional program," insists that when included "they should be clearly labeled as such . . . These materials should be used only to demonstrate the evils, fallacies, and contradictions of Communism."[5] Nebraska, even more prescriptively, after announcing that "Communism's goal is to enslave the world," demands that schools awake pupils to "the deadly threat of Communism to America and the rest of the world."[6] Generally speaking, state legislation pertaining to the teaching about communism constitutes a paradox: in one breath, it holds up scholarly objectives as the guiding standard of instruction; in another breath, it announces what scholarly objectivity should consist of, namely, a depiction of Communism as harmful and malicious, if not actually diabolical.

Apart from legislation, the quantitative facts about international communism are reason enough for the schools to bestir themselves to action. It is a movement that holds political sway over almost one billion of the world's inhabitants. It also is a movement with the announced purpose of captivating the minds and lives of the remaining two billion people. With data like these literally begging for social interpretation, forward-looking schools actually have no intelligent alternative but to incorporate the teaching about communism into the framework of general education. Any other alternative places education, or the society, or both, in a position of retreat from reality.

Identifying Features of Communism

First we elect to examine a profile of communism which presents the ideological hard core of the movement. The purposes, in this regard, are twofold: to provide the nonspecialized reader with a capsuled picture; and to establish an abstract base that will give perspective to generalizations scheduled for appearance later in the chapter. This profile is not intended as a suggested curriculum. That sort of presentation would require much more substantive detail, would need content to be pitched at a different level, would require the inclusion of a broad listing of primary and secondary references, and would require elaboration in the area of teaching method.

Now to the question: What are the essential cornerstones of communism?

[4] *Ibid.*
[5] *Ibid.*
[6] *Ibid.*, p. 72.

The Theories of Marx and Engels.   Communism, wherever practiced in the world today—in Russia, in Red China, in Yugoslavia, in Albania, or elsewhere—rests in great part on the hard-rock theory of Karl Marx and Joseph Engels. Both men were expelled from Germany and, after much moving around on the Continent, finally sought and gained asylum in England, where they did the majority of their writing. The two collaborated on the most basic of all communist documents, *Manifesto of the Communist Party*, 1848. This brief treatise of some forty pages is the bible of communism. Other of their writings include *Capital, Theses on Feuerbach,* and *Toward the Critique of Hegel's Philosophy of Right*—all by Marx; and *On Historical Materialism,* and *Socialism: Utopian and Scientific*—both by Engels.

The ensuing constitute the most basic tenets of the two political philosophers.

1. *Historical materialism.*   In the words of Engels, the term historical materialism connotes "that view of the course of history which seeks the ultimate cause and the great moving power of all important historic events in the economic development of society, . . ."[7] More specifically, it is the concept that economic forces dictate the nature of any society—whether tribal, slave, feudal, capitalistic, or communistic.

2. *Dialectic materialism.*   The concept of the dialectic, Hegelian in origin, carries the proposition that every social force precipitates a countering social force. The inevitable result becomes a third force, which then acts to set the dialectic process once more in motion. Marx and Engels took this concept and applied it to their dogma about the pivotal status of materialistic values. The composite led them to conclude that the face of any organized society is no more than a mask reflecting the underlying conflicts within the economic structure.

3. *Theory of surplus value.*   Reaching to the heart of their economic position is the theory of surplus value, which can be summarized in the following propositions: (*a*) labor alone creates value; (*b*) the difference between what labor earns and what it receives is surplus value; (*c*) this difference is put to legitimate use only when invested by the communistic state for the welfare of all the people; it is put to illegitimate use when invested for self-gain by private enterprisers. Surplus value employed in this latter way, say Marx and Engels, leads first to resentment and ultimately to open rebellion on the part of those exploited.

4. *Theory of the class struggle.*   As the rebellion graduates in intensity, it sooner or later loses its individual nature and becomes a class

[7] Joseph Engels, "On Historical Materialism," in *Basic Writings on Politics and Philosophy,* edited by Lewis S. Feuer (Garden City: Doubleday and Company, 1959), pp. 53–54.

concern—thus the term, theory of the class struggle. According to this theory, every social group, as it moves toward the ideal of the true communist society, lives in a turbulent state of conflict between the "haves" and the "have-nots"—conflict which is a product of the dialectical process. The struggle, Marx and Engels predicted, will mount in intensity until the proletariat emerge as conquerors. The following subpropositions are basic to this tenet: the bourgeoisie are grasping exploiters; thus the exploited proletariat have a moral right to take what is rightfully theirs; they will need to employ violence to accomplish this end, destroying capitalism in the process; then with the proletariat alone remaining, communism will become its potential.

Always sensational stylists, Marx and Engels wax particularly melodramatic when writing of the class struggle. They categorize labor as "privates of the industrial army," and as "slaves of the bourgeois state . . . daily and hourly enslaved by the machine."[8] The old-line ruling classes they castigate as "the social scum, that passively rotting mass."[9] And in the final lines of the *Manifesto,* they reach their highest pitch:

The communists . . . openly declare that their ends can be attained only by the forcible overthrow of all existing social conditions. Let the ruling classes tremble at the communistic revolution. The proletarians have nothing to lose but their chains. They have a world to win.

WORKING MEN OF ALL COUNTRIES, UNITE![10]

All such statements as this pertaining to the inevitability of revolution remained to plague Marx and Engels in their later years. Noting that political and economic changes without armed conflict were taking place in England, Holland, and the United States, Marx in 1872 grudgingly conceded that communism in certain places might be achieved without revolution.

5. *Communism, a process of evolution.*   As conceived by Marx Engels, Lenin, and others, communism is a process of evolution, with the social order already having moved sequentially from the tribal, to the slave, to the feudal, and most recently to the capitalistic state. Projected for the future are the following events. The proletariat, in their struggle against capitalism, will "wrest, by degrees, all capital from the bourgeoisie, . . . centralize all instruments of production in the hands of the state, i.e., of the proletariat organized as the ruling class,

[8] Karl Marx and Joseph Engels, "Manifesto of the Communist Party" in Feuer, *Basic Writings on Politics and Philosophy,* p. 14.
[9] *Ibid.,* p. 18.
[10] *Ibid.,* p. 41.

and . . . increase the total of productive forces as rapidly as possible."[11] Then, after the social conflict has been resolved favorably for the communists, the proletariat "will lose its political character," will abolish "its own supremacy as a class," and will flower "in an association in which the free development of each is the condition for the free development for all."[12]

The assumption that violent means will lead inexorably to peaceful ends constitutes one of communism's many paradoxes. At the practical level, however, it conveniently justifies totalitarianism in communist government as an alleged expediency measure, pending the time that capitalism comes to heel and reluctant communists convert to selflessness.

6. *The criterion of work and reward.* Once the bourgeoisie has withered, the standard of work and reward will be, as stated in the frequently quoted maxim of the two political philosophers: "From each according to his ability; to each according to his need." It is interesting to note, in this regard, however, that communism as it is being practiced today in Russia and elsewhere has yet to put this ideal into practice. In fact, wage differences on an order of 30 to 1 are not at all uncommon.[13] The communist explanation for this discrepancy goes back to the tenet on social evolution. The system, so say its advocates, is as yet in a transitional state. Thus man is only in the process of liberating, but has not yet completely liberated, himself from such ignoble purposes as self-interest and external incentives. But higher goals, they aver, are definitely in the making.

7. *The family is subordinate.* A seventh doctrinal belief of Marx and Engels, to be touched on only lightly here, pertains to the status of the family in the communist social order. Fundamentally, they portray the family as a bourgeois institution, which, like the bourgeois class itself, ultimately will disintegrate when the socialistic state becomes dominant. They rhetorically ask: "On what foundation is the present family, the bourgeois family, based?" They answer: "On capital, on private gain. In its completely developed form this family exists only among the bourgeoisie." The proletarian family, they continue, is well nigh nonexistent by reason of the fact that the bourgeois males prostitute the proletarian females; and industry prostitutes the proletarian children.[14] Marx and Engels, on this family issue, did what was probably their poorest writing. Their case throughout rests on devious logic; and their manner of expression often lapses into the inarticulate.

[11] *Ibid.,* p. 28.
[12] *Ibid.,* p. 29.
[13] Baldwin Lee, *Capitalism And Other Economic Systems* (Washington, D.C.: Council for Advancement of Secondary Education, 1959), p. 40.
[14] Marx and Engels, "Manifesto," in Feuer *Basic Writings,* pp. 24–25.

8. *Materialism, the fundamental value.*   A final tenet of Marx and Engels, and one that is probably the most controversial of all, relates to value theory. Dialectical materialism, it is to be recalled, holds the economic factor to be responsible for all other value outcomes. In this connection, the two communist thinkers postulated that when economic worth is distributed evenly in the world, all other values will fall into their proper places. This is in contrast to the Judeo-Christian Ethic of the Western World which also holds equitable (although not necessarily equal) economic distribution to be a legitimate goal, but which insists that it be subordinated to and grow out of such other values as love, peace, care for the helpless, sacrifice, and legal justice. The world of communism starts with economic equity and projects toward the idealistic intangibles; the Western World starts with the idealistic intangibles and projects toward increasing economic equity.

The Theories of Lenin.   Following the death first of Marx and afterward of Engels, in the latter part of the nineteenth century, communism took two paths. The first was the path of "revisionism," espoused both by the so-called Menshevists in the Russian Communist party and by the British Labourites outside the party. The basic postulate of the revisionist group was that the working class can and should achieve its proper status by peaceful, democratic means, characterized by gradualness.

The second path was the one espoused by Vladimir Ilyitch Ulyanov, more commonly known as Lenin. Like Marx and Engels, he believed in the absolute inevitability of the class struggle; but, unlike them, he sought faster action than the natural course of history might achieve. For this reason, he is often dubbed an impatient Marxist. Until his death in 1924, he was ever the advocate of strikes, infiltration, sabotage, artificially created revolution, and civil war—these, in his opinion, being needed partners of history in the class struggle.

His second claim to eminence was as a communist theoretician. Aware that Marx and Engels, in selected instances, had been inaccurate prophets, Lenin saw the need to explain away some of their more obvious inconsistencies. In particular, he felt compelled to explain why the democracies of long standing were gaining, not losing, ground in the so-called class struggle. He explained this phenomenon by injecting the issue of imperialism into the dogma of Marx and Engels. In the process, he depicted the class conflict as being not an individual but a world-wide matter. Second, he identified the protagonists more as colonialist and imperialist nations than as proletarian and bourgeois groups. Third, he identified the cause of the conflict more as the disappearance of large-scale frontier markets than as economic deprivation at a local level. And fourth, he prophesied that the colonialist nations would become communistic victors as a result of the imperialistic nations destroying one another in their search for new world markets. Thus, according to Lenin, prosperity in the long-standing democracies was nothing more than a temporary phenomenon which would disappear with the drying up of the last frontier sources of supply.

Lenin made a third significant contribution to the cause of communism when, following the Russian Bolshevik revolution in 1917, he provided leadership for the new communist movement. For the first time, communist words had to become communist deeds, and theory had to be translated into operational practice. For a half century, history has been evaluating the successes and failures of this translation of theory into the realities of everyday living. And it is understatement to report that the last word is far from having been written about it.

The State Is Dominant. Regardless of the garments in which communism appears, it needs to be recognized for what it fundamentally is: a way of life wherein the state is supreme and the individual is subservient. And the state, with the U.S.S.R. as an example, consists not of all the people but only of the approximately ten million Communist Party members. In the U.S.S.R., actually the state is virtually synonymous with the hard core of the Party elite who belong to the Council of Ministers and to the Central Committee. And with communism a single party system, these elite constitute a self-perpetuating in-group. They employ the method of democratic centralism in making policy—that is, of decision by vote of the party hierarchy. Once the majority has spoken, the point of view of the minority, at least theoretically, ceases to exist.

The communist state, from its position of supremacy, is the master planner, the master policy maker, and the master implementer of all policy that it makes. Furthermore, it owns and controls all means of production and distribution. Within such a framework, the individual exists as a servant of the state. If the state needs workers in one area and not in another, it holds the right to transplant individuals and families to suit its purposes of the moment. If the state needs fewer merchants than it does mechanics, it holds the right to draft merchants to become mechanics. This is not to say that communist rulers are capricious or malicious. It is rather to establish the dominance of the state over the desires and preferences of individuals who exist to serve the state.

Communism Is International and Evangelistic. Until recently, the term state, at least in theory, connoted the entire world organization of communists, with the seat of the movement located in the U.S.S.R. In such a context, nationalism as well as individualism was expected to concede to the monolithic communist authority. The state, in effect, was the worldwide Communist party, not a political unit. In 1948, however, international communism had its first loss to so-called national communism when Yugoslavia's Tito withdrew his country's allegiance from the U.S.S.R. Preemptorily expelled from the party, but reinstated later, Yugoslavia by its action foreshadowed slightly more than a decade later the defection of Communist China, Albania, and a number of other communist national groups.

In whatever form communism appears—whether as a single international entity or as a loose federation of entities—its goal is to convert to its cause all nations and all peoples. It is an evangelistic movement. In this regard, Alfred Meyer draws an interesting parallel between communism and puritanism. Each, he says, espouses liberty over tyranny but employs autocratic means to achieve liberty's goals. Each champions brotherhood and equality but, in practice, ends up with inequalities of reward. Each claims "overriding justification" for its causes: historical inevitability and God, respectively. Each is a liberation movement, he says, which has "gone sour." Each conceives of its membership as the chosen few destined to set others free. Each has a *bête noire:* capitalism and Satan, respectively. Each is ascetic and evangelistic. And each is alternately otherwordly and materialistic.[15]

Whether this comparison is authentic or forced, communism takes seriously its role of evangelist. But in all fairness, let us ask whether the United States has not been just as evangelistic in its many attempts to convert nondemocratic nations to the democratic way. Germany after both world wars and various South American nations come to mind here. The issue, however, revolves around the legitimacy of the means of conversion that either ideology employs. To the extent that the means bear the stamp of brute force and misrepresentation, victories of the moment, with the passage of time, may well prove more illusory than real. History surely will have to judge both communism and the democracies on the ethics of their efforts to convert others to their respective causes. The goals themselves are just part of the picture. In this connection, for 10 million Russians to attempt to coerce 200 million other Russians into brotherhood is both a ludicrous and tragic paradox. But was it any less tragic a paradox for the democracies to colonize by force and then to "Christianize" the colonials into ways of peace?

Communism Is Atheistic.   Communism, even though evangelistic, is evangelistic in a nonreligious and even atheistic sense. Marx and Engels early made this clear in their declaration that "communism abolishes eternal truths, it abolishes all religion, and all morality."[19] Throughout communism's history, religion in general and Christianity in particular have been passed off by the various communist theoreticians as bourgeois devices designed to perpetuate economic inequality.

[15] Alfred Meyer, *Communism*, pp. 3–7.
[16] Marx and Engels, "Manifesto," in Feuer, *Basic Writings*, p. 27.

Being avowedly unmoral, communism in international political matters consistently has demonstrated little or no compunction about misrepresenting facts, just so long as such misrepresentation served the cause of the state. In this connection, we ask how long any nation, or complex of nations, can maintain tenable relationships with other nations when truth is not a basic ingredient. But by the same logic, we even more strongly assert that any nation which espouses a conventional moral and ethical code is all the more obligated, when dealing with other nations, to live up to the demands of that code.

Issues Raised by Communist Dogma

In this hard core of communist dogma, what parts appear to be specious or unconvincing? Or asked in a different way, what questions does the dogma raise that it does not answer satisfactorily? In response to these related questions, we identify the following issues pertaining to communism which the ideological movement has to date resolved hazily, if at all. Any mature high-school group should face all of them; and pupils in the upper elementary grades should face many of them.

1. First and foremost, with communism anchored to the deductive postulates of Marx and Engels, the validity of communism can be little greater than the validity of the conceptualizations of these two theoreticians. The fact that Marx himself revised some of his own ideas, and that Lenin, Stalin, Khrushchev, and Kosygin later revised others, calls for a posture of skepticism about the validity of the ideas in the first place. Better the cumulative process of induction as a method of reasoning than deduction revised to a point of absurdity. For instance, it makes little sense for dogma to demand revolution in 1848, nonrevolution in 1872, revolution again during the Lenin and Stalin periods, and peaceful coexistence during the Khrushchev and Kosygin periods.

2. Second, assuming that the dialectic to date has decided the course of history, by what logic is communism projected as terminal? Why is the dialectical process not projected beyond communism into infinity?

3. If fewer than 10 million Communist party members in Russia control 200 million nonparty communists, and fewer than 40 million party members in the world control approximately 900 million nonparty communists, what is this but an oligarchic rather than a communistic way of life? That the few will ultimately convert the remaining many, as alleged, stretches the limits of credulity.

4. Furthermore, what body of theory or what events of history support a conclusion that power once possessed will become power voluntarily relinquished? The explanation that equitable economic distribution will automatically lead to this outcome has yet to be demonstrated.

5. If communism continues to coerce and to affront human personality in other ways, how can peace and the finer virtues become ultimate realities? The avenging angel does not predictably convert to the dove of peace, and the "set upon" does not customarily become docile before his erstwhile oppressor.

6. The democracies assume almost all adults to be rational enough to formulate social policy; communism at the present time assumes only the chosen few to be this rational. Specifically, what characteristics do the few in communism possess that the many do not equally possess? And are these characteristics such as to lead to greater rationality? For instance, does greater party loyalty necessarily lead to this outcome? Or does more power? Or does more material worth? Or does less individualism?

7. If communism is the convincing and inexorable force its advocates claim it to be, why have Lenin, Stalin, Khrushchev, Kosygin, and others been so aggressive in their attempts to alter the natural course of its development? Also why are conversions to the Communist party so limited: totaling 4 per cent in Russia and only 1 to 2 per cent throughout the entire world?

8. In the Communist World, as stated earlier, morality rests on the relative criterion of what at any time is good for the party. In the Western World, morality rests more on established principles. How can the two worlds when operating from these disparate moral positions ever reconcile their differences?

9. Can any group that forces on its members a policy of atheism long survive? Can individualism be this completely suppressed?

10. And finally, once the Iron Curtain drops and other ways of life ventilate into the world of communism, will the latter be equal to the test of comparison?

Teaching about Communism in the Schools

The chapter's focus to this point has been on communism as a body of theory, and on the practical issues that it raises. Now the focus shifts to the teaching about communism in the schools. And we go on record at the beginning that education's efforts should be over *the how, the what, the who,* and *the when.* Debate over *the whether* should be a thing of the past.

Program Requisites.   Four essentials need to undergird any programming effort that touches on communism in more than a superficial way. First, a school needs to keep all interested parties—school-board members, parents, individuals in key community positions, and pupils—informed of what is going on in that area of the curriculum. Sound public relations before the fact of program implementation are certainly preferable to resistance after the fact. This is not to suggest obsequiousness on the part of a school that seeks support for the teaching about communism. It is rather to conclude that the success of the venture will increase as the school and the community work more closely together in achieving their common goal.

A second essential is qualified teachers to give professional leadership to the planned program. Ideally, they should be qualified at the time of hiring. Short of this ideal, the school should arrange some kind of well-designed inservice training program to compensate for any serious shortcomings that they might have. As with any other controversial curriculum element, the topic of communism in the hands of uninformed teachers can have grisly consequences. But in the hands of the qualified, the topic can lead to rewarding outcomes.

A third essential is the availability, as needed, of adequate curriculum materials for instructional purposes. If in written form, they should meet this three way test: run a gamut of many diverse points of view, include both adequate primary and adequate secondary sources, and extend across a wide range of reading abilities.

Finally, in their selection of subject matter, schools should adhere closely to the criteria of pupil readiness, pupil interest, significance of the content, and authenticity of the content. This topic will undergo further development later in the chapter.

To Indoctrinate or Not to Indoctrinate. Those in the schools who teach about communism recurringly have to decide the extent to which they should attempt to mold student opinion on this important subject. However, this issue, not at all restricted to the topic of communism, rises to plague at many points of contact with any curriculum. In this connection, education appears to be nearing consensus on the following generalizations pertaining to it.

The pivotal assumption is that teaching itself is a form of indoctrination. It is indoctrination in these two ways. First, when a curriculum by its very nature delimits the scope of learning, it indoctrinates in the sense that it chooses the fields of concentration for the learner. Second, when a given teacher within the then narrowed field makes content and methods choices, he also indoctrinates to a degree.

Within this broad frame of reference, a teacher next has to elect one alternative from the following three. In effect, he can expose learners only to what he or authority figures around him believe pupils need to know. This alternative presupposes that authority figures are the only proper ones to make choices for students and to decide on methods of implementation. This approach is particularly harmful to the causes of reflective thinking and learning by discovery.

A second possible alternative is one wherein a teacher from a position

of detached neutrality exposes curriculum content—including the controversial—to the open view but eschews any effort to influence the
points of view of the learners. This alternative presupposes that inherent
values of first-rank significance are not at stake; or that the learners,
by reason of personal readiness and curriculum adequacy, can and will
reach mature conclusions about them on their own; or that less mature
conclusions reached independently are preferable to more mature ones
reached at the sacrifice of independence. The weakness of this position
is that authority figures, by assuming a posture of neutrality before
important values, may thereby encourage students to adopt a similar
posture. This possibility, when related to the teaching about communism,
poses this fundamental question: can authority figures in the Western
world afford to remain neutral before such basic issues as individualism
and freedom—the very cornerstones of the Occident's way of life?

A third possible position is one wherein an instructional figure unashamedly espouses the values of individualism and freedom and employs them as guarantors of the open encounter in regard to all curriculum issues. In such a frame, he stimulates learners to think critically, demands that they conclude from breadth of data, maintains a climate
of skepticism toward absolutism, and worries little when a few of his
personal biases show through. The beauty of this position is in its consistency; it employs the identical values which it espouses. And when
teacher biases occasionally do reveal themselves, pupils have the right
to question and appraise them. It is understatement for me to identify
this position as the one that I wholeheartedly support. Of the three, it
alone harmonizes with the prevailing philosophy of this book on the
emergent in curriculum.

Advocates of the first position—the one which rests on deduction and
didactic indoctrination—have been highly verbal over the issue of teaching about communism. And they tend either to expose the ideology as
completely beyond the pale of consideration by the intelligent mind;
or they oversimplify with capsulation and the color phrase.

This first position is the one which William Buckley regularly assumes.
In the early 1960's, for instance, Yale University invited Gus Hall, the
secretary of the Communist party in the United States, to speak to the
student body, but subsequently withdrew the invitation as a result of
conservative counterpressure. Buckley defended the withdrawal on the
grounds that because a communist, by definition, has renounced "the
bond that holds people together,"[17] he is therefore not a bona fide member of the human race. In developing his case, Buckley attacked the
would-be anticommunist listeners as well as the would-be communist

---

[17] William F. Buckley, Jr., "Inviting Communists to Speak at Colleges," *National
Review*, 15 (October 22, 1963), p. 345.

listeners (if any), charging both with sordid intentions. Then, via an imperative strangely tinged with the zeal of a crusade and the fair play of a sports arena, he concluded his attack with this strange bit of advice: "Fight him, fight the tyrants everywhere; but do not ask them to your quarters merely to spit upon them; and do not ask them to your quarters if you cannot spit upon them: to do the one is to ambush a human being as one might a rabid dog; to do the other is to ambush oneself—in disregard of those who have *died* trying to make the point—to force oneself to break faith with humanity."[18]

The oversimplified, capsular approach is the one taken particularly by the many primers on communism that have recently appeared in increasing numbers on the reading market. These serve a worthwhile purpose when employed as one of a diverse ensemble of resources; but when employed alone, the generalization too often stands without sufficient supporting evidence, thereby denying the reader a scholar's right to interpret from a broad base. Here is an illustration from one such primer: "According to communist ideology, the communist movement has a double objective: to destroy all democratic and other non-communist governmental systems and ways of life and to replace them with the universal rule of the communist system, under the leadership of the U.S.S.R."[19] On a black and white basis, this statement has enough face validity to be marked "true" on an alternate-response examination. But it says nothing about communism's existing because tsarism was failing at the turn of the century, because economic distribution had broken down, and because Russia's industrial revolution was a half century behind that of the Western World.

Heavy sarcasm is also a characteristic of those who express themselves through capsulation and the bright phrase. Here is an example: "If it is our objective to coexist with the Soviet empire, we must, of necessity, retreat every time the Soviets move forward. Otherwise, we would 'antagonize' the U.S.S.R., 'bypass' the United Nations, and be guilty of 'war action.' "[20] The sweeping, unsupported assertion replaces sarcasm in the next one: "It is said that Marx became suspicious of everyone; he was quarrelsome; he developed an outward arrogance possibly due to his inner feelings of inferiority. Envy and bitterness were his constant companions. He seemed to know little of tolerance."[21]

---

[18] *Ibid.*, p. 370.
[19] Moshe Decter (editor), *The Profile of Communism: A Fact-by-Fact Primer* (New York: Collier Books, 1961), p. 19.
[20] Anthony T. Bouscaren, *A Guide to Anti-Communist Action* (Chicago: Henry Regnery Company, 1958), p. 38.
[21] Rodger Swearingen, *The World of Communism: Answers to the 100 Questions Most Often Asked by American High School Students* (Boston: Houghton Mifflin Company, 1962), p. 46.

Countering this tendency by many to oversimplify and then to propagandize from assumed positions of detached unassailability is enlightened scholarship, which more and more is addressing itself to the issue of communism. And the confrontation invariably carries with it a vote of confidence in youth's ability to engage in evaluative thinking even on the more controversial aspects of the ideology. The confrontation similarly carries with it a vote of confidence in the common sense of teachers to exercise intellectual integrity once they have been pronounced qualified to instruct in the sensitive area of communism. In this connection, a report in 1963 to the School Board of Winnetka, Illinois, from the Lay Advisory Committee on Teaching the Values of Freedom in a Divided World contains just such a ringing vote of confidence. It recommends that each teacher who is involved in the consideration of totalitarianism in the classroom have "freedom to determine the focus, content, and scope of his or her teaching. We understand this policy to be based on the premise that originality and effectiveness in teaching require an atmosphere free from restraints and limitations on candor and from pressures to compromise intellectual integrity. In the committee's view, such permissiveness is a vital prerequisite to an effective school system. As lay citizens of the Winnetka community, the members of the committee recommend continued full adherence to such policy with respect to teaching about freedom, totalitarianism, and communism."[22]

This voice of enlightened maturity resists, for several fundamental reasons, the many efforts of schools to indoctrinate students with unequivocal points of view. The first reason we commented upon previously. It is that a democracy conceived in and dedicated to individualism in a free market of ideas cannot with impunity, except in dire circumstances, adopt methods of thought control. One writer, with an obvious excess of emotionalism, impugnes such methods because they bear the "brand of rigidly righteous anticommunism which capitalizes on the hates, fears, and anxieties that arise out of present-day world conflicts." And he regrets that they are "now being impressed upon the minds of the grade school subteens and teenagers through the use of emotional and anti-intellectual and derationalizing propaganda devices."[23]

A second equally fundamental reason harkens back to the earlier chapters on mental health, creativity, and problem solving. In these chap-

[22] Unpublished report from The Lay Advisory Committee, Mr. Gifford Foley, Chairman, to Mr. William R. Kinnaired, President Board of Education, May 15, 1963.
[23] Haig A. Bosmajian, "Anti-Communism in the Grade Schools," *School and Society*, 91 (February 3, 1963), p. 93.

ters, individualism was stressed as a cherished personal-social value. However, equal stress was laid on the benefits of teaching through discovery. In deference to both mental-health and learning values, a mounting chorus in support of this method of rational discovery is being heard, a chorus that I hope will increase in volume.

The third case against indoctrination is just as convincing as the other two. It is that the free way of life is its own champion, secure in validated traditions and established values. The following quotation expresses the case crisply and well. "I do not believe it is necessary or desirable to go so far as to brainwash our youth on the evils of communism or the superiority of our system . . . It seems to me that the factual evidence in comparing the political systems and philosophies comes out so strongly in favor of the system under which we are privileged to live that there is really very little need to indoctrinate, to make dogmatic statements which oversimplify."[24]

Our Way of Life First. To this point in the chapter's development, we have alluded several times to pupil readiness as an indicator of when a school should introduce the topic of communism. Unfortunately, in this regard, most readiness criteria are vague and elusive. Fortunately, in this instance, however, one criterion stands out as both specific and identifiable. In brief, it is the postulate that no school should introduce an ideology strange to pupils until the school has first grounded those same pupils in the democratic way of life—including the values, institutions, and practices of that way of life. In such a sequence, pupils become acquainted first with the known before the unknown rises to challenge them. And even more fundamental, a preliminary familiarity with the democratic way of life enables them to forge a value system that they later can employ in assessing other ways of life, including communism.

The orientation to democracy, of necessity, must stress the preeminence of individualism, civil liberties, the duties of citizens as well as their privileges, minority rights, faith in human progress, the methods of peaceful change, and social mobility. In addition, the orientation should leave students well grounded in the basic facts and *modus operandi* of America's major institutions: governmental, economic, social, and religious. This grounding should be characterized by increased realism as children advance sequentially through the grades. It is better for pupils, in the controlled atmosphere of the school, to face certain of life's shortcomings than for the school to lose its integrity by concealing or rational-

[24] R. Barry Farrell, an unpublished address entitled "Some Problems In Teaching About the Cold War," delivered at the Conference on Cold War Education, Tampa, Florida, June 13, 1963.

izing these same shortcomings. After all, what is there to fear? Freedom
even though imperfectly practiced still towers as a value unequalled, as
yet, in history's annals.

Programming.   Pupils thus armed with a realistic appraisal of American values and institutions are ready for the open encounter with other
cultures. What still remains is for education to integrate the subject of
communism into the school's curriculum—a far from simple task. At the
heart of the problem is the newness of the topic of communism to education, and the resulting paucity of precedent for it. Furthermore, the task
of programming is complicated by the tendency of well-meaning but
ill-prepared individuals to get into the act. Among these are legis-
lators, politicians, civic organizations, and chauvinists from many sources,
who too often confuse propaganda with learning, and substitute expediency for thoughtful scholarship. The need of the future is for the teaching about communism to leave the province of the political and enter,
to stay, the province of the scholarly-educational. In a few systems, this
transition has been made: For instance, in Hawthorne, California;
Winnetka, Illinois; and Baltimore County, Maryland. But these definitely
are exceptions, not the rule.

The ideal approach to program planning is multi-level and multi-disci-
plinary, with a team of individuals possessed of complementary strengths
and backgrounds joining in a collective effort. Members of such a team
might well consist of the following: one or more elementary-school
social-studies teachers, one or more secondary-school social-study teachers, a school administrator, a college specialist on communism, one or
more state-department representatives, and selected qualified lay citizens.
Each would contribute from his field of competency while acting as an
antidote to possible extremism within the group.

In general, program planning should move from the incidental to the
direct, from communism as related to our own way of life to communism
as an independent way of life, and from the restricted safe to the open-
encounter controversial. Such a flow follows the line of increasing developmental readiness.

From kindergarten through grade 4, we recommend an adherence to
the incidental, with the teacher neither dodging the issue of communism
nor attacking it frontally. By the same logic, however, when a current-
events project, a fact of history, or a curious pupil exposes the issue
to view, instructional leaders have little or no choice but to respond
factually—but only within the limits of the curriculum situation itself.
Then in grade 5 (or grade 6 in some schools), where the focus of the
social-studies program is on such topics as "The Building of America"
or "Where Our Ancestors Came From," the study of people who came
to America from communist as well as from noncommunist countries

follows logically. This program of grade 5 (or 6) flows smoothly into a study of early European and Asiatic civilizations in the next grade, with Russia being singled out for specialized treatment. Particular attention at this level should be given to tsarist rule, foreign trade, geographical phenomena, the Russian class system, Russia's ethnic diversification, and the cultural life of the many peoples.

With this historical background established, a comfortable shift can then be made in grades 7 or 8, or in both, to modern Russia—Russia of the period from approximately 1800 to the present. The curriculum for these grades should logically include content such as the following:

1. Russian geography (a review); terrain, arable and nonarable land areas, other natural resources, climate, population distribution, and neighboring land masses.

2. Economic factors: the generally low standard of living, impoverished farm lands, a relatively backward technology, an industrial revolution that was a half century behind England's, and a limited foreign trade—by Western standards.

3. Social-political factors: the tsarist traditions including suppression of individualism and freedom, the class struggle, the theory of Marxism, the practical implementations of Lenin, the Revolution of 1905, and the end of tsarism.

4. The contemporary picture: The thread of communist dogma from Lenin, to Stalin, to Krushchev, to the present; life in Russia today; the worldwide spread of communism; the evangelistic nature of communism and its threat (or challenge) to the West.

5. The many rifts which recently have appeared in the communist block, and their possible implications.

6. A comparative study of the three ideologies of: fascism, communism, and democracy.

7. The challenge that confronts the West, namely, that the democratic way must always remain virile and dynamic, that status-quoism must ever make way for social change.

Finally, at the senior-high school level, it is my considered belief that the topic of communism, as contextually appropriate, should be at least an incidental component of all social-studies courses; but, in addition, that it should constitute the discrete motif of at least a four-to-six week unit in a designated course. So as to reach the entire student body, the unit should be part of a curriculum constant; of problems of democracy or world history, unless these are electives, in which event United States History would be the alternative.

The central theme of the unit would be communism as a current reality: a reality with ideological, economic, political, social, and ethical implications for America and the entire world. The unit should emphasize and reemphasize that communism to be lived with must be communism rationally comprehended. Forming the content of the unit would be those concepts and issues delineated and briefly discussed earlier in the chapter, translated, however, into more acceptable learning format. The following concepts would receive special billing: that communism is opposed to freedom and individualism; that it is evangelistic and thus international; that its relationships with countries dedicated to other ideologies rest often more on practical expediency than on enduring ethical and moral values; that the state is the political and economic overlord; and that communism promises the good life to all who are loyal to it.

Overshadowing all other outcomes of the unit, in my opinion, would be an open encounter by students with communism—an encounter which would elicit the deepest of reflective thought. Facts are essential but they are not enough. Second-hand interpretation has its place, but it too goes only so far. In the final analysis, the student himself has to think through communism to a point of conclusion. Allies in the process would be extensive primary resources; a satisfactory cross-section of secondary resources; a teacher who broadly guides rather than one who narrowly indoctrinates; a climate removed from hysteria and fear; in brief, a learning situation where the reflective-thinking process has free rein—or at least a fair approximation thereof. Deterrents to the process would be an absence of, or too few, primary resources; a slanted selection of secondary resource materials; authority figures who substitute indoctrination for thought; a climate of fearfulness; and a too great reliance on deductive concepts.

Suggested References

For readers who themselves desire an open encounter with communism, I suggest an extensive and diversified reading program that projects across the two conflicting ideologies of communism and democracy. And for those who, from the start, view freedom as a supreme value, the experience should be a rewarding one. To facilitate such an opportunity, I have included a fairly lengthy annotated bibliography with captioned headings—this is in lieu of the unannotated bibliography customarily included at the end of most chapters. A sampling of readings from each of the listed categories is recommended.

1. Readings on the many aspects of communism, characterized, for the most part, by scholarliness and objectivity of treatment

Adams, Arthur E. (ed.), *Readings in Soviet Foreign Policy*. Boston: D. C. Heath and Company, 1961. A collection of points of view regarding Russia's methods of dealing with the Western World.

Bereday, G. Z., William W. Brickman, and G. H. Read, *The Changing Soviet School*. Boston: Houghton, Mifflin and Co., 1960. The title is self-explanatory.

Bosmajian, Haig A., "Anti-Communism in the Grade Schools," *School and Society*, 91 (February 23, 1963), pp. 93–95. The author decries the slanted programs and slanted resources pupils are being exposed to in many schools which teach about communism.

Brickman, William W., "Teaching About Communism in the Schools," *School and Society*, 91 (January 6, 1963), p. 30. Is more conservative than I am regarding the open encounter with communism. Brickman stresses the importance of readiness as a prerequisite.

Counts, George, *The Challenge of Soviet Education*. New York: McGraw-Hill Book Company, Inc., 1958. A factual presentation and treatment of Soviet education by a long time scholar on the subject.

Dallin, David, *Soviet Foreign Policy After Stalin*. Philadelphia: Lippincott and Company, 1961. Treats of the shift from Russian bellicosity under Stalin to the theme of peaceful coexistence under Khrushchev.

Fainsod, Merle, *How Russia Is Ruled*. Cambridge: Harvard University Press, 1953. A thorough-going study by a first-rate scholar on Soviet affairs.

Fraser, Dorothy M., *Deciding What To Teach*. Washington, D.C.: National Education Association, 1963, pp. 154–174. An excellent discussion of the schools' role in regard to controversial issues in general and communism in particular.

Gray, Roland R., "Teaching About Communism: A Survey of Objectives," *Social Education*, 28 (February, 1964), pp. 71–72. Summarizes the legislation and the curricula about communism that the various state departments of education are advocating.

Griffith, William E., *Albania And the Sino-Soviet Rift*. Cambridge: The M.I.T. Press, 1963. Traces the Chinese-Russian conflict and Albania's Sino-oriented role; employs primary Russian documents in presenting his case.

Gunther, John *Inside Russia Today* (Rev. Ed.). New York: Harper and Row, 1962. An interesting and kaleidoscopic overview in Gunther's somewhat newsy style.

Gunther, John, *Meet Soviet Russia: Land, People, Sights*. New York: Harper and Row, 1963. Same as above.

Hook, Sidney, *Marx and The Marxists*. New York: Van Nostrand, 1955. A scholarly treatment of Russian theory and practice by a liberal unafraid to speak his mind.

Iverson, Robert W., *The Communists And The Schools*. New York: Harcourt, Brace, and Company, 1959. A highly readable account of the attempt by the communist party in the United States to infiltrate education at all levels, particularly the universities. Such well known names as John Dewey, Harry Gideonese, Theodore Brameld, and Robert Lovett are discussed as past targets of communist efforts to convert. Only Lovett, the author alleges, proved vulnerable.

Joint Committee of the National Education Association and the American Legion, *Teaching About Communism: Guidelines for Junior and Senior*

High School Teachers. Indianapolis: The American Legion, 1962. A non-controversial booklet with helpful hints and suggestions to instructional leaders engaged in, or to become engaged in, teaching about communism.

Meyer, Alfred G., *Communism.* New York: Random House, 1960. A unique treatment by almost any standards. Draws a particularly interesting parallel between the evangelism of puritanism and of communism.

Miller, Richard I., "An Approach to Teaching About Communism," *Phi Delta Kappan,* 43 (February 1962), pp. 189–192. Should be helpful to a high school engaged in programming on the subject of communism. Is down to earth and meaningful.

Moos, Elizabeth, *Education in the Soviet Union.* New York: National Council of American-Soviet Friendship, 1962. Title is self-explanatory.

Rieber, Alfred J. and Robert C. Nelson, *A Study of the U.S.S.R., An Historical Approach.* Chicago: Scott, Foresman and Company, 1962. The work of two competent scholars: one a professor at Northwestern University and the other the Midwest Editor of the *Christian Science Monitor.*

Zagoria, Donald S., *The Sino-Soviet Conflict.* Princeton: Princeton University Press, 1962. Exposes the conditions and issues between China and Russia that led to the recent split in communist ranks.

2. Possible textbooks and recommended supplementary student readings in units on communism.   In general, we are opposed to the narrowness of most textbooks on communism. Those in this section, however, meet reasonably high standards.

Caldwell, John C., *Communism in Our World.* New York: The John Day Company, 1962. An uncomplicated treatment of communism throughout the world; also of N.A.T.O., S.E.A.T.O., and our many allies. Appropriate for grade 7 or 8.

Editors of Scholastic Book Services, *The Soviet Union.* New York: Scholastic Book Services, 1963. Contains excellent maps, study questions, and other helpful aids. Appropriate for grade 8 or 9.

Evans, Eva Knox, *Why We Live Where We Live.* New York: Little, Brown, and Company, 1953. For use in connection with the study of the many races who settled in America. Appropriate for grades 5 or 6.

Glendenning, Robert M., *Eurasia.* Land of People and the World Series. New York: Ginn and Co., 1961. Emphasizes the interdependence of nations and peoples. Appropriate for grade 7.

Jackson, W. A., and William O. Douglas, *Soviet Union.* Grand Rapids: Fideler Co., 1962. Relates the social development of the Russian people to geographical and political factors: land, climate, government. For grade 7.

Lee, Baldwin, *Capitalism And Other Economic Systems.* Washington, D.C.: Council for Advancement of Secondary Education, 1959. An excellent comparative study of the East and West. Sharpens up issues and relates them to historical developments. For the high school.

Lovenstein, Meno, *Capitalism, Communism, Socialism*. Minneapolis: Curriculum Resources, Inc., 1962. An objective, comparative study of the three ways of life. For the high school.

Miller, W. J., Henry L. Roberts, and Marshall D. Shulman, *The Meaning of Communism*. New York: Silver, Burdett, and Company, 1963. Traces important landmarks in Russia leading to the present state of Soviet development. Stresses the communist challenge today. For grade 8.

Nazaroff, Alexander, *The Land of the Russian People*. Philadelphia: J. B. Lippincott Company, 1960. Primarily concerned with early Russian history, its government, and peoples. Covers the current scene briefly in the final section. For grade 6 or 7.

Rockefeller Brothers Fund, *Prospect For America: The Rockerfeller Reports*. Garden City: Doubleday and Co., Inc., 1961. Presents the points of view toward American foreign-policy and domestic issues of leading American citizens and scholars. For the high school.

Vandivert, Rita and William, *Young Russia*. New York: Dodd, Mead, and Company, 1960. Treats of Russian children by word and picture. For grade 6 or 7.

3. Simple primers and profile books

Anti-Defamation League of B'nai B'rith, *The Profile of Communism*. New York: Freedom Books, 1961. A relatively unslanted, terse yet factual thumbnail sketch of communism and the issues it raises.

Decter, Moshe (Ed.), *The Profile of Communism, A Fact-By-Fact Primer*. New York: Collier Books, 1961. A terse, overly-simplified treatment.

4. Slanted treatments of communism

The listings in this section portray communism almost exclusively from the Western World point of view. Their apparent intent appears to be, primarily, arousal of the emotions. The listed publications freely employ the color word or phrase (hate-mongers, masters of duplicity, purveyors of fear, etc.), name dropping, and oversimplification.

Bouscaren, Anthony T., *A Guide to Anti-Communist Action*. Chicago: Henry Regnery Company, 1958. A crusading document.

Colgrove, Kenneth and Hall Bartlett, *The Menace of Communism*. New York: D. Van Nostrand Company, Inc., 1962. A one-sided picture from the West's point of view.

Cronyn, George, *A Primer on Communism: 200 Questions and Answers*. New York: E. P. Dutton and Co., Inc., 1960. A simple but slanted treatment.

Dennen, Leon, *The Soviet Peace Myth*. New York: National Committee For A Free Europe, Inc., 1951. A classic of overstatement.

Hoover, J. Edgar, *Masters of Deceit*. New York: Henry Holt and Company, 1958. Tries desperately to be objective but is unsuccessful.

National Review. A weekly periodical under the editorship of William F. Buckley, Jr. Its selection of content and overall style could scarcely be more stereotyped or extreme.

Overstreet, Harry and Bonaro, *The War Called Peace: Khrushchev's Communism*. New York: W. W. Norton and Co., 1961. A factual treatment of the cold war but from the Western point of view only.

Platig, Raymond E., *The United States And the Soviet Challenge*. Chicago: Science Research Associates, 1960. The verbal pictures are fairly straightforward, but the cartoons and chapter-end questions are definitely slanted.

Swearingen, Rodger, *The World of Communism: Answers To the 100 Questions Most Often Asked By American High School Students*. Boston: Houghton Mifflin Company, 1962. Slants primarily by oversimplification.

5. *Primary sources.* In this section we include original sources in their entirety, collections put together by anthologists, and selected digests.

Adams, Arthur E. (ed.), *Readings in Soviet Foreign Policy*. Boston: D. C. Heath and Company, 1961. Title is self explanatory.

Daily Worker. The official weekly organ of the Communist party in the United States. It is a masterpiece of propaganda effort.

Feuer, Lewis S. (ed.), *Basic Writings on Politics and Philosophy: Karl Marx and Frederich Engels*. Garden City: Anchor Books, Doubleday and Company, Inc., 1959. Available in paperback edition.

Inkeles, Alex and Kent Geiger, *Soviet Society: A Book of Readings*. Boston: Houghton Mifflin Company, 1961. A selection from Soviet documents and commentaries on them by specialists from the Western World.

Joint Committee on Slavic Studies, *The Current Digest of the Soviet Press*. New York: Columbia University. A weekly publication which condenses Soviet news releases.

Lenin, Vladimir I., *Selected Works*, 12 Vols. New York: International Publishers, 1935. Title is self explanatory.

Molotov, V. M., *Problems of Foreign Policy*, Speeches and Statements. Moscow: Foreign Languages Publishing House, 1949. A collection of Molotov's addresses on foreign affairs, approved for publication by the Soviet.

Schwartz, Harry (ed.), *Russia Enters the 1960's. A Documentary Report on the 22nd Congress of the Communist Party of the Soviet Union*. Philadelphia: J. B. Lippincott Company, 1962. Speeches and other primary documents which underwrite Russia's alleged current policy of peaceful coexistence and anti-Stalinism.

Whitney, Thomas P., *The Communist Blueprint For the Future*. New York: E. P. Dutton and Co., Inc., 1962. A history of communist dogma lifted from the basic primary sources of origin.

6. *Bibliographies*

Department of Public Instruction, Harrisburg, Pennsylvania, *World Communism: A Selected Annotated Bibliography, 1958*. Compiled by the Library of Congress. This lists 200 publications.

Gray, Roland F., "Teaching About Communism: A survey of Objectives," *Social Education*, 28 (February 1964), pp. 71–72. Contains an excellent listing of the resources available in the various state departments of education on the teaching about communism.

Hartshorn, Merrill F., and T. Marcus Gillespie, *A Selected Annotated Bibliography To Assist Teachers in Teaching About Communism.* Washington, D.C.: National Council for the Social Studies, 1962. A descriptive listing of approximately forty publications for the use of students.

Perdew, Richard M., "Source Materials for Teaching About Communism," *Social Education,* 28 (February 1964), pp. 81–83, 118. An excellent listing of government reports, periodicals, films, film strips, and other resources pertaining to the teaching about communism—for teachers and advanced students.

A Final Word

Communism in a very real sense casts a shadow over the visage of the world. The shadow silhouettes two contrasting ways of life. One stands for individualism; the other stands for statism. One entrusts freedom to the masses; the other entrusts it only to the select few. One views the affective values as primary; the other views the materialistic values as primary.

The hope for the future is that this confrontation will motivate the Western World to reappraise, methodically and thoughtfully, its fundamental beliefs, values, and practices. The reappraisal predictably will reveal that the Western World has made a too weak commitment to its own values; that it has not translated into altruistic action the humanistic tenets to which it purportedly subscribes. The reappraisal also predictably will convince that the good life needs to be for the underprivileged as well as for the privileged.

If these are the outcomes, mankind will have been served well by the confrontation. In such a frame, communism's role in activating the conscience of the Western World may redound ironically as its greatest single contribution. But these outcomes are possible only when education permits an open encounter with all sides of the issue. In such an encounter, the inward look of democracy at itself is as essential as its outward look at the ideology of communism.

For Further Thought

1. Our only question here is this: Should education progressively enlarge the encounter with communism to a point of complete openness at the high school level, or should it set limits? If the latter, what limits should be set?

part V

Organizational Practices

chapter 14

Team Teaching

In this the last section of the book, our locus of attention is three organizational arrangements—team teaching, the nongraded classroom, and the Advanced Placement Program—all of which have a direct bearing on the innovational in curriculum. Each, in effect, is an organizational extension of a curriculum point of view.

Standing first in order of treatment is team teaching, an instructional scheme that has recently assumed a position of importance in the nation's schools. Little more than a theoretical consideration in 1956, it has important practical significance today. A reasonable estimate, in this connection, is that well over 200 school systems throughout the country employ it in one form or another. One source, reporting on team-teaching projects in existence as of 1961, lists 43 then in operation at the elementary-school level, 22 at the junior-high level, 73 at the senior-high level, and 24 at the college level. These totals undoubtedly have increased since 1961. This same source lists 48 books or pamphlets relating completely or in part to team teaching, and 108 periodical articles relating exclusively to the same topic.[1]

School systems whose team-teaching programs appear most widely in educational literature are located as follows: (1) elementary schools—Jefferson County, Colorado; Norwalk, Connecticut; Englewood, Florida; Auburn, Maine; Lexington, Massachusetts (where at the Franklin School the first organized team-teaching experiment in the country was started in 1957); and Carson City, Michigan. (2) junior-high schools—San Diego, California; Decatur, Illinois (Lakeview School); Racine, Wisconsin; and Duchesne and Ogden, Utah. (3) high schools—San Diego, California; Jefferson County, Colorado; University

[1] Judson T. Shaplin and Henry F. Olds (eds.), *Team Teaching* (New York: Harper and Row, 1964), pp. 379–421.

of Chicago Laboratory School, Chicago, Illinois; Cicero, Illinois; Decatur, Illinois; Evanston, Illinois; Norridge, Illinois; Park Forest, Illinois; Newton, Massachusetts; Wayland, Massachusetts; Madison Heights, Michigan; Easton, Pennsylvania; and Snyder, Texas. (4) Colleges or Universities—Claremont, George Peabody, Harvard, New York University, and the University of Wisconsin.

The existence of team teaching in so many of the country's school systems does not mean, however, that practices everywhere are uniform. To the contrary, as will be developed later, practices vary greatly from place to place. Nor is this suprising in view of team teaching's relative newness. In this regard, extensive variation during this early stage of the movement is wholesome. It is wholesome because variety tends to encourage more careful analysis that ultimately, in turn, should lead to a separating of the authentic from the spurious.

And if the growing prevalence of team teaching in the schools has not led to uniformity of practice, neither has it demonstrated, as yet, that the newer configurations are necessarily better or worse than what they organizationally replaced or are replacing. At the moment, team teaching is an experiment and should be regarded as just that. It may be redirectional but it is not a new organizational essence; it may be a refinement of the old, but it is not by any stretch of the imagination a complete replacement of the old. Above all else, it is an attempt at improvement but not a panacea. In regard to the latter—as with programmed learning and the nongraded classroom—too many friends of team teaching have harmed more than they have helped by their patently unwarranted and overstated claims in regard to it.

What Is Team Teaching?

Although, as indicated previously, team teaching is not a discrete entity, it more often than not appears with selected common characteristics. Some of these are visible in the definitions which follow; others will be identified specifically and receive comment later in the section.

First of all, we offer these three definitions:

Team teaching exists when two or more teachers *regularly, purposefully,* and *deliberately* work co-operatively in the planning, the presenting and the evaluating of learning experiences.[2]

Team teaching is a type of instructional organization, involving teaching personnel and the students assigned to them, in which two or more teachers are given responsibility, working together, for all or a significant part of the instruction of the same group of students.[3]

[2] Melvin P. Heller, *Team Teaching: Questions and Answers* (Cleveland, Ohio: Educational Research Council of Greater Cleveland, 1963), p. 1.
[3] Shaplin and Olds, *Team Teaching,* p. 15.

Specifically, a teaching team is a group of several teachers (usually between three and six) jointly responsible for planning, carrying out, and evaluating an educational program for a group of children.[4]

Teachers Share Instructional Responsibilities. From these definitions as well as from a denotation of the word team itself, one conclusion emerges: team teaching involves two or more individuals sharing a common effort. Nor is this a novel organizational phenomenon in education. Lancaster and Bell, a century and a half ago, built an entire system of education around it. Their teaching team consisted of a professional teacher and selected precocious students utilized as teacher helpers. More recently, Bay City, Michigan, in 1955, embarked on a project wherein several classroom teachers shared the services of a teacher aid in a kind of team arrangement. At the teacher-education level, whenever a classroom teacher accepts a student teacher from a nearby college and shares teaching responsibilities with him, this in a very definite sense is team teaching.

As of the late 1950's, the term team teaching became more a specialized trade term than a general semantic one. As a trade term, it came to be employed (as it generally still is) to denote an organizational arrangement wherein two or more *certified* teachers, with or without the services of noncertified personnel, share a common bond of instructional responsibility. The relationship must be a planned, structured one, not an incidental one. Within the framework of this new usage, casual, spur-of-the-moment organizational sharing, strictly speaking, does not fall within the province of team teaching.

The advent of the modern version of team teaching has recast the role of teacher. In his new garments, he loses much of the autonomy he possessed as a single classroom performer. As recasted, he works—at least is expected to work—cooperatively with his organizational co-workers on such tasks as planning a curriculum, dividing instructional responsibilities, and evaluating the results of pupil learning. And with most teams consisting of three, four, or five individuals (three or four most often in elementary education, and four or five in secondary education), this new requirement of cooperative effort assumes significant dimensions—so much so that only cooperative personalities should become members of a teaching team. Intelligence and technical competence are not enough. In addition to these qualities, team teachers need to have a high tolerance for criticism, enjoy the give-and-take of the group process, be able to listen as well as talk, be willing to concede as well as engage in the hard sell, be patient, be curious, and be open-minded. Probably the greatest overall single need of the team teacher is flexibility.

[4] Robert H. Anderson, "Team Teaching," *NEA Journal,* **50** (March 1961), p. 52.

Curriculum Planning Is Essential.   A primary task that habitually confronts teachers associated in a team-teaching effort is curriculum formulation. This is a task common to all teachers in all school settings, regardless of organizational differences, but it assumes added significance in a team situation. This is not to imply that in team teaching administrative authority automatically transfers all responsibility for curriculum decision-making to a predetermined group of individual teachers. Such is rarely the case. But it is to state that team teachers, of necessity, have to operate across a more extensive range of curriculum decision-making than do their counterparts in more conventional organizational arrangements. As stated by one writer, team teachers must ask out loud and far more frequently, "What are we trying to accomplish with the children and why? . . . In varying degrees, they [have to discover] the underlying rationale of the curriculum which has been in their books for several decades or more."[5] And, because of the social-professional nature of a team group, self-justification of a given plan of curriculum action is usually not enough; the plan, more often than not, has to meet the collective approval of the group. It is at this point that a strong defense based on educational purpose becomes a requisite. It is at this point, likewise, that status quoism for its own sake has to concede to critical appraisal.

Team Patterns Vary.   Curriculum purpose not only determines the academic directions of teaching teams but their organizational shapes and characteristics as well.[6] Customarily, teams form on the basis of one or more of the following criteria: (1) short-term or long-term curriculum intent, (2) grade-placement level of students, (3) subject-matter content, (4) desired learning outcomes related to the size of the student group, (5) personal and professional attributes of the team members, (6) the pattern of leadership within the team (7) scheduling factors, and (8) space factors.

The Criterion of Short-Term or Long-Term Curriculum Intent.   One factor that shapes or modifies any team organization is the duration of any given curriculum project. The duration might be short-term or long-term. An illustration of the first is the occasional joining together for a common purpose of two or more otherwise independent groups: for instance, one class of high-school juniors in the area of English and another class of juniors in the area of the United States history. The common interest topic might be Shakespeare and his times, or literature and the Civil War. Another instance would be the joining of two or more

[5] Joseph C. Grannis, "Team Teaching and the Curriculum," in Shaplin and Olds, *Team Teaching,* p. 130.
[6] See John A. Brownell and Harris A. Taylor, "Theoretical Perspectives for Teaching Teams," *Phi Delta Kappan,* 43 (January 1962), pp. 150–157, for an excellent, although somewhat theoretical, treatment of team-teaching structure and organization.

fifth- or sixth-grade classes, or a combination of both, as a basis for planning a mutual camping-out project. In either event, the academic fusion—if actually a fusion at all—would be temporary, with each group, once the common mission had been accomplished, going its own separate way. As indicated previously, whether such an arrangement actually would be team teaching at all depends on definition. In contrast to short-term arrangements such as the aforementioned, most team-teaching groups operate on a fairly long-term basis (usually for a year). In these latter, curriculum planning, curriculum implementation, and pupil evaluation have to pass the test of continuity and time.

The Criterion of Grade-Placement Level. Quite commonly in elementary education, and occasionally in secondary education, team-teaching groups form around the factor of grade placement. An uncomplicated illustration of this approach would be a team made responsible for 120 first-grade pupils, or another team made responsible for 90 first-, second-, and third-grade pupils combined. In either event, the teaching team would be obligated to plan curriculum outcomes and assume professional responsibilities for their accomplishment. Interesting in this regard, a pioneer team-teaching school—the Franklin School of Lexington, Massachusetts—has employed both the single and the multigrade arrangements from its experimental beginning in 1957–1958. The Norwalk, Connecticut School System, on the other hand, has tended consistently to cut across two or more grade levels. Within either the single or the multigrade framework, the teaching team has had to plan the curriculum; divide the total body of pupils into various subgroups, or keep them together, depending on curriculum purposes; and make an appropriate division of labor within the team.

The Criterion of Subject-Matter Content. At the high-school or junior-high-school level, subject-matter content usually substitutes for grade placement as a basis for group formulation. For instance, two teachers of sophomore English at the Andrew Hill High School, San José, California, recently assumed team responsibility for a group of 75 students. Such other high schools as those of Newton, Massachusetts, and of Evanston, Illinois, have been experimenting since the late 1950's with single-discipline teams involving groups totaling as many as 120 to 150 students.

At a more ambitious level, selected schools as long ago as the 1930's employed team teaching in core programs that cut across subject-matter lines. In these latter, it was not unusual for teachers—one each, for instance, in the fields of English, social studies, and art—to plan and cooperatively implement a series of curriculum experiences for a given group of core students. A more recent counterpart to this approach is described by Singer: "In Racine, Wisconsin, the junior high school established a team teaching system under an English—social studies block organization. Students attended double periods of English and social studies in three sections during the same period in the morning and again in the afternoon. A seventh-grade team of three teachers handled the morning and afternoon blocks of ninety students per block. They then planned the curriculum, schedule, teacher assignment, and evaluation procedure cooperatively."[7] A cross-discipline team such as this is more common at the elementary-school and junior-high-school levels than at the senior-high-school level.

Desired Learning Outcomes Related to the Size of the Student Group. In any school, irrespective of its organization, a curriculum rarely becomes operative until one or more instructional figures energize it. And the audience of potential learners, depending on curriculum purpose, can range from as few as the single pupil to as many as the total school population. In the conventional classroom setting, the top of the range is usually not in excess of 25 to 35. In the team-teaching setting, however, the top can extend to as many as 90, 120, or even more. This greater potential population accentuates the need for education in general, and teaching teams in particular, to ascertain more clearly than either has done to date the relatedness of the three educational variables: learning outcomes, teaching methods, and size of learning groups.

Apropos of the relationship of the size of learning groups to learning outcomes, education without benefit of valid supporting evidence has long assumed the desirability of a classroom ratio of 25 pupils to 1 teacher. And at times educators have adhered to this idea regardless of the learning purposes of the moment. Skeptical of this kind of rigidity, many have uncovered evidence that purportedly casts the validity of the ratio in doubt. These latter, however, invariably anchor their conclusions almost exclusively to gains in achievement; rarely, if at all, to gains along other learning dimensions such as the creative, the social, and the emotional. Thus their counter inferencing may be comparably specious.

Aware of the inconclusiveness both of research findings and of subjective evidence relating to the optimum size of the group to be taught, team-teaching experimenters have been encouraged to work with learning groups which deviate, at times even dramatically, from the traditionally respected stereotype of 25. And in so doing, they have been on safe ground so long as they have remained modest about their claims. Unfortunately, however, many soon announced counter claims that were every bit as unsupportable as those which long had related to the number 25. One of the greater offenders in this regard has been the Commis-

---

[7] Ira J. Singer, "What Team Teaching Really Is," in David W. Beggs, III, *Team Teaching: Bold New Venture* (Indianapolis: Unified College Press, Inc., 1964), p. 20.

sion on the Experimental Study of the Utilization of the Staff in the Secondary School, an agent of The National Association of Secondary School Principals.

Undeniably, the Committee deserves credit for spearheading in secondary education many curriculum innovations that often have been noteworthy. Unfortunately, however, it has tended on occasions to confuse postulate with fact. For instance, one of its claims is that groups of over 15 are too large to permit effective discussion. Another is that in most team-teaching projects, "independent study will average 40 per cent of the school's schedule for students."[8] A third is that "if a class is to hear a presentation by a teacher or some other speaker on a face-to-face basis, 150 students will be the maximum class size."[9] And a fourth, just as unsupportable, is that "Tomorrow's schools, with more flexible scheduling, will be able to arrange as many large classes as curriculum plans require. Combined, these purposes suggest that about 40 per cent of a student's time in school will be spent in large classes."[10] The harm of these and other such patently unsupportable conclusions lies in their implied absolutism. A preferable approach, we contend, is for theoreticians and practitioners to keep their conclusions tentative and modest during this present period of experimentation.

What most perplexes team-teaching experimenters at the moment is the issue of when they should employ large-group, small-group, and individual instruction. A valid answer, we are convinced, can never lie in fixed percentages detached from curriculum purposes, but only in the purposes themselves. And with formal research evidence inconclusive, the answer usually can rely for validation only on observation and empiricism.

A growing consensus is that the *large group is best* for the following kinds of curriculum activities: to introduce units, to present deductive concepts, to explain the meaning of terms, to present salient facts, to demonstrate scientific and related phenomena, to show visuals, to teach note-taking, to utilize the services of outside consultants, to correlate interdepartmental subject matter, to review subject matter, and to administer certain types of tests. The same growing consensus supports the thesis that *the small group is best* for discussion, the probing of controversial issues, the give-and-take between and among differing personalities, the placing of pupils from differing backgrounds in juxtaposition, and the refinement of language expression. In this connection, The Association of National Advertisers (although not without ulterior motive,

[8] J. Lloyd Trump and Dorsey Baynham, *Guide to Better Schools* (Chicago: Rand McNally and Company, 1961), p. 27.
[9] *Ibid.*, p. 28.
[10] *Ibid.*, p. 30.

we admit) avers that "people retain only 20 per cent of what they hear, 50 per cent of what they see and hear, but 70 per cent of *what they say*."[11] The *self-instructional method* is alleged to be best for reading, problem solving, library research, reinforcement and overlearning, application, and creative endeavor.

The Criterion of the Personal and Professional Roles and Attributes of Team Members. A fifth and once again important distinction among teaching teams revolves around the status of the personnel who make up the teams. In this connection, some schools, in deference to the complexities of the organizational arrangement, restrict a team's membership to professional individuals only. Other schools open a team's membership additionally to quasi-professional individuals including one or more of the following: teacher aids, student teachers, clerk-secretaries, or paper graders. The rationale behind the inclusion of one or several nonprofessional individuals from one or more of these categories is that they free teachers from the less important professional tasks, and thus permit them to spend greater time on the more important ones. At Norwalk, Connecticut, for instance, a team usually consists of a teacher-leader, teacher, and teacher aide. At Jefferson County, Colorado—at least at the beginning of the experiment—a team consisted of a teacher leader, two teachers, and a clerk.

Regardless of the exact makeup of any team, the job description of each member should emanate from curriculum intent and should be articulated before any final determination of team organization is made. In contrast, teams, not infrequently, are first put together and then told to hammer out their respective functional roles.

The first requisite for effective team endeavor is the desire by participants to be partners in it. A second requisite is the possession by team members of those personality attributes essential to it. A third requisite is the possession by team members of the specialized talents demanded by it. In this latter connection, the overriding purpose of many team-teaching arrangements is the exposure of a greater number of students to the specialized talents of selected teachers. Team teaching conveniently lends itself to this outcome. For instance, if four team-teaching colleagues in the field of high-school English have specialities in the fields of the drama, the novel, English composition, and poetry, respectively, each can increase the outward reach of his speciality by projecting it, in the appropriate curriculum context, to a larger than class-size group. Or if at the elementary-school level, three fourth-grades are united in a team effort and the three teachers, respectively, have

[11] Harold S. Davis, *Why Team Teach?* (Cleveland, Ohio: Staff Utilization Project, Educational Research Council of Greater Cleveland, 1964), p. 6.

strengths in science, children's literature, and teaching the slow learner, each of the three is better able to exploit his specialty.

The Criterion of the Leadership Pattern within a Group.   Yet another factor which distinguishes between and among teaching teams is the posture of leadership within teams. Team leadership manifests itself in two ways: as a line-and-staff entity and as a cooperative entity. When it manifests itself in the guise of the former, one team member, having been designated by higher authority to play a dominant administrative role, has line authority over the other members. When it manifests itself in the guise of the latter, team members share leadership, all acting cooperatively to accomplish their joint mission.

The line approach is probably best for teams which include one or more of the quasiprofessional individuals commented on in the last section. It also is probably best for teams organized around an experienced-inexperienced teacher arrangement. As a general rule, however, we underwrite the nonline approach to leadership for teams that consist exclusively of capable and experienced teachers. Our reason is that line authority tends to suppress and to stultify. Shared leadership, in contrast, if maturely exercised, tends to liberate and to generate. It is even possible that those individuals who are not ready for cooperative leadership are not ready for team membership at all.

The Criterion of Scheduling.   A seventh factor that differentiates among teaching teams is scheduling. Three approaches are operative throughout the country. The first consists of a temporary arrangement between or among teachers that brings classes together on a planned but yet strictly *ad hoc* basis. A case in point, similar to the illustration cited earlier, would be a several-week unit on Tudor England taught cooperatively during a common period by a teacher of English and a teacher of world history. The second consists of an organizational pattern wherein a role specialist moves from group to group. The specialized teacher of art, music, or creative dramatics in any one of hundreds of elementary schools through the country would be illustrative. In each instance, the classroom teacher and the curriculum specialist would constitute a team—a team at least in one sense of the word. The third is the one that conforms to the definitions spelled out at the beginning of the chapter. It commits a given number of teachers to share for a fixed period of time, usually a year, the instructional responsibilities for a given body of students.

Within the framework of this third organizational arrangement, patterns vary. In the elementary school, a growing practice is for teacher teams to be responsible during the entire school day for a combined group of pupils, with the latter being grouped and subgrouped in various ways throughout the day. Under such a plan, the problem of scheduling is an internal one, placed squarely on the shoulders of those responsible for the learning outcomes. And what could be more ideal? Yet this delegation of responsibility obligates the teaching team to professionalism in every sense of the word. By extending the base of decision making, it places greater demands on team teachers: in the planning for learning, in the grouping of pupils, in the choice of teaching method, and in the evaluation of pupil growth. In such a situation, the professional rewards can be greater, but the errors in judgment can also be more costly.

At the junior-high and senior-high levels, scheduling for team teaching is customarily of three types: back-to-back, alternate-period, and single-large-group. In the first, a school schedules two or more teachers for different groups which meet at a common time. The basic unit is the class, but the back-to-back composition permits classes to combine in various ways for common purposes. In the second method, two or more teachers have classes which meet during alternate periods and which likewise have alternate free periods. For instance, English 3-A meets the seventh period but is free the eighth; and U.S. History meets the eighth period but is free the seventh. This arrangement enables the two classes to combine, as the curriculum warrants, for double-length as well as for single-length class periods. In the third method, a team of teachers assumes a long-term shared responsibility for a single large group of pupils. From the beginning, all major decisions regarding scheduling are in their hands.[12]

The Criterion of Space. The factor of space as an influence on team-teaching activities is the last one to be covered in this section. Simply stated, if pupil groups which number from 100 to 150, from 25 to 30, and from 5 to 10, or which meet as individuals, are to learn effectively by the team method, adequate instructional space must be available. Furthermore, if instructional areas, particularly the large ones, are not to be vacant much of the time, they need to be structurally flexible—flexible in the sense that they can be made to adjust either to large-group or small-group specifications. The auditorium, lunch room, or gymnasium fall almost totally short of small-group specifications while just barely meeting large-group specifications. What is far preferable is a classroom with movable walls or one possessed of some other type of constructional flexibility that will permit easy conversion from small to large space areas, and vice versa. In this regard, the ideal team-teaching arrangement begins with the curriculum idea and ends

[12] We recommend the reading of Chapters 4 and 5, on the topic of organization, by Edward G. Buffie and Eugene R. Howard, respectively, in David W. Beggs III (ed.), *Team Teaching: Bold New Venture* (Indianapolis: Unified College Press, 1964).

with a building constructed around that idea. Most schools, falling short of this ideal, have to improvise. And the curriculum suffers in proportion to the amount of improvisation required.[13]

Accomodations for teacher-planning purposes are also vitally important. Provisions for such accomodations are lacking in many, if not in most, team-teaching situations. If teachers have to plan together, as they do, a minimum requirement is for education to provide them with facilities conceived along professional lines.

Advantages of Team Teaching: Real or Alleged

Team teaching had its birth in several basic educational postulates. One was that teachers are more effective when performing collectively than when performing individually. A second was that pupils, even younger ones, are less in need of a single "mother-image" figure than previously supposed. A third related one was that pupils can adjust more maturely, than previously presumed, even to a complex organizational setting.

Confident of the soundness of these postulates, team teaching was born, has survived the early stages of its existence, and increasingly is claiming the following as advantages.

Grouping Flexibility Is Inherent in Team Teaching.   Standing high on the list of advantages—real, not alleged, in my opinion—is the characteristic of grouping flexibility afforded by most team-teaching formulations. To begin with, the larger any team group of pupils happens to be, the greater its diversity is likely to be, and these two factors of size and diversity in and of themselves play into the hands of grouping.

If we consider just the factor of size, four teachers responsible, for instance, for 120 elementary or high-school pupils enjoy almost unlimited mathematical possibilities for grouping. At one extreme, a single teacher might teach the entire 120 while the remaining three played subordinate helping roles. Or the same teacher might teach 117 pupils while each of his colleagues counseled individually with a single student. Conversely, he might serve as one of the three counselors while one of his colleagues assumed the role of large-group leader. Or, one of the four could teach 90 pupils while each of the remaining three taught ten. Or, again, the four could teach 30 pupils each. These are only five of a much greater number of alternatives.

This characteristic of flexibility is a function not only of size but of diversity which customarily is a correlate of size. Generally speaking,

---

[13] For a detailed treatment of this factor of space, we refer the reader to two excellent sources: Evans Clinchy, *Schools for Team Teaching* (New York: Educational Facilities Laboratory, 1961); and Cyril G. Sargent, "The Organization of Space," in Shaplin and Olds, *Team Teaching*, Ch. 7.

the larger the total group, the greater the likelihood that a given school will be able to form subgroups around such diverse factors as ethnic differences and needs, emotional differences and needs, and social differences and needs, as well as around the more widely accepted traits of intelligence and achievement. A teaching team might group slow and fast learners together at certain times and keep them divided at other times. The same team, on certain occasions, might separate certain ethnic groups for social purposes; and on other occasions, keep selected ethnic-group members together for academic purposes.

However manifested, grouping flexibility is a pearl of great value in team teaching. It can exist along lines of numerical class size, curriculum purposes, teacher competencies, choice of teaching methods, and pupil differences. The same cannot be said for homogeneous grouping patterns in most other organizational settings throughout the country. With this characteristic of flexibility so important, teaching teams are remiss when they fail to exploit it to the hilt.

The Reach of Teacher Strengths Is Extended.   A second advantage of team teaching, real or alleged, is the effective use it can make of the specialized personal and professional competencies of teachers. For instance, as stated earlier, if one elementary school teacher is more knowledgeable than his team colleagues in a single academic area, he can extend this asset, via various grouping plans, throughout the entire group. In the area of teaching method, team teaching similarly permits the capable lecturer to do more large-group lecturing, the effective discussion leader to meet more often with seminar-sized groups, and the specialist in personal counseling to work more often with individual pupils. Yet it needs to be noted here that too much specialization within a team can weaken the basic structure of the team itself, which gets much of its strength from cooperative give-and-take relationships and shared endeavor.

In-service Education Is a By-product.   A third advantage, undoubtedly real in many or most team situations, is the in-service growth experienced by team members as a result of their close associations with fellow team members. One avenue to such growth is along the path of the respective specialties of the participating members. Each of the latter, at least so the conjectural thesis goes, can learn from the specialized talents of his team colleagues just as he learned many times from the demonstrated talents of a college professor or other instructional figure in a college or other kind of controlled academic setting.

A second avenue to in-service growth is down the path of give and take among team members who learn from each other by thinking together, by planning together, by differing together, and by making decisions together. Although not unique to team teaching, these habitually characterize team teaching because the latter rests on a social base.

Generally speaking, we more readily attest to the in-service benefits of team teaching as by products of the approach than as the *raison d' être* of the approach. Rarely, if ever, should a team-teaching pattern come into being solely to enable less experienced teachers to learn from more experienced ones. In such an arrangement, pupils are short-changed to the extent that one or more teachers are learners rather than professional instructional figures. The fundamental purpose of team teaching is pupil learning, not teacher learning, important though the latter indisputably is.

Teachers Have More Time for Professional Duties in Team Teaching. As indicated earlier in the chapter, many schools, spurred on by the Bay-City teacher-aid experiment in 1955, have assigned to teaching teams one or more noncertified personnel assistants. At the elementary-school level, these latter customarily take over such academic tasks as helping children with their wraps, taking the roll, supervising playground activities, collecting lunch money, and supervising in the lunch room. At the high-school level, these assistants engage in many of the tasks listed above while also performing obth clerical duties and designated professional ones. For instance, at the Evanston Township High School, an experiment has been going on for several years wherein instructors of English dictate, into an electric recorder, critical comments about English themes, comments which a secretarial aide later transcribes to the themes themselves. In this same general area, many schools farm out the entire task of paper-grading to college-trained, but noncertified, team members.

When team aides perform the lesser academic functions, certified team members, so the thesis goes, will gain valuable time which they then will devote to their more strictly professional functions. The counter thesis is that teachers who delegate to others such so-called menial tasks as paper grading and pupil conferences dull the edge of their professionalism as a result. Although leaning toward this counterthesis, I admit to some ambivalence, which only further thought and future educational experimentation can resolve.

Team Teaching Neutralizes the Effect of the Ineffective Teacher. A fifth advantage claimed for the team-teaching approach is that the ineffectiveness of "weak" teachers tends to be neutralized when averaged in with the assets of more competent team members. In this connection, however, which of the two following alternatives is less offensive: the concentration of professional inadequacy in one group of 30, or the dilution of adequacy across a range of 120 pupils? Perhaps a better answer than either is a third alternative whereby teacher inadequacy is dealt with administratively, not via curriculum manipulation. After all, team teaching, in view of the greater demands inherent in it, should depend on the best efforts only of competent people.

Pupils Become More Independent under Team Teaching.   A final advantage of team teaching, proclaimed by some, is that with pupils made to change their academic environments more often, they grow toward independence faster because they have more opportunity to practice independence. Once again, however, this advantage is most comfortable in the "alleged" category because little solid evidence exists to support or refute it. We prefer thus to withhold judgment about it.

Some Possible Limitations of Team Teaching

Despite the rather convincing body of logic on which the advantages of team-teaching rest, equally respectable authority has built up a body of counterlogic that oftentimes is no less convincing. And many who oppose all or certain aspects of team teaching are administrators and teachers who have worked with the method and found it wanting. In the following, we present the case for this opposition group.

Sustained Cooperation Is Difficult to Achieve.   High on the list of difficulties inherent in team teaching is the problem of the human equation. Stated at the most primitive level, certain teachers are just not mature enough to work cooperatively and productively with their colleagues in a team-teaching situation. Nor should this be surprising in view of the demands that the approach makes on the team members. First of all, it places them in a close family-like relationship wherein their paths cross hundreds of times in the course of a year. Second, within the framework of this close relationship, it asks them to resolve their major curriculum differences to the end of a workable consensus on fundamental issues. Third, team teaching confronts teachers frequently with the unexpected, requiring decision making at odd times and under unplanned conditions. Fourth, teachers have to perform under the critical eyes of their colleagues, which is a disturbing experience for many. And finally, because of the experimental nature of team teaching, the professional participants are called on consistently to justify their curriculum choices before administrators, parents, and the general public.

In view of these complexities, team members need to be unusually well-adjusted individuals who meet the high standards of mental health discussed in Chapter 4. The paradox of team teaching is that it expects team members at one and the same time to be individually creative and collectively outgoing. Although these outcomes are not mutually exclusive, they are attainable only by the more mature.

Curriculum Issues and Class Size.   Almost as difficult to resolve as the human problem in team teaching, is the curriculum problem of what should be taught in what way to what sized groups. And until this problem is solved to a point of reasonable satisfaction, teaching teams will lose much of their operational effectiveness. As mentioned earlier in the chapter, we reject any fixed mathematical solution, contending instead that the nature of learning outcomes, the nature of learning content, and the nature of the learners alone can decide when large-group, small-group, and individual methods are called for.

The assumptions on which we predicate a solution are those which constitute the basic platform of the entire book, namely, (1) that education is not only cognitive but social, emotional, ethical, and physical as well; (2) that any group of 90 to 150 pupils will differ widely on all these traits; (3) that oral-verbal methods can reach the entire group for certain, but not all, aspects of cognitive content; (4) that even when oral-verbal methods reach the entire group, it will reach them in different ways; and finally, (5) that extensive small group and individualized approaches will need to serve as controlling influences in deference to the multipurposes of education and the wide differences among learners. Because of the imponderables of the issue, no teaching team will ever know for a certainty just what curriculum components go best with what sized groups. But every teaching team is culpable when it fails to resolve the issue in the light of the best insights it has at any given time.

Other Possible Disadvantages or Unresolved Issues. We terminate this section on limitations by identifying and touching lightly on the remaining ones. Some actually are more unresolved issues than they are demonstrated disadvantages per se.

1. *Team teaching and the small school.* The problem of scheduling for team teaching mounts in inverse relationship to the size of any school. Back-to-back scheduling is obviously impossible where two or more sections of a given grade or content area do not exist. Thus in a very small school, team teaching which cuts across grade-level or subject matter lines is the only feasible solution. This constitutes a definite limitation, forcing team teaching, by necessity, into some core type of orgnizational pattern.

2. *The danger of pupil detachment.* With large-group endeavor characteristic of any team-teaching arrangement, an ever-present danger is that the individual will become isolated from needed personalized attention. This is more of an operational than an inherent limitation, however.

3. *The problem of planning time.* High on the list of unresolved issues in team teaching is the one pertaining to teacher planning. First of all, teachers need a common time during which to plan. For this time to be scheduled regularly after school hours poses difficulties. And for it to be scheduled during a commonly assigned "free" period poses no

fewer difficulties. Second, if planning is to be other than cursory, as well it should be, teachers need time released from other responsibilities to make it profitable. This latter constitutes an administrative problem in general and a budget problem in particular.

4. *The problem of facilities.*   The problem of facilities relates to large-space and individual-space needs. The ideal arrangement is for initial school construction to provide for these needs. Short of this ideal, most team groups throughout the country are preempting conventional space areas for team-teaching purposes. When these areas (such as a lunch room for a large-group meeting place) fall too short of the desired mark, team goals suffer.

5. *The issue of team leadership and whether it should be financially recognized.*   Currently a subject of debate in academic circles, as earlier indicated, is the issue of what pattern of leadership is most conducive to success in team teaching: the cooperatively-shared type or the line type? My preference is decidedly for the former. Schools which prefer the latter, however, face this additional issue: Should the leader receive compensatory pay for the leadership functions he performs? Axial to the issue is the age-old controversy regarding the relative importance of administration on one hand and scholarship on the other. Our general conclusion, which takes reality into account, is that administration which rests on a foundation of scholarship is justification for differential pay; but that administration without a scholarship basis has tenuous justification. In the cooperative leadership arrangement, however, this controversy is academic—as it should be.

6. *Teacher training as a problem.*   Finally, teacher members of teams should be qualified in advance for the professional responsibilities which they will have to assume. This means that teacher-training institutions need to face more realistically than they have to date the task of helping teacher candidates get ready for their new roles. This is not to deprecate the value of in-service training. It is rather a plea for a better foundation for it to build on.

Selected Evaluations of Team Teaching

Earlier in the chapter, I made note of the paucity of research on team teaching. Thus, this final assessment admittedly is subjective, relying for substance on the opinions of educational theorists and the observations of practitioners.

An assessment by Judson Shaplin of Washington University is a good one to start with. He states first that team teaching too prevalently is described in "highly general terms" against a badly distorted negative stereotype of more traditional patterns. Then he follows with this interesting allegation:

An attempt is also frequently made to surround team teaching with the aura of science. This creates a barrier between the projects and the potential critics who risk the label of antiscientific if they choose to assault the barrier. All projects have become experiments, and objectives are frequently stated as hypotheses. However, in most cases the projects are merely educational demonstrations of preferred practices with few of the variables identified, much less controlled in any experimental sense, and with the hypotheses stated so generally that it is impossible to establish operational conditions under which they can be tested.[14]

Brownell and Taylor, claiming five to six years of functional experience with team teaching, are agnostic, although not skeptical, of its merits, announcing: "We recommend closer analysis of assumptions, more explicit models, better research design, and more penetrating evaluation of results of team experimentation so that schoolmen will be able to make sound judgments about teaching teams."[15]

Anderson, after working for four years with the original pioneer team-teaching project at the Franklin School of Lexington, Massachusetts, under the auspices of Harvard's SUPRAD (School and University Program for Research and Development), concludes as follows:

Data reported to date show that team teaching results are no less satisfactory than those from typical conventional teaching in elementary and secondary schools. There are some slight indications that team teaching is particularly beneficial to markedly advanced and retarded pupils, and also signs that certain children find greater stimulation and security within team-teaching situations.[16]

Clinchy, commenting on the same project, makes such conservative statements as these: "Team teaching is feasible," "the children's achievement results did not suffer," "The children's personal, emotional, and social adjustments are at least as good as before—and there are indications that gains have been made." And finally, "The building definitely influences program possibilities; a conventional building operates against the efficient working of a team program."[17]

Another writer, Heller, first sanguine and then more cautious, announces that:

Competent, albeit subjective, evaluations of team teaching are resoundingly in favor of pupil gains in terms of social attitudes, interest in further education, increased verbal articulation, development of curiosity, and knowledge and

[14] Shaplin, and Olds, *Team Teaching*, p. 7.
[15] John A. Brownell and Harris A. Taylor, "Theoretical Perspectives for Teaching Teams," *Phi Delta Kappan*, 43 (January 1962), p. 157.
[16] Anderson, "Team Teaching," p. 54.
[17] Clinchy, *Schools for Team Teaching*, p. 40.

skill in small group discussions. Until standardized tests and/or teacher-made tests can give objective data to support this evaluation, these subjective conclusions are the best that can be offered.[18]

An emerging synthesis, although without the support of research, is that team teaching is accomplishing the outcomes of learning, broadly conceived, as effectively as do the more traditional plans. The essential drawback seems to be increased pupil detachment. The essential assests seem to be a highly flexible base for grouping and a better utilization of teacher strengths. Team teaching is no panacea, but neither have been the various plans associated with the single-teacher arrangement. In our opinion, the merits of team teaching for years to come will rest almost exclusively on educational theory and subjective experience. The reason is that the variables of team teaching are too multitudinous to be controlled properly in any conclusive research attempt. This is not to discourage research in the area, but only to reduce future expectations to modest proportions.

The following excellent summary statement provides an appropriate conclusion for this section:

The heart of the concept of team teaching lies not in details of structure and organization but more in the essential spirit of cooperative planning, constant collaboration, close unity, unrestrained communication, and sincere sharing . . . Inherent in the plan is an increased degree of flexibility for teacher responsibility, grouping policies and practices, and size of groups, and an invigorating spirit of freedom and opportunity to revamp programs to meet the educational needs of children.[19]

For Further Thought

1. If asked to make a choice, would you elect to become a member of a teaching team or to become a classroom teacher in the more conventional understanding of the term? Give your reasons.

2. I have emphasized the importance of personality adjustment for members of teams. Do you regard this factor in the same light? If not, defend your stand.

3. Which of the three approaches—large-group, small-group, or individual —would you recommend for the following learning outcomes: teaching a controversial topic, breaking down social or economic barriers, helping an aggressive pupil to become less belligerent, teaching grammar, teaching creative writ-

[18] Melvin P. Heller, *Team Teaching Questions and Answers* (Cleveland, Ohio: Educational Research Council of Greater Cleveland, 1963), p. 11.
[19] Stuart E. Dean and Clinette F. Witherspoon, "Team Teaching in the Elementary School," *Education Briefs*, OE-23022 (Washington, D.C.: U.S. Department of Health, Education, and Welfare, 1962), p. 4.

ing, teaching *Julius Caesar* to nonverbal students, helping the gifted to intensi-
fy their understanding of biochemistry, teaching reading to third graders, encouraging art interests in a first grade? These are just a few of the grouping
decisions that teaching teams have to make.

4. If team-teaching and conventional-teaching methods led to identical academic achievement outcomes, might the latter still be regarded as superior?
If so, in what way? If not, why not?

5. Describe in what ways, if any, team teaching might be effective in meeting the needs of exceptional children?

6. Do you envision team teaching as being more appropriate at certain
school levels (primary, intermediate, junior-high, and senior-high) than at
others? Explain your point of view.

7. List all the duties which you think are appropriate for a teacher aide
to perform at a given school level. Then defend each as not detracting unduly
from the strength of the teacher from whom they have been removed.

8. If you believe in differential pay for team members in the light of the
duties they perform, create and defend a hierarchy of job or duty categories
from high to low. Then justify your choices in terms of "more important" or
"less important."

References

Anderson, Robert H., "Team Teaching," *NEA Journal,* **50** (March 1961), pp.
    52–54.

Beggs, David W. III (ed.), *Team Teaching: Bold New Venture.* Indianapolis:
    Unified College Press, Inc., 1964.

Brownell, John A. and Harris A. Taylor, "Theorctical Perspectives for Teaching
    Teams," Phi Delta Kappan, **43** (January 1962), pp. 150–157.

Clinchy, Evans, *Schools For Team Teaching.* New York: Educational Facilities
    Laboratory, 1961.

Davis, Harold S., *Planning A Team Teaching Program.* Cleveland, Ohio: Staff
    Utilization Project, Educational Council of Greater Cleveland, 1964.

Davis, Harold S. *Why Team Teach?* Cleveland, Ohio: A Staff Utilization Pro-
    ject, Educational Council of Greater Cleveland, 1964.

Dean, Stuart E. and Clinette F. Witherspoon, "Team Teaching in the Ele-
    mentary School," *Education Briefs,* OE-23022. Washington, D.C.: U.S.
    Department of Health, Education, and Welfare, January, 1962.

Dearborn, Michigan Public Schools, *Analysis of a Team Teaching And of a
    Self Contained Homeroom Experiment in Grades 5 and 6,* 1962.

Hamilton, Andrew, "Is Team Teaching For Your Child?" *The PTA Magazine,*
    58 (May 1964), pp. 4–6.

Heller, Melvin P., *Team Teaching: Questions And Answers.* Cleveland, Ohio:
    Educational Research Council of Greater Cleveland, 1963.

Hoppock, Anne, "Team Teaching: Form Without Substance? *NEA Journal,*
    50 (April 1961), pp. 47–48.

Lambert, Philip, "Team Teaching for the Elementary School," *Educational
    Leadership,* **18** (November 1960), pp. 85–88.

Shaplin, Judson T. and Henry F. Olds, (eds.) *Team Teaching*. New York: Harper and Row, 1964.

Stafford, James, *An Exploration into Team Teaching in English And the Humanities*. New York: The National Council of Teachers of English, 1963.

Stoltenberg, James C., "Team Teaching in Junior High School," *Educational Leadership*, 18 (December 1960), pp. 153–155.

University of Maine, College of Education Team Teaching Project, *A Second Annual Report to the Ford Foundation on Team Teaching in Maine*. Orono, Maine: University of Maine, January, 1964.

chapter 15

The Nongraded Classroom

Another controversial aspect of organization is the nongraded classroom. Like team teaching, the nongraded classroom involves a break with tradition in the grouping of pupils for learning. Unlike team teaching, however, it has been slow to catch on as an approved organizational pattern. Its successes in the primary grades, although limited in number, have been qualitatively significant. Its successes in the intermediate, junior-high, and senior-high-school grades, however, have ranged from the modest to the insignificant.

The nongraded classroom movement becomes most understandable against a historical backdrop. Beginning with the classical period, and continuing for the better part of two millenia, teaching and learning had their organizational roots in the tutorial process. A Socrates, a Quintilian, a Saint Augustine, or some other teacher-scholar would customarily tutor selected students individually; occasionally, two or three children in a single family; but rarely, or never, more than a small select group of learners. The tutoring method generally was so expensive as to be beyond the reach of all but the affluent. For this reason, the educated slave was valuable merchandise when up for barter in the market place.

Society gradually came to realize that if education was to become the property of the masses, group methods for the underprivileged many would need to parallel, or replace, tutorial methods for the privileged few. This insight was translated differentially into practice as the third estate of feudalism and the later evolving middle class grew in numbers and stature. Early attempts at instruction of the masses took place in learning groups which, along the lines of almost any trait dimension, were notoriously heterogeneous. This purturbed surprisingly few at a time when learning's focus was on content, not on the learner. When the focus began to veer toward the learner, however, education felt a comparable need for learning groups to possess a firmer core of homogeneity.

One practical manifestation of this need was the graded classroom. This latter had its origin in Europe when, in 1537, John Sturum converted a school in Strassburg, Germany, to the graded pattern. Sturum employed age as the basis of grouping, seating pupils on benches according to their grade or "form." Three centuries later, encouraged by the successes which Germany had had with the graded organizational pattern, and motivated by the need to substitute the more economical large-group approach for the more expensive tutorial or small-group approach, Horace Mann recommended the graded plan for America. John Philbrick took Mann's recommendation and brought it to fruition in 1848 when he made the Quincy School of Boston into the first graded school to open in this country.[1] It should also be mentioned here that the appearance in the first part of the nineteenth century of graded, or partially graded, textbooks gave Mann and Philbrick added reason for their espousal of the graded school plan. The Warren Colburn Arithmetic textbooks of 1821 and the more famous McGuffey Eclectic Readers of 1836 are illustrative in this regard.

Whatever the exact reasons for the graded classroom, once it appeared in America, it became within two or three decades the conventional school organizational pattern.[2] Conceived as an antidote to heterogeneity within learning groups, its more avid proponents consistently placed too much faith in its ability to neutralize, via the process of age classification, this same heterogeneity. Grading with age as a unilateral criterion assumes falsely that children of similar ages not only have similar interests and abilities, but have had similar cultural experiences as well. Reality, in contrast, reveals that the mental-age range of a typical first-grade class is as great as four years. And, as stated by Goodlad and Anderson, "By the time children complete the fourth grade, the range in readiness to learn (as suggested by the M.A.) in most areas of achievement is approximately the same as the number designating the grade level."[3]

As early as 1870, the newly adopted graded pattern was subjected to attack by such well known educators as Francis Parker, Charles W. Eliot, William Rainey Harper, and John Dewey. Like their numerous counterparts of today, they rebelled against the artificial division of curriculum into fixed segments, and against the subsequent superimposition

---

[1] We give credit for the details of this paragraph to B. Frank Brown, *The Nongraded High School* (Englewood Cliffs, N.J.: Prentice-Hall, Inc., 1963), pp. 27–28.

[2] For a more complete treatment of grading, see William J. Shearer, *The Grading of Schools* (New York: H. P. Smith Publishing Co., 1899).

[3] John I. Goodlad and Robert H. Anderson, *The Nongraded Elementary School* (Harcourt, Brace & World, Inc., 1963), p. 13.

of these same segments on learners who, even though grouped by age, remained none the less diversified on most counts. Goodlad, Anderson, and Brown of the current educational scene identify this practice as no different in principle from Procustes' practice of fitting people of all heights to a single-length bed. To achieve a proper fit, he cut down the tall and stretched the short to conform to the bed's linear dimensions. In comparable manner, a graded organizational system when operating traditionally forces a given body of learners into a preconceived curriculum niche; and it retains them there, theoretically at least, until they have met the standards of the niche. For most, the retention time is usually of a single year's duration; for a few at each of the polar ends, the retention time is for a period shorter than or longer than a year's duration. For the few who are retained longer than one year, the assumption is made that at a later date they then will be able to advance to, and perform successfully at the level of, the next curriculum rung. This line of reasoning, while alluring by its plausibility, almost consistently breaks down in practice.

The Antidote of the Nongraded System

Perturbed by the manifest shortcomings of the graded school, a small but convicted group of educational theorists and practitioners recently forged into being a countermovement, dedicated to the establishment—more accurately, to the re-establishment—of the nongraded school. At a surface level, this had the appearance of a reactionary return to the past: for instance, to the Dame or District School of colonial times, or to the Little Red School House of more recent times. All of these were nongraded schools—and none was more than passably successful. However, the actual purpose of this group was liberal rather than reactionary. The purpose was liberal in the sense that, although they looked back to the nongraded plan with all its recognized disadvantages, they looked forward to the inherent but previously unexplored possibilities of the plan. The were very much intrigued by the hitherto untapped potentials of nongrading, very little intrigued by the practical traditions of the plan itself.

For the past thirty years or thereabouts, theory and practice pertaining to the nongraded school movement have become increasingly integrated and mutually supportive. Nor is this at all surprising since sound theory, with rare exception, anchors the base of operational practice. And in the same scheme of affairs, operational practice serves to distill error from existing theory. Such has been the interlocking relationship between theory and practice with respect to nongrading. When the latter was reborn in the 1930's, its theory was vague and diffused. Since that time, its theory has been refined by Anderson, Brown, Goodlad, Kelly, and others. During the same period, nongrading has extended its practical horizons noticeably if not extensively.

In terms of operational practice, Western Springs, Illinois, in 1934, adopted the nongraded pattern but dropped it shortly thereafter.[4] Milwaukee, Wisconsin, in January of 1942, initiated a nongraded program that is still in operation. In 1960 it was in operation "on a voluntary basis" in 114 of the 116 Milwaukee schools.[5] Appleton, Wisconsin, embarked on the new plan in 1947, and Coffee County, Georgia, in 1950.[6]

An accurate estimate of the number of elementary school systems or schools that currently operate along lines of the nongraded organizational pattern is difficult to come by. For one reason, the movement is too new for valid data to be readily available. For a second significant reason, a number of schools that profess to operate on a nongraded plan are not necessarily nongraded in the real meaning of the term. In this regard, Goodlad and Anderson—who are the most prolific and articulate spokesmen for the nongraded program in elementary education—estimate that approximately 50 communities[7] and 550 schools[8] are operating on the nongraded pattern. Brown, one of the newer and also one of a selected few secondary-education spokesmen for the nongraded program, specifically refers to only five secondary schools or school systems that are organized around the new pattern. These Brown cites as the Melbourne High School in Florida, of which he is principal; The Brigham Young University Laboratory School; the Middletown High School of Newport, Rhode Island; the Hamilton Junior High School of Newton, Massachusetts; and the high school, as well as the lower grade schools, of Borregon, California.[9]

Just What Is a Nongraded School Organization?

So far in this chapter, the terms nongraded school, nongraded school organization, and nongraded classroom have appeared primarily as abstract symbols. Furthermore, the emphasis has been more on what they contrast to—the graded school organization—than on what they themselves stand for. Now we raise the fundamental question: Just what is

[4] Leonard B. Wheat, "The Flexible Progress Group System," *The Elementary School Journal*, 38 (November 1937), pp. 26–28.
[5] Florence C. Kelly, "Ungraded Primary School," *Educational Leadership*, 18 (November 1960), pp. 79–81.
[6] Lillian Gore, "The Nongraded Primary Unit," *School Life*, 44 (March 1962), pp. 6–9.
[7] Goodlad and Anderson, *The Nongraded Elementary School*, p. 55.
[8] John I. Goodlad and Robert H. Anderson, "Educational Practices in Nongraded Schools: A Survey of Perceptions," *The Elementary School Journal* 63 (October 1962), p. 33.
[9] Brown, *The Nongraded High School*, pp. 33–34.

the nongraded plan? And relatedly, what are some of its theoretical and functional dimensions and characteristics?

Definitions

At the start, I wish to make clear that the nongraded organizational plan is not a discrete entity with identical features wherever found. Rather, even though the many instances of implementation have much in common both in terms of theoretical rationale and practical manifestations, the nongraded pattern is basically a lengthened shadow of the philosophies and experiences of those doing the implementing. School patterns vary over such practices, for instance, as the initial and subsequent grouping of pupils, over how long a given teacher will remain with a given class group, over methods of effecting vertical pupil progress, and over pupil retention. The following definitions mirror a few such differences as well as a basic core of commonality.

Gore, who is elementary oriented and who in that frame of reference has related to nongrading essentially at the level of the primary grades, defines it this way:

> The Nongraded Primary Unit is one that follows a design or plan of organization which disregards grade-level designations and expectations. Such a plan places children in flexible groups and allows each child to progress at his own optimum rate . . . In the mind of many educators, it has much value for mental health practice.[10]

Thompson, also elementary oriented, opines that:

> The ungraded unit is an organizational pattern adopted primarily to provide continuity in learning. It recognizes the sequential development of skills and the importance of success or mastery at each stage.[11]

Brinkman, Superintendent of the Dobbs Ferry School System of New York State, writing from his individualized orientation avers that:

> The essence of the ungraded school is a plan to group youngsters on the basis of age, certain abilities, and other related factors and then let them move ahead at their own speed. Such a built-in flexibility enables a youngster not only to work with his own class and teacher but to cross the hall and work with another class—in arithmetic, for example, where there may be a better match for his capacity.[12]

[10] Gore, "The Nongraded Primary Unit," p. 9.
[11] Ethel Thompson, "The Ungraded Plan: Today and Tomorrow in Elementary and Secondary Education," reprinted from *The NEA Journal* (January 1958), p. 5.
[12] Albert R. Brinkman, "Now Its the Ungraded School," *The PTA Magazine,* 105 (June 1961), p. 24.

Brown, from an exclusive orientation in secondary education, describes nongrading along similar lines:

The innovation of the nongraded high school is out of the hothouse. What is a nongraded school? A nongraded school is a place which makes arrangements for the individual student to pursue any course in which he is interested, and has the ability to achieve, without regard either to grade level or sequence.[13]

Specific Characteristics of Nongrading Plans

With these definitions meaningful enough to frame but not specific enough to delineate—a typical shortcoming of highly condensed abstractions of almost any kind—a needed clarifying next step is for us to list and discuss the specifics that make up the nucleus of nongraded curriculum organizations.

Conventional Grade Designations Are Omitted. A universal attribute of nongrading, intrinsic in the term itself, is that it avoids grade designations as conventionally conceived and employed. Thus the usual labels of Grades 1, 2, and 3, in a primary nongraded unit, or Grades 4, 5, and 6 in an intermediate nongraded unit, are consigned, in theory at least, to oblivion. In their place appear such substitute labels as Mrs. Smith, Primary, or Mr. Jones, Intermediate. Admittedly, this transposition of labels in and of itself is no more than symbolic, revealing nothing about the educational practices that take place under cover of the labels. Yet as an initial step of a process aimed in fact as well as in name at the ultimate elimination of grade lockstepping, the transposition is far more than mere facade.

The Yearly Block Gives Way to a Three- Or Four-Year Block. Eschewing the time-honored yearly grade period as an organizational concept, nongraded units employ in lieu thereof block periods of longer duration as indices of school status. These they usually label with the terms primary or intermediate in the elementary school. Nongraded patterns in the secondary school are as yet too infrequent to have earned any comparable label. In the typical nongraded primary or intermediate unit, pupils customarily spend 3, and occasionally 2 or 4, years before moving on to the next unit, or to the next grade-level sequel, as the case may be. In this connection, Brown envisions American education of the future as divided into five organizational subparts; the nongraded primary, the nongraded intermediate, the nongraded junior high school, the nongraded high school, and the nongraded college. In effect, says he, this would reduce 16 grades into 5 general areas.[14] Needless to say,

[13] Brown, *The Nongraded High School*, p. 43.
[14] Brown, *The Nongraded High School*, p. 47.

Brown's vision of the future of secondary and college education is not shared by the overwhelming majority of educators. Yet, if properly implemented at the classroom level in terms of educational practice, there is no sound reason why the proposed organization would not work.

Most Nongrading Occurs in Primary Units. The incidence of nongrading is greatest at the primary level of elementary education, shrinks significantly at the intermediate level, and becomes only a fractionated phenomenon above the intermediate level. A fundamental reason why nongrading is most at home with primary-age children resides in its great sensitivity to variations in the developmental growth patterns of the young. In this connection, it is an accepted phenomenon that young children mature more unevenly and thus less predictably than do their older counterparts. Maturation in some 6-, 7-, and 8-year-olds proceeds at a more or less steady pace; in others, it appears to leap forward at times and almost to stand still at other times. And a few slow starters inevitably pass up others who matured faster during an earlier growth period.

If the processes of maturation in young children are notoriously uneven and unpredictable, growth for these same young children along almost any learning progression is just as uneven and unpredictable. Learning depends too much on pupil readiness for the relationship to be otherwise. Thus, an organizational arrangement such as nongrading, which relies almost for its very existence on keeping learning and readiness closely attuned, has special appeal for teachers of children where this affinity conceivably is of greatest importance. Apart from the specialized nature of pupil readiness in younger children, however, the same grounds that justify nongrading at the primary level equally justify it at the intermediate and maybe even higher levels.

Continuous Pupil Progress Is Fundamental. The goal of every nongraded organizational scheme is the sequential progression of each pupil toward outcomes uniquely appropriate for him. A curriculum that takes cognizance of this goal thus has to be elastic enough to provide a high floor and a high ceiling for the gifted, and a commensurately lower floor and lower ceiling for the slow. Each pupil in such a scheme, theoretically at least, starts and ends at a different point.

With nongrading this closely attuned to the individual, a related issue is whether it is ever attuned, and if so to what degree, to standards outside the individual. Theoreticians who serve as spokesmen for nongrading generally touch lightly, if at all, on this issue. Classroom teachers and school administrators, however, face up to it more realistically. When they predict, as most do, that the majority of students will spend three years in a nongraded unit, they come close to admitting the existence of objective standards. Then when they announce verbally, or in administrative fine print, that a few selected pupils will be able to complete the program in two years and that a few others will require four years to complete it, they even more strongly reveal, even though indirectly, the existence of external standards.

However, even when both nongraded and graded units operate within the framework of external standards, the professional personnel involved tend to relate to the standards in contrasting ways. Those in nongrading tend to treat the standards more broadly as guides; those in grading tend to treat them more narrowly as prescribed sequences. Furthermore, the former relate them more specifically to the individual; the latter relate them more generally to the larger group.

Bases of Grouping

Irrespective of the exact pattern of educational organization, whether graded or nongraded, schools have no choice but to group children in some defensible way to get them into class-sized clusters. This necessitates a careful determination and employment of grouping criteria. The typical graded elementary school employs the criterion of age in its selection of children for the first grade. State law, in this regard, universally sets the minimum age limit. From Grade 1 and beyond, such other factors as achievement, ability, social readiness, and emotional maturity join with age as the more commonly employed criteria of selection.

The nongraded organization shares with its graded counterpart concern over the criteria that schools should employ in bringing class-sized groups into being. Although not unique to nongrading, the latter has made extensive use of the five following bases.

1. *General reading ability.*   Standing high on the list is reading ability which, according to Goodlad and Anderson, constitutes the criterion in fifty per cent of nongraded primary organizations.[15] Even though other sources place their estimates at 10 to 15 per cent lower than this, the reading criterion remains a significant one.

2. *Age.*   As in graded organizations, age is also an important criterion in nongraded organizations. In this regard, a few schools in grouping for nongraded primary units separate the incumbent pupils into two age groups: those who are over 6 years but who are under 6 years 6 months; and the remainder who are at least 6 years 6 months, but who are under 7 years.

3. *Social homogeneity.*   A few schools, again mostly those at the primary level of elementary education, employ social development—if not as the sole criterion, at least as a supporting criterion.

[15] Goodlad and Anderson, *The Nongrade Elementary School*, p. 34.

4. *Deliberately imposed heterogeneity.* A number of schools, such as the public elementary schools of Appleton, Wisconsin, and the Englewood School of Saratosa County, Florida, deliberately strive for heterogeneity in their nongraded units by operating within a broad frame of human differences. The stated aim of the Englewood School, for instance, is a "multigrade, multiage" classroom organization. In a comparable way, the aim of the Milwaukee system is an admixture of the chronological, the social, and the emotional.[16]

5. *Achievement.* Eschewing heterogeneity, Brown, from his orientation exclusively to secondary education, defends achievement unequivocally as the sole grouping criterion. He announces forthrightly: "There are many factors besides native intelligence that determine the rate of student progress, but achievement is superior to any other criterion."[17]

In the last analysis, grouping not only for a nongraded situation but for a graded one is a function of educational purpose. If growth along a broad personality spectrum is the goal, groups probably need to be more heterogeneous; if growth in a narrower outcome such as achievement is the goal, groups conceivably need to be more homogeneous. We hedge deliberately on this issue because no view is correct or incorrect apart from underlying philosophical assumptions.

An Evaluation of Nongrading

Since most nongraded classes have been using the nongraded pattern of organization for only a short time and since very little research data are available about it, the task of assessment becomes that much more difficult. The vast majority of the evaluative evidence currently available is a product either of practical experiences that are too local or too biased to be convincing; or, at best, is a product of common-sense inference. Thus, because of the instability of the evaluative evidence, our conclusion at the moment is that a posture of questioning neutrality toward nongrading is the only defensible one for the academic world to assume. Even the two outstanding advocates of nongrading, Goodlad and Anderson, confess candidly that "there is no evidence to suggest anything."

In contrast to this conservative position, school administrators and teacher practitioners who are actively involved throughout the country in a nongraded situation not infrequently exude almost unrestrained enthusiasm about it. I commend their optimism while urging that it not lead to premature judgment. What is needed instead is for claims of superiority to await the results of a longer period of careful experimentation and assessment. In the meantime, empirically based conclusions will have to suffice. These constitute the central theme of the present section.

[16] Lillian Gore, "The Nongraded Primary Unit," p. 10.
[17] Brown, *The Nongraded High School*, p. 35.

Advantages: Real or Alleged. One of the most frequently alleged advantages of nongrading is that it permits pupils to progress at their own individual rates in an unbroken curriculum progression. Whether this is, or is not, an advantage, however, depends on how closely the curriculum of the nongraded program is integrated and articulated. Irrespective of grading or nongrading, articulation can take place through two methods of staff utilization. One is by a teacher's remaining with a group of children for a period longer than a year, conceivably the entire three years, in a nongraded unit. The other is by a careful teacher exchange of complete and meaningful pupil personnel information at such time as pupils move from one organizational level to another, either from grade to grade or from one nongraded unit to another. When a teacher remains with a group longer than a year, he becomes his own articulator; but in the process, this plan deprives pupils of additional teacher contacts, even penalizing them seriously when a given teacher is professionally inept. When different teachers in any kind of school organization instruct at different levels, the sought-after resultant of graduated pupil progress depends fundamentally on how effectively the several teachers are able to integrate their respective efforts. Thus, to our way of thinking, growth continuity in a nongraded curriculum organization is not at all an inherent feature of the organizational medium; rather, it is a product of curriculum quality and a school's effectiveness in the process of articulation.

A second advantage of the nongraded plan—and this we regard as intrinsic—is that decisions on retardation of pupils automatically are delayed for three years. This delay permits teachers to appraise with a constantly growing body of cumulative evidence. In any graded organization where pupil promotion is not automatic, each teacher at the end of any given year has to decide who will pass or fail. This is a sobering task at any time, and is a particularly disturbing one in grades 1 and 2 where delayed readiness ever lurks as a plausible reason for substandard performance. In the nongraded plan where retardation can be delayed for three years, decisions tend to have more clinical defensibility.

A third advantage, alleged, is that teachers in a nongraded-school organization have more flexibility in the selection of subject matter, in establishing its sequence, and in assigning time allocations to it than do their "graded" counterparts. Generally speaking, this appears to be a valid advantage, hemmed in as most teachers in graded schools are by superimposed curriculum prescriptions and limitations. Yet in a well planned curriculum of an enlightened graded school, the difference would be minuscule.

A fourth often asserted advantage of the nongraded plan is that actual pupil achievement, not time spent in school, constitutes the basis of evaluation. This is a point Kelly makes in her description of the Milwaukee School System.[18] This claim rather left-handedly implies that teachers in graded units conceive evaluation primarily in terms of time spent. A few may, but the majority, in my opinion, do not. If this advantage were stated in shadings rather than in stark contrasts, I might accept it; otherwise, I tend to reject it as too categorical.

A fifth advantage identified by many—and this relates usually only to the primary unit—is that greater progress in reading is made under the nongraded than under the graded plan. What casts doubt on this purported advantage is that research is as yet too unsubstantial to support the allegation. A number of studies, such as one by Skapski[19] in Burlington, Vermont, claim support for the allegation, but these lack the experimental controls necessary to establish the findings as other than artifactual. What is needed is more matched-pair experiments of graded and nongraded children wherein strict controls are exercised over pupil ability, over time spent in reading, over teacher selection, and over methods of instruction. Until such experiments are forthcoming, honest skepticism about this alleged advantage constitutes the better part of wisdom.

Shortcomings Real or Alleged. Now we turn to the shortcomings, real or alleged, of the nongraded plan. And in my opinion, the most controversial issue revolves around the question of what vertical sequence pupils will follow, and in what way will they follow it, as they progress through a two-, three-, or four-year nongraded curriculum. In essence, if children are to move along a graduated curriculum sequence, they will need the services of a curriculum which is ever sensitive to their individuality including their respective needs, interests, and rates of progress.

This means that nongraded settings should have curricula that extend quantitatively from less to more content, and qualitatively from less to more intensity. They should be of such nature as to challenge the fast while not leaving the slow in a state of frustration. But above all, they should be graduated so as to enable pupils both to move into and through learning experiences at varying rates and in varying qualitative ways.

A curriculum whether in a graded or nongraded setting can meet the needs of children and youth in only these two procedural ways. One is when knowledgeable curriculum workers formulate a curriculum outside the context of specific situations and allow each teacher flexibility—even extensive flexibility as the occasion warrants—to apply it in individualized ways. The other is when a given teacher, endowed with

[18] Kelly, "Ungraded Primary School," pp. 79–80.
[19] Mary King Skapski, "Ungraded Primary Reading Program," *The Education-Digest*, **26** (January 1961), pp. 45–47.

proper administrative authority, first studies a learning group and then brings a curriculum into being. Although the second is the preferable way, it is also the idealized way, making almost insurmountable demands on teachers.

Irrespective of the exact method of implementation, most nongraded schools espouse the goal of vertical sequence for each pupil but few elaborate on it descriptively, and even fewer reveal the specifics of its implementation. If vertical sequence is as obscure in practice as paucity of comment would indicate, one of the major justifications for nongrading rests on a tenuous foundation.

A second possible soft spot of at least a few nongraded plans is that after eliminating conventional grade labels they proceed to add others that may be no better than the ones they replace. For instance, Milwaukee has divided its primary curriculum into twelve levels of achievement. This is a step in the right direction provided these levels serve the cause of vertical progression. But to the extent that they substitute twelve different hurdles for the three grade hurdles which they replace, what is this but grading merely under a greater number of labels?

A third sensitive area, which is equally a problem of both graded and nongraded organizations, relates to the process of grouping children for instructional purposes. And in this connection, irrespective of organizational pattern, schools have yet to find the "right" answer. As indicated earlier in the chapter, the criteria used as grouping bases in one or more nongraded schools are these: reading, chronological age, social development, planned heterogeneity, and achievement. No single one or combination of several of these is right or wrong apart from a philosophy of education to back it up; but each or all are wrong without such a philosophy. Nongrading needs to speak out more articulately on this grouping issue.

A fourth issue regarding nongrading, although not necessarily a shortcoming, concerns the uncertainty of its appropriateness for certain departmentalized school settings. In one sense of the term, nongrading is already operative when a seventh- and an eighth-grader are enrolled in the same typing course, or when a ninth- and an eleventh-grader are enrolled in the same Spanish I or basic industrial-arts course. But these are incidental rather than planned occurrences.

Generally speaking, a nongraded plan within any general-education area is as defensible for the customarily departmentalized grades 7 through 12 as it is for the self-contained classroom grades K through 6. Common ingredients would be a time block longer than a year, vertical scheduling, sequential pupil progression through a given body of content, and teacher flexibility. However, nongrading rests less sure-footedly in the curriculum electives, where a single semester or year of enrollment is commonplace and where the refinements of curriculum sequence and pupil progression through it would pose a serious problem.

To my knowledge, the only methodical treatment of nongrading in secondary education appears in B. Frank Brown's book in 1963, *The Nongraded High School.* And I seriously question whether Brown conceives nongrading in the same way as do those theoreticians and practitioners who speak for nongrading in elementary education. Brown's book actually is more a description of the specialized curriculum and organizational practices of the public high school—a school of which Brown is principal—of Melbourne, Florida, than it is a contribution to the institution of nongrading as conventionally conceived.

The Melbourne High School divides its student body into five Phases, with Phase I containing the remedial students and Phase 5 "students with exceptional ability who are willing to assume responsibility for their own learning and go far beyond the normal high school level."[20] Students merit assignment as a result of their respective performances on standardized achievement tests. The total curriculum, according to Brown, is characterized by a variety of curriculum materials and a minimum of adherence to conventional textbooks. The Melbourne system requires students to enroll in six courses. The students do not have study halls. Up to this point, very little in the description relates directly to nongrading in the accepted meaning of the term.

Generally speaking, Brown seems to have lifted the symbolic term nongrading from its familiar academic context and reapplied it to suit his subjective purposes. To most, nongrading connotes standards that reside in each individual learner; to Brown, despite lip service to the contrary, it apparently connotes standards implicit in a fixed curriculum. To most, nongrading presupposes no set posture toward grouping practices; to Brown, it presupposes the adoption of homogeneous grouping practices with achievement the criterion. To most, nongrading does not imply an essentialist orientation; to Brown, apparently it does.

To summarize here, I believe that nongrading has had very little impact on secondary education. Nor for the near future do I envision any significant increase in the size of the impact.

A Point of View

In conclusion, I synthesize the case for nongrading this way. Neither grading nor nongrading in and of itself is unequivocally superior or unequivocally inferior to its counterpart. Each succeeds or fails depending on the supporting philosophies and operational practices of the professional personnel who give it leadership. Labels per se do not make organizations successful; attitudes and wisely chosen activities do. Thus, de-

[20] Brown, *The Nongraded High School,* p. 50.

pending on given circumstances, either or neither pattern can know success.

Oblivious to this viewpoint or holding it to be specious, a number of writer-analysts of nongrading have concluded too hastily—too hastily at least in my opinion—that grading and nongrading lie at opposite poles. Having so concluded, they then strike out with black and white contrasts. And quite predictably, they make grading the bête noire. In the process, grading becomes a symbol for large-group teaching habitually practiced, for fixed curriculum standards, and for automatic pupil retardation. Conversely, nongrading becomes a symbol for small-group or individualized teaching habitually practiced, for flexible curriculum standards, and for commendable achievement by nearly every pupil. All evaluations such as these are inaccurate by the very nature of their onesidedness.

One often reported by-product of nongrading is the growth experienced by teachers and school administrators engaged in readying themselves for its demands. Faculties that probe assiduously in the areas of child growth and development, curriculum, and learning cannot help being better informed people and cannot help bringing into being a better educational product as a result. But it is just as possible that faculties and curricula of graded organizations would improve comparably under parallel circumstances.

In my opinion, nongrading finds its best niche in elementary education. In this niche, it enables teachers to work with pupils over a reasonably long period of time with these results: possibly better curriculum integration and delayed pupil retardation. The first is a feature common to all levels. The second is a feature especially germane at the primary level where differences of readiness and maturation have unique significance.

For Further Thought

1. For teachers with new pupil groups at the beginning of each year, describe ways these teachers should integrate and articulate their curriculum efforts with teachers of the previous year.

2. Weigh the pros and cons of teachers remaining with pupil groups for periods of longer than one year. Under this arrangement, what advantages, if any, would a nongraded plan have over a graded plan?

3. Review the characteristics of the nongraded organizational plan, and then decide which ones could be applied, and in what way, to a high-school nongraded organization.

References

Anderson, Robert H., "Some Types of Cooperative Teaching in Current Use," *The National Elementary Principal* 44 (January 1965), pp. 22–26.

Brinkman, Albert R., "Now It's the Ungraded School," *The P.T.A. Magazine*, 105 (June 1961), pp. 24–26.

Brown, B. Frank, *The Nongraded High School*. Englewood Cliffs, N.J.: Prentice-Hall, Inc., 1963.

Cook, Walter W., *Grouping and Promotion in the Elementary School*. Minneapolis: University of Minnesota Press, 1961.

Goodlad, John I. "Individual Differences and Vertical Organization," *Sixty-First Yearbook of the National Society for the Study of Education*. Chicago: University of Chicago Press, 1962, pp. 209–238.

Goodlad, John I. and Robert H. Anderson, "Educational Practices in Nongraded Schools: A Survey of Perceptions," *The Elementary School Journal*, 63 (October 1962), pp. 33–40.

Goodlad, John I. and Robert Anderson, *The Nongraded Elementary School* (rev. ed.). New York: Harcourt, Brace & Company, 1963.

Gore, Lillian, "The Nongraded Primary Unit," *School Life*, 44 (March 1962), pp. 6–9.

Graft, Patricia C., *A Study of Various Nongraded Primary Plans And a Program of Abilities Recommended to the Barrington Schools*. Masters Thesis, Northwestern University, 1961.

Kelly, Florence C., "Ungraded Primary School," *Educational Leadership*, 18 (November 1960), pp. 79–81.

Lane, Howard, and Mary Beauchamp, *Human Relations in Teaching*. Englewood Cliffs, N.J.: Prentice-Hall, Inc., 1955, pp. 298–303.

Larsen, Martha, *The Criteria Used to Establish Grouping in the Ungraded Primary*. Masters Thesis, Northwestern University, 1960.

Skapski, Mary K., "Ungraded Primary Reading Program," *The Education Digest*, 26 (January 1961), pp. 45–47.

Thompson, Ethel, "The Ungraded Plan," *Today and Tomorrow in Elementary and Secondary Education*. reprinted from the N.E.A. Journal (January 1958).

Wheat, Leonard B., "The Flexible Progress Group System," *Elementary School Journal*, 38 (November 1937), pp. 26–28.

chapter 16

The Advanced Placement Program

Just after midcentury, education embarked once more on the innovational by adopting for experimental purposes the Advanced Placement Program. Like many other programs to follow, this was an effort by the nation's schools to relate more closely to the needs of the gifted which many believed had been treated too casually for too long a time. A creation of the College Entrance Examination Board, The Advanced Placement Program had as its original purpose—a purpose which remains unchanged today—the updating of the school's curriculum as a means of challenging the best in the most talented students. In this ambitious venture, education apparently was undaunted by the long history of debate, controversy, and conflicting experience which for decades had characterized other homogeneous-grouping attempts.

As stated in the preceding chapter, from the day that instruction shifted from the one to the many, education had to devise a method, or methods, of organizing a given student body into learning units. Lancaster and Bell experimented with large class-sized groups of a hundred or more, utilizing pupil assistants to compensate for the resulting unwieldiness. More recently, the class of twenty to thirty pupils has become the vogue. Irrespective of size, however, each class unit comes into being as a result of a plan, with the grouping criteria differing from time to time, and from school to school. And the criteria, irrespective of their specific nature, fit into one of the following grouping categories.

1. *Homogeneous grouping.* Under this arrangement, schools group pupils around such governing criteria as intellectual ability, academic

aptitude, reading ability, social maturity, emotional maturity, physical characteristics, or additional factors. Regardless of the specific criterion or combination of criteria, the thesis underlying this approach is that pupils will learn better if the school narrows the range of human differences within any given learning group.

2. *Heterogeneous grouping.* Under this arrangement, heterogeneity constitutes an incidental or planned-for outcome. Practically speaking, grouping with the factor of age or grade level as the criterion always results in extensive heterogeneity. But under such circumstances, this outcome is more accident than the result of preplanning. For any group to be heterogeneous by deliberate plan, selected trait-differences within a larger group need first to be identified and then distributed more or less evenly throughout a number of smaller groups. The traits themselves might be one or more of those mentioned under 1 above, and might include age, sex, and ethnic background as well.

3. *Flexible grouping.* This approach is one wherein a school groups pupils in different ways at different times depending on the intended learning outcome or outcomes. Team teaching best exemplifies this approach. In a team arrangement involving 120 pupils, 10 pupils, for instance, might be congregated at 9 A.M. for drill in one of the academic skills; and then at 9:45 A.M., the larger group might be divided three or four ways into groups of 30 to 40 each for purposes of discussion. Later at 11 A.M., the 120 pupils might be assembled in a single body for large-group instructional purposes. In similar vein, any classroom teacher who as the occasion warrants organizes instruction around small groups also engages in flexible grouping.

The Advanced Placement Program logically fits into the category of homogeneous grouping and consequently falls heir to its long traditions. These latter constitute a mosaic of optimism, skepticism, and honest doubt when mirroring homogeneous grouping's record of performance. It is fair to state that reactions have varied, and continue to vary, from time to time, from place to place, and from grade level to grade level. Greater skepticism toward homogeneous grouping usually is evidenced by instructional leaders in self-contained classrooms, more optimism by instructional leaders in departmentalized settings. The greatest single reason for the difference resides in the selection of grouping criteria. In the self-contained classroom, criteria that might be appropriate in one curriculum situation are never equally appropriate, if appropriate at all, in another situation. Thus such frequently tried criteria as general ability, overall achievement, reading ability, or social readiness have not worked out satisfactorily. In a departmentalized school organization, however, with each class usually concentrated in a single content area, grouping criteria are somewhat easier to come by and apply—although this is not to imply that the task is ever performed with ease or with a surety of correctness.

Birth and Early Development of the Program

According to the College Entrance Examination Board, The Advanced Placement Program originated in 1951. This and other pertinent information concerning the Program's birth, purposes, procedures, and developmental growth can be secured from the College Entrance Examination Board, Box 592, Princeton, New Jersey; or from Box 27896, Los Angeles, 27, California. One of the Board's mimeographed publications is "The Advanced Placement Program—A Brief History," which traces the Program's first decade of existence.

It relates that in the early fifties, the Fund for the Advancement of Education provided financial support for two experiments. One had to do with the conception and implementation of a revised program of general education for the high school. The active participants were three high schools: Andover, Exeter, and Lawrenceville; and three universities: Harvard, Princeton, and Yale.

The second experiment, which came to be known as the Kenyon Plan, actually constituted the starting phase of the Advanced Placement Program itself. Its purpose was to test out the plausibility of the awarding by an institution of higher learning of advanced standing to students who had completed a specialized type of high-school program—a program mutually agreed to in advance by a given school and a given college. This school-and-college study took substance when the presidents or deans of twelve colleges organized themselves into a Committee on Admission with Advanced Standing. Joining this Committee shortly thereafter were twelve secondary-school administrators. The first chairman was the late Gordon Chalmers, President of Kenyon, who was succeeded by William Carnog, then President of Central High School of Philadelphia, and who now is Superintendent of the New Trier Township High School of Winnetka, Illinois.[1]

In 1952, the committee assigned to approximately eight school and college teachers the task of forming subject-matter subcommittees to prepare individual course outlines. In 1953, the twelve colleges involved in the study approved a plan to award college credit to selected high-school students who met certain predetermined criteria. In 1954, the College Entrance Examination Board further "approved a proposal to give a series of advanced examinations following initially the general design of those used by the Study and to be given in 1956." In 1955,

[1] College Entrance Examination Board, "The Advanced Placement Program—A Brief History" (unsigned) August, 1962, pp. 1–2.

the committees were transferred to the organizational auspices of the College Board—with little change of membership.[2]

Moving backward one year to 1954, we note that the first subject-matter conference was held between high-school teachers and their college counterparts—in the single field of the social studies. This conference took place at Williams College and was attended by 48 teachers from 27 secondary schools and 12 colleges.[3] In 1955, conferences took place in 11 subject-matter areas. The conferences were first a phenomenon of the East Coast; then, in 1957, extended westward to Northwestern University; and in 1958, further westward to Stanford University.[4]

By 1960, the Program had spread to 24 of 50 large cities with populations of 200,000 or more;[5] and by 1961–1962, had extended into 1358 schools of varying sizes throughout the country. This revealed a significant increase from the earlier total of 104 schools in 1955–1956. The colleges which participated in the Program increased in number from 130 in 1955–1956 to 683 in 1961–1962.[6]

The Program Itself

In general terms, the fundamental purpose of the Advanced Placement Program is to help high schools relate more closely to the needs of capable students. To facilitate this process, the Program performs the function of catalytic agent in high schools and colleges. Through this function, it unifies and makes more efficient the efforts of both. There are also two other partners in the multiheaded enterprise, namely, the College Entrance Examination Board and the Educational Testing Service of Princeton, New Jersey; the latter is a nonprofit organization. All these institutions, with the school necessarily playing a pivotal role, have the following common concerns: (1) to develop a curriculum for the high school that will challenge the gifted while at the same time meeting the standards of cooperating colleges and universities, (2) to select the proper students for that curriculum, (3) to encourage parental support for the newly conceived curriculum, and (4) to prepare and administer

[2] *Ibid.*, p. 2.
[3] Charles R. Keller, "The Advanced Placement Program Now Has a History," *The Bulletin of the National Association of Secondary-School Principals*, 42 (December 1958), p. 6.
[4] *Ibid.*, p. 11.
[5] Nancy C. Ralston, "Advanced Placement Policies in Large City School Systems," *The Bulletin of the National Association of Secondary-School Principals*, 45 (September 1961), p. 130.
[6] College Entrance Examination Board, *A Guide to the Advanced Placement Program*, 1962–1963 (Princeton, N.J.: College Board Advanced Placement Examinations, 1962), p. 9.

examinations which, accurately and economically, will evaluate student performance and program adequacy.

With advanced curriculum placement in college the goal, high schools provide several avenues that lead to it. The customary one is the college-level course which meets college specifications but which also operates as an integral part of a given high school's curriculum. A second avenue is independent preparation by the talented for Advance Placement Examinations. This path is trod by only a small percentage of students. A third avenue, which lies outside the province of this chapter, is academic work taken by a given student in a nearby university during the time that he is still enrolled in a high school program. Several instances of this third method, a noteworthy one involving the University of Miami, Coral Gables, Florida, are highlighted in the March, 1963 issue of *The Bulletin of the NASSP.* Our concern in this chapter is almost exclusively with the first avenue.

Most schools that participate actively in the Advanced Placement Program go through a series of preliminary procedural steps that unfold more or less as follows:

1. Early in the planning phase, the school sends a request to the College Entrance Examination Board for descriptive written materials pertaining to the Advanced Placement Program. By early return mail, it can expect to receive some or all of the following.

(a) *A Guide To The Advanced Placement Program,*

(b) *Advanced Placement Program: Course Descriptions,*

(c) *The College Board Today.*

(d) *Bulletin for Students, Advanced Placement Examinations,*

(e) Testimonials to the Program's quality via selected articles written by the Director of the Program.

2. The school requests from the national office the services of a consultant. As stated in C above, "the program now has over 100 volunteer consultants who are available to visit schools interested in offering these college-level courses for the first time. The volunteers, all of them teachers or administrators in school or college, have had extensive experience with advanced placement courses which they are prepared to share; their expenses are borne by the College Board."[7]

3. An interested school gains community support for the Program by explaining and publicizing it. As the *Guide* in A above states: "Without understanding and tangible help from the community, and this includes state education departments and neighboring colleges, the best intentions

---

[7] College Entrance Examination Board, *The College Board Today* (Princeton, N.J.: 1962), p. 22.

and the strongest efforts of the teachers and administrators are handicapped, if not defeated."[8]

4. If the school has not previously engaged in ability grouping, it customarily adopts this pattern for Program students. Throughout the literature from the College Board, the implication is strong that although pupils can be readied for the Program examinations through organizational efforts and patterns other than ability grouping, such counter procedure is rare.

5. Next the school addresses itself to the problem of selecting students for the Program. The guide suggests adherence to the following check list:

(*a*) Is he a volunteer who is interested, willing, and able to extend himself?
(*b*) Do his parents approve of his taking the courses?
(*c*) Is his past record good enough?
(*d*) Does he have the recommendations of his former teachers?
(*e*) And has he been interviewed by the teacher and found acceptable by him?[9]

Most schools have established a minimum eligibility I.Q. score of around 120, although a few have set it lower. Fritz, in a description of the Advanced Placement Program as it operates at the Highland Park High School of New Jersey, states that only students with I.Q.'s of 120 or higher are eligible, and that these represent the upper 15 per cent of all high-school children.[10] This is essentially Conant's attitude regarding the ability limits of the gifted child as expressed in *The American High School Today*. Ralston, without setting I.Q. limits, reports that teachers who have worked in the Program unanimously agree "that a high level of ability . . . [is] definitely necessary in order to succeed in such a vigorous program." Perseverance, she concedes, may compensate somewhat for lesser ability, but it will stretch only so far. Furthermore, she says that the student "should come to advanced placement classes with the understanding that he will face a long pull and receive heavier assignments. He must be willing to work very hard in the advanced-placement subject." Other attributes that Ralston recommends are a sincere interest in the subject being studied, self-reliance, creativity, and emotional stability. However, she concedes that he can be either introvert or extrovert, a follower-type or a leader type.[11]

[8] College Entrance Examination Board, *Guide*, p. 12.
[9] *Ibid.*, pp. 13–14.
[10] William D. Fritz, "Advanced Placement Courses As Seen by a High School Instructor," *School Science and Mathematics*. **63** (April 1963) pp. 343–344.
[11] Nancy C. Ralston, "Teachers Play an Important Role in Advanced Placement," *The Bulletin of the National Association of Secondary-School Principals*, **47** (March 1963), pp. 103–104.

6. Once a faculty has agreed on the criteria of selection, it will next need to face a related issue, namely, the number of college-level courses in which it will permit any given student to enroll at any given time.

A few schools throughout the country, on occasions, have allowed such enrollments to spread widely across a student's schedule. "Most of the students," however, as indicated by the College Board, "enroll in college-level courses . . . in only one or two subjects; very few planned to finish college in fewer than four years."[12] In this regard, a school must avoid the danger of permitting a student to overextend himself lest the legitimate outcome of academic fulfillment be lost to diffused effort.

7. Somewhere along the time line, which starts with planning and terminates with implementation, a school will need to select a teacher or teachers for the Program. According to the *Guide,* these teachers "must be, like their students, able and ambitious."[13] The unfortunate, even though perhaps unintentioned, implication here is that teachers of the slow and average do not have to be comparably able and ambitious. To avoid the possibility of such an odious interpretation, we state simply that teachers of college-level courses should be scholars competent in the designated curriculum area for which they are to be responsible, and instructional leaders capable of teaching the knowledgeable pupils with whom they will work.

8. Also at some place along the time line, questions over curriculum selection and teaching method will arise. When they do, the heavy hand of the college or university will occasionally manifest itself. Nor should this outcome prove surprising in view of the strongly vested interest of higher education in the Advanced Placement Program. After all, a college-level course needs to be at a college level. Yet within this framework of admitted dictation, college representatives in the Program press toward curriculum flexibility. In the process, their stated goal is course outlines that "are for the most part kept purposely general, as little restrictive as possible, in order to allow the instructor the sort of individual freedom that most college teachers are allowed."[14]

In confirmation of this goal, the course description in English, for example, allows considerable teacher choice. He has latitude to select *one tragedy* from the five: "Othello," "Hamlet," "Macbeth," "Oedipus Rex," and "Antigone"; and one comedy from among five authors: Shakespeare (3 choices), Sheridan (1), Goldsmith (1), Wilde (1), and Shaw (3). The course outline, after affirming that "one work of fiction should be

[12] College Entrance Examination Board, *Advanced Placement Program: Course Descriptions* (Princeton, N.J.: 1962), p. 17.
[13] College Entrance Examination Board, *Guide,* p. 15.
[14] *Ibid.,* p. 14.

closely analyzed in class," allows a choice from eight selected authors (Swift, Fielding, Austen, Dickens, Hawthorne, Twain, Hardy, Conrad) and from ten of their literary productions.[15]

Past examinations for the various courses, like the course descriptions themselves, are made available to interested schools, upon request, by the College Board. Five-member committees: three members from selected universities and colleges, one from a public school, and one usually from an eastern private preparatory school, prepare all examinations. The readers also come both from schools and colleges, but the "chief reader," in each of the subject-matter areas in which examinations are given, is a college representative. The examinations themselves are usually of the essay type, whenever this type is feasible. They take place yearly during the period, May 13 to May 17, and are of three-hours duration each. The rating scale consists of a graduated five-point continuum: "5 (high honors), 4 (honors), 3 (good), 2 (credit), and 1 (no credit)."[16] A candidate for each examination first pays a registration fee of $5.00, and later a fee of $10.00.

9. A highly important essential for all schools is that they effect a harmonious relationship among students, teachers, and the respective curricula to the end of optimum student learning. How well most schools achieve this goal, however, is conjectural. Subjective opinion and the later success of students in college are the only available criteria. And regarding the second of these, the outcome of college success could be almost habitually predicted from the high caliber of students initially selected.

10. During the summer following the termination of any given course, the College Board forwards both to the school and to the appropriate college all available data, the most important being the examination results. The college, then, depending on its policy, decides on the proper level of placement for the student when he arrives; likewise, on the amount of credit, if any, it will grant him when he arrives.

Advantages: Purported or Real

Any school or school system looking forward to future involvement in the Advanced Placement Program should first assay its assets. The ones most frequently highlighted by past and present participants are these: (1) products of the Program make successful records in college; (2) the Program has a salutory effect on a school's curriculum, predictably updating it; (3) school faculties that participate in the Program grow professionally as a result of their in-service efforts; and (4) products

[15] College Entrance Examination Board, *Course Descriptions*, p. 55.
[16] College Entrance Examination Board, *Guide*, p. 18.

of the program enjoy a better articulated curriculum while in college, graduate earlier, or both.

College Success of Students.   High on the list of the Program's stated assets is the success enjoyed in college by students who formerly were enrolled in it. Generally speaking, when academic achievement, as customarily conceived, is the criterion, products of the Program do as well in college classes as do their somewhat older counterparts who are not products of the Program. However, the University of Chicago and selected other collegiate institutions anticipated this finding several decades ago. But none of these sources, as yet, has adequately answered such fundamental questions as the following: How much acceleration is good and how much is harmful? Does a demonstrated proficiency by students in the area of the detached abstract necessarily connote a comparable level of proficiency in the deeper level of cognitive, social, and ethical meanings which lie beneath or beyond? And third, does a demonstrated readiness for advanced academic status connote a comparable readiness for advanced status in other essential developmental growth areas? Until Program personnel are able to answer such questions as these, with at least a semblance of positive assurance, their academic success story should stop with the modest.

Curriculum Updating.   Also high on the list of the Program's stated success is the alleged significant contribution it makes to the cause of curriculum updating. This along with the in-service growth of teachers—a topic to receive treatment next—we regard as probably the most noteworthy of the Program's basic values. Simply stated, when any faculty collectively squares off to reassess its efforts, curriculum improvement becomes almost an inevitable result.

The process, as described by many, reportedly effects improvement along an extensive educational line. The initial focal point is the gifted secondary-school pupil himself, with curriculum effort directed forthrightly at his specialized interests and needs. The curriculum-revision process, however—at least as stated by those who articulate the position—soon enlarges to include pupils and issues that lie outside as well as inside the Program's primary focus.

The point made by these individuals is that curriculum change can never take place and remain in isolation; it inevitably has to spread out. And as it spreads out, so the proposition goes, the gifted secondary-school child sooner or later becomes just one of a large constellation of curriculum concerns that reach downward into the elementary school grades, upward to the college grades, and horizontally throughout the several secondary-school grades.

To the extent that this thesis is a realistic one in the sense that curriculum change for the gifted can take place without a school's neglecting the needs of the more numerous nongifted, it is none other than laudable.

After all, what is the purpose of any well-conceived curriculum but to meet the needs of any and all members of a student body? But to the extent that the thesis is a whitewash to conceal an operational neglect of the nongifted, the society needs to inventory its basic values.

In the process, education will emerge, as it generally has throughout most of its recent history, as an institution for all children who can profit from it. When, in contrast, it lavishes a disproportionate share of its rich, but not inexhaustible, resources on a specialized few, it sacrifices the right of the remaining many to develop to their optima. This sacrifice the society cannot afford to let education, however well intentioned, make.

When, however, curriculum revision for the gifted broadens its horizons to include a comparable revision for the nongifted, the process of articulation is the winner. In discussing this issue of articulation, Lloyd Michael, Superintendent of the Evanston Township High School, describes its development since 1900 as taking place in three phases. Around 1900, says he, unity existed between schools and colleges because college preparation for the bright constituted a synthesizing influence. Then, later, when secondary education reached out to embrace a wider range of ability levels, unity gave way to division, with the high schools veering tangentially away from intellectualism and the colleges moving too onesidedly toward it. The third phase, Michael views as existing in the present, with the Advanced Placement Program constituting "one of the most promising developments in curriculum articulation."[17]

In-service Faculty Growth. A third stated asset of the Program is that successful curriculum revision almost universally results not only in the greater growth of pupils but in significant growth among professional participants as well. When high-school and college personnel meet together each June at the various conferences sponsored by the College Entrance Examination Board, in-service growth can scarcely help taking place. When representatives of any two educational levels hammer out a mutually conceived course program, in-service gains again are a predictable result. Even when philosophical and other professional differences stand as a temporary barrier, an often-heard claim is that efforts to resolve them customarily culminate in greater mutual understanding and insight. Quite likely, when the final results of the Advanced Placement Program are in and tabulated, it may well be that the in-service value of the Program to teachers will be a major outcome.

A Better Articulated College Program for Students. The same individuals who profess that student products of the Program achieve commendable success in college just as consistently profess that the products

[17] Lloyd S. Michael, "Articulation Problems with Lower Schools and Higher Education," *The Bulletin of the National Association of Secondary-School Principals*, **43** (February 1959), pp. 51–55.

reap the benefits of a curriculum better suited to their needs. And with the freshman year an amorphous one in most colleges, advanced placement of the gifted, if carefully effected, requires no defense. In the academic year 1962–1963, Harvard University, for instance, from a total of 500 Advanced-Placement entering students declared 130 eligible for sophomore standing.[18]

In the light of this unquestioned asset of improved curriculum articulation, the issue of how much credit a given college should grant for Advanced-Placement work taken in high school fades into relative unimportance. Some give no credit; others give token credit. In 1956, the University of Michigan awarded up to 16 hours of credit for Program students who were enrolled in the College of Literature, Science, and the Arts.[19]

Whether the granting of a sizeable amount of college credit for work taken in high school is an advantage or disadvantage is a moot issue. Assuming social as well as cognitive readiness for advanced college experiences, and a world of industry and business unprejudicial toward the 19- or 20-year-old-college graduate, the practice has prima facie merit. The question still remaining unanswered, however, is the maximum amount of credit that any institution of higher standing should grant. Might even two years be feasible for some? We doubt it! Individual readiness only, however, can provide exact clues.

The practice of effecting advanced placement without necessarily giving actual college credit is too patently logical for any to seriously question. If the so-called college-level curriculum in the high school is correctly conceived in the first place, a next level of curriculum exposure during the freshman year of college should be none other than axiomatic. This practice places a proper emphasis on curriculum articulation, where it properly belongs, rather than on college credit to be given.

Disadvantages: Purported or Real

Leading proponents of the Advanced Placement Program, who at one and the same time are predictably the leading spokesmen for it, are prone to dwell heavily on the advantages while glossing lightly over the possible shortcomings. Avoiding this onesidedness, we single out and make selective comments on the four following possible disadvantages of the Program. One is the tendency of the Program to overemphasize the cognitive in curriculum content to the neglect of other important learning outcomes. A second is the danger of possible adverse effects

[18] College Entrance Examination Board, *Guide*, p. 19.
[19] Alice L. Beeman, "High School Students Earn Credit Toward University Entrance," *The Bulletin of the National Association of Secondary-School Principals*, **42** (February 1958), pp. 86–88.

of the Program on nongifted students. A third is the danger of possible adverse effects of the Program on the nonacademic subjects. A fourth possible disadvantage—the one inherent in any fixed homogeneous-grouping arrangement—is discussed in a later section.

The Tendency of the Program to Overemphasize the Cognitive. High on the list of possible shortcomings of the Program is the tendency of many, if not most, Advanced-Placement courses to relate disproportionately to cognitive outcomes while neglecting or ignoring such other important outcomes as the emotional and the social. The strictly intellectual orientation of higher education is, with little question, responsible for this phenomenon. Whether this orientation is proper even for higher education, we have serious doubts; and regarding its appropriateness for secondary education, we view it unequivocally as misplaced. In this connection, if the total-personality or mental-health orientation is the proper one for education to espouse in general, as we believe it is, then we regard it as the proper one for every facet of education to give service to in some tangibly significant way. The glib and frequent high-school answer of: "We do it this way because the colleges expect us to do it this way" is more evasive rationalization than convincing reason.

Yet this point of view set forth here is far from universally accepted. Conant, just one of a sizeable number, would take forceful exception to it, as the following statement clearly reveals: "The elementary school today, then, is child centered; the college, subject-matter centered. And this is as it should be, I think all well-informed educators would declare." He continues with the declaration that by grade 8, the shift to subject matter should be well underway.[20]

If Conant is to be taken literally, one thus has to conclude that educators who espouse a total-personality position for either secondary or higher education are plainly not well informed. While passing over this implied conclusion as unintended, I cannot comparably pass over Conant's supreme faith in subject matter as an educational cure all. The mental-health premises on which this book rests lead, in fact, to the following strong rejoinder. No curriculum, irrespective of level, is, can be, nor should be oriented exclusively to subject-matter content. Such an orientation places too much faith in cognition per se. It implies either that cognition alone will eventuate in personality fulfillment or that the school has responsibility only for the cognitive.

The orientation, I contend, is in error on three important counts: first, the society expects schools to produce not one-sided intellectual products, but well-rounded many-sided products; second, the way to personality fulfillment, an accepted goal of education, is multi—not single-di-

[20] Quoted in Jack N. Arbolino, "Proper Placement—Key to Articulation," Reprint from *College Board Review*, 44 (Spring 1961) p. 1.

mensioned; and, third, cognition is not a discrete essence that can be dealt with in isolation. Why not, instead, a curriculum that, without downgrading the mental, relates in a balanced way to the affective and psycho-motor, as well?

The Danger of Adverse Effects on the Nongifted.   A second possible disadvantage, although not intrinsic in the Program, resides in the tendency of many schools to invest a disproportionate amount of time and energy on the highly gifted few to the neglect of the less gifted many. The issue, in reality, is one of democratic values applied to human differences. Apropos here, a fundamental democratic tenet is that all children, regardless of intellectual or other differences, should share in an equitable (although not necessarily in an arithmetically equal) manner the nation's educational resources and opportunities. Thus, to the extent that education has a balanced concern for all children and youth, it fulfills its humanistic mission. But to the extent that it becomes badly one-sided in favor of any single group, it fails this same mission. Admittedly, in the twenties and thirties, education shortchanged the talented student by a too great preoccupation with concerns of the slow learner. However, the present countertrend is no more defensible, and probably not less one-sided. Either extreme constitutes a value distortion. The constructive compromise is a balanced educational program for all students with no one group singled out for special dispensation. If articulation, then, needs to characterize the Advanced Placement Program, it needs no less to characterize the curricula for the slow and average. And if teachers need to be "hand picked" for students in the Program, teachers need to be just as carefully hand picked for students who are not in the Program.

The Danger of Adverse Effects on the Non-academic Subjects.   A third possible disadvantage is that the nonacademic subjects, which appear never or sparingly in the Program, lose the status battle to the academic subjects that constitute the life blood of the Program. As of 1962, for instance, the Program covered the following specific courses: "American History, Biology, Chemistry, English, European History, French, German, Latin, Mathematics, Physics, and Spanish."[21] An easily drawn inference here is that such other content areas as music, art, physical education, and agriculture are less worthy of college-level treatment than their academic opposites. Business education, interestingly, has recently made an appearance in the Program in a few schools throughout the country.

The Issue of Homogeneous Grouping

In the last analysis, the Advanced Placement Program, separating students as it does on factors of ability and achievement, cannot escape

[21] The College Entrance Examination Board, *Course Descriptions,* p. 14.

the impact of research and attitudes pertaining to homogeneous grouping. And the case for or against this organizational practice is anything but conclusive. In support of this statement, we submit the following as a reasonable synthesis of existing evidence.

1. Homogeneous grouping reduces human variability along the lines of the criterion employed, but it leaves a broad range of variability in other areas.

2. Research differs regarding who, if any, is helped most by grouping: the slow, the average, or the fast. Goodlad reports that the "dull" are helped most.[22] Wilhelms and Gibson,[23] and Eckstrom[24] concur. On the other hand, Passow[25] and French[26] report just the reverse.

3. Students who have been grouped homogeneously in high school do not do significantly better in college than do their ungrouped counterparts.[27]

4. Grouping on the criteria of ability and achievement tends to divide students along lines of such social factors as race and economic-status.[28]

5. Generally speaking, teachers at the high-school level favor the practice of grouping; teachers at the elementary level and educational theoreticians are most often opposed.

A Point of View

In the opinion of the author, the Advanced Placement Program has made its most significant contribution to education by encouraging those engaged in it to analyze and criticize themselves and school practices in many areas. The essential outcomes have been curriculum updating and in-service growth of the participants at all levels. All this is on the credit side.

What is on the debit side, however, is the tendency by many to overemphasize intellectual outcomes to the neglect of other equally important value outcomes. If carried too far, this trend could lead to a cast system with intellect the single criterion. In a democratic society, all individuals,

[22] John I. Goodlad, in *The Encyclopedia of Educational Research* (New York: The Macmillan Co., 1960), p. 224.
[23] Fred T. Wilhems and D. W. Gibson, "Grouping: Research Offers Leads," *Educational Leadership*, 18 (April 1961), p. 411.
[24] Ruth B. Ekstrom, "Experimental Studies of Homogeneous Grouping: A Critical Review," *School Review*, 69 (Summer 1961), p. 216.
[25] *Ibid.*, p. 220.
[26] John W. French, "Evidence from School Records on the Effectiveness of Ability Grouping," *Journal of Educational Research*, 54 (November 1960) pp. 83–91.
[27] David A. Abramson, "The Effectiveness of Grouping for Students of High Ability," *Educational Research Bulletin*, 38 (October 1959), pp. 169–182.
[28] Maurice J. Eash, "Grouping: What Have We Learned?" *Educational Leadership*, 8 (April 1961), p. 430.

not just the intellectually favored, have an equal right to develop into their potentials.

Also on the debit side are the extravagant claims for the Program made by selected of its ardent supporters. Several years ago, the Director of the Program, in a moment of unbridled optimism, averred that: "This Program is not a panacea, but it is directed toward making us whole."[29] Equally sanguine was another's unvarnished assertion that: "Few faults, if any, have been found in it by students, teachers, or administrators, whether on the secondary or college level; praise and satisfaction have been well nigh universal."[30] Such unvarnished claims as these are scarcely in harmony with the avowed scholarly nature of the Program itself. Education unquestionably needs to study and to evaluate the Advanced Placement Program, but it should do so in an atmosphere wherein quiet judgment and mature values dominate. Only in such an atmosphere will the authentic win over the spurious.

For Further Thought

1. What is gained by the term "college level" in connection with the Advanced Placement Program? What are the specific credits and debits of the caption?

2. Are personality and social development as essential for the talented student as for the slow learner? Defend your response.

3. React to the suggestion that before college personnel assume responsibility for curriculum development in the high school, they should have some formal preparation for the assignment, including experience in a high-school program.

4. What do you recommend as a ceiling for college credit earned at the high school level? Defend your point of view. Or do you recommend only curriculum enrichment apart from acceleration?

5. What if a student were "bright" enough to compete favorably in college after one year of high school, what would be the pros and cons of his being "promoted" to college at that time?

References

Angermann, G., "Advanced Placement, Present and Future," *The Bulletin of the National Association of Secondary-School Principals,* Vol. 45, Nov. 1961, pp. 49–51.

Arbolino, Jack N., "More Flies Should Practice Law," *Journal of Secondary Education,* Vol. 37, Apr. 1962.

Arbolino, Jack N., "Proper Placement—Key to Articulation," *College Board Review,* No. 44, Spring, 1961.

[29] Jack Arbolino, "Proper Placement—Key to Articulations," p. 2.
[30] Frank Copley, *The American High School And the Talented Student* (Ann Arbor: The University of Michigan Press, 1961), p. 33.

Arbolino, Jack N., "What's Wrong with the Advanced Placement Program?" *The Bulletin of the National Association of Secondary-School Principals,* Vol. 45, Feb., 1961.

Beeman, Alice L., "High School Students Earn Credit Toward University Entrance," *The Bulletin of the Association of Secondary-School Principals,* Vol. 42, Feb., 1958, pp. 86–88.

Cameron, Ben F., "Advanced Placement Examinations," *Educational Leadership,* Vol. 20, Oct., 1962, pp. 30–33.

College Entrance Examination Board, *A Guide to the Advanced Placement Program 1962–63.* Princeton, N.J., 1962.

College Entrance Examination Board, *The College Board Today,* Princeton, N.J., 1962.

Dodes, Irving A., "Advanced Placement in Mathematics: Another View," *High Points,* Vol. 44, Jan. 1962, pp. 16–23.

Evans, Richard W., "Acceleration Prior to Advanced Placement," *The Clearing House,* Vol. 37, Dec., 1962, pp. 560–566.

Fritz, William D., "Advanced Placement Courses as Seen by a High School Instructor," *School Science and Mathematics,* Vol. 63, Apr., 1963, pp. 343–347.

Keller, Charles R., "The Advanced Placement Program Now Has a History," *The Bulletin of the National Association of Secondary-School Principals,* Vol. 42, Dec., 1958, pp. 6–12.

Michael, Lloyd S., "Articulation Problems with Lower Schools and Higher Education," *The Bulletin of the National Association of Secondary-School Principals,* Vol. 43, Feb., 1959, pp. 51–55.

Nadel, Max, "Advanced Placement in English," *High Points,* Vol. 45, March, 1963, pp. 19–23.

Ralston, Nancy C., "Advanced Placement Policies in Large City School Systems," *The Bulletin of the National Association of Secondary-School Principals,* Vol. 45, Sept., 1961, pp. 130–133.

Ralston, Nancy C., "Teachers Play an Important Role in Advanced Placement," *The Bulletin of the National Association of Secondary-School Principals,* Vol. 47, March, 1963, pp. 102–105.

AUTHOR INDEX

(Persons)

AUTHOR INDEX

(Institutions)

SUBJECT INDEX